On the Edges of Whiteness

ON THE EDGES OF WHITENESS

Polish Refugees in British Colonial Africa during and after the Second World War

Jochen Lingelbach

berghahn
NEW YORK • OXFORD
www.berghahnbooks.com

First published in 2020 by
Berghahn Books
www.berghahnbooks.com

© 2020, 2023 Jochen Lingelbach
First paperback edition published in 2023

All rights reserved. Except for the quotation of short passages
for the purposes of criticism and review, no part of this book
may be reproduced in any form or by any means, electronic or
mechanical, including photocopying, recording, or any information
storage and retrieval system now known or to be invented,
without written permission of the publisher.

Library of Congress Cataloging-in-Publication Data
Names: Lingelbach, Jochen, 1980- author.
Title: On the edges of whiteness : Polish refugees in British colonial
    Africa during and after the Second World War / Jochen Lingelbach.
Description: New York : Berghahn Books, 2020. | Includes bibliographical
    references and index.
Identifiers: LCCN 2020006097 (print) | LCCN 2020006098 (ebook) | ISBN
    9781789204445 (hardback) | ISBN 9781789204476 (ebook)
Subjects: LCSH: Polish people--Africa, East. | Polish people--Africa,
    Southern. | World War, 1939-1945--Deportations from Poland. | World War,
    1939-1945--Refugees--Poland. | World War, 1939-1945--Refugees--Africa,
    East. | World War, 1939-1945--Refugees--Africa, Southern.
Classification: LCC DT429.5.P65 L56 2020 (print) | LCC DT429.5.P65
    (ebook) | DDC 305.891850676--dc23
LC record available at https://lccn.loc.gov/2020006097
LC ebook record available at https://lccn.loc.gov/2020006098

British Library Cataloguing in Publication Data
A catalogue record for this book is available from the British Library

ISBN 978-1-78920-444-5 hardback
ISBN 978-1-80073-912-3 paperback
ISBN 978-1-78920-447-6 ebook

https://doi.org/10.3167/9781789204445

Contents

List of Illustrations — vi
Preface — vii
List of Abbreviations — xii

Introduction — 1

Chapter 1. How the Poles Came to Africa — 19

Chapter 2. The Postwar Refugee Regime and the Imperial Order of Things — 65

Chapter 3. Comparing Colonialisms in Africa and Poland — 104

Chapter 4. 'An Incredible Pool of Femininity': Gendering the Refugees — 130

Chapter 5. Polish Refugees as Part of Colonial Society — 171

Conclusion. On the Edges of Whiteness — 257

Bibliography — 267
Index — 285

Illustrations

Figure 1.1. Distribution of refugees among the East and Central African territories, 31 December 1944.   27

Figure 1.2. Polish camp Tengeru, Tanganyika. Anonymous drawing.   32

Figure 1.3. The Polish Church in Nyabyeya/Masindi, Uganda, 2013.   35

Figure 1.4. Where did the Polish refugees go?   48

Figure 2.1. Ship with Polish soldiers and civilians arriving from the Soviet Union via the Caspian Sea at the port of Pahlevi, Iran, 1942.   69

Figure 2.2. 'Run Down of Refugees in East Africa, July 1947–December 1948'.   77

Figure 3.1. Polish and African staff of the camp bakery in Koja, Uganda, 1944.   121

Figure 4.1. Group of Polish children and teachers in front of their school in Tengeru, Tanganyika, 1945.   134

Figure 4.2. Group of refugee women in the hills above Koja camp, Uganda, 1948.   140

Figure 4.3. Young Polish women and Ugandan men on a boat trip on Lake Victoria next to Koja camp, Uganda, 1943.   159

Figure 5.1. Group of Polish and African farmworkers at the Polish pig farm in Koja, Uganda, 1944.   175

Figure 5.2. Church celebration, probably Corpus Christi in Masindi, Uganda, 1944.   197

Figure 5.3. Parade of Polish refugees, presumably on the occasion of 3 May, Polish Constitution Day, Tengeru, Tanganyika, 1948.   204

Figure 5.4. A group of Polish and African fieldworkers, probably in Tengeru, Tanganyika.   223

Figure 5.5. Drawing of the Mukama of Bunyoro by visiting painter Feliks Topolski, Masindi, Uganda.   238

Preface

It all started with Mzee Asman. We were sitting in the shady courtyard of the old man's house in the Kijitonyama neighbourhood of Dar es Salaam in 2009. His wife and some young neighbours had joined the conversation, and only a few roaming chickens disturbed the quiet setting. I was conducting an interview for my diploma thesis on the urban structure of the town and the influence of its colonial segregation on the present-day perception of one particular neighbourhood.[1] In the conversation with Mzee Asman I was simply asking who had lived in which part of the town during the late colonial period. Going mentally through the different neighbourhoods of town he mentioned that some Poles used to live in one area. I was not sure if I had got him right and so asked again. He explained that they had been refugees from the Second World War in Europe and they stayed in the area around Ocean Road in a place called 'Poland House'. I was immediately struck by this information and thought no one had ever heard or written about this episode before. I was never able to track 'Poland House' or its exact location. Wanderings and enquiries around Ocean Road led to no result.[2] There had, however, been a transit camp for Polish refugees near Dar es Salaam, which I read about much later.

Hearing from Mzee Asman about the unexpected sojourners in East Africa, this story drew my interest. After finding out more about the way and reasons for their coming to Africa I was wondering how this story would fit into the history of colonial rule. I had always taken the racial division and hierarchy of colonial societies for granted. The presence of white refugees contradicted the conventional image of societies where whites ruled and profited while Africans were exploited. I enquired further into their history, and revised this schematic concept of colonial society. Coming from an African studies background I also started to learn about Polish history – a history that was much closer to my own family history than I had earlier thought. My maternal grandmother grew up in Wrocław at a time when it was a German town called Breslau. She had been an active supporter of the Nazi regime, but later deeply regretted her involvement. What was my position in this regard?

I thought I was an outside observer of a story that had only distant links to myself. It turned out, however, that the entangled history of war displacements and colonialism had come full circle. People had been deported due to the combined aggression of Soviet and German forces, then released because of the German attack on the Soviet Union. Many of them became part of the forces that eventually liberated Germany. Some of the civilians found a safe place in a former German colony where I arrived sixty years later as an exchange student. It is an enmeshed, small world indeed.

Ever since Mzee Asman hit me on the topic, there were friends and colleagues who spent time and energy to keep my enthusiasm high and help me focus on the interesting issues. Over the years I refined my short version to the surprising question of why and how Polish refugees ended up in Africa. It was a long process, but I never lost interest in this astonishing story. Along the way, the so-called 'refugee crisis' reached European headlines and my obscure topic drew more interest. The story of the Polish refugees in Africa does not, however, only offer a simple narrative of reversing flight directions. Its complexity urges us instead to critically engage with both, simple analogies as well as the short-sighted ignorance of history. But before delving into this fascinating story I wish to thank some of the people without whom I would never have been able to write these pages.

First of all I have to thank the organizers of the DFG research training group 'Critical Junctures of Globalization', Matthias Middell and Ulf Engel, for the generous funding that gave me the material basis to conduct my research. Apart from the financial support, it was a pleasure to take part in the vibrant discussions of the group. The seminars, colloquia, Winterklausuren and Summer schools influenced my own theoretical approach and provided great opportunities to discuss wider issues and to present draft chapters of this study, which helped to clarify my argumentation.

My PhD supervisor, Adam Jones, was always there when I needed support and encouragement. His rigorous and critical approach towards sources, his meticulous way of history writing and his broad knowledge of African history deeply influenced my own research. Twice a year I had the honour to make the long journey to his idyllic home in the village of Polenz. It was always a wonderful occasion to discuss issues with an inspiring group of colleagues in a relaxed but concentrated atmosphere. In Polenz I presented drafts of most chapters of this book and received numerous useful comments that always gave me food for thought, and ideas about how to refine my texts. Many of the Polenz people have followed my writing from the first proposal until the last drafts. Among them were Tina Kramer, Silke Strickrodt, Joram Tarusarira, Anne Beutter, Dmitri van den Bersselaar, Geert Castryck, Rose Marie Beck, Michaela Unterholzner, Hatice Uğur, Peter Lambertz, John Njenga Karugia and many more. Luckily, Stefan Troebst agreed at short notice to act as my second supervisor. His extensive knowledge of the entangled history of East Central Europe helped me to better grasp the Polish part of this history, of which I had been no specialist at all.

In 2016 I had the opportunity to work with Joël Glasman in his project 'The Invention of Refugee Camps' (funded by the DFG as part of the SPP 1488 'Adaptation and Creativity in Africa') at the Centre Marc Bloch in Berlin. Thanks to his support, and the openness of the centre's director, Catherine Gousseff, and colleagues, I profited from discussions on aspects of this study and enjoyed the welcoming atmosphere at the centre. In 2018, on the invitation by Kerstin Stubenvoll, I took part in a project on refugee history at the memorial site 'House of the Wannsee Conference' in Berlin. Through the writing of short texts and selection of primary documents on the Polish refugees for educational use in schools, I learned another, more accessible, way to impart historical knowledge.[3]

During the writing and rewriting of this book I had numerous informal exchanges and discussions with my colleagues in our Berlin office community. Lunchtimes especially were often an opportunity for personal exchanges and encouragement that helped me to finally finish this project. Friends and colleagues like Manuela Bauche, Jan Zofka, Frank Usbeck and Katarzyna Nowak gave me crucial feedback on various parts of the manuscript. Another special group of people were the members of the 'project clinic' African history. It helped a lot to have this protected forum of mutual aid, both from a professional and personal perspective.

On two occasions I visited the National Archives of the United Kingdom in secluded Kew, the archives of the former Polish government-in-exile in the Polish Institute and Sikorski Museum and the library of the lively POSK in Hammersmith. The national archives in Dar es Salaam and Nairobi both offered invaluable material from the local administration. My sincerest thanks to Alexander Makulilo at the University of Dar es Salaam for providing me with the support for the Tanzanian research permit clearance. One brief but fruitful research trip brought me, rather unexpectedly, to the French national archives in Paris where the records of the International Refugee Organization are stored. And one last trip led me to Oxford where I consulted some private papers in the special collections of the Bodleian Libraries. While these archives differed greatly in terms of their technical facilities and financial means, the people working there were invariably welcoming and helpful.

A special experience was the trip to the sites of the three largest refugee camps in Tengeru, Koja and Nyabyeya, and conversations with people who had been there at the time. Without the willingness of people to guide me and share their knowledge I would never have been able to get a glimpse of events from their perspective. In Uganda, Edward Wakiku, the caretaker of Koja cemetery, was a wonderful host who introduced me to interview partners in the vicinity of the former camp. He was furthermore a congenial companion on the trip to Nyabyeya where he introduced me to Ochau Paito Caesar, the caretaker of the local Polish cemetery. Caesar accompanied me to meet more people who remembered the Poles. Edward furthermore introduced me to Professor Lwanga-Lunyiigo, who had researched the Polish refuges in Uganda over two decades ago, and he shared some of his extensive knowledge on the topic. I hope this book will live up to his expectations. In Tengeru, cemetery caretaker Simon Joseph patiently answered my questions and introduced me to Edward Wojtowicz, the last Pole to have lived in Arusha since the 1950s and whose mother had once stayed in Tengeru camp.

For making this book look the way it does, I want to thank Fatimah and Amena Amer for generously allowing me to use one of the private photographs of their grandmother, Katarzyna Oko, for the cover. Moreover, I am grateful to Teresa Topolski for her generous permission to reproduce one of her father's drawings within these pages. Eminent expressionist painter and draughtsman Feliks Topolski had once visited to the Polish camps in Uganda and Tanganyika. There, as throughout his astonishing travels around a world in turmoil, he documented his impressions in fascinating drawings and paintings.

At Berghahn Books I found a wonderful home for my manuscript. It was greatly improved by the work of its editors Chris Chappell, Mykelin Higham and Caroline Kuhtz. The engaged and thorough reviews by Lynne Taylor, Brett Shadle and a third, anonymous reviewer were extremely helpful. They hinted me to flaws in my argumentation, additional aspects I had overlooked and thereby greatly enhanced the quality of the final book's content. Nigel Smith's careful and thorough copyediting greatly increased its readability. All the mistakes that I managed to hide from their view are, however, my own.

Last but not least, I wish to thank my family for their stamina in supporting and enduring me in critical moments. They are the base for everything that I do. My parents never gave up the hope that I would one day finish writing. Anne always lent me an ear and a critical opinion on my numerous questions and endless digressions. I began working on this project when Kito, my eldest child, started going to kindergarten. Now Nana, the younger one, is nearly going to school, and I have finally finished reading old letters and asking old people about former times, and the book is complete. Although it has few pictures, is written in English and features no ninjas or unicorns I hope they will one day enjoy reading it.

Notes

1. Published as Lingelbach, *Oyster Bay*.
2. In 2013, Ocean Road was renamed Barack Obama Drive.
3. My contribution to this project is published as Lingelbach, 'Der Sturm trieb uns weit um die Welt'.

ABBREVIATIONS

CO	Colonial Office
DC	District Commissioner
DP	Displaced Person
DSM	Dar es Salaam
EAGC	East African Governors' Conference
EARA	East African Refugee Authority
EAS	*East African Standard*, Nairobi
FO	Foreign Office
GP	*Głos Polski*, Nairobi
IRO	International Refugee Organization
ITS	Archives of the International Tracing Service, Bad Arolsen
KNA	Kenya National Archives, Nairobi
MERRA	Middle East Relief and Refugee Administration
MSS Afr	Bodleian Libraries: Commonwealth and African Collections, Oxford
NKVD	People's Commissariat for Internal Affairs (interior ministry of the Soviet Union)
NP	*Nasz Przyjaciel*, Nairobi
PC	Provincial Commissioner
PCIRO	Preparatory Commission for the International Refugee Organization
PISM	Polish Institute and Sikorski Museum, London
POW	Prisoner of War
PRO	The National Archives of the UK: Public Record Office, London
TNA	Tanzania National Archives, Dar es Salaam
UNA	United Nations Archive, New York
UNRRA	United Nations Relief and Rehabilitation Administration

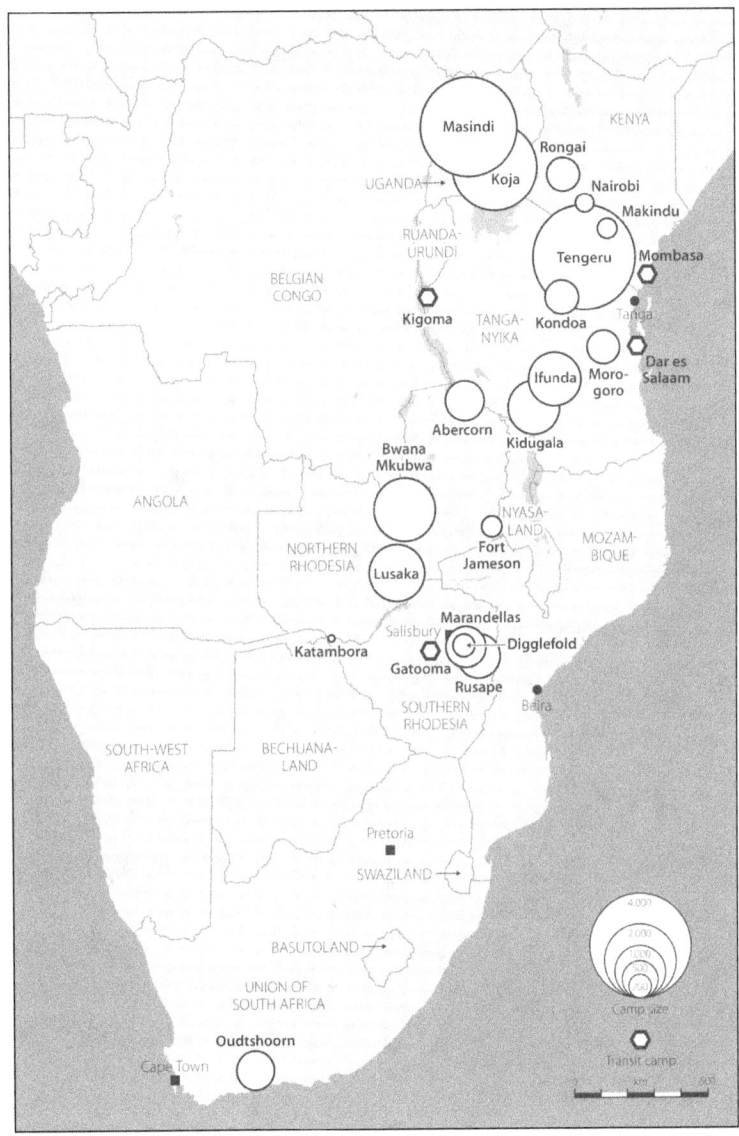

Polish refugee camps and areas of concentration in Africa. Created by Erfurth Kluger Infografik (Berlin) based on numbers compiled from PISM: Kol 18/2: 'Stan liczbowy Uchodzcow [sic] Polskich w Afryce na 31.XII.1944'; TNA: W3/31299, p. 52, Pennington to Chief Secretary, DSM, 22.03.45; PISM: Kol 147/11, 'Kronika – Afryka Rodezja Północna – Polskie osiedla uchodźce', transport list, n.d.; Zins, *Poles in Zambezi*, 78; KNA: AH/1/49, p. 44A, Director of Aliens & Internees: 'Refugee Strengths by Camps', 30.07.45; Bożena Masojadówna-Piłacka in Piotrowski, *Polish Deportees*, 179.

Introduction

White refugees are not the expected inhabitants of African colonies. From 1942 to 1950, however, nearly twenty thousand Poles[1] lived in refugee camps in the British colonies of East and Central Africa.[2] They were hosted in such diverse societies as Uganda, Kenya, Tanganyika and Northern and Southern Rhodesia, and lived in over twenty camps ranging in size from a few hundred to nearly four thousand. How did they fit into the racial hierarchies of colonial societies? Were they part of the colonizers due to their European origin? Or had they more in common with the colonized? After all, they came from Poland, a country that some West Europeans regarded as oriental as well. Or did they occupy a neutral third position in the Manichean world of colonialism? And what about their precarious refugee status? They were no permanent settlers but highly dependent on decisions in the higher echelons of power. It was not their choice to go to the colonies and live in refugee settlements. To what extent did they influence decisions about their fate? Furthermore, the group consisted mainly of women and children. What did this mean in the colonial context? The women were white, but not the wives of colonial administrators or settlers. This book endeavours to answer these diverse questions. The understanding of refugees as an integral part of the hosting society, the importance of race for the hierarchical structure of colonial societies and the importance of gendered experiences all underline this approach.

Before starting to think about their place in colonial societies, the very presence of the Poles in Africa needs some explanation. As it turned out, the reasons for their coming to Africa were no less complicated than their position in the colonial societies. They did not simply run away from war, but were initially deported from the eastern part of Poland by Soviet forces. The people who ended up in the African settlements were part of a much larger group who were forcibly deported to work in labour camps and special settlements in the Soviet interior from 1940 onwards. There they fought for survival under harsh conditions until the Germans attacked the Soviet Union. Suddenly in dire need of support, the Soviet government reached a British-brokered agreement with the Polish government-in-exile in London. This agreement, the Sikorski–Maisky Agreement, included the release of all Polish citizens in the Soviet Union in order to form a Polish army fighting against the German aggression. Owing to disagreements between the Polish and Soviet governments, the released Poles were evacuated to Iran where the British army accommodated the emaciated Poles in makeshift camps. The men (and some women) who were fit for military service formed the Second Polish Corps under General Anders. The rest of the group, mainly women, children and elderly men, were stuck in Iran. As the British administration considered the country to be too close to the war theatres and the refugees potentially in the way, they sought safer places for them. The British colonies in Africa and India provided the closest practicable refuge.

The colonial governments were not happy with the influx, but the moral obligation to contribute to the Commonwealth war effort made them accept the Poles. They established refugee camps in remote, but accessible, corners of their colonies and established a dual administrative structure with superior British officers supervising an internal Polish administration. The Poles were largely confined to live in the assigned settlements, but they soon gained strength and health in the peaceful environment. As it became apparent after the war that the communists would dominate Poland and the refugees' home region was incorporated into the Soviet Union, most of the refugees refused to return. They were again stuck, but the colonial governments were not willing to host them much longer. Colonial rule came under increasing pressure from the colonized, and colonial governments had no interest in the settlement of a large group of potentially poor whites. Most of the Poles had to leave eventually; only about one thousand were allowed to settle permanently in Africa. Most refugees joined the Polish soldiers who were demobilized and settled in Britain. Some were accepted for resettlement into Canada or Australia, some opted for voluntary return to Poland and others found opportunities individually in other countries.

Exile, Immigrant or Colonial History?

There are many ways to tell this story. Most who wrote about this episode have told it as part of Polish national history, some have inserted it into the immigration history of the countries where the refugees eventually settled. Only a few have told it as part of the colonial history of the hosting African countries. The existing literature on the topic can thus be grouped according to the historiography into which this episode is put. I call them: the Exile Story, the Immigrant Story and the Colonial Story.

First, the *Exile Story* places the Poles into the larger context of Soviet occupation, deportations and flight. Tadeusz Piotrowski's edited volume of recollections is the most outstanding English-language publication in this regard.[3] While Piotrowski gathered first-hand accounts of former refugees from nearly all African camps, his main focus is on the deportations, which he described as one of the many 'monstrous measures' that befell the Poles during the Second World War.[4] He clearly regards the refugees as part of the Polish nation, upholding their Polishness in exile. Interaction with other people is only mentioned in passing in some of the recollections. The only German-language publication on the topic follows the same line of reasoning.[5] Another prominent book is the memoir of Łucjan Królikowski.[6] He was a Polish priest and himself part of the refugee group. He took care of a group of orphans and eventually went with them from Tengeru, Tanganyika to Canada. Królikowski writes from memory, based on religious and anticommunist convictions, with the clear aim to denounce the crimes of the Soviet Union during the Second World War.[7] Janusz Wróbel wrote a comprehensive Polish-language book on the whole group of evacuees from the Soviet Union. He devotes, like Piotrowski, one chapter to the sojourn in Africa and thereby puts it in a comparable frame. He describes the migrations that followed the deportations as 'probably the most unusual chapter in the history of the Polish diaspora', bringing Poles to 'remote and exotic regions'.[8] Wróbel uses a range of Polish and some British sources for an account of the whole trajectory starting with the evacuation from the Soviet Union. The research of Hubert Chudzio and colleagues at the Pedagogical University in Kraków has been conducted in a comparable national context of the deportations.[9] They concentrate mainly, however, on interviewing and thus preserving the memories of the former deportees.

A second way of telling the story stems from the destination countries, mainly Canada and Australia. This *Immigrant Story* is mainly interested in the way people with Polish backgrounds arrived in their new countries and how they were integrated there. Clearly in this line is the book by Allbrook and Cattalini about a group of Poles who eventually settled in Australia.[10] Their research was funded and published by the Australian Immigration authorities and based on interviews with former refugees. It tells the story of the whole odyssey starting with the deportations, but the main interest lies in the end point of the journey. Even better documented is the story of a group of Polish orphans who eventually settled in Canada. Apart from Królikowski's memoirs, Lynne Taylor wrote an excellent book on their journey and the diplomatic row the decision over their fate caused in the context of the emerging Cold War.[11] Taylor based her account on a range of interviews with the former refugee children and archival sources from Canada, Britain and international organizations. Other authors took the Polish refugees as a case study in articles about specific aspects of their migration, like Monica Janowski on foodways as a way of performing Polishness outside of Poland.[12] Ewa Stańczyk highlights the question of the children's experience of forced migration, and psychologist Amanda Chalupa is working on the way the refugee children coped with trauma.[13]

In both strands of literature, the African context serves mainly as a background to a story of suffering and survival. Interactions with the host population and administration are merely side notes, and the Poles are largely depicted as self-sufficient and rather isolated communities. They are mainly based on interviews with the former refugees and on archives in Europe and North America. Sources that capture perspectives from Africa are considered in neither of them.

The third – and smallest – strand of literature comes from an African studies background and tells the *Colonial Story*. It consists only of articles covering the sojourn, or an aspect of it, in one colonial territory. Martin Rupiah gives an overview of the refugee and internment camps in Southern Rhodesia and their use afterwards.[14] In a more recent article, Tavuyanago, Muguti and Hlongwana point to the marginal position of the Poles in Southern Rhodesia. In an attempt to keep the white community British, the Polish refugees were discriminated against and denied the right to settle permanently.[15] For Uganda, Samwiri Lwanga-Lunyiigo published in 1993 a conference paper on the history of the Polish refugees, pointing again to their rather marginal position.[16] In the conference, as elsewhere, the Polish refugees form the prelude to the long history of refugee hosting in Uganda.[17] Kiyaga-Mulindwa published a short article on the refugees in Uganda, arguing that the colonial government's opposition to white settlement led to the isolation of the Poles and hence a lack of impact or impression.[18] For Tanganyika, only a brief text from 1952 by the colonial official who was in charge of the refugees is available.[19] In the history of Tanzanian refugee hosting, the Poles are, however, left out.[20] For Northern Rhodesia, Alfred Tembo researches the history of the Polish refugees and a Master's thesis looked at the history of one of the refugee settlements.[21] Apart from this, there are scattered references to the Polish refugees in the literature on African colonial history, but they are often confined to a sentence or a footnote.

This book is thus the first comprehensive study of the Polish refugees and their interaction with the different actors of the hosting colonial societies. The few articles that tell the *Colonial Story* all cover only one country. The books that tell the *Exile Story* treat the host societies only as a backdrop – an exotic stopover on the long odyssey of the Polish exiles. The literature telling the *Immigrant Story* traces the background of a part of the immigrant population. All three strands of literature operate within a national frame – only the nations differ. The *Exile Story* views the refugees as part of the global Polish diaspora, that is firmly committed to the national cause. In the *Immigrant Story* the Poles are incorporated into Canadian or Australian history, countries where immigration is an essential part of the national narrative.[22] Literature of the *Colonial Story* focuses on one postcolonial African nation, incorporating the refugee hosting into the historiography of that nation and its colonial predecessor.

By contrast, *On the Edges of Whiteness* tells another story. It covers not only the whole range of places and colonies in East and Central Africa that hosted the refugees, but also takes none of the actor groups for granted. While my main interest is in colonial social history, I will not ignore the pre- or post-history of this episode. To understand the Poles' social position with regard to the hosting societies it is necessary to know where they came from; and to understand what some of them later said and wrote about their time in Africa, it is necessary to know where they went afterwards. In contrast to the articles about individual colonies and their policies towards the refugees, I do not insert the story into any national narrative but deliberately take a regional perspective.

An Entangled History of Colonial Whiteness

Based on 'global history' approaches, this study does not confine itself to the historiography of one nation.[23] It focuses on the entanglements and interaction between people from different places around the world, without reducing them to mere representatives of 'their' nation. This does not mean that national or local identifications are not important or that all things and people are the same. Hierarchies and differentiation are no less important through interconnectedness. With regard to my case, global history means, first of all, that it is a history that crosses borders.[24] But more than this, my understanding of the refugee group is not as an integral, homogeneous part of the Polish nation in exile. Some of them worked hard to keep up this sense of belonging, while others were less committed to do so. They were furthermore not completely isolated from their surroundings. There was considerable interaction between the Polish refugees and members of the host population, although the authorities tried to minimize it. Just like in European displaced person camps of the time, the Polish refugee camps in Africa 'manifested a degree of porosity'.[25] The links of the refugees (and colonial officials) were furthermore not confined to their hosting colony. They were connected to each other, and to the central refugee administration in Nairobi, the Colonial Office, the Foreign Office, the Polish government-in-exile in London, and international refugee and diaspora organizations.[26] Although this interaction is generally acknowledged in national historiographies, it has so far not been the focus of enquiry.

Focusing on the manifold interactions, this study takes inspiration from Werner and Zimmermann's *Histoire Croisée* approach. They developed their approach as a critique of both static comparisons of national entities and unidirectional transfers between two nations. According to Werner and Zimmermann:

> *Histoire croisée* breaks with a one-dimensional perspective that simplifies and homogenizes, in favor of a multidimensional approach that acknowledges plurality and the complex configurations that result from it. Accordingly, entities and objects of research are not merely considered in relation to one another but also through one another, in terms of relationships, interactions, and circulation.[27]

Bringing the intersections between objects into central focus, they urge us to consider not only the changing nature and the criss-crossing of transfers, but also to view the objects or entities *through* each other. I am hence not only recounting what happened between these actor groups, but also how they saw each other. I will thus focus on the interaction, the encounters, the conflicts and the mutual perceptions and influences.

The inherent danger in such an approach is, obviously, the one that Gorge Luis Borges sketched in 1946 in his one paragraph short story *On Exactitude in Science*.[28] In trying to make more and more precise maps, the cartographers of a fictional kingdom made such an exact map that it finally had the same size as its territory. Realizing that this huge map was useless, later generations simply dumped it into the desert. In order to evade the same fate, this study will not only describe as precisely as possible (within the limits of the available sources), but will also generalize from the findings.

The history of colonialism is in itself an entangled history of encounter, transfers, boundary making and mutual influences.[29] It is not a simple transfer of European social models into the colonies. As Ann Laura Stoler notes: 'Colonial cultures were never direct translations of European society planted in the colonies, but unique cultural configurations'.[30] While different colonial societies functioned differently, there were certain commonalities. Colonial rule rested, as Frantz Fanon noted, on a Manichean division into colonizer and colonized, corresponding with the racialized division into white and black.[31] Partha Chatterjee remarks accordingly that many signs could be taken to divide colonial societies, but 'race was perhaps the most obvious mark of colonial difference'.[32] While the difference between the colonizer and the colonized was maintained through the construction of racial difference, the dividing lines were never precise. Frederick Cooper rightfully cautions that this 'racialization of difference' in nineteenth-century imperial polities was not only significant but also unstable.[33] He consequently argued that at the heart of colonialism was 'the *politics* of difference'.[34] While colonial ideology constructed a clear-cut difference between white and black, the colonially ruled world did not conform to this ideal: 'The Manichean world of high colonialism that we have etched so deeply in our historiographies was thus nothing of the sort'.[35] There is an important difference between the discursive world of colonialist ideology and the empirically and locally grounded history of colonial societies. The two are closely linked, but not the same. Poor white refugees from the rural periphery had no place in the ideal colonialist world, but they were there. So, where did they fit in?

A simple answer is not possible for such a variety of places. But all of them were part of the British Empire that rested on the assumption of European superiority. One could expect the social position and perspective of the Polish refugees to be a neutral third position in the fractured world of colonialism. They were neither colonizers nor colonized, and before arrival they had personal experiences themselves of being declared an enemy of the state by the Soviets, and part of a subhuman race (*Untermenschen*) by the German Nazis. They could have been rather sympathetic to the plight of the colonized. But as Albert Memmi pointed out in 1957: 'The colonial situation manufactures colonialists, just as it manufactures the colonized'.[36] For this case, Memmi's statement could be understood as the impossibility of a position outside the colonial dichotomy for the Polish refugees. Comparing different perspectives on the refugees' social position offers a way to take a closer look at the complex empirical realities of British late colonial societies. Just as Africans were not a homogenous group, nor were the Europeans.

Examining white people in colonial society connects to the flourishing field of critical *whiteness studies*. The simple starting point of whiteness studies as an academic field was the observation that studies of race or racism usually examined the people who were discriminated and not the people who were privileged. W.E.B. Du Bois was one of the first writers already tackling this issue in his classic essay *The Souls of White Folk* in 1910.[37] However, just with discussions in the 1990s in the United States, whiteness has come under increasing scholarly scrutiny. David Roediger and other historians have studied why white workers did not join their black colleagues in a common class struggle, as Marxist reasoning would expect, but advanced their position by forming white-only unions.[38] East and South European immigrants to the United States, who had previously been classified into different racial groups, became 'white' after the turn of the twentieth century.[39] Their rewards were the 'wages of whiteness', which were not only financial but also public and psychological.[40] Being white brought privileges in the workplace and in the public sphere. Sociologist Ruth Frankenberg critically engaged with fellow white feminists for ignoring race, and emphasized the importance of scrutinizing the seemingly neutral position of whiteness. Starting from the premise that any system of differentiation shapes the privileged as well as the oppressed, she states: 'Naming "Whiteness" displaces it from the unmarked, unnamed status that is itself an effect of its dominance'.[41] She thereby points to the usually ignored role of whiteness as 'unmarked marker', the position from which white people speak about others. As a relational category, whiteness can only function in differentiation towards being black. Whiteness, however, is no timeless monolithic entity, but is historically situated in specific times and places.[42]

The focus of most studies on the US context has subsequently been challenged by scholars who point to the transnational nature of whiteness. Taking up Du Bois' famous notion of the 'colour line' as the problem of the twentieth century, they traced the evolution and spread of 'whiteness as a transnational form of racial identification'.[43] Frankenberg also clarified that the position of whiteness as 'invisible norm' only applies to very specific contexts, namely when 'white supremacy is hegemonic'.[44] Most of the time and, even more importantly, to most people, it is quite clearly visible.[45] This is obviously the case for colonial societies where whites formed a tiny but powerful minority. Satya Mohanty even claims that 'colonial rule generated a dominant image of the white man as spectacle'.[46] Whites were highly visible in the colonies, and attached a high importance to the impression they made on the colonized.[47] Brett Shadle showed that Kenyan settlers were preoccupied with white prestige as a kind of barrier to protect them against rebellious Africans.[48] Settlers believed that as long as Africans thought whites were superior, they would not dare to rise against them.[49] It was therefore of utmost importance to maintain white prestige by appropriate behaviour. Although British settlers distinguished and looked down on other whites, they were convinced that Africans could not distinguish. The individual failure by *some* whites to maintain white prestige led to a threat to *all* white people in the colony.[50]

This leads us directly to the margins of white colonial societies. The liminal whiteness of the Polish refugees offers a case to interrogate the drawing of racial boundaries within colonial societies. The Poles thereby resemble two categories of people that Stoler pointed out as threatening and defining 'the boundaries of European (white male) prestige and control': poor whites and white women.[51] The Polish refugees were mainly women and 'largely peasant folk'[52] who were completely dispossessed through the deportations. Their lice-ridden, emaciated appearance upon arrival was a far cry from the quasi-aristocratic lifestyle of settlers. They had more in common with other people whom Harald Fischer-Tiné termed 'subaltern whites'. In his study on white vagrants, criminals, prostitutes and lunatics in India, he showed that they were privileged as well as marginalized.[53] The problem of poor whites in colonial societies was, following Stoler, generally tackled with three measures: isolation, material support and removal.[54] To have them out of sight of the colonized, specific institutions to isolate European criminals and lunatics were set up. Secondly, poor whites got financial and technical support as well as access to better education to lift them above Africans.[55] And thirdly, colonial governments kept out the unwanted less affluent whites through immigration restrictions. Impoverished Europeans were, furthermore, sent back home.

The studies about white subalterns or poor whites are, however, mainly based on examples from the period of high colonialism. When the Poles arrived in Africa it was a different time. To be sure, discourses and convictions did not change at once; even in the late colonial period there were concerns over poor whites and racial transgression.[56] Furthermore, the increased regimentation during the Second World War led to growing tensions in the colonies. More Africans were demanding improved conditions and eventually self-government, while Indian independence loomed large as a precedent. The shift towards a rhetoric of 'racial partnership' led to an avoidance of overtly racist tones in the official administrative correspondence.[57] The superiority of whites, however, still formed the basis for policies of postwar 'developmental colonialism'.[58] Although the explicit goal of these efforts was 'to raise the standard of living of colonized people',[59] the idea was that superior Europeans were guiding inferior Africans on the way to eventual self-government. But the question of when this was to be achieved was contested between the colonial rulers and the leaders of the independence movements.[60] Some settlers insisted that Africans would never be capable of ruling themselves.[61] The rising tensions were a threat to the continuity of colonial domination and to the creation of friendly African-led successor states as well. An image of white superiority and prestige was thus not only important in the overtly racist discourse of high colonialism, but also in the late colonial discourse of development and African welfare. Africans would only follow Europeans as long as the latter were regarded as superior. As David Killingray and Richard Rathbone note poignantly on the impact of the Second World War on Africa: 'If colonial power in Africa had always rested on a mixture of bluff and force, the bluff proved to be a busted flush and the force more questionable than it had appeared before 1939'.[62] Cracks in the image of white superiority were but one of the factors that eventually led to the end of colonial rule, but maybe not the least important.

This study is not only about colonial whiteness, but about forced migration as well. In the scholarly writing about migration, 'identity' and the possibilities of renegotiating and remaking 'identities' is a central topic. The entry into a new social setting necessitates a renegotiation of the migrant's social position, but I caution here against the use of the term 'identity'. Brubaker and Cooper provide an influential critique of the widespread use of 'identity' as an analytical category.[63] They reject the 'hard' essentialist understanding of 'identity' (as a thing that individuals primordially have) as well as its 'soft' constructivist understanding (as 'constructed, fluid, and multiple').[64] What is subsumed under the term identity, however, is not a given, eternal thing, and nor can everyone choose identity categories at will. While 'identity' is an important 'category of practice', it is not a useful analytical category, as it is imprecise and it blurs 'constructivist language and essentialist argumentation'.[65]

As an alternative to the term, Brubaker and Cooper propose three more precise clusters of analytical terms that help to better describe what is usually subsumed under 'identity'. First, categorization and identification are processes of placing other people (or oneself) into a category. This processual term underlines the importance of agents that do the identification.[66] Secondly, self-understanding and social location describe the sense of who one is. In contrast to self-identification, this does not need to be discursively articulated.[67] A third cluster is commonality, connectedness and groupness. These terms describe the emotionally laden feeling of belonging to a distinctive group of people. It is what gives 'identity talk' its power to hold people together as well as to exclude others. To be sure, the three clusters are closely interrelated. If people are categorized by a state or discourse into a certain identity group, this may well lead to their feeling of groupness or belonging together, but this is not necessarily so. For the overarching question of this study it cautions us to analyse who places whom into which category, and how these categorizations differ relationally.

Scattered Sources

In order to trace different perspectives on the Polish refugees in colonial societies it is not enough to go to just one place. As the refugees travelled the globe, the documents that can recount their history are scattered far and wide. Accordingly, this study relies on a varied source base that can be grouped according to four perspectives from which the sources were produced. I will give a short overview of them here.

The perspective of different layers of the British colonial administration is captured through archival material from the national archives in London,

Dar es Salaam and Nairobi.[68] In London the sources consist mainly of correspondence of the Colonial Office (signature CO) with the respective colonial governments, but also of files from the Foreign Office (FO), the Ministry of Education (ED) and the National Assistance Board (AST)[69] responsible for the welfare and integration of Poles in Britain. In Nairobi, as in Dar es Salaam, the files are correspondence and reports from the respective provincial and district commissioners as well as from the secretariat of the central government. Unfortunately, there are no complete files from the camp commandants or the government officials in charge of the refugees in the archives;[70] as a consequence, these records are fragmentary and sketchy. In the basement of Nairobi's McMillan Memorial Library, I went through some issues of the *East African Standard*, the leading (settler-dominated) newspaper in the region. Additional information was obtained from the Commonwealth and African Collections at the Bodleian Libraries in Oxford where some of the British officials, who had worked with the refugees, deposited their private papers.

Perspectives of the Polish refugees were captured through two Polish newspapers – *Nasz Przyjaciel* and *Głos Polski* – published by and for the refugees in Nairobi.[71] Additional sources from the Polish perspective are found in the archives of the former Polish government-in-exile – the Polish Institute and Sikorski Museum (PISM) in London.[72] Although I did no interviews with former refugees themselves, I consulted a range of recollections and memoirs of former Polish refugees. While the nature of these sources makes them not unproblematic, they offer the possibility to approximate the perspective of the 'average' refugee and not only the elites. As outlined above, most of the existing secondary literature on this episode is based on interviews with former refugees, so there was already a large literature I could build on.

To trace African perspectives I conducted interviews with former workers and neighbours of the Polish camps in the vicinity of the three biggest refugee settlements (Tengeru, Koja and Masindi/Nyabyeya) as well as in Dar es Salaam. As I was not able to trace written primary sources by Africans regarding the Polish refugees, this was the only possibility to capture these perspectives. While there might be contemporary African newspaper articles on the Poles, the search for such material would be like looking for a needle in a haystack. The challenges of using oral sources alongside written ones will be discussed in Chapter 5.

A fourth set of sources is found in the records of the International Refugee Organization (IRO), stored in the Archives Nationales in Paris. This corpus provides yet another perspective on the whole issue, and was revealing because it introduced a fourth set of actors: the staff of international organizations. From 1947 to 1950 the Polish refugees were under not only the dual Polish and colonial administration but were the responsibility of the IRO as well. Additionally, I was provided with some copies from the archives of the International Tracing Service (ITS) in Bad Arolsen and the records of the United Nations Relief and Rehabilitation Administration (UNRRA) from the United Nations archives in New York.[73] A valuable report on the camps by an American Red Cross official as well as the papers of one IRO official were consulted in the Bodleian Libraries in Oxford.

As this brief overview suggests, there is no single or complete corpus of primary sources to answer all the questions raised in this study. The multi-perspective approach of my research and the broad geographical range of this history call instead for an assemblage of source types. Each type has its limitations, gaps and biases, which I will address in the respective chapters.

Outline

This book is divided into three parts, giving the background (Chapter 1), three issues (Chapters 2, 3, 4) and three perspectives (Chapter 5) on the Polish refugees' sojourn. In the Conclusion, the findings and arguments are summed up, evaluated and an outlook is given.

Chapter 1 provides a descriptive narrative of the Polish refugees' journey to Africa, descriptions of all refugee settlements, their administrative set-up and the refugees' further trajectories. It provides the basis for understanding why there were Poles in Africa, where and how they lived, and where they went afterwards. The chapter thereby forms the necessary basis for the more problem-centred, argumentative chapters that follow. It therefore draws on a broad range of primary and secondary sources to give accurate descriptions and impressions of the different settlements.

Chapters 2 to 4 each address one aspect of the Polish refugee group, and connect their story to another scholarly debate. All three chapters start with a literature review of this discussion, to which the Polish refugees in Africa serve as cases.

Chapter 2 understands the Polish refugees as one group among the millions of refugees and displaced persons (DPs) produced by the Second World War. While they were initially deportees, they became refugees in the African settlements. They were placed under special legislation, and in the postwar period came under the care of newly established international organizations. I argue that the officials of these new organizations differed in some regards from the colonial officials hitherto in charge of the Poles. While the colonial officials based their decisions on the basic assumption of fundamental differences between different (ethnic, racial) groups, the assumed principle guiding the IRO officials was a universalist and technocratic understanding of the subjects of their social intervention. Despite the universalist aspiration, the

IRO was, in fact, confined to assisting European refugees only, no matter where in the world they were located.

Chapter 3 focuses on the national history of the refugees. It contributes to a discussion in the historiography of East Central Europe and its recent conceptual opening towards transnational or global history. In the conflicting field between Polish national historiography and postcolonial approaches, a debate about the understanding of Poland as a former colony of Germany and/or Soviet-Russia has evolved. In particular, the reading of Soviet dominance as colonial rule over the region has led to fierce discussions. The chapter takes the Poles' sojourn as a kind of test case for the thesis of the equation of Poland as colony, brought forward by some in this debate. Enquiring whether the Poles sided with the colonizers or the colonized, I argue that the Polish elites, at least, identified and portrayed themselves as members of Western Europe, and hence were on the colonizers' side.

Chapter 4 looks at the gender aspect of the refugee group. As most refugees were women and children, this focus contributes to the historiography of white women in colonial societies. It further draws inspiration from interpretations of the history of the Polish diaspora and migration studies that take gender as an important social category. The gendered analysis of the situation shows that the women were basically in a position of dependence on the male soldiers in the army as well as the male Polish and British administrators. These men regarded them as an asset for potentially stabilizing their communities, but also as a threat if they crossed the boundaries of the community. Officials' reactions towards transgressive refugee women show that these boundaries were most of all racially defined. But the women were also actors in their own right, deliberately making their way. Some profited from employment opportunities provided by war conditions and the racially defined colonial division of labour. The women made the most of their constrained and dependent situation.

Chapter 5 contrasts three perspectives on the social position of the Polish refugees in regard to the hosting colonial societies. The first section asks how the British members of the colonial societies dealt with the influx of refugees, and how they inserted them into the colonial setting. Thereby I put stronger emphasis on the specific local conditions and socio-economic models, and differentiate between the perspectives of administrators and settlers. To capture the latter's perspective, I drew on newspaper correspondence in Nairobi's *East African Standard* as well as on memoirs and secondary literature. Generally speaking, the Polish refugees were regarded and treated by the British part of the colonial societies like subaltern whites. They were isolated, materially lifted and sent away as soon as feasible. While some officials and settlers were sympathetic with the Poles' plight, there was the widespread conviction that they should not become a permanent part of society. Reasons for this were the threat to the image of white superiority, the possibility of the establishment of a numerous competitor for political power, and the fear of stirring up opposition from the colonized. All this was informed by a class-based understanding of the Poles as European peasants, who did not fit into colonial societies in Africa.

The second section examines Polish perspectives on the sojourn. Again, I first show that the Polish refugee group was no uniform block of exiles as national historiography portrays them. Within the group there were cleavages of class, gender, religion and political affiliation. The elite Poles, who wrote in the newspapers, underlined their position as European allies on an equal footing with the British. By contrast, the memory literature and recollections of former refugees paint a more egalitarian picture in regard to Africans. After surviving the deportations, the Polish refugees presented themselves as simple human beings and less arrogant than members of the colonial white community. They nevertheless underlined their distance from the Africans. The Catholic faith played an important role in the everyday life in the settlements. While it strengthened the bond between the Poles it also provided ground for interaction with fellow believers of other races and nationalities. In the colonial situation the Poles thereby echoed some traits with the self-perception of missionaries; the paternalistic position of helping the 'poor heathens' by bringing the allegedly superior faith.

The last section is based mainly on interviews with former African camp workers and neighbours, and on some traces of African perspectives in secondary literature. The interviewees provide, again, differing assessments of the refugees, who are seen as no homogeneous group. The bigger Polish settlements were major sites of employment, attracting thousands of workers for the initial construction. Some hundreds who built the camps arrived also involuntarily as conscript workers. The settlements were furthermore large markets for local producers, providing them with an opportunity for selling fresh products. The sites of the settlements became thus not only places of encounter between Africans and Poles, but between Africans from many places as well. To generalize a bit, the Poles were described, in retrospect, as friendly white people with superior knowledge who were, however, controlled and isolated by the distanced, arrogant British administrators. The religious encounter played an important role for African Catholics, corresponding with the Polish self-perception as missionaries. But in some instances, the Poles were also portrayed as a threatening group, causing fear among their neighbours. Taken together, the material improvement of the Poles' situation, together with their humbler attitude, seem to have made an impression.

Contrasting the different perspectives and experiences of the Poles' nearly eight-year stay in East and Central Africa shows the value of the chosen approach. The refugees were not in a neutral third position outside the colonial dichotomy, but somewhere on the lower rungs of white society. In the Conclusion, these thoughts are taken up, and the relevance for a better understanding of the complex social dynamics of colonial societies are touched upon. While some individual Poles managed to become accepted respectable members of white society, the majority were placed somewhere on 'the edges of whiteness'.

Notes

1. Please note that I use 'Poles' as a shorthand for 'Polish citizens', as not all of them were considered to be ethnically Polish – an issue I will return to later.
2. By 'Central Africa' I am referring throughout this book to the historical region of 'British Central Africa', consisting of the British colonies of Northern Rhodesia, Southern Rhodesia and Nyasaland.
3. Piotrowski, *Polish Deportees*. Most of the recollections in the Africa chapter of Piotrowski's volume are taken from Sulkiewicz, Bartkowiak-Drobek and Fundacja Archiwum Fotograficzne Tułaczy, *Tułacze dzieci. Exiled children*.
4. Piotrowski, *Polish Deportees*, 2.
5. Julia Devlin's small book is largely based on secondary literature and only draws on a few primary sources. See Devlin, *Deportation und Exil*.
6. Krolikowski, *Stolen Childhood*. The original Polish version was published in London in 1960 (Królikowski, *Skradzione dzieciństwo*) and translated into English in 1983. Please note, when I refer to him as 'Krolikowski' (and not 'Królikowski') I refer to his translated book.
7. Krolikowski, *Stolen Childhood*, xv.
8. Wróbel, *Uchodźcy polscy*, 7. Unless otherwise stated, all translations from Polish, German, Kiswahili and French are by myself.
9. See the volume published after a 2010 conference of the same title: Chudzio, *Z mrozów Syberii pod słońce Afryki*. On Tengeru camp, see the book by another member of the research group: Hejczik, *Sybiracy pod Kilimandżaro*.
10. Allbrook and Cattalini, *The General Langfitt Story*.
11. Taylor, *Polish Orphans*. See also Kévonian, 'Histoires d'enfants' and the MA thesis of Payseur, 'I Don't Want to Go Back'. On the same topic there are some short articles by a member of the group. See Tomaszewski, 'Snows of Siberia'; Tomaszewski, 'Shade'.
12. Janowski, 'Food in Traumatic Times'. Her article is based on interviews with former Polish refugees in Britain.
13. Stańczyk, 'Exilic Childhood'. Chalupa is working with interviews in an ongoing PhD project in psychology. See http://storytelling.concordia.ca/content/chalupa-amanda (last accessed 6 December 2019).
14. Rupiah, 'History of the Establishment of Internment Camps'.
15. Tavuyanago, Muguti and Hlongwana, 'Victims'. Mlambo makes a comparable point, but draws comparisons to other white groups as well. See Mlambo, 'Some Are More White'.
16. Lwanga-Lunyiigo, 'Uganda's Long Connection'.
17. For a recent example, see UNHCR and World Bank, 'Assessment of Uganda's Progressive Approach'.
18. Kiyaga-Mulindwa, 'Uganda: A Safe Haven'.
19. Pennington, 'Refugees in Tanganyika'.

20. Chaulia, 'Politics of Refugee Hosting'.
21. Alfred Tembo, University of Zambia, did research on the Poles in the Zambian National Archives (he generously shared a draft chapter of his forthcoming book with me). Mary-Ann Sandifort wrote her Master's thesis about Abercorn camp (Sandifort, 'World War Two').
22. Gabaccia has termed and criticized this 'immigrant paradigm' in the United States from a transnational perspective. See Gabaccia, 'Is Everywhere Nowhere?'
23. On global history and related approaches generally, see Conrad and Eckert, 'Globalgeschichte'.
24. Duara, 'Transnationalism', 43.
25. See Gatrell, 'Homeland' to 'Warlands', 15.
26. For the colonial officials it makes sense to speak of networks or webs of empire (see Lester, 'Imperial Circuits'; Ballantyne, *Webs of Empire*). The Poles, in turn, were part of these networks, but at the same time part of Polish diaspora networks (see Jaroszyńska-Kirchmann, *Exile Mission*; Pacyga, 'Polish Diaspora').
27. Werner and Zimmermann, 'Beyond Comparison', 38.
28. For the English translation, see Borges, 'On Exactitude in Science'.
29. See Conrad and Randeria, 'Geteilte Geschichte'.
30. Stoler, 'Rethinking Colonial Categories', 135.
31. Fanon, *Die Verdammten dieser Erde*.
32. Chatterjee, *The Nation and Its Fragments*, 20.
33. Cooper, *Colonialism in Question*, 29.
34. Ibid., 23.
35. Cooper and Stoler, 'Between Metropole and Colony', 8.
36. Cited here from the English translation in the 2003 edition. Memmi, *The Colonizer and the Colonized*, 100.
37. Du Bois' essay 'The Souls of White Folk' was published in 1910 and in a revised version again in 1920. It is reprinted in Du Bois, *Social Theory*, 32–37. On the text see also Rabaka, 'The Souls of White Folk'.
38. Roediger, *The Wages of Whiteness*, 6. For a critical overview of historical whiteness studies, see Kolchin, 'Whiteness Studies'.
39. Barrett and Roediger, 'Inbetween Peoples'; Jacobson, *Whiteness of a Different Color*; Zecker, 'Negrov Lynčovanie'.
40. Roediger, *The Wages of Whiteness*, 12.
41. Frankenberg, *White Women, Race Matters*, 6.
42. Ibid., 21. See also Steyn, *Whiteness Just Isn't What It Used To Be*.
43. Lake and Reynolds, *Drawing the Global Colour Line*, 3. In the same direction, some are arguing for closer attention to the connections between the histories of whiteness and colonial rule. For this argumentation, although focusing mainly on settler colonialism in Australia, see Boucher, Carey and Ellinghaus, *Re-Orienting Whiteness*.
44. Frankenberg, 'Introduction', 5.
45. For the US context, see hooks, *Black Looks*. For the image of whites in African oral and written literature see Schipper, *Imagining Insiders*, 30–55.
46. Mohanty, 'Drawing the Color Line', 314.
47. The 'hypervisibility' of whites is an important issue in present-day Africa as well. For a recent overview of the field, see Zyl-Hermann and Boersema, 'Introduction'.
48. Shadle, *The Souls of White Folk*, 5.
49. Kirk-Green makes a comparable point to explain the authority of colonial administrators in Africa. See Kirk-Greene, 'The Thin White Line', 42.

50. Shadle, *The Souls of White Folk*, 5.
51. Stoler, 'Rethinking Colonial Categories', 139.
52. Pennington, 'Refugees in Tanganyika', 54.
53. Fischer-Tiné, *Low and Licentious Europeans*.
54. Stoler, 'Rethinking Colonial Categories', 150.
55. E.g. for Southern Rhodesia see Kennedy, *Islands of White*, 169.
56. E.g. Carina Ray's study on interracial relationships in late colonial Gold Coast shows that the public legitimation of interracial marriages was, although not forbidden, still widely regarded as problematic. See Ray, *Crossing the Color Line*, 135.
57. Jackson, 'Dangers to the Colony'; Wolton, *Lord Hailey*, 3.
58. For Tanganyika, see Iliffe, *Modern History of Tanganyika*, 436. On the reconstruction and shifting policies in the French and British African empires, see Cooper, 'Reconstructing Empire'.
59. Cooper, 'Reconstructing Empire', 204.
60. Chakrabarty, *Provincializing Europe*, 8.
61. E.g. one Tanganyika settler estimated in 1934 that it would take at least a century until Africans could rule themselves. See Reid, *Tanganyika without Prejudice*, 34.
62. Killingray and Rathbone, *Africa and the Second World War*, 3.
63. Brubaker and Cooper, 'Beyond "Identity"'.
64. Ibid., 1.
65. Ibid., 6.
66. Ibid., 14.
67. Ibid., 18.
68. I did not visit the national archives of Uganda, Zambia or Zimbabwe, but refer to secondary literature based on these three archives.
69. These abbreviations feature in the PRO's internal system indicating the origin of the archive files.
70. The responsible officials (the Director of Refugees in Tanganyika, the Director of Aliens and Internees and War Refugees in Kenya) as well as the camp commandants are, however, prominent in the correspondence with local officials.
71. Please note that I have looked at only a fraction of the Polish newspapers covering the period from 1945 to 1947. Going through the *Polak w Afryce* newspaper, which ceased publication in 1945, could add further valuable insights into the early years of the refugees' stay in Africa. All three papers are held by the library of the *Polski Ośrodek Społeczno-Kulturalny* (POSK) in Hammersmith, London. As the Nairobi newspaper print shops were not able to print Polish diacritics, the articles were printed without them. Throughout this book I cite the original titles without correcting these mistakes. I further cite the original spelling of names in the English files, which usually did not include diacritics and sometimes anglicized first names (e.g. Joseph instead of Józef).
72. There are more Polish sources that I did not consult, e.g. in the archives of the *Ośrodek KARTA* and the *Archivum Akt Nowych* in Warsaw, as well as in the Hoover Institution in Stanford which holds some material from the Polish government-in-exile. They already form, however, the base of other publications to which I refer in this book.
73. My sincerest thanks to Katarzyna Nowak for providing me with invaluable copies from these two archives.

Chapter 1

HOW THE POLES CAME TO AFRICA

The journey of most Polish refugees started in the early morning hours with a knock on the door. It was a freezing winter morning in February 1940 when Soviet NKVD (secret police) men and soldiers forced the Poles at gunpoint to pack a few belongings and gathered them at the nearest train station. From there the odyssey started in almost unbearable circumstances, locked up in cattle wagons, fighting for survival. At this time none of them would have guessed that three years later they would be living in camps in the British colonies of East or Central Africa. One of the refugees later remembered the moment, when she was forced to leave home: 'It was bitterly cold and I felt fear, fear of the unknown'.[1]

British officials in the East and Central African colonies were not aware of this drama unfolding in eastern Poland. For them the story started on 26 June 1942, when Thomas H. Preston, the head of the Middle East Relief and Refugee Administration (MERRA), came to Nairobi. His mission was to convince the governors to take in some of the Poles who were at that time staying in camps in Iran.[2] The colonial governments were supposed to set up camps where the Polish refugees could stay for the duration of the war. The newspaper-reading public in the colonies was asked for donations and support.[3] One former policeman remembered seeing the Poles when the first ship arrived a few months later in Dar es Salaam: 'Some 1000 women and children came on the first ship; they were distressingly dirty and debilitated and none spoke English'.[4]

For Africans living in the vicinity of the refugee camps, the story began a month later with a call for construction work. Within ten days after Preston's visit, the Tanganyika government had made arrangements to take possession of a farm in northern Tanganyika near Arusha and asked the provincial commissioner to start construction work for a refugee camp 'forthwith'.[5] Three months later, in October, the first Polish refugees arrived on the site, where construction was to continue until late the following year. Eventually around four thousand workers erected some twelve hundred buildings.[6] In Northern Rhodesia the district commissioner of Abercorn asked people to cut grass for roofs without informing them who would eventually sleep under them.[7] In Uganda hundreds of workers literally had to cut the site for Masindi camp out of the forest.[8] In the end, two thousand were employed in the construction of the camp and another one thousand in that of the other Ugandan camp in Koja.[9] Many others were later employed in the upkeep of the camps or their supply with food products. One Ugandan camp worker later remembered: 'When they came, we used to fetch firewood for the Polish refugees. We made sure the firewood was split, the logs, we washed for the Polish bosses'.[10]

Deportations from the Eastern Borderlands

The 19,200 Polish refugees who eventually lived in Africa for some years were a small part of a bigger group whose ordeal started with the Soviet invasion at the beginning of the Second World War. They were victims of the mass deportations that Soviet forces carried out in the eastern parts of Poland. Under the Hitler–Stalin pact, Poland was divided into two parts and both occupation forces carried out massive deportations. From 1940 to 1941 the Soviet NKVD organized the deportation of over three hundred thousand Polish citizens from the region that was to become incorporated into the Byelorussian and Ukrainian Soviet Socialist Republics.[11] Before the war this ethnically mixed region was called the eastern borderlands or '*kresy*', and had been part of the Second Polish Republic since the Polish–Soviet War of 1919–21.[12] The deportations aimed to crush Polish political and social life in order to safeguard Soviet domination, and were targeted not only at the Polish elites, but at Poles of all social categories, from peasants to the intelligentsia.[13] But it was not only ethnic Poles who were deported, but Polish citizens of Jewish, Ukrainian and Belarusian nationality as well.[14] The deportations were aimed at all people who were suspected of being a potential threat to the new political order.

After early arrests in 1939 of those Poles who were associated with the state apparatus, the bulk of the others were deported in early 1940.[15] The first mass deportation was carried out by the NKVD in February 1940 and took most of its victims by surprise. Soviet soldiers usually came in the early morning hours. Within a moment, the life of the deportees had taken a violent turn – they were forced from their homes, loaded onto lorries or sleighs or had to walk to the next train station. The victims of the February deportations were mainly *osadnicy* (settlers or colonists, i.e. Poles who had received land from the Polish state after the Polish–Soviet war) and forestry workers, together with their families.[16] These first deportations were the most severe, as they took place in freezing temperatures and the victims were completely unprepared.[17] Some elderly and children died on this cold morning on their way to the trains.[18] After these first deportations, other people in the region were aware about what could happen, and so some already had their luggage packed when the second and third waves of deportation took place in April and June 1940. The April deportations targeted the families of those already arrested and those who had evaded arrest, as well as tradespeople, small farmers and prostitutes.[19] Refugees from the German-occupied part of Poland, mainly Jews, were the target of the June deportations. The last deportation wave one year later was aimed at those who had escaped earlier attempts. It was, however, cut short by the German attack on the Soviet Union.[20]

All four deportation waves followed a common procedure. In the stations, freight trains stood ready for the deportees to be locked inside and transported eastwards. The trains consisted of forty to fifty wagons, each filled with fifty to sixty people. The conditions of the journey were terrifying. The deportees were kept unaware of where the trains were heading and an unknown number perished due to overcrowding, insufficient nourishment and insanitary conditions. In the winter it was bitingly cold, and in the summer unbearably hot.[21] Although whole families were arrested, the male household heads were usually separated from the rest of the family.[22] Depending on the final place of deportation, the transport could take several weeks. In the recollections of the deportees, these days in the trains formed the second traumatizing event after the forced removal from their homes.

When the trains finally arrived, things got no better. Depending on their status, the deportees fell into three categories. First, those who had been formally arrested and sentenced by NKVD courts were brought to corrective labour camps of the Gulag administration. Second, the ones who were seen as a generally 'anti-Soviet element' were brought to 'special settlements' in distant regions where they were obliged to stay and work.[23] Although this was not under the harsh conditions and direct control of closed camps, the circumstances were usually just as bad, and escape from these remote places was not a viable option. The third rubric included the so-called 'free deportees': mainly women and children who were not regarded as capable of heavy work. They were typically dropped off at far-off train stations and then brought from there to collective or state farms, where they were obliged to work for their own upkeep. Free deportees were treated like other Soviet citizens, and had (in comparison to the other categories) the most freedom. Nevertheless, they had to endure tough times in the struggle for daily survival in the remote regions of northern Kazakhstan or the Altai Krai.[24] Many deportees later referred to this period as 'Gehenna' – a biblical term roughly equivalent to hell.[25]

The deportees had to live under these severe conditions until the Sikorski–Maisky Agreement was signed on 30 July 1941. The pact, an agreement between Sikorski, the president of the Polish government-in-exile, and the Soviet ambassador Ivan Maisky, was reached with British mediation in London. It included the release of all Polish citizens in the Soviet Union and the formation of a Polish army to join the fight against Germany. The British government wanted to close ranks against the Nazi threat and end the conflict between the Polish and the Soviet government. The Soviet interest was urgent, as the USSR needed all possible support in its defence against the advancing Nazi troops. The Polish government-in-exile was eager to get its people out of the Soviet labour camps and special settlements. It also wanted to improve its political standing through the creation of a Polish army that would one day liberate Poland. The government was convinced that its army would become important in negotiations with the Allies during and after the war.[26]

News of the 'amnesty' sometimes only reached the deported Poles after weeks of delay. As there were no provisions made apart from the immediate release, most people just headed south to gathering points of the Polish army, using whatever means of transport they could find.[27] The journey took place under chaotic conditions and most had nearly no provisions for the long trip. The transport situation was further complicated by the simultaneous mass movement of people fleeing eastwards from the advancing German troops and the Soviet military moving westwards to the front.[28] The whole country was in a chaotic state with the German troops advancing and the Soviet mobilization running high. Train stations became overcrowded transit places for refugees, while the military had prior access to transport capacities. In this second 'voluntary' mass movement of people, the mortality was probably even higher than in the initial deportations that had brought the Poles to the Soviet Union.[29]

While the prospective soldiers were making their way to the gathering points of the Polish army, the relations between the Polish and Soviet officials were deteriorating. Additionally, the Polish soldiers faced severe supply problems. As a result, the army, which was in the process of formation, was transferred to Iran from March 1942 onwards. Food in the Soviet Union was generally short and the British needed troops to fight back the Axis forces in North Africa and secure the Iranian oilfields.[30] The transfer was mainly conducted across the Caspian Sea, with some smaller numbers of people taking a land route. One of the evacuees remembered being 'packed like sardines'.[31] When the first overcrowded ships arrived in the Persian port of Pahlavi (today Bandar e-Anzali), the British and Polish authorities were surprised to find civilians (women and children) among the evacuees.[32] The British authorities had prepared to receive 27,000 soldiers in the first evacuation, but instead about 33,000 soldiers and 11,000 civilians came. Faced by a humanitarian drama, and realizing that it would destroy the morale of the soldiers if their relatives were not taken care of, the British officials unwillingly accepted them. In the second evacuation in July 1942 there were circa 44,500 soldiers and 25,500 civilians.[33] As the Foreign Office wrote in a note to Winston Churchill: 'The morale of these troops could hardly be good had those with wives and children been compelled to leave them behind in the USSR'.[34]

For most of the Poles the arrival in Iran was a moment of relief and happiness. As one of them remembered it: 'Immediately things were better'.[35] For the first time since the initial knock on the door, they met officials who regarded them not as enemies but as part of an allied nation. The British army set up a makeshift tented camp directly on the shore of the Caspian Sea, and provided food and medical support for the lice-ridden, exhausted and emaciated refugees. To contain the spread of diseases, all arrivals were first quarantined and shaved, and all their clothes were burnt. Although more than two thousand died in Iran due to diseases and the after-effects of malnourishment during the journey, for the survivors a period of physical healing started.[36] One former refugee child remembered: 'In the new settlements a time of therapy and return to life began after the horrible experiences in Russia'.[37] The Poles capable of military service were separated from the civilians and transferred to Iraq and Palestine, where they were trained to eventually fight alongside the British in North Africa and Italy.[38]

For the civilians a time of waiting and anxiety began. First, they were transferred to more permanent camps in the vicinity of Tehran. These camps were organized by officials of the Polish government-in-exile. While negotiations and plans were made at the international level, the refugees were waiting, accommodating and hoping for solutions. As it became clear that they would have to go somewhere else, rumours about the possible destinations spread in the camps, and options were discussed.[39] The option of going to Africa was remembered by one of them as 'the move most feared', especially among the mothers.[40] Apart from the general reluctance to move further into the unknown and the desire to stay close to the Polish soldiers, images of a wild and dangerous continent seem to have been prevalent. Although there were attempts on the side of the Poles to influence their paths, the decisions were by and large made by the British authorities. The Poles who eventually landed on the African shores did not come by their own choice, but were forced by circumstances.

The Cyprus Group

Apart from the vast majority of Polish refugees, there was another, smaller group whose journey to Central Africa was rather different: the 'Cyprus group'. These were around five hundred Poles who had fled directly after the Polish defeat in 1939, via Romania to Cyprus.[41] In Cyprus the group was accommodated in luxurious top-class hotels. In July 1941 they were evacuated from Cyprus and brought via Palestine and South Africa to Northern Rhodesia.[42] By July 1942, there were 423 of them staying in Northern Rhodesia under the direct responsibility of the British Foreign Office.[43] Besides their different way of arriving in Africa, they had a different social composition. In contrast to the other Poles there were slightly more men in the group than women. Furthermore, while most of the Polish refugees had a rural background, the 'Cyprus Poles' were mainly part of the educated elite and close to the pre-war government, the biggest professional group among them being civil servants.[44] Their educated urban background was a problem for the local authorities, as the Northern Rhodesian Director of War Evacuees and Camps explained: 'The root of the trouble is that the type of evacuee sent to us is a town-dweller, quite unprepared to make the best of, let alone, enjoy life in what is still a pioneer country'.[45] According to the Northern Rhodesian governor, John Waddington, the evacuees started a hunger strike after they received one instead of two eggs per person for breakfast (in addition to liver, porridge and ham). He added that there existed 'a strong feeling of class-consciousness and of anti-Semitism' among them.[46] In the beginning they were housed in the Fort Jameson settlement and in hotels and boarding houses along the railway line between Livingstone and Lusaka.[47] Owing to the desire of the Polish authorities to have the Cyprus Poles separated from the main group, efforts were made to concentrate the former in one settlement in Livingstone.[48] Nevertheless, the majority lived scattered in hotels and private accommodation. Because of their educated background, those who found employment worked in government departments, private firms or the Polish administration of the camps.[49]

Why Africa? The Rationale behind the Refugee Hosting

To answer the question of why the colonial governments agreed to host the Polish refugees, we have to consider the war situation in early 1942. At that time German troops were advancing on Soviet territory and towards Egypt, and the outcome of the war was far from clear. The Allied forces were in dire need of support, and the Polish soldiers were a welcome reinforcement. While it seemed that nothing could stop the German advance towards the south-east, the British Middle East Command was short of manpower, and strategists feared the area could become the next major battlefield.[50] Anita Prażmowska notes: 'The manpower issue was crucial. Churchill and the Middle East Command in particular needed Polish soldiers, both in North Africa but also in Iran'.[51] To have these soldiers on their side it was important to take care of their relatives and compatriots who had been released with them from the Soviet Union. The people who were not regarded as fit for military service were largely women, children and elderly men. Although some Polish women joined the army's auxiliary service, most were stranded in the British camps in Iran. Of the over 110,000 Poles who arrived from the Soviet Union, nearly 40,000 were civilians.[52] While the soldiers came under the command of the British armed forces, these civilians had to be taken care of. Apart from the strategic interest in the soldiers, taking care of the Polish civilians was also a moral obligation. Once these destitute people had arrived on the Persian shores the British officials were obliged to look after them.

In July 1942, Anthony Eden, the Secretary of State for Foreign Affairs, explained the refugee situation in the Middle East to the War Cabinet. He indicated that there were already 13,000 Polish civilians in Persia and that the Polish government wanted to send another 50,000 women and children who were 'stated to be starving in the Soviet Union', adding: 'Without meeting the Polish Government on this point it may prove impossible to obtain the three divisions of Polish soldiers which the Russians said they would be willing to permit to leave and whose services are urgently required by our Military Authorities'.[53] Eden further claimed that these 'abnormal additions of war refugees ... are embarrassing to our military effort' and he underlined: 'The problem ... is not so much humanitarian but military and political'. Nairobi's *East African Standard* newspaper explained to its readers that the refugees had to be removed, 'as they were liable to clog what might be a potential war area'.[54] The director of the East African Refugee Administration (EARA) later underlined that the hosting of the Polish civilians had made possible 'the transfer from Soviet Russia to the Middle East front, at a most critical moment of the war, of thousands of additional Polish bayonets'.[55]

There were three reasons for their relocation from Iran. First, refugees were seen as a liability in a strategically important area. Vital supply lines to the Soviet allies ran through the 'Persian Corridor', and British strategists regarded the refugees as potentially disturbing the military logistics. The second reason was that Iran was quite close to the war theatres, and the danger loomed that it would become a battlefield itself. The third reason was food shortages in Iran, that were exacerbated by the presence of the refugees.[56] The strategic importance of getting refugees out of the way was a lesson learned from the summer 1940 advance of German troops, in which refugees had hindered the Allied military logistics.[57]

Following these considerations, the British administration became aware that they had to take care of the Polish civilians and move them further away from the war. Uganda and Tanganyika agreed to take in 10,000 refugees after they were approached in June 1942, and the Government of India declared itself willing to receive a thousand Polish children. Eden's further recommendations for relocation of Polish civilians were to request the South African Union to take in 50,000 refugees, the East African colonies and the Rhodesias to take 30,000, and to send a non-specified number to Canada on returning US ships.[58] Interestingly, the South African government was seemingly very reluctant, as it finally admitted a mere five hundred children. Canada did not participate in any of the refugee hosting during wartime.[59] One can only speculate as to the reasons for this, but the geographical distance to Canada and the position of both as independent dominions could have contributed to their reluctance. Seen from Iran, India and the East African coast were much closer and part of the historically integrated region of the western Indian Ocean. The South African Union had furthermore already been hosting close to one hundred thousand Italian prisoners of war (POWs) since early 1941.[60] The colonies of the British Empire were less independent in their decision making and more obliged to contribute to the war effort.

The close connection to the war effort and the Polish army's contribution becomes clear when contrasted to the British reluctance to accept European Jews fleeing from Nazi prosecution. As Michael Marrus states in his seminal book on European refugees: 'In striking contrast to what was claimed about the Jews, namely, that there was no room anywhere for them, space was somehow found for the Polish civilian exiles, seen as co-belligerents against Hitler'.[61] The strategic interest in the army was the decisive factor. Antisemitism among the local European settler community may have been another reason for the acceptance of these mostly Catholic refugees. In 1938 a proposal for Jewish settlement in Northern Rhodesia had faced strong antisemitic opposition from settlers.[62] Kenyan efforts to fend of Jewish refugees are a further case in point.[63]

The Poles were subsequently 'dispersed in a way probably never before seen in history'.[64] Eventually about 4,000 went to India[65] (half of these were later sent to Mexico)[66] and about 7,000 to the Middle East (Palestine and Lebanon). The biggest group, consisting of 19,000 Poles, eventually passed through the British colonies in East and Central Africa.[67] According to numbers published in the *East African Standard*, on 1 July 1944 around 18,000 Polish refugees were in the African colonies, distributed as follows:

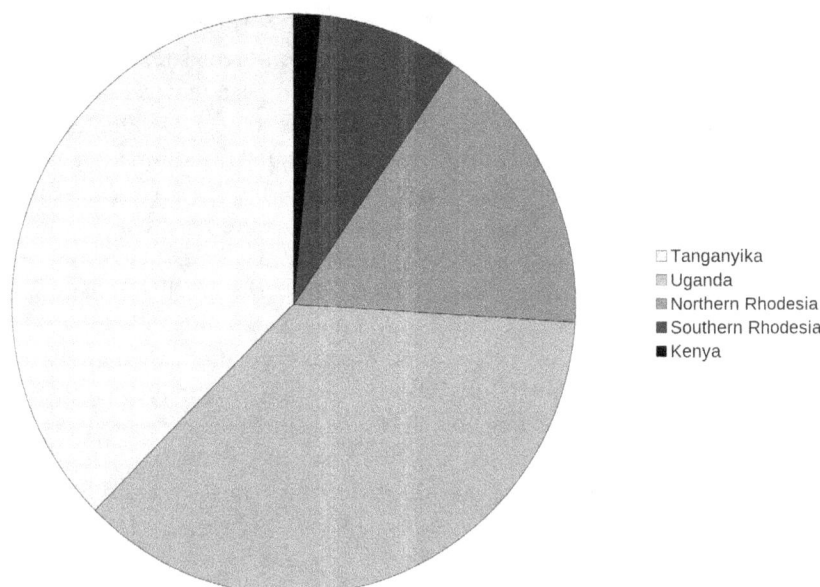

Figure 1.1. Distribution of refugees among the East and Central African territories, 31 December 1944. Chart created by the author with numbers from PISM: Kol 18/2: 'Stan liczbowy Uchodzcow Polskich w Afryce na 31.XII.1944'.

6,250 in Tanganyika, 6,250 in Uganda, 2,850 in Northern Rhodesia, 1,350 in Southern Rhodesia and 780 (in transit) in Kenya (see Figure 1.1).[68] The low numbers for Kenya were due to the fact that there were already a large number of Italian POWs in the country from the East African Campaign that had ended in 1941.[69] The war with Italy in neighbouring Ethiopia had brought Kenya close to the war theatre, and it hosted not only POWs but Commonwealth military personnel as well. The importance of Kenya as an economic and military hub for the operations against Italy and later Japan could have been another reason. It appears to have already contributed its fair share to the Commonwealth war effort. Uganda, Tanganyika and Northern Rhodesia had so far been less engaged and their position was less independent from the metropole. The low numbers of refugees in Southern Rhodesia seem to confirm the observations in regard to Kenya. While it never had dominion status, Southern Rhodesia was a self-governed colony with considerable independence from Britain in its domestic affairs, including defence.[70] The Southern Rhodesian army and air force were fighting in the war, and over five thousand interned enemy aliens were hosted alongside the Polish refugees.[71]

The colonial governments do not seem to have been eager to host the Polish refugees, despite the fact that the refugees were not their financial liability as all costs were reimbursed by the British Treasury, which in turn was hoping to get reimbursed by the Polish government later. It is not too far-fetched to relate the reluctance to host East European refugees to a general reluctance to accept East European immigrants as settlers. For the Southern Rhodesia case, Mlambo shows that there was a general discrimination against non-British white immigrants, aimed at Afrikaners and Jews, as well as immigrants from Eastern and Southern Europe. They were regarded as a threat to the image of white superiority and thus colonial rule.[72] Generally, the bigger the white population in the colony was, the smaller the number of Polish refugees accepted. Uganda and Tanganyika, with their tiny white communities,[73] hosted most of the Poles whereas the settler colonies – Kenya, Southern Rhodesia and the South African Union – accepted comparatively small numbers. Although it is not clearly documented in the sources, the existence of a powerful white settler lobby might be the reason behind this. While there was a politically powerful 'settler voice' in Kenya and Southern Rhodesia, this voice was weak in Tanganyika and nearly absent in Uganda.[74]

The Polish Settlements

In contrast to the sudden arrival of the Poles in Iran, the inhabitants and administration in the colonies had some time to prepare for the refugee influx. Through newspapers, the general public was asked to help and welcome them. Directly after the East African Governors' Conference (EAGC) had met with Thomas H. Preston, the *East African Standard* published an editorial explaining that the refugees were the wives and children of the 'gallant Polish fighters' and that there was no alternative place for them to stay, categorically stating: 'To them we owe a duty. To look after their wives and families will be a pleasure'.[75] In the article the Poles were portrayed as refugees fleeing the advancing German troops who joined the allied 'forces of freedom' and therefore 'they and their families are marked down by the enemy'. This explanation avoided the problematic mentioning of forced deportation by the Soviet ally. One month later the same paper reported that Tanganyika was ready to host five thousand Polish refugees for the duration of the war, and asked the local people to 'extend to these people ... the kindness and understanding sympathy [that] their plight deserves'.[76] And so they did.

The Poles experienced the arrival in East African ports as a moment of relief from their initial fears and anxiety about the unfamiliar destination. One of the refugees later remembered that 'fantastic tales' of cannibals, wild animals and poisonous snakes circulated among the passengers. Upon arrival in Dar es Salaam port, however, they were greeted by friendly black people: 'The overjoyed crowd threw exotic fruits onto the decks. For the first time in their exile, the refugees saw smiling faces'.⁷⁷ Another remembered the arrival in Tanga as a moment when they were 'relieved that [they] had encountered such a friendly people'.⁷⁸ The arrival in Beira, Mozambique was seemingly less enthusiastic, as only one Polish priest and a few Africans greeted the refugees.⁷⁹

After this cordial reception in the port cities of Mombasa, Tanga, Dar es Salaam or Beira the refugee groups were accompanied by colonial officials and brought by rail to the scattered refugee camps upcountry. In Dar es Salaam a transit camp was established on the premises of a former internment camp for Germans at Pugu Road.⁸⁰ After a short stay they were further distributed. For the trips to faraway camps, overnight stays were organized. The refugees were surprised about the warm welcome from both black and white people on a stopover in Nairobi, where a reception was arranged with food and fruits spread on tables and a small orchestra played.⁸¹ While British officials organized the transportation and hosting of the refugees, these social events were largely organized by European women's welfare organizations.⁸² In Tanga, for example, the Women's Service League collected and donated toys and clothes for the refugees.⁸³ All this proceeded with 'British efficiency', as one former refugee remembered.⁸⁴ Only one instance was rather disturbing to the refugees: as one of the first groups of arrivals left Dar es Salaam by train, they were accidentally 'attacked' by British soldiers in an exercise – a frightening experience and a reminder of the ongoing war elsewhere in the world.⁸⁵ Apart from this incident the transfers were uneventful. While the younger ones were mostly curious and enthusiastic to see the exotic 'Black Land' and its wild animals, the adults were more concerned about health problems, their lost relatives and their accommodation on this unfamiliar continent. While some camps could be reached directly by train, the last leg of the trip to the remote settlements was often made by lorry. Part of the way to Masindi camp in Uganda was even by a steamer on the River Nile.⁸⁶ Upon arrival the refugees started to get used to the new settlements and slowly made them their 'wartime homes'.⁸⁷

Although there was a great variety in the size and location of the refugee settlements, some general remarks can be made. First of all, there was no choice; every refugee was obliged to live in the refugee camp he or she was assigned to. The camps were mostly located in rather remote areas, but close enough to railways or roads. The camps were not tented, but permanent structures ranging from barrack-type accommodation to little round houses, made from a variety of materials. All settlements had at least one Polish primary school, and the bigger ones even had secondary schools. In the bigger camps there was often a central quarter, where the British and Polish officials worked, and some kind of social centre (usually run by the YMCA). Some place for worshipping was found in every camp, and Catholic priests were central figures in everyday life. The camps were not usually fenced in, and refugees were generally allowed to leave them. If they wanted to work or live outside, however, they needed a permission from the camp commandant.

Tanganyika

Tanganyika hosted more than a third of the Polish refugees; it had not only the biggest refugee settlement, but also the one that lasted longest. The refugees lived in five regular Polish settlements, and one transit camp in Dar es Salaam.

One of the smallest settlements in Tanganyika was *Morogoro*, about 200 km inland from Dar es Salaam, with around four hundred inhabitants.[88] It was attached to the Catholic Holy Ghost Fathers mission station in Bigwa, and used for two short periods for Polish refugees. Poles from the very first refugee contingent stayed there from September to December 1942 before being transferred to other settlements.[89] It was available at short notice, as the original plan to host Italian evacuees (women and children) from Ethiopia had been abandoned.[90] Afterwards it was used for Greek refugees and Italian prisoners of war.[91] In 1944 another group of Poles stayed there for one or two years.[92] The brief and interrupted existence was due to the unhealthy surroundings, especially a nearby swamp that was a breeding ground for mosquitoes. Attempts were made to drain the swamp, for which local farmers had to be compensated.[93] The missionaries, however, were unenthusiastic about this drainage, as they used the swamp for growing rice – but they accepted it.[94] Nevertheless the conditions remained unfavourable and the refugees were removed. The orphans were brought to Rongai, Kenya, and the others allocated to various camps in Tanganyika.[95] From 1946 on, the structures in Bigwa were used as a training centre for demobilized African soldiers.[96]

Like Morogoro, *Kondoa* settlement was rather small, attached to a mission and used for the very first arrivals. It was located in the Central Province in an arid region about two kilometres from Kondoa town, and became home to over four hundred refugees.[97] As in Morogoro, the settlement was supposed to be used for Italian evacuees and was therefore readily available.[98] It was attached to an Italian mission of the Passionist Fathers, of whom Benedetto Barbaranelli served as priest for the Poles as well.[99] The refugees were hosted in groups of twenty in rather simple mud barracks with banana-leaf roofs, later divided into five rooms housing four people each.[100] Despite its small size and the rather uninviting environment, Kondoa did not close down until late 1948 when the remaining inhabitants were moved to Tengeru.[101] According to one unconfirmed report, the majority of refugees in Kondoa were ethnically not Polish, but Belarusian or Ukrainian – an issue we will return to later.[102] Furthermore, Kondoa had a Polish camp commandant, Dr Zamenhof (Kidugala was the only other settlement to be run by a Pole) and thus for a while from mid-1943 it had no British official in its administrative structure.[103] Zamenhof and his wife, who was also a medical doctor, were responsible for the well-run camp hospital and established an exemplary care and diet programme for children who had arrived ill and undernourished.[104]

Kidugala was maybe the most remotely situated of the Tanganyika camps. It lay in the southern highlands of Tanganyika, with the closest town of Njombe more than one hundred kilometres away. From 1942 to 1948 this – according to a Polish article – 'pleasant centre'[105] became home to over a thousand Poles.[106] Kidugala consisted of two parts located on opposite sides of a small river and with vastly differing standards of construction. The inferior part was heavily criticized by a visiting British official who noted that an 'effective township authority ... would not accept the buildings in the better parts of its native townships'.[107] Again we have the connection to a mission station, but this time with another twist: the settlement was established on the premises of the Berlin Missionary Society, which had been confiscated when the war broke out. The German missionaries were interned or sent back to Germany while the African employees of the mission seem to have been sent away from the station when the Poles were settled there.[108] According to a newspaper article from 1942, the German pastor had earlier spread Nazi propaganda among the Africans. The irony of the situation was not lost on the Polish writer: 'Now the Germans are in a concentration camp and the bungalows [of the mission] have been handed over to the Poles, who are told to consider this as the first "reparation" for the villages destroyed in Poland'.[109] Due to the remote location and the absence of a British commandant it seems to have been run fairly independently from the colonial administration.[110] The initial British camp commandant was replaced by a Pole in 1943,[111] and it was the only settlement where Poles established a YMCA centre specially for Africans. The Poles seem to have somehow stepped into the footprints of the German missionaries, giving handicraft courses, among others, to Africans in this little school.[112]

With up to a thousand inhabitants,[113] *Ifunda* was about the same size as Kidugala and seems to have likewise been built on the confiscated lands of a German mission station.[114] Initial pastoral care was again provided by an Italian priest from a nearby mission, but then taken over by a Polish priest who arrived from his exile in Canada.[115] The settlement was enclosed by bush, opening on one side to a panoramic view over marshland. It consisted of well-spaced living huts with thatched roofs divided into two rooms, each accommodating four to five refugees.[116] Flower and vegetable gardens between the houses created the atmosphere of a 'pleasant, tidy village'.[117]

Figure 1.2. Polish camp Tengeru, Tanganyika. Anonymous drawing. From Archiwum Fotografii Ośrodka KARTA, Signature: FOK_0051_0002_0021, online.

The houses were organized into six blocks, each equipped with a canteen, kitchen, laundry, wash- and bathroom.[118] Due to its altitude it had a temperate climate that was described by the Polish camp leader as 'easy to bear for Europeans'.[119] In contrast to Kidugala, it was less remotely located and seems to have been run less independently. It was the only settlement that had, at least for some time, a Tanganyika police officer stationed there.[120] While the efforts of the Polish officials were praised in one Polish article,[121] there seem to have been more problems with the British administration as there was quite some rotation of posts and the district commissioner voiced severe complaints about their mismanagement.[122] In July 1948 the camp was officially closed and the buildings handed over to the Overseas Food Cooperation to accommodate workers of the ill-fated 'groundnut scheme'.[123]

With about four thousand inhabitants, *Tengeru* was not only the biggest Polish settlement but also the last to close down in all of Africa.[124] For this reason, many refugees were transferred there when other places were closed down, so many more passed through it.[125] While Nairobi was the Polish administrative centre, Tengeru became the social centre of Polish life in Africa. Tengeru settlement was built on farmland at the foot of Mount Meru in northern Tanganyika, near the town of Arusha and the railway line from Tanga. The erection of the settlement was a major operation, drawing on the labour of four thousand Africans to build the first twelve hundred thatched rondavel huts.¹²⁶ When the first Poles arrived by train from Tanga in October 1942, this building activity was still ongoing.¹²⁷ As one former inhabitant remembered: 'The whole looked like a large African village, except that whites lived there'.¹²⁸ There was lots of lush greenery between the small houses and a pleasant temperate climate. Quarters for the African workers, who did most of the heavy work, were built next to the refugee settlement. As a third of the settlement population were children, a Polish school centre with primary, secondary ('lyceum') and technical schools was organized.¹²⁹ Further central facilities were a hospital, three community centres,¹³⁰ a music school,¹³¹ a bakery, an orphanage, two churches (Catholic and Orthodox) and even a small synagogue.¹³² Furthermore, a farm was operated by the refugees, and expanded subsequently to help to supply the settlement with vegetables and meat.¹³³

While the basic food supplies were obtained and distributed centrally, for other shopping needs a 'camp bus' went twice a day to Arusha,¹³⁴ leading to higher prices and quite some discontent among the region's white residents.¹³⁵ Head of the settlement was the British camp commandant John Minnery, who was much liked by the refugees.¹³⁶ Towards the end the numbers of Poles gradually declined as many found permanent resettlement opportunities elsewhere; Tengeru was officially closed in December 1951.¹³⁷ On the premises the government established the Natural Resources School and its officials pressed in mid-1952 for the removal of the last eleven Polish families still living there.¹³⁸ Many of the structures still stand today and are used as an agricultural college. A little way apart from the college one can find the well-preserved Polish cemetery and a small memorial hall that serve as a reminder of the Polish sojourn.

To sum up the situation in Tanganyika, there was one big Polish settlement in the Northern Province, an area signified by its concentration of white settlers. Many refugees passed through Tengeru, and those who had problems in finding permanent residence elsewhere stayed there until the end. Apart from Tengeru, the four other settlements were all connected to mission stations and were rather remotely located. The two medium-sized settlements (Kidugala and Ifunda) were established on confiscated German missionary land in the Southern Highland Province. The two smallest (Morogoro and Kondoa) were attached to existing Catholic missions in the Central Province and Eastern Province respectively.

Uganda

Uganda, like Tanganyika, hosted more than a third of all Polish refugees in Africa. In contrast to the five camps in Tanganyika, the Poles in Uganda were concentrated in only two settlements, both large and remotely located, and not attached to any existing institution. The choice of the camp sites was influenced by the availability of land and transport connections, but for some colonial officials it was also important to find 'districts where the Poles, a European and white race, could till the land out of the sight of natives'.[139] Both Masindi, in a forest of the thinly populated kingdom of Bunyoro, and Koja, on a peninsula of Lake Victoria, largely met these criteria.

Masindi settlement sat rather isolated on a hill near Nyabyeya village in the midst of Budongo forest, some thirty kilometres from Masindi town, and housed over 3,600 refugees.[140] When the first group arrived in late 1942, African workers were still cutting back the forest to erect the buildings. After an initial stay in temporary accommodation, the Poles were distributed among the six villages that made up the settlement.[141] In contrast to Tanganyika, both Ugandan settlements were constructed under the supervision of Polish engineers.[142] One British visitor described her first impressions of the settlement as follows: 'The cottages are mud-built in native style, and it was strange to see white faces instead of black ones peering out of the doorways'.[143] A former inhabitant depicted it as a 'secluded, peaceful world' and a 'green paradise' with lush gardens around every hut.[144] Set apart from the residential villages, there was a central compound where British and Polish camp officials lived. Attached to this compound were the central institutions: a 120-bed hospital with four doctors,[145] grammar, commercial and technical schools,[146] a small post office, and a community centre equipped with a library and a radio, around which the inhabitants gathered every evening to hear the news. Slightly outside the settlement compound, overlooking a nearby valley, a church was built by the inhabitants.[147] The church is today used by the local Catholic parish, and stands as an impressive reminder of the Polish settlement (see Figure 1.3). In May 1948, Masindi camp was closed down and the remaining refugees were sent to Koja.[148] The buildings were taken over by the government for the establishment of a forestry college, which is still located there today.

Although closer to the Ugandan capital Kampala than Masindi, *Koja* (also Kojja or Koya) settlement was nevertheless quite isolated from the surrounding villages. With about three thousand inhabitants it was also slightly smaller.[149] The settlement stood on a picturesque peninsula on Lake Victoria, thus surrounded by water on most sides, and with only a small, controlled and gated opening to the hills on the mainland. It was built on the land of a former livestock farm under the direction of an architect from Warsaw.[150] The well-planned settlement had a remarkable street grid like a spiderweb.[151] In its centre stood a large open church on a hill featuring an altar painting reminiscent of the Ostra Brama in Vilno.[152] The 'grandiose' building was thatched

Figure 1.3. The Polish Church in Nyabyeya/Masindi, Uganda, 2013. Photo: Jochen Lingelbach.

with papyrus and, according to the British commandant, 'looked more like a Buddhist temple with wings' than a Catholic church.[153] The rectangular residential houses had three rooms, each holding one family, and were built of clay with whitewashed walls, and roofs of elephant grass.[154] Apart from this structure, there was a compound on a hill where the administrative workers lived in houses of a better standard – the 'high life' as it was called by the inhabitants.[155] Koja's sociocultural life revolved around the four social centres where a choir, folk and theatre groups practised, and where piano lessons as well as English courses were conducted.[156] Furthermore there were schools, a hospital, regular festivities on Polish national and church holidays (including a lakeside stage for theatre performances) and political organizations like the 'Association of the Eastern Lands of the Polish Republic'.[157] Outside the Polish settlement lived African workers who did most of the heavy work as well as providing the security services.[158] By 1951, Koja and Tengeru were the only Polish refugee settlements left in Africa. Koja's last inhabitants were eventually transferred to Tengeru.[159] All the buildings were taken down, and today only a recently rebuilt cemetery serves as a reminder of this large settlement.

Kenya

The role of Kenya in the refugee hosting was different from its East African neighbours, as there were no regular Polish settlements. In Kenya were three small and specialized camps, and a substantial group of Poles lived and worked in *Nairobi*. If Tengeru was the social centre of the Polish community, Nairobi was its political capital. The town was the centre of the British as well as the Polish refugee administration. In April 1945 there were seventy Polish officials there, working as delegates for a range of Polish ministries and welfare organizations.[160] Some of them became clearly accepted members of Nairobi's white community, like the Polish Red Cross director and former foreign minister, Prince Eustachy Sapieha.[161] During the war, a further eighty-five young Polish women lived and worked for the Royal Air Force auxiliary service at its base in the Eastleigh suburb.[162] After the war, Kenyan officials pressed hard to get the Poles back to their 'parent camps' in Uganda and Tanganyika.[163] Nevertheless at least fifty-five Polish refugees lived and worked individually in Nairobi in 1947.[164] Their presence was so significant, that Polish was one of the languages typically heard on Nairobi's streets.[165]

Starting in January 1946, at English Point in the Nyali part of *Mombasa*, a transit camp was set up where Poles stayed while awaiting transportation by ship for either repatriation or resettlement elsewhere. Directly on the beach, the site had been used as a navy rest camp and by an Indian swimming and rowing club until it was taken over for the Polish refugees.[166] The location of the transit camp was chosen due to its proximity to Mombasa port. There was a scarcity of shipping space, so by waiting close to the port, any available space could be utilized at short notice.[167] The camp was managed by

UNRRA and then IRO representatives and two British officers with a small Polish staff. It provided 600 places in barracks and 120 in tents, but was at times overcrowded with more than one thousand inhabitants.[168] After some thousands of Poles had passed through, the transit camp was closed down late in 1950.

Makindu was the smallest camp in Kenya, with roughly one hundred inmates.[169] Located on the railway line between Mombasa and Nairobi, it was first used as a transit camp for arriving Poles before their distribution to the other settlements.[170] Later some grown-up boys from other settlements gathered here on their way to join the Polish army in the Middle East.[171] Starting in late 1943, a section of Makindu, hosting up to forty Polish men, was used as a 'special' camp for troublemakers from other camps. At a conference of British and Polish refugee officials in November 1943 it was recognized that special arrangements had to be made for the removal of 'persons whose influence in main camps is subversive to good order'.[172] The Kenyan representative in the conference emphasized that Makindu was no 'penal camp', and furthermore rejected the acceptance of prostitutes from other territories.[173] The camp became a place for those who had 'made trouble' in other camps, and were sent to Makindu together with their wives and children.[174] Although it was fenced in with barbed wire[175] and had a strong police presence,[176] it was not a prison camp, and featured an elementary school as well as a cultural centre.[177]

The biggest settlement in Kenya was the school settlement *Rongai* hosting around three hundred Polish children and a hundred adults.[178] It was established for children (mainly orphans) from the other settlements late in 1944, and built by Italian prisoners of war who stayed in a camp next to the site.[179] Unlike most other settlements, Rongai did not look like a village, but like military barracks. It consisted of spacious, bright mud-dried brick buildings with tarred hessian roofs and concrete floors, which were taken over from the military base.[180] Owing to the temperate climate, there was a relative absence of malaria and other diseases, and accordingly the hospital was described as nearly empty. Apart from teachers and administrative staff, there were also some Polish nuns taking care of the orphans.[181]

With the exception of the Rongai school settlement, Kenya served mainly as a transit point for Poles in and out of East Africa. Nairobi was the centre of decision making for the British as well as the Polish, and it therefore had a strong presence of Polish officials as well as some individual workers who were allowed in because of wartime labour shortages. In comparison to their East African neighbours, Kenyan officials seem to have been more hostile towards any Polish presence in the colony.

Northern Rhodesia

With about three thousand Polish refugees, Northern Rhodesia was the third largest host to Polish refugees in Africa. The first refugees in the country were members of the so-called 'Cyprus group', arriving from August 1941 onwards.[182] Like Uganda and Tanganyika, the colony had quite a small white population, but its economic structure was rather different and was signified by the mining industry of the Copperbelt. The Poles were accommodated in four settlements of varying size and scattered across the territory.

Fort Jameson, with 160 inhabitants, was the smallest of the five Polish settlements in the territory. It initially housed 100 Poles of the Cyprus group in 1942, and was later used for Poles of the larger group from Iran.[183] Located at the border to Nyasaland and a three-day bus ride from the next railway station, it was also rather remotely situated.[184] The small town of Fort Jameson (today Chipata) itself was divided into three: one part for the English inhabitants and administration, then the Polish settlement in the middle, and next to that a neighbourhood of Indian merchants. The Poles were housed in rectangular three-room cottages with a veranda on one side, and a separate toilet that was cleaned daily by African workers.[185] The general layout was rather spacious, with grass and flower beds between the houses – one inhabitant praised the settlement in a newspaper article in the highest tones.[186] In the cultural centre, regular lectures about history, nature and current politics were given, and the Polish priest led an active parish.[187]

Abercorn settlement had nearly 600 inhabitants and was located about two miles from the small town of the same name (today Mbala) in the peripheral northern highlands of Northern Rhodesia close to the Tanganyika border.[188] Initial plans in 1941 to host Italian internees from Somalia and Ethiopia there were abandoned, as they did not come.[189] The remote location 'in this isolated native reserve' was an argument that the Provincial Commissioner put forward against the erection of the settlement.[190] It was nevertheless built (albeit smaller than initially planned) on a hilltop, and was described by one inhabitant as hidden in the deep forest and far away from any cultural centres.[191] Before arrival of the Poles, local inhabitants were asked by the district commissioner to cut grass for the thatched roofs of the whitewashed clay buildings.[192] The refugees arrived in Abercorn via Dar es Salaam, Kigoma and by ship over Lake Tanganyika in two transports in August and September 1943.[193] Despite the modest size, lively religious and national activities developed around the parish priest Antoni Wierzbiński, the community centre and the church.[194] One IRO official praised the work of the British commandant, and described Abercorn as a 'garden city where the sun is warm and the earth gave forth its fullness in food and flowers'.[195] The Poles lived in the settlement until 1948 when the buildings were handed over to the district commissioner. Today only one overgrown tombstone and some artefacts in the local museum serve as reminders of the settlement.[196]

Lusaka camp was located just outside the small but growing newly established Northern Rhodesian capital Lusaka.[197] About 1,300 people lived in the camp, arriving mainly by train from the port of Beira from January 1943 onwards.[198] The small rectangular houses, with grass roofs, whitewashed clay walls and a garden patch attached, stood in neatly arranged in rows, each holding four people.[199] It looked like a garden suburb with trimmed lawns and occasional trees. Owing to its proximity to Lusaka town, the settlement was less secluded than others, the city centre being within walking distance. The school director, however, tried to keep the youth under strict control, prohibiting them from going to the movies in town or riding bicycles.[200] The YMCA centre was thus the central location for social life, with its weekly film screenings, local news broadcasts, concerts, social games and dance parties.[201] From February 1945 on, the settlement became the secondary school centre for Polish children from the region, featuring a lyceum and a boarding school.[202] One of its teachers even established a small natural history museum.[203] Lusaka was the last of the Northern Rhodesian camps to close down in 1950.[204]

With around 1,500 inhabitants, *Bwana Mkubwa* (also Bwana M'Kubwa) was the biggest settlement in Northern Rhodesia.[205] It was situated in an abandoned mining town in the Copperbelt, near the railway centre of Ndola. The refugees arrived in four transports via Beira from April 1943 onwards. The settlement consisted of small houses with elephant-grass roofs – each holding one or two families – and tropical green vegetation giving it 'the appearance of a beautiful garden'.[206] In the centre of the settlement was the administrative building, a Polish flag flying in front of it. The camp commandant, Captain Shannon Grills, and his Polish wife lived in a 'lovely house surrounded by beautiful, tropical gardens', which were cared for by his 'many servants'.[207] Grills was praised as the best and sincerest friend of the Poles. According to one Polish official, his leadership was the reason for the good conditions in the camp and the abundance of food.[208] For the more than four hundred children, a kindergarten, an elementary school and two vocational schools (for mechanics and sewing) were established. The four doctors (one British and three Polish) at the hospital were kept busy with treating malaria and sunstroke.[209] The religious life revolved around the Catholic church, led by a Polish priest, and the spacious community centre; and there was close cooperation with the African Catholic parish in neighbouring Ndola, led by an Italian Franciscan.[210] In the settlement, the sociocultural activities ranged from theatre groups and choirs to regular lectures about Poland, as well as the running of English courses. On top of that, there was a library and even a small radio station.[211]

The small and short-lived settlement of *Katambora* had an exceptional status. It was established in 1944 as a reaction to a series of burglaries, assaults and prostitution by Polish refugees from Bwana Mkubwa and Lusaka settlements.[212] To segregate the problematic refugees, the farm Katambora was acquired from a British farmer. It was picturesquely located on the Zambezi river, 35 miles upstream from Livingstone in a sparsely populated area.[213] Katambora consisted of six farmhouses and two warehouses, and was meant to house fifty Polish inmates, a small African police detachment (in separate quarters) and administrative staff, but the scheme did not really work out as planned. The anonymous Polish authors of the handwritten *Kronika* ascribe the failure to the naive Britons who were not able to cope with the ruthless gang of petty criminals. While the British officials tried to make polite gentlemen out of them, the Polish criminals did everything to terrorize the authorities and get out of Katambora as soon as possible. First, they feigned severe sicknesses until the doctor gave up and was removed, and then they brought unfounded charges against the British commandant. In court the Poles conspired and lied under oath to the judge, who believed them and allowed them back to the normal settlements.[214] The *Kronika* authors argue that the British authorities kept the whole settlement secret as it allegedly conflicted with 'British liberalism'. To cover up the whole affair, they suggested that Katambora had to be closed because the Polish authorities could not provide another doctor.[215] It further seems that Katambora was never filled according to plan; the only precise number of inmates I found was seventeen.[216] In March 1945 the Polish YMCA representative suggested to the British authorities that they use the beautiful farm as a normal settlement.[217] This suggests it was already being underutilized at that time.

The camp situation in Northern Rhodesia was thus rather diverse. It featured two of the bigger camps; one of them adjacent to the new capital, the other one in an abandoned mining town. There were furthermore two smaller, rather remotely situated camps. The brief existence of the 'segregation camp' Katambora and the presence of the majority of Poles from the 'Cyprus group' are the main differences from the other colonies.

Southern Rhodesia

Like Kenya, Southern Rhodesia had a large white settler community, and like Kenya it also hosted comparably few Polish refugees. Around fifteen hundred Poles stayed in two regular settlements and one school centre.[218] All three were located in the eastern part, along the railway from the Mozambican port town Beira up to the capital Salisbury.

With over seven hundred inhabitants, *Rusape* (also Rusapi) was the biggest Polish settlement in Southern Rhodesia.[219] The first group of five hundred refugees arrived via Beira in February 1943, and others followed in later transports.[220] The settlement consisted of small brick houses with tin roofs that were organized like a village and situated in a healthy environment with little disease. Maybe thanks to the pro-Polish camp commandant, Major Francis Bagshawe, the Poles of Rusape seem to have lived in quite comfortable conditions. There was electric light, food rations were abundant, and African workers emptied the latrines daily. The settlement farm and the well-equipped tailor shop produced not only for the Poles but for the local market as well.[221] A visiting delegate of the International Red Cross even complained that maybe 'too much money [was] spent too easily'.[222] A Polish newspaper article confirms the favourable impression, as it is full of praise for the leadership of the settlement, the 'good-looking small houses' and the centrally located church, consisting of three connected rondavels.[223] After the closure in 1946–47, the settlement was used for African housing and developed into the Vengere township of Rusape.[224]

Like Rusape, nearby *Marandellas* was situated just outside a small town (present-day Marondera) along the railway line to the capital, and the first Poles arrived at the same time. With over six hundred residents it was only slightly smaller.[225] To make room for the refugees, the African residents of the 'model village Marandellas' were evicted from forty houses, with the help of a white women's organization.[226] The organization had protested against the placement of white women and children next to Africans, and urged the eviction of the inhabitants.[227] The refugees moved not only into the forty existing round houses, but a further seventy-two 6-person square houses were built, all with thatched roofs, brick walls and cement floors. In the centre of the settlement stood the 'Polish Home', a community centre, the canteens, kitchen, laundry, baths, church, grammar school and a parade ground featuring flower beds containing the Polish and the Rhodesian emblem.[228] Marandellas farm produced meat, eggs and vegetables, and some thirty refugee women made sun hats that sold well.[229] A Polish newspaper article described the settlement as 'one of the culturally best and nicest settlements' due to its proximity to Salisbury and the excellent leaders.[230] This praise was shared by a visiting Red Cross official who claimed: 'Were I a Polish refugee, my choice of a camp in which to live for the duration of the war would be Camp Marandellas … a thriving village of contented, busy people, and not a storage depot for refugees at all'.[231] He stressed that nearly all refugees were employed in one of the camp activities. The earlier mentioned 'friend of the Poles', Major Bagshawe, was camp commandant of Marandellas as well.[232] After the refugees had left at the end of 1946, the settlement was used again as an African location, whose environment and recreational facilities were described as good, despite the poor living conditions of its inhabitants.[233]

Located only fifteen kilometres from Marandellas was the Polish School Centre of *Digglefold*.[234] It was an entirely Polish secondary and high school for nearly 190 girls from the Polish settlements in both Rhodesias.[235] Around fifty adult Poles lived and worked in the settlement, which had opened in September 1943.[236] Established on a formerly British-owned farm, it had a large central school building, several dormitories, teachers' quarters, laundry, dining hall, a garden, a carpentry and a bicycle repair shop.[237] Under the strict and caring leadership of General Ferdynand Zarzycki, the teachers and students worked hard to make up for their missed school years since deportation, finishing a one-year curriculum in six months.[238] While scouting was popular in most settlements, Digglefold seems to have been especially active.[239] Encouraged under the leadership of Zarzycki and the teachers, and as means to discipline the youth, the Digglefold scout teams were in contact with the British scouts from Salisbury and Marandellas.[240] Reportedly, the discipline made a huge impression on the Southern Rhodesian governor at an official visit, and the newspapers were apparently full of praise for the Digglefold youth.[241]

Towards the end of 1946, conditions for the Poles in Southern Rhodesia deteriorated. The friendly official Major Bagshawe was removed from his post and the three settlements were closed down by the Rhodesian authorities.[242] The remaining refugees were sent in January 1947 to the former Italian internee camp *Gatooma* (today Kadoma). One former refugee described the houses in Gatooma in his recollections as 'clay cabins ... very small and hot'.[243] A visiting IRO official called it 'one of the grimmest encampments imaginable'.[244] After strong protests about the conditions, a joint Polish–British mission went on inspection to Gatooma and found that insufficient food and a poor health situation were leading to undernourishment and the spread of tuberculosis.[245] Blame for the bad conditions was put on the chief accountant at the Ministry of Justice, who allegedly hated the Poles and so had deliberately cut rations and supplies to try to force them to leave.[246] He was consequently removed from his post. The supervisor of the camp was Lieutenant Mollie Rule, who had earlier led an internment camp for Germans.[247] Around ninety Poles from the camp worked for low wages in a nearby textile factory.[248] The Digglefold school was continued in Gatooma under Zarzycki, but in less favourable conditions.

The settlement landscape in Southern Rhodesia consisted thus of two pleasant mid-sized camps under benevolent British leadership and a school settlement along the railway line. With the subsequent relocation of the Poles, barely two years after the war, the conditions deteriorated seriously with the closure of these camps and the concentration of all refugees in Gatooma.

South African Union

There was only one Polish settlement in the South African Union, hosting five hundred children and about sixty caretakers and teachers.[249] The establishment of the school centre was the result of direct negotiations between the Polish consul general in Pretoria and the South African government. The whole group arrived from Iran on one ship in April 1943 at Port Elizabeth.

The Polish Children's Centre (also called 'Southern Cross' or 'Krzyż Południa') was set up in an unused part of an army camp in the small town of *Oudtshoorn* in the Cape Province, halfway between Cape Town and Port Elizabeth. The settlement consisted of around forty comfortable brick accommodation barracks. Other barracks served as a chapel, recreation hall, YMCA centre, hospital and kitchen.[250] The children spent their days in a kindergarten, two primary schools and three technical secondary schools. Even a Polish scoutmaster was sent to Oudtshoorn to organize the scouting activities there.[251] The Polish Children's Centre was well integrated into white South African society, with regular invitations, visits and donations, as well as theatre and folk-dance performances by the children. The children toured the whole Union with their exhibition of traditional handicraft works, accompanied by a show of Polish songs and dances in traditional costumes.[252] Relations to the African kitchen personnel seem to have been close as well, no doubt helped by how quickly they learned the Polish language. The school centre was administered by local Polish officials and a South African superintendent. Growing up, the young Poles gradually left Oudtshoorn for further education or employment. The Polish home was closed in June 1947.[253]

The Refugee Administration

> It is hoped that, with the exception of two temporary reception officers ... no staff will need to be provided by this Government for the maintenance and supervision of the refugee camps.[254]

These were the words of A.L. Pennington, a government official in Tanganyika, before the arrival of the first refugees. His hopes were shattered, as he became the director of refugees and thereby head of a British staff responsible for the Polish refugees during their stay in Tanganyika. Apart from this British administrative structure, there was a large Polish administration and some non-governmental and international organizations. The Polish refugee settlements were generally administered through a dual Polish–British structure. While the colonial governments were responsible for the establishment of the settlement and all matters relating to the outside, Polish officials were responsible for the internal organization. Both had a parallel hierarchical structure, from Nairobi, to the colonial capitals, and down to the settlements. The Polish internal administration then went further down into subsections of the settlements. In the following, the administrative set-up will be explained, from the top to the bottom.

The East African Refugee Authority (EARA), a branch of the East African Governors' Conference (EAGC) in Nairobi, formed the top layer coordinating the British refugee administration in all territories.[255] In the respective colonial governments the post of director of refugees was established.[256] He oversaw all matters relating to the Polish refugees, including accommodation, provisions, employment and transportation. He was also concerned with all problems that arose between the refugees and any other inhabitants, officials or government departments. In the establishment of the refugee settlements, the colonial governments were partly connecting to their earlier experience with internees and prisoners of war. In Tanganyika, for example, the initial planning for food rations and African labour required for the construction was done according to experiences with the Italian camps in Tabora and Kigoma.[257]

Mirroring the British refugee administration, Nairobi became the capital of 'Polish Africa'.[258] The Polish refugee administration was part of the Polish government-in-exile in London, which sent a range of officials to eastern Africa. Apart from the consul general and his staff, there were delegates from different Polish ministries in the town. The most important was the delegation of the Ministry of Labour and Social Welfare, responsible for the reception, welfare, organization and administration of the settlements, in close cooperation with the EARA commissioner.[259] The delegate of the Ministry of Religion and Public Education administered the entire Polish school system, with up to eight thousand pupils and more than three hundred teachers scattered over all territories.[260] A delegate of the Ministry of Finance was sent in 1943 to deal with financial matters,[261] and further delegates of the Ministry of Interior Affairs, Ministry of Justice and the Polish Army Chief Paymaster were present.[262] The Foreign Ministry established consular posts in the respective colonial capitals, and some deputy delegates were sent there from the ministries in Nairobi. With the de-recognition of the Polish government-in-exile in July 1945 the whole official structure collapsed. The most important and best-liked delegates and consuls were taken over by the British administration as 'Polish advisers' – many others, however, were relegated to the rank of ordinary refugees.[263] The former delegate responsible for the school system became 'Chief Polish Educational Adviser'. In April 1946 the Polish elite in Nairobi, with support from all Polish settlement councils, formed a political body, the Polish Civic Committee.[264] It was in line with the Polish government-in-exile, and represented all Polish refugees who were not willing to return to Poland 'under the current political circumstances' (that is, communist rule).[265] Although EARA officials had some sympathy for the committee, it was never officially recognized as this would have contradicted official British foreign policy.[266]

Apart from the Polish and British government officials there were also representatives of non-governmental organizations engaged with the refugees. The Polish Red Cross had an office that was mainly concerned with the correspondence between different refugees and the tracking of lost relatives.[267] The African branch of the Polish YMCA was established in mid-1943 and had its chief representative in Nairobi. It was responsible for the recreational centres in all Polish settlements.[268] The church was further represented by the head of the Catholic Chaplaincy, Władysław Słapa, who served as director of the American War Relief Service (WRS) in Nairobi and published a biweekly Catholic newspaper.[269] After the derecognition of the Polish government-in-exile, these organizations remained active, but new international organizations appeared. From August 1946 the United Nations Relief and Rehabilitation Administration (UNRRA) became the officially responsible organization in charge of the Polish refugees. The administrative work, however, remained the same, and the task of the UNRRA representative was to supervise and pay.[270] While UNRRA's main task was to assist the voluntary repatriation to Poland, its successor, the International Refugee Organization (IRO), additionally arranged resettlement missions. From 1947 to 1950 the IRO had an office in Nairobi from where its regional representative Hubert Arnold Curtis supervised its activities in East and Central Africa.[271]

Let us go down from this higher level to the local administration in the refugee settlements themselves. One can find the same dual structure here, but this time with many more Poles than Britons. Head of the settlement administration was the British camp commandant, often a former army officer.[272] He was appointed by the director of refugees, and was responsible for the administration of the camp, especially the buildings, supplies, and the control of the refugees. He had the power to give or deny the refugees the permission to leave camp,[273] and he could also order individual 'troublemakers' to be transferred to another camp.[274] Furthermore, he was in charge of the African labour force, employed in the settlements.[275] African security guards were mainly responsible for the external security, but patrolled inside the settlements as well. When complaints about the settlements from other departments reached the director of refugees, he could order the camp commandant to take action.[276] In some camps another British official was employed as quartermaster, or the wife of the commandant served as 'Women Supervisor', but the number of British personnel was very limited.

When the refugee groups arrived, they were usually already organized in groups with leaders and their own medical and other staff.[277] In the settlements the Polish administration was larger, but it was still subordinated to the British commandant. Only in two instances – in Tanganyika in 1943 – were Polish camp commandants appointed 'on an experimental basis', so that no British official was present anymore.[278] In 1944, one visiting Red Cross representative criticized this arrangement in Kondoa, because the Polish commandant's 'position seemed uneasy' as he was subject to 'group pressure' from the refugees. The representative argued: 'He is so near the people that it is difficult for him to see the forest from the trees'.[279] It is not clear how this experiment worked out, but the Polish commandant in Kidugala was removed in May 1945, and by 1947 Kondoa had a British commandant again.[280] Apart from this, the highest Polish position in the settlements was the Polish settlement leader, who was responsible for the internal organization of the settlement. The British commandant communicated through him with the Polish refugees. The settlement leader was appointed by the Polish delegate in Nairobi and could himself appoint the other Polish functionaries, apart from the educational, medical, sanitary, cultural welfare and work organization staff.[281] The settlement leader served also as chairman of the settlement council, a body that was elected by all inhabitants of the settlement. All refugees were organized into 'sections' of sixty to eighty adults, and these sections were in turn put together into 'groups' of five to six sections. At these two levels again a leader was appointed, so there was a hierarchical structure from the settlement leader through the group leader to the section leader. Apart from this administrative structure, the schools, labour, religion and cultural welfare services were under direct supervision from the respective ministry delegate in Nairobi. By contrast, the settlement hospitals were under the supervision of the medical department of the particular colony. A Polish settlement police force was responsible for the internal order.[282] This internal organization was not really affected by the changes after the derecognition in 1945. It was only dismantled slowly and progressively in line with the departure of the refugees.

Let me conclude this administrative overview by asking: Who paid for the Polish refugees? While guests of the British Empire, the refugees and the payment of their upkeep were, until its derecognition in July 1945, theoretically the responsibility of the Polish government-in-exile in London. In practice, however, the British government advanced money to the Polish government, which planned to pay it back after the war. As the government-in-exile did not return to Poland until the fall of the communist regime, the UK had to negotiate with the communist Polish government in Warsaw, which refused to cover the debt of its political enemies. In 1946 it was agreed in British–Polish negotiations that the Polish (communist) government should pay back a smaller part of the debt.[283] However, as the Cold War deepened, it became clear that the British government would never get its money back, as at least one official recognized in 1951.²⁸⁴ The colonial governments in Africa never had to pay for the upkeep of the Poles, as they were reimbursed by the British Treasury. From 1 August 1946, UNRRA took over the financial responsibility and reimbursed the costs in relation to the refugees.²⁸⁵ After the winding up of UNRRA, the financial responsibility was taken over in July 1947 by its successor, the International Refugee Organization.²⁸⁶ The IRO's main aim was to resettle the remaining refugees and liquidate the camps, which it nearly accomplished when it closed its offices in Tengeru, Koja and the transit camp in Mombasa.²⁸⁷

Departure and Resettlement

The initial understanding of the colonial governments was that they would host the Polish refugees for the duration of the war only. When the war ended, however, most of the refugees were reluctant to go home. After the celebrations of VE Day in the African camps they soon became disillusioned about the outcome of the war. The continuing Soviet domination in Poland and the westward shift of its territory led to a feeling of disappointment and betrayal by the Western Allies. Prince Sapieha, the Polish Red Cross director in Nairobi, explained the reasons for the reluctance in a letter to the editor in the *East African Standard*.²⁸⁸ He emphasized that the refugees did not want to return to a Poland under communist rule, adding that if these conditions changed, they would willingly go. The deportees had gone through terrible times in the Soviet Union, and even if they had not been anti-Soviet before, they must have become so in the labour camps and special settlements. Furthermore, over 80 per cent of the Polish refugees came from those Polish provinces that belonged to the Soviet Union after the war.²⁸⁹ Their houses had been confiscated following their deportation, and they would have been denied the right to return to the places they came from. Most of the Poles were thus stranded in Africa after the brief happy moment of the war's end. While anxiety about their fate was prevalent among the refugees, the British authorities were quick to underline that there would be no forced deportations. In the end, only 2,800 of the Polish refugees opted for repatriation to Poland.²⁹⁰

The departure of the Poles from the refugee camps was not a collective mass movement, but rather a successive departure of groups, followed by the step-by-step closure of camps and the rearrangement and inter-camp transfer of the remaining refugees. In the end, about two-thirds of the refugees were eventually settled in the UK (for an overview of their destinations, see Figure 1.4). The largest group to leave were the ones who had relatives among the Polish soldiers and were therefore permitted to join them under the Polish

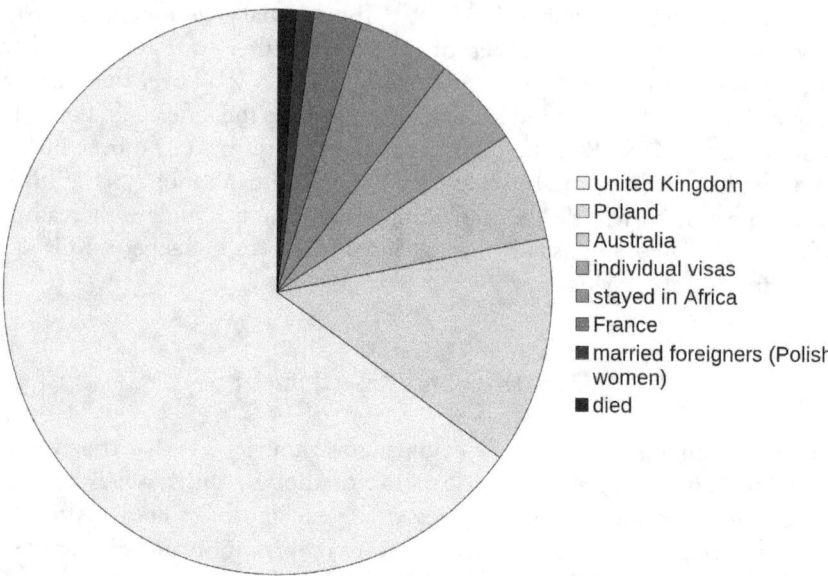

Figure 1.4. Where did the Polish refugees go? Chart created by the author with numbers from Królikowski, 'Operation Polejump', 186.

Resettlement Act of 1947. The soldiers who had fought with the British army had already been allowed to settle in Britain. Their preferential treatment reflected the political obligation towards the group, but it was also a measure to offset labour shortages in the postwar era.[291] In the so-called 'Operation Polejump' the War Office brought around 9,000 Polish refugees to Britain during the first half of 1948.[292] Their departure was an important caesura, as the refugee population nearly halved in the course of six months. As camps were being closed, it became clear to the remaining Poles that their stay was coming to an end.

While some Poles with relatives elsewhere in the world were successful in individually applying for visas, the IRO tried to arrange mass resettlement opportunities in other countries as well. The problem for the IRO, however, was that most selection missions from resettlement countries went to Europe only. From among the millions of displaced persons, they could select the most suitable candidates. In 'Operation Cherry', therefore, 620 Poles were even transferred to France to meet selectors there.[293] Some 400 were chosen by a Canadian resettlement mission that actually came to East Africa in July 1949, and 150 orphans were taken care of by the Canadian Catholic Church.[294] The second selection mission that came to Africa was also the last one: an Australian mission accepted 1,200 Poles, who left Mombasa port on the MS *General Langfitt* in February 1950.[295]

In 1950, with the IRO's mandate coming to an end, the colonial governments were eager to get rid of the last remaining 1,698 Polish refugees. On 21 March, a meeting at the Home Office in London finally came to the conclusion that it was necessary to accept this last group into the UK.[296] It was paramount to remove them fast, as the IRO was still paying for the transport, and the group was regarded as a nuisance by the colonial governments. Although these refugees were not directly related to the Polish army, as the earlier accepted Poles had been, they came 'under the provisions of the Polish Resettlement Act'.[297] Only a small number of mental and bedridden cases, as well as those with criminal records or classified as a 'security risk', were not accepted and thus stayed put, maintained by the UK government. These very last Poles living under refugee status were finally admitted to Britain after the independent government of Tanganyika urged the British administration to take them in. In May 1967 the last Polish family from Tanganyika arrived at Ilford Park Polish Home.[298]

Fewer than one thousand Poles were allowed to stay as residents in Africa. At a conference at the IRO office in Nairobi on 10 July 1948 the colonial governments agreed on 'Polish quotas' – the numbers of Polish refugees they were ready to accept as permanent residents. These were 300 in Kenya, 250 in Tanganyika, 250 in Northern Rhodesia and 150 in Southern Rhodesia.[299] Despite efforts by the IRO representatives, the Uganda government refused to accept any Poles, explaining this with the general rejection of white settlement in the protectorate. Uganda was not considered a 'white men's country'. IRO officials furthermore failed to increase the quota for Southern Rhodesia, as the government generally opposed non-British immigrants.[300] By contrast, the five hundred Polish children and youths from Oudtshoorn had been accepted willingly in South Africa in 1947.[301] Reasons for their ready acceptance were not only their youth, training and manageable size, but also the government's eagerness to accept white immigrants after the war. Hopes of the IRO that South Africa would accept many more Poles from the other colonies, however, were shattered by a shift in the country's immigration policy. While Prime Minister Jan Smuts had encouraged white immigrants to come to the country in 1946, the 1948 election of the Afrikaner nationalist government under F.M. Malan put a halt to this policy. To safeguard Afrikaner-domination, the nationalists closed the doors on European immigrants.[302] IRO efforts to settle more refugees in the country thus came too late.

In 1968 Roman Królikowski took stock of the Polish community in East and Central Africa.[303] In Uganda and Tanzania there did not seem to have been a sizeable Polish community after the settlements had closed down. In Kenya, where he lived, most of the Poles who had established themselves there left when the country gained independence. Farmers sold their possessions, and those who worked for the colonial administration left their jobs. In Zambia there were some dozen Polish families, working in mining or industry. In Rhodesia, a few had become rich tobacco growers, and a Polish Association was still in existence at the time he wrote. By then, Rhodesia was the only one of the former host countries in East and Central Africa that was still being ruled by a white minority.

As far as I know, there are not many of these Poles left in East Africa today. When I was in Uganda and Tanzania and tried to trace some, I was only able to meet one old man, who still lived in Arusha. According to him he was the only former refugee still living in Tanzania.[304] His mother was one of the nine refugees who had remained in Tengeru after the camp's closure in order to run the former Polish farm, by then taken over by the government.[305] I further heard of a woman in the same town, who was reportedly the descendant of a Polish-African marriage. In Masindi I heard of two other Polish women who had supposedly married one rich African, but I was not able to contact their children. Some of the children from Oudtshoorn are still living in South Africa.[306] Apart from these people, the memories, buildings and cemeteries, there was not much left in Africa from the Polish sojourn.

Notes

1. Chappell and Milek, *Persian Blanket*, 71.
2. *East African Standard* (hereafter EAS) 1.07.42: 'Finding Homes for Polish Refugees. "Orderly, Patriotic and Hardworking People"'.
3. EAS 28.07.42: 'Ready for Refugees' Reception – Tanganyika to Give Homes to 5,000 Poles'; *Uganda Herald* 23.09.42: 'Polish Refugees'.
4. Macoun, *Wrong Place, Right Time*, 21.
5. Tanzania National Archives (hereafter TNA): 69/787, p.2, Chief Secretary to Provincial Commissioner, Arusha, 6.07.42.
6. '"History" of Tengeru Camp' written by Miss Jowitt, attached to TNA: 69/782/IV, p.743, Camp Commandant Tengeru to East African Refugee Authority, Nairobi, 6.11.43.
7. Sandifort, 'World War Two', 43.
8. Porajska, *From the Steppes*, 107.
9. Lwanga-Lunyiigo, 'Uganda's Long Connection', 7.
10. Interview with Mukeera Kasule, Koja, 16.04.2013.
11. Overall there were about seven hundred thousand people affected by various forms of Soviet-induced forced migrations (Ahonen et al., *People on the Move*, 25–26). The exact number of deportees has long been disputed. Piotrowski discusses varying numbers ranging from 320,000 to 1,692,000, and Sword offers a comparable range of numbers, while Jolluck writes of circa 1 million civilians and up to 1.8 million Poles in total. See Piotrowski, *Polish Deportees*, 4–5; Sword, *Deportation and Exile*, 25–27; Jolluck, *Exile and Identity*, 9–10.

12. Over 90% of the Polish refugees in Africa came from the following eight pre-war provinces (in descending order): Wołyń, Tarnopol, Lwów, Polesie, Białystok, Nowogródek, Wilno, Stanisławow (Bodleian Libraries: Commonwealth and African Collections, Oxford (hereafter MSS Afr.) s. 1366/9, p.180, 'East African Refugee Administration. Distribution in Poland and Other Countries before the War', n.d.).
13. Piotrowski, *Polish Deportees*, 5.
14. According to estimates of the Polish authorities, 52% of the deportees were ethnic Poles, 30% Jewish, and 18% Ukrainian and Belarusian (Gross, *Revolution from Abroad*, 199; see also Piskorski, *Die Verjagten*, 128–29). Please note that *citizens* of the Polish Second Republic had different *nationalities* (that is, ethnicities). See Taylor, *In the Children's Best Interests*.
15. Sword, *Deportation and Exile*, 5–15.
16. Ibid., 15.
17. Ibid., 16.
18. Gross, *Revolution from Abroad*, 214.
19. Jolluck, *Exile and Identity*, 15.
20. Ibid., 16.
21. Ibid., 18.
22. Sword, *Deportation and Exile*, 19–23.
23. On the 'special settlements' within the Gulag system, see Schnell, 'Gulag als Systemstelle', 143–47. On the Gulag, see Applebaum, *Gulag: A History*.
24. Sword, *Deportation and Exile*, 24.
25. Siberia had, earlier, already been associated with the suffering in the 'Gehenna' (e.g. 1902 in Fraser, *The Real Siberia*, 45.) One example of usage of the term is in an article describing mothers who cried at a communion festivity in Abercorn for their children who had died in the 'Gehenna of exile' (*Nasz Przyjaciel* (hereafter NP) 15.01.46: 'Abercorn ku czci Chrystusa Krola' by 'H.C.'). Later 'Gehenna' or the 'inhuman land' became standard terms to describe the time in the Soviet interior among the Polish 'Sybiracy' (= 'Siberians'; a self-description used by those who had survived the deportations).
26. Prażmowska, 'Polish Refugees as Military Potential', 219–20.
27. These ranged from walking and trains to makeshift rafts to travel down a river. See Anita Paschwa (née Kozicka) in Piotrowski, *Polish Deportees*, 91.
28. Sword, *Deportation and Exile*, 43.
29. Ibid., 44.
30. Prażmowska, *Britain and Poland 1939–1943*, 108.
31. Ryszard Tyrk in Piotrowski, *Polish Deportees*, 103–4. Wesley Adamczyk vividly describes the conditions onboard in Adamczyk, *When God Looked the Other Way*, 131–33.
32. It was mainly General Anders' initiative to evacuate the civilians with the army. Before the second evacuation the British authorities were informed and agreed to receive the civilians as well (Prażmowska, *Britain and Poland 1939–1943*, 131–47; Adamczyk, *When God Looked the Other Way*, 111–12.)
33. An additional 2,600 Poles arrived over land in the Iranian town of Mashad in September 1942. For detailed numbers of the evacuated, see Table 3 in Wróbel, *Uchodźcy polscy*, 42.
34. Cited in Sword, *Deportation and Exile*, 68.
35. Chappell and Milek, *The Persian Blanket*, 139.
36. Piotrowski, *Polish Deportees*, 10.
37. Gabiniewicz, 'Na tułaczym szlaku', 16.

38. See Anders, *An Army in Exile*.
39. Kelly, *Finding Poland*, 188.
40. Krolikowski, *Stolen Childhood*, 77.
41. In his memoirs, Krolikowski writes of a thousand Cypriot group members in Southern Rhodesia (Krolikowski, *Stolen Childhood*, 85), but these numbers are not confirmed in the literature or sources I found. There seems to have been only five hundred Polish refugees in Cyprus in 1940. See Dimitrakis, *Military Intelligence in Cyprus*, 40.
42. My sincerest thanks to Alfred Tembo for providing me with these details from his unpublished draft chapter on the Polish refugees in Northern Rhodesia (cited in the following as Tembo, 'Strangers in Our Midst'). See also Królikowski, 'Operation Polejump', 152–54; Królikowski, 'Polacy w Afryce Wschodniej', 138.
43. The National Archives of the UK: Public Record Office (hereafter PRO): CO 795/125/15, p.38ff, Report of Colonel Gore-Browne, Director of War Evacuees and Camps, Lusaka 3.7.1942. In March 1944 there were 414 'on strength' in Northern Rhodesia, of whom over 100 were not in the territory (PRO: CO 795/132/4, Officer Administering the Government, Northern Rhodesia to Secretary of State for the Colonies, London, 22.03.44).
44. Of the 212 listed men, 44 were civil servants, followed by 15 merchants and 14 clerks; see PRO: CO 795/125/15, p.38ff, Report of Colonel Gore-Browne, Director of War Evacuees and Camps, Lusaka, 3.7.1942.
45. Ibid.
46. Waddington deliberately left these remarks out of the above-mentioned report in case it were to be read outside the Colonial Office. PRO: CO 795/125/15, p.36, John Waddington, Governor of Northern Rhodesia, to Arthur Dawe, Colonial Office, London, 29.7.42.
47. Ibid.
48. In March 1944, there were 176 Cypriot Poles staying at Livingstone, 98 in hotels and 118 in houses or rooms (PRO: CO 795/132/4, Officer Administering the Government, Northern Rhodesia, to Secretary of State for Colonies, London, 22.03.44). The background of this wish for separation is not entirely clear, but it was possibly their marked class difference and expected living conditions that caused friction.
49. There were 127 of them in employment (PRO: CO 795/132/4, Officer Administering the Government, Northern Rhodesia, to Secretary of State for the Colonies, London, 22.03.44); Krolikowski, *Stolen Childhood*, 85.
50. Prażmowska, *Britain and Poland 1939–1943*, 139.
51. Ibid., 108.
52. Holborn, *International Refugee Organization*, 176.
53. PRO: CAB 66/26/29: 'War Cabinet. Evacuation of Polish and Greek Refugees from Middle East', Memorandum by the Secretary of State for Foreign Affairs, 14.07.42.
54. EAS 1.07.42: 'Finding Homes for Polish Refugees. "Orderly, Patriotic and Hardworking People"'.
55. MSS Afr s 1366/9, p.10, 'Refugees in the East African Territories and Northern and Southern Rhodesia', by C.L. Bruton (EARA) to Ministry of Information Offices, Nairobi, 20.09.44.
56. Sword, *Deportation and Exile*, 84. Mohammad Gholi Majd even argues that the influx of Polish refugees contributed to the outbreak of diseases, a massive hunger crisis and bread riots in Iran. See Majd, *Iran under Allied Occupation*, 2.
57. Holborn, *International Refugee Organization*, 18–19.

58. PRO: CAB 66/26/29: 'War Cabinet. Evacuation of Polish and Greek Refugees from Middle East', Memorandum by the Secretary of State for Foreign Affairs, 14.07.42.
59. The British government had already approached the United States and several Latin American countries in vain. None of them was willing to take any Poles. Sword, *Deportation and Exile*, 84.
60. Moore, 'Unwanted Guests', 68; see also Fedorowich and Moore, *British Empire*, 51–71.
61. Marrus, *The Unwanted*, 246.
62. In 1938 a group of Rhodesian settlers sent a letter to the governor vehemently rejecting any Jewish immigration: PRO: CO 795/111/8, Letter from Muizenberg, Cape Province, to John Maybin, Governor of Northern Rhodesia, 17.12.38. See also Gann, *A History of Northern Rhodesia*, 332; Shapiro, *Haven in Africa*, 66.
63. See Chapter 2.
64. Holborn, *International Refugee Organization*, 176.
65. See Bhattacharjee, *The Second Homeland*.
66. Nearly 1,500 Poles stayed in Santa Rosa camp in Mexico, see Kesting, 'American Support'; Lukas, 'Polish Refugees in Mexico'. For first-hand accounts by a Felician sister and an American Catholic relief worker, see D'Arc, 'Colonia Santa Rosa in Mexico'; Egan, *For Whom There Is No Room*, 11–86.
67. Numbers from Holborn, *International Refugee Organization*, 176.
68. EAS 14.07.44: 'Refugees in East Africa'. The sometimes diverging overall figures are due to the fact that there was some fluctuation between refugee camps in different regions. In March 1948, a group of 700 Poles came from India to Uganda and another 100 former Polish official staff changed into refugee status later. While 18,200 was the biggest number of Polish refugees at any one time in Africa, the total number passing through the refugee settlements was around 19,000 (PRO: T 220/724, H.A. Curtis, Chief of Mission, International Refugee Organization East Africa, Notes on Memorandum to the High Commission, 19.08.49). The Polish Liaison Officer in charge of the resettlement to the UK mentioned 19,400, including 209 children who had been born and 116 who had died in Africa between 1943 and 1949 (Królikowski, 'Polacy w Afryce Wschodnie', 141).
69. In December 1942 there were over fifty thousand Italian POWs in Kenya (Fedorowich and Moore, *British Empire*, 49). This reason was also given by T.H. Preston in an interview for the *East African Standard* to explain why Uganda and Tanganyika had agreed to take five thousand refugees each but Kenya had declined (EAS 1.07.42, 'Finding Homes for Polish Refugees. "Orderly, Patriotic and Hardworking People"').
70. On the concept and installation of 'responsible government' in Southern Rhodesia, see Chanock, *Unconsummated Union*, 149–53.
71. In September 1944 there were 5,369 German and Italian internees in Southern Rhodesia (PRO: CAB 66/57/8, 'War Cabinet. Measures taken by the British Commonwealth to provide Asylum for Refugees', 30.10.44). On the Southern Rhodesian military contribution, see also Killingray and Plaut, *Fighting for Britain*, 65–68.
72. Mlambo, 'Some Are More White', 141.
73. There were 3,448 Europeans in Uganda and 10,648 in Tanganyika (PRO: CO 822/145/5, Draft Notice, Colonial Office [Harris, Dawson, Scott, Rogers] to Cabinet, London, 26.7.50).
74. For a more nuanced treatment of the different colonial societies and the role of their white settler communities, see Chapter 5.
75. EAS 30.06.42: 'Refugees from Persia'.

76. EAS 28.07.42: 'Ready for Refugees' Reception – Tanganyika to Give Homes to 5,000 Poles'.
77. Plawski, *Torn from the Homeland*, 140.
78. Zarzycki and Buczak-Zarzycka, *Kwaheri Africa*, 25.
79. Chappell and Milek, *The Persian Blanket*, 153.
80. TNA: 61/685/14, p.44, Neil Stewart, Commissioner for Aliens and Internees, 23.10.42. Macoun, *Wrong Place, Right Time*, 21.
81. Interview with unnamed male Polish refugee, then resident in Australia; cited in Evert, 'War Experiences', 382.
82. One former British policeman in Tanganyika remembered that his wife was involved (Macoun, *Wrong Place, Right Time*, 21) and one former refugee remembered that 'English ladies' organized the reception in Nairobi (Porajska, *From the Steppes*, 103). Refugees en route to Masindi camp in Uganda were welcomed by the wives of colonial officials during a stopover in Namasagali (Kiyaga-Mulindwa, 'Uganda: A Safe Haven', 67). And the Federation of Women's Institutes in Southern Rhodesia played an important role in the welfare of Polish refugees (Kufakurinani, *Elasticity in Domesticity*, 124).
83. TNA: 69/782/4, Elsa Bonavia, Chairman Women's Service League, Tanga to Camp Commandant, Tengeru, 27.10.42.
84. Plawski, *Torn from the Homeland*, 140.
85. Macoun, *Wrong Place, Right Time*, 135–36.
86. Kiyaga-Mulindwa, 'Uganda: A Safe Haven', 67.
87. '"History" of Tengeru Camp' by Miss Jowitt, attached to TNA: 69/782/IV, p.743, Camp Commandant Tengeru to EARA, Nairobi, 6.11.43.
88. TNA: 26/60/1, p.2, 'Survey of Morogoro Refugee Camp' by P.M. v. H., Medical Entomologist, 16.10.44.
89. TNA: 61/685/14, p.54, Pennington for Commissioner for Aliens and Internees to Provincial Commissioner, Dar es Salaam (hereafter DSM), 17.12.42.
90. TNA: 61/685/14, p.16, Chief Secretary DSM to Provincial Commissioner DSM, 8.09.42.
91. Ibid., and Zdzisława Wójcik in Piotrowski, *Polish Deportees*, 164.
92. Zdisława Wójcik in Piotrowski, *Polish Deportees*, 164.
93. TNA: 26/60/1, p.2, 'Survey of Morogoro Refugee Camp' by P.M. v. H., Medical Entomologist, 16.10.44. TNA: 26/60/1, p.14, Camp Commandant, Morogoro, to the Procurator Holy Ghost Fathers, 7.02.45.
94. TNA: 26/60/1, p.12, Pennington to Camp Commandant, Morogoro, 20.01.45.
95. They were distributed to Tengeru, Ifunda and Kidugala. See Zdisława Wójcik in Piotrowski, *Polish Deportees*, 164; TNA: W3/31299, p.52, Pennington to Chief Secretary, DSM, 22.03.46.
96. TNA: 26/182, p.11, Acting Director of Training, DSM to all District Commissioners, District Officers, Labour Officers, Civil Dispersal Officers, 22.08.46.
97. Irena Bartkowiak-Drobek in Piotrowski, *Polish Deportees*, 160. According to a report from 1947 there were 435 refugees in Kondoa (Archives Nationales: Records of the International Refugee Organization, Paris (hereafter IRO): AJ/43/781, Curtis, PCIRO Nairobi to Ag. Chief PCIRO, 'Mr. Harazin's report on Polish Camps in Tanganyika', 29.08.47).
98. TNA: 61/685/14, p.16, Chief Secretary DSM to Provincer DSM, 8.09.42. The claim that the buildings had been used for 'Italian prisoners of war during the First World War' (Irena Bartkowiak-Drobek in Piotrowski, *Polish Deportees*, 160) is not supported by any other sources.

99. NP 1.12.45, 'Swietlica Katolicka W.R.S. w Kondoa'; according to Krolikowski, Barbaranelli spoke Polish perfectly after five years of service to the Polish community. See Krolikowski, *Stolen Childhood*, 147.
100. Irena Bartkowiak-Drobek in Piotrowski, *Polish Deportees*, 160.
101. TNA: W3/31299, p.78, Pennington to Chief Secretary, DSM, 28.06.48.
102. IRO: AJ/43/781, Curtis, PCIRO Nairobi to Ag. Chief PCIRO, 'Mr. Harazin's report on Polish Camps in Tanganyika', 29.08.47. I will come back to this report and the internal differentiation of the 'Polish' refugee group in Chapter 5.
103. TNA: 69/782/IV, Pennington, for Director for Aliens and Internees to Camp Commandants Tengeru, Kondoa, Ifunda, 11.06.43.
104. MSS Afr. s. 116, p.1, Report '*Camp Kondoa*' by Russel R. Johnston, American Red Cross, 27.01.44.
105. *Głos Polski* (hereafter GP) 2.12.45, 'Z Osiedli', p.10.
106. In early 1946 there were 1,051 refugees in the settlement (TNA: W3/31299, p.52, Pennington to Chief Secretary, DSM, 22.03.46); according to a Polish newspaper article later the same year there were 1,116 (GP 28.07.46, 'Bez komentarza').
107. MSS Afr. s. 1378, Box 2, file 8, Report 'Kidugalla [*sic*] Polish Refugee Camp as seen on 15.01.43' by Bertram Wilkin, senior medical officer, p.14.
108. In files of the Berlin Mission there is an inventory of the stores 'at time of confiscation' ('Inventar-Verzeichnis Kreislager Kidugala bei Beschlagnahme', n.d.) as well as mention of a letter from Ananidze Mwa Kyungu, an African member of the mission, who wrote on 19.7.49 that all church members were now scattered; however, he was hoping to return to the station as the Poles had by then left ('Komitee', 11.10.49). Archiv des Berliner Missionswerks (BMW): bmw 1/ 6046, Band 1 'Missionsstation Kidugala'. Retrieved from: http://kab.scopearchiv.ch/detail.aspx?ID=90776 (last accessed 10 December 2019).
109. MSS Afr. s. 705, 'Haven for Poles in E. Africa. 8,000 moved from Russia', from a Polish correspondent, late 1942, newspaper clippings of Charles M.A. Gayer, title of publication missing [most likely *Tanganyika Standard* or *East African Standard*].
110. The relative absence of Kidugala in the British files indicates this.
111. TNA: W3/31299, p.15, Pennington to Chief Secretary, DSM, 8.09.43.
112. GP 14.10.45, 'Z Osiedli', p.10.
113. The 1,055 inhabitants mentioned in early 1946 seems to have been the highpoint (TNA: W3/31299, p.52, Pennington to Chief Secretary, DSM, 22.03.46), while in mid-1947 there were 856 Poles in the camp (TNA: 24/80/37 Vol.III, p.723, Camp Commandant Ifunda to DC Iringa, 9.08.47).
114. Although not mentioned in other sources, social scientist Peter Worsley writes this in his autobiography. He worked for the 'groundnut scheme' in Ifunda after the Poles had left; see Worsley, *Academic Skating on Thin Ice*, 60.
115. Polish Institute and Sikorski Museum, London (hereafter PISM): Kol 174/2, 'Duszpasterstwo w Ifundzie' by Jan Sajewicz. See also Sajewicz's recollections: Sajewicz, 'Wspomnienia'.
116. PISM: Kol 174/2, p.55, 'Ogolny rzut na historie osiedla Ifunda', by Aleksander Czerny, Settlement Leader, 15.10.46.
117. MSS Afr. s. 116, p.1, Report 'Camp Ifunda' by Russel R. Johnston, American Red Cross, 29.01.44.
118. Filomena Michałowska-Bykowska, in Piotrowski, *Polish Deportees*, 162.
119. PISM: Kol 174/2, p.55, 'Ogolny rzut na historie osiedla Ifunda', by Aleksander Czerny, Settlement Leader, 15.10.46.

120. TNA: 24 /80/37 Vol.III, p.722, Walden, District Commissioner Iringa to Camp Commandant, Ifunda, 12.07.47
121. NP 01.08.46, 'Perelki (Opowiesc o Ifundzie)' by Podhalanin.
122. At least four British camp commandants were employed in Ifunda. Walden, the district commissioner of Iringa, criticized especially the first commandant, Douglass, of mismanagement, and pressed for his removal (TNA: 176 /87, p.12, S.A. Walden, DC Iringa to PC Southern Highland Province, Mbeya, 13.04.46).
123. TNA: 24 /80/37 Vol.III, p.786, E.K. Biggs, Camp Commandant Ifunda to Director of Refugees, 6.07.48. The 'groundnut scheme' was a major postwar development project by the colonial government that turned out to be a huge failure.
124. See Piotrowski, *Polish Deportees*, 11; TNA: 69/782/IV, p.850, Ag. Director of Refugees, Tengeru to Member for Law and Order, DSM, 22.09.48. The highest precise number in the Polish files was from December 1944 and stands at 4,018 (PISM: Kol 18/2, 'Stan liczbowy Uchodzcow Polskich w Afryce na 31.XII.1944'). According to a British file from October 1944 there were 3,814 refugees in the Northern Province of which 45 lived outside camp (TNA: 69/782/IV, p.809, PC Northern Province to Chief Secretary, DSM, 13.10.44).
125. Apart from the other African settlements, some Poles arrived in 1948 from India, which was regarded unsafe after independence; see Bhattacharjee, 'Polish Refugees', 1753; Taylor, *Polish Orphans*, 56.
126. By January 1944 there were already 2,712 completed living huts (MSS Afr. s. 116, Report 'Camp Tengeru' by Russel R. Johnston, American Red Cross, 25.01.44.)
127. '"History" of Tengeru Camp' by Miss Jowitt, attached to TNA: 69/782/IV, p.743, Camp Commandant Tengeru to EARA, Nairobi, 6.11.43.
128. Wisia Reginella (née Danecka), in Piotrowski, *Polish Deportees*, 156.
129. Stefania Burczak-Zarzycka in ibid., 151.
130. The three were 'Scout, Catholic and Polish YMCA'. See Zdzisława Wójcik in ibid., 157.
131. The music school was led by Jadwiga Marko, a Lwów conservatory graduate, and had 157 students (GP 2.12.45, p.9, 'Szkola muzyczna w Tengeru').
132. '"History" of Tengeru Camp' by Miss Jowitt, attached to TNA: 69/782/IV, p.743, Camp Commandant Tengeru to EARA, Nairobi, 6.11.43; there were 37 Jews in Tengeru in 1943 (Carlebach, *Jews of Nairobi*, 61). Today the small and unimpressive synagogue building is home to a mosque.
133. It eventually became quite a large enterprise with an 'excellently run' herd of over one hundred milk cows (TNA: 471/999, p.1, T.M. Revington to Member for Agriculture and Natural Resources, Arusha, 12.01.50) and was taken over by the colonial government in 1950 together with nine Polish employees, who continued working there (TNA: 471/999, p.4, Regional Assistant Director of Agriculture, Arusha to Senior Provincial Commissioner, Chairman, Natural Resources Committee, Northern Province, 26.07.50).
134. '"History" of Tengeru Camp' by Miss Jowitt, attached to TNA: 69/782/IV, p.743, Camp Commandant Tengeru to EARA, Nairobi, 6.11.43. In 1947 the bus service was used by about fifty Poles every day (IRO: AJ/43/781, Detailed Half-Year Report on Tengeru by Camp Commandant Minnery, 29.04.47).
135. See e.g. TNA: W3 /31798, p.1A 'Ex-Service', Arusha to Editor, *East African Standard*, Nairobi, forwarded to Chief Secretary, DSM on 1.12.43.
136. GP 2.12.45, p.10, 'Z Osiedli'; Jadwiga Morawiecka-Zabrowska in Piotrowski, *Polish Deportees*, 158. John Minnery (born 1894 in Barrhead, Scotland) had served during the First World War in France and later in British Somaliland. In 1928 he was appointed

as game ranger in Tanganyika. After serving as camp commandant he lived as a farmer near Arusha. See http://johnminnery.blogspot.com/2014/02/introduction.html (last accessed 19 February 2019).
137. TNA: 69/782, Quartermaster Polish refugee camp, Tengeru to Director of Refugees, 5.12.51.
138. TNA: 69/782, D.S. Troup, Provincial Commissioner Northern Province to Director of Refugees, 15.05.52.
139. MSS Afr. s. 1366/9, 'The East African Refugee Administration', handwritten report by C.L. Bruton, no date. Bruton disagreed with these unspecified officials on this point, as he noted in brackets: 'Note. In my opinion all nonsense'. His handwritten document formed the basis of a report he sent to the Ministry of Information in Nairobi explaining EARA's work. Neither the quote nor Bruton's critical remark, however, found their way into his submitted report (MSS Afr. s. 1366/9, 'Refugees in the East African Territories and Northern and Southern Rhodesia', C.L. Bruton to Ministry of Information Offices, Nairobi, 20.09.44).
140. At the end of 1944 there were 3,635 Poles in Masindi (PISM: Kol 18/2, 'Stan liczbowy Uchodzcow Polskich w Afryce na 31.XII.1944'), and in a 1945 newspaper article the number is estimated at 'around 4,000' (NP 30.03.45, 'Pod znakiem obrony całości i niepodległości ojczyzny. Z Osiedla Masindi – Uganda' by Kornel Makuszyński).
141. Porajska, *From the Steppes*, 107; Henryka Utnik-Łappo in Piotrowski, *Polish Deportees*, 146.
142. Two Polish engineers were sent in August 1942 from the Polish Army in France to Uganda in order to build the settlements there (Jerzy Skolimowski to Masindi, and Michał Makowski to Koja). See Królikowski, 'Operation Polejump', 158.
143. Huxley, *The Sorcerer's Apprentice*, 238.
144. Porajska, *From the Steppes*, 113, 117.
145. Ibid., 115; Adela Konradczyńska-Piorkowska in Piotrowski, *Polish Deportees*, 142.
146. Adela Konradczyńska-Piorkowska in Piotrowski, *Polish Deportees*, 143.
147. The church was consecrated on 1 November 1945 (NP 01.12.45, 'Wspanialy Kosciol zbudowano w Masindi' by Władysław Słapa).
148. Lwanga-Lunyiigo, 'Uganda's Long Connection', 18.
149. At the end of 1944 there were 2,800 inhabitants in Koja (PISM: Kol 18/2, 'Stan liczbowy Uchodzcow Polskich w Afryce na 31.XII.1944').
150. MSS Afr s. 1652, p.1, 'A Polish Interlude in Africa – 1943–1944. A Personal Account of the Polish Refugee Settlements Established in Uganda during the War Years' by Rennie Bere, November 1978. The architect Michał Makowski became a friend of British camp commandant Rennie Bere, as both shared a passion for mountaineering.
151. Królikowski, 'Operation Polejump', 177.
152. GP 2.12.45, 'Uroczystosci Matki Boskiej Ostrobramskiej w Osiedlu Koja' by T. Zemoytel.
153. MSS Afr s. 1652, p.8, 'A Polish Interlude in Africa – 1943–1944. A Personal Account of the Polish Refugee Settlements Established in Uganda during the War Years' by Rennie Bere, November 1978.
154. Vala Lewicki (née Miron) in Piotrowski, *Polish Deportees*, 146.
155. Bogdan Harbuz cited in Allbrook and Cattalini, *The General Langfitt Story*, n.p.; Krolikowski, *Stolen Childhood*, 170.
156. GP 14.10.45, 'Z Osiedli', p.10.
157. 'Związek Ziem Wschodnich Rzeczpospolita Polska' organized events and passed resolutions against the annexation of eastern Poland by the Soviet Union (GP 15.–30.07.45,

'Uchwała'; GP 30.08.45, 'Zagadnienie Europy Srodkowej' by T. Zemoytel; GP 1.07.46, 'Zebranie Informacyjne Kola Zw. Ziem Wschodnich R.P. w Koji' by T. Zemoytel). Branches existed in several Polish settlements, but the one in Koja was especially vocal.

158. Guards came mainly from the northern Ugandan Acholi region, while people from Buganda did the other jobs. Some tax defaulters were also employed at the Polish settlement (Interview with Mukeera Kasule, former settlement worker, Koja, 16.04.2013).
159. In July 1951 there were only 152 Poles left in Koja (PRO: CO 822/350, p.48, J. Hathorn Hall, Uganda to Secretary of State, Colonial Office, 23.07.51).
160. The Polish Consulate tried to increase the number to 87, but the Kenyan officials insisted on the 70-person limit (KNA: AH/1/51, p.22, A. Zawisza, Polish Consul General, Nairobi to Chief Secretary, Nairobi 28.04.45).
161. The EARA commissioner described him as an 'old type of Polish Aristocrat' (MSS Afr. s. 1366/9, 'Prince Eustace Sapieha' [sic], n.d.). Sapieha later owned a sawmill in Kipkarren and stayed in Kenya until his death in 1963 (KNA: AH/3/3, p.178, E.M. Gare, Secretary Board of Agriculture, Nairobi to Chief Secretary, 26.02.48).
162. KNA: AH/1/51, p.61, J.S. Coney, for Director of Aliens and Internees, Nairobi to Chief Secretary, Nairobi, 08.09.45. Królikowski even writes that 135 Polish girls had worked there (Królikowski, 'Operation Polejump', 163).
163. KNA: AH/1/51, p.61, J.S. Coney, for Director of Aliens and Internees, Nairobi to Chief Secretary, Nairobi, 08.09.45.
164. The responsible Kenyan official was not able to give exact numbers, but stated that in four hotels in the Parkland area alone there were 55 Polish refugees (KNA: AH/1/51, p.112/1, Caldwell, Ag. Director of Aliens and Internees and War Refugees, Nairobi to Commissioner East African Refugee Authority, 23.09.47).
165. In her travelogue, Elspeth Huxley mentions Polish among other languages that made up the 'cacophonous' sounds of Nairobi's streets in the first half of 1947 (Huxley, *The Sorcerer's Apprentice*, 3).
166. KNA: CA/12/23, p.5, T.J. Inamdar, President Indian Swimming and Rowing Club, Mombasa to Provincial Commissioner, Mombasa, 14.08.49; KNA: AH/3/3, p.66, Director of Aliens and Internees to Captain in Charge of Naval HQ, Kilindini, 18.01.46.
167. KNA: AH/3/3, p.59A, Record of Discussion with UNRRA Representatives and Deputy Commissioner, EARA on 27.12.45.
168. KNA: AH/1/49, p.255/1, H.A. Curtis, Senior PCIRO Representative East Africa and Rhodesia to Director of Aliens, Internees and War Refugees, Nairobi 17.03.48.
169. GP: 4.11.45, 'Z Osiedli', p.10.
170. Zdisława Wójcik in Piotrowski, *Polish Deportees*, 140.
171. TNA: K6/31882, p.3, Pennington, Director of Refugees, DSM to Polish Consul, DSM, 15.06.44. Makindu was furthermore used as transit camp for Greek refugees on their way from the Congo back to Greece in 1945 (KNA: AH/3/3, p.49, Director of Aliens and Internees to Chief Secretary, Nairobi, 7.09.45).
172. PISM: Kol 18/2, p.5, Conference of Directors of Refugees in East Africa, Nairobi, 17.–18.11.43.
173. Ibid.
174. In July 1945 there were 41 men, 39 women and 21 children in Makindu (KNA: AH/1/49, p.44, Director of Aliens and Internees: Refugee Strengths by Camps on 30.07.45).

175. Vala Lewicki (née Miron) in Piotrowski, *Polish Deportees*, 140.
176. One police inspector, five Polish police officers and thirty African policemen were employed in Makindu (KNA: AH/1/49, p.32C, 'Makindu Polish Refugee Camp. Detailed Estimate of Expenditure for 1945' n.d.).
177. GP 14.10.45, 'Z Osiedli', p.10.
178. In July 1945 there were 420 Poles in Rongai (KNA: AH/1/49, p.44, Director of Aliens and Internees: Refugee Strengths by Camps on 30.07.45).
179. KNA: CS/1/5/150, p.39, Director of Public Works to Chief Secretary, Nairobi 17.02.48.
180. Królikowski, 'Operation Polejump', 159.
181. NP 30.05.45, 'Osiedle Szkolne – w Rongai' by Podhalanin; according to Królikowski there were 21 nuns working in Rongai (Królikowski, 'Operation Polejump', 159).
182. There were 2,850 Polish refugees in the camps of the colony by 1944 (EAS 14.07.44, 'Refugees in East Africa' (numbers as of 1.7.44); PISM: Kol 18/2, 'Stan liczbowy Uchodzcow Polskich w Afryce na 31.XII.1944'). Considering that many of the (initially 500) Cypriot Poles were staying in hotels or private accommodation, we arrive at a total number of more than 3,000.
183. The settlement was under construction when the Cypriot Poles arrived there (PRO: CO 795/125/15, p.38ff, Report of Colonel Gore-Browne, Director of War Evacuees and Camps, Lusaka 3.7.1942).
184. GP 31.03.46, p.12, 'Fort Jameson' by 'Mieszkaniec Osiedla'.
185. Ibid.
186. Ibid.
187. NP 15.02.47, p.10, 'Kronika Osiedlowa'.
188. On the Polish settlement in Abercorn, see Sandifort, 'World War Two'.
189. Rotberg, *Black Heart*, 235.
190. Cited in Sandifort, 'World War Two', 40.
191. NP 01.–15.01.46, 'Abercorn ku czci Chrystusa Krola' by 'H.C.'.
192. Interview with Joshua Sinyangwe, cited in Sandifort, 'World War Two', 43.
193. Wanda Nowosiad-Ostrowska in Piotrowski, *Polish Deportees*, 172; PISM: Kol 147/11, 'Kronika – Afryka Rodezja Północna – Polskie osiedla uchodźce', n.d.
194. NP 01.–15.01.46, 'Abercorn ku czci Chrystusa Krola' by 'H.C.'. Father Wierzbiński was sent from the United States to Abercorn and later moved on to Tengeru (Wanda Nowosiad-Ostrowska in Piotrowski, *Polish Deportees*, 173).
195. Lush, *A Life of Service*, 255.
196. Sandifort, 'World War Two', 56.
197. Although Lusaka became the capital of Northern Rhodesia in 1935, it still had less than 20,000 inhabitants in the mid-1940s. Being the administrative centre of the colony, the refugees were close to the Polish and Northern Rhodesian refugee officials.
198. Andrzej Szujecki in Piotrowski, *Polish Deportees*, 165. Numbers fluctuated. At the end of 1944 there were 968 in Lusaka (PISM: Kol 18/2, 'Stan liczbowy Uchodzcow Polskich w Afryce na 31.XII.1944'), and in June 1945 a further group of 205 Poles of the Cypriot group arrived from Livingstone (PISM: Kol 147/11, 'Kronika – Afryka Rodezja Północna – Polskie osiedla uchodźce', n.d.).
199. Chappell and Milek, *The Persian Blanket*, 155.
200. Andrzej Szujecki in Piotrowski, *Polish Deportees*, 166.
201. GP 18.11.45, 'Z Osiedli (z dzialalnosci YMCA)'.
202. Andrzej Szujecki in Piotrowski, *Polish Deportees*, 166.

203. Dr Witold Eichler was an entomologist and made the most of his stay in Central Africa by collecting insects as well as ethnographic objects, which he donated to the city museum of Pabianice when he returned to Poland (ibid.).
204. Tembo, 'Strangers in Our Midst'.
205. Maria Gabiniewicz in Piotrowski, *Polish Deportees*, 170.
206. Ibid., 169.
207. Jadwiga Sokołowska-Galas in ibid.
208. Korabiewicz, *Kwaheri*, 26–27.
209. Maria Gabiniewicz in Piotrowski, *Polish Deportees*, 170.
210. Ibid., 171. The community centre was financed by the American Catholic organization War Relief Service (NP 15.06.46, 'Fragmenty dorobku War Relief Services NCWC w Afryce Brytyjskiej').
211. Maria Gabiniewicz in Piotrowski, *Polish Deportees*, 171–72.
212. The exact date of its establishment remains unclear. While the decision to set up the settlement had already been made in February 1944, in September the houses for the African policemen were yet to be built (PRO: CO 795/132/4, P. Mason, Foreign Office, Refugee Department, London to Józef Ruciński, Polish Embassy, London, 6.09.44). At a conference in November 1944 it was stated that the 'special camp' Katambora had already been instituted (PISM: Kol 18/2, Conference of the Directors of Refugees in East Africa, Nairobi, 6.–8.11.44).
213. PRO: CO 795/132/4, p.63, Waddington, Acting Governor, Lusaka to Stanley, Secretary of State for the Colonies, London, 28.02.44.
214. PISM: Kol 147/11, 'Kronika – Afryka Rodezja Północna – Polskie osiedla uchodźce', chapter 'Katambora', n.p, n.d.
215. Ibid. The Northern Rhodesian governor explained the closure with the impossibility of finding a replacement for the medical doctor who had suffered a nervous breakdown (PRO: FO 371/51150, E. Waddington, Governor Northern Rhodesia, Lusaka to Oliver Stanley, Secretary of State for the Colonies, London, 16.02.45).
216. There were 11 men, 5 women and one youth in Katambora at the end of 1944. PISM: Kol 18/2, 'Stan liczbowy Uchodzcow Polskich w Afryce na 31.XII.1944'.
217. PRO: ED 128/103, Jan Baranski, Polish YMCA, Nairobi to Director of War Evacuees and Camps, Lusaka, 6.03.45.
218. At the end of 1944 there were 1,437 Polish refugees present in Southern Rhodesia (PISM: Kol 18/2, 'Stan liczbowy Uchodzcow Polskich w Afryce na 31.XII.1944'). According to Tavuyanago, Muguti and Hlongwana ('Victims', 952), there were altogether 1,624 Poles in the country.
219. Numbers range between 726 at the end of 1944 (PISM: Kol 18/2, 'Stan liczbowy Uchodzcow Polskich w Afryce na 31.XII.1944') and 657 in September 1944 (PRO: FO 371/51150, 'Colonie de réfugiés polonais de Rusape. Visité le 4 septembre 1944 par M.G.C. Senn', 25.04.45).
220. PRO: FO 371/51150, 'Colonie de réfugiés polonais de Rusape. Visité le 4 septembre 1944 par M.G.C. Senn', 25.04.45.
221. Marta Marczewska-Jankówska in Piotrowski, *Polish Deportees*, 174.
222. PRO: FO 371/51150, 'Colonie de réfugiés polonais de Rusape. Visité le 4 septembre 1944 par M.G.C. Senn', 25.04.45.
223. NP 15.04.46, 'Rusape' by 'X.W.S.' [Ks. Władysław Słapa].
224. Rupiah, 'History of the Establishment of Internment Camps', 139.
225. At the end of 1944 there were 622 Poles in Marandellas (PISM: Kol 18/2, 'Stan liczbowy Uchodzcow Polskich w Afryce na 31.XII.1944').

226. According to its 1943 annual report, the Federation of Women's Institutes of Southern Rhodesia was active in the 'eviction of natives from model village Marandellas, installation of Polish women in village from which natives have been evicted'. Cited in Kufakurinani, *Elasticity in Domesticity*, 125.
227. Zins, *Poles in Zambezi*, 68–69.
228. Bohdan Ławiński in Piotrowski, *Polish Deportees*, 176–77.
229. GP 21.10.45, 'Z Osiedli'; MSS Afr. s. 116, Report 'Camp Marandellas' by Russel R. Johnston, American Red Cross, 19.02.44.
230. NP 15.10.46, 'Marandellas' by 'X.W.S.' [Ks. Władysław Słapa].
231. MSS Afr. s. 116, Report 'Camp Marandellas' by Russel R. Johnston, American Red Cross, 19.02.44.
232. Apparently he was commandant of all Southern Rhodesian settlements simultaneously (MSS Afr. s. 1366/9, p.23 'List of names of Directors and Camp Commandants and P.O. Adresses', n.d.).
233. Hodder-Williams, *White Farmers in Rhodesia*, 196.
234. Bohdan Ławiński in Piotrowski, *Polish Deportees*, 174.
235. In 1946, 189 girls were attending school in Digglefold, of which 90 came from Marandellas and 52 from Rusape (Zins, *Poles in Zambezi*, 78).
236. Counted together, Ławinski mentions 45 employees (in Piotrowski, *Polish Deportees*, 175), while a table from the end of 1944 mentions 61 adults (PISM: Kol 18/2, 'Stan liczbowy Uchodzcow Polskich w Afryce na 31.XII.1944'). Echo z Digglefold, No. 2, September 1944 ('Echo z Digglefold' was a 100-copy typewriter-style newsletter of the Digglefold scouts, and is archived in the POSK library in London).
237. PISM 174/1, 'Digglefold (Pld. Rodezja). Poczatki Digglefoldu', n.d.
238. See Romanko, 'From Russian Gulag'. Zarzycki came to Southern Rhodesia as Sejm member with the Cypriot group; he was an experienced schoolmaster, a Doctor of Philosophy, a former soldier in Piłsudski's Polish Legions and a former minister of industry and trade. See Dall, 'Generał Ferdynand Zarzycki'.
239. Nearly all students seem to have been in the scout teams, as the 'Echo z Digglefold' wrote of 135 scout members in November 1944 (Echo z Digglefold, No. 4, 15.11.44).
240. Bohdan Ławiński in Piotrowski, *Polish Deportees*, 175. The description of one of the friendly visits by English boy and girl scouts is in: Echo z Digglefold, No. 3, May/June 45, p.7–9, 'Przyjmujemy Gości' by Mila Panachowna.
241. NP 01.10.45, 'J.E. Gubernator Rodezji Poludniowej wśród polskiej mlodziezy szkolnej w Digglefold. (Korespondencje z osiedli)' by 'J.K.'; and Echo z Digglefold, September 45, p.10–14, 'J.E. Gubernator Poludniowej Rodezjii w Digglefold', by 'E.D.'. The good impression of the school was shared by other Rhodesian officials. See Zins, *Poles in Zambezi*, 79.
242. Bagshawe was removed from his post in September 1946 after he had proposed in July to settle some Polish refugees permanently in Southern Rhodesia. On the plan, its enthusiastic reception by Polish officials, and the vehement rejection by the colonial authorities, see Chapter 3.
243. Romanko, 'From Russian Gulag', n.p.
244. Lush, *A Life of Service*, 253.
245. Zins, *Poles in Zambezi*, 83–85.
246. Ibid., 85.
247. Rupiah, 'History of the Establishment of Internment Camps', 151. Mollie Rule later became the IRO representative in Tanganyika, and afterwards a professional refugee relief worker with the World Council of Churches. See Gatrell, *Free World?*, 148.

248. IRO: AJ/43/652/45/2, Office of the Minister of Internal Affairs and Justice, Salisbury to M.S. Lush, IRO Cairo, 4.12.47.
249. Bożena Masojadówna-Piłacka in Piotrowski, *Polish Deportees*, 179. A complete list of the children, derived from files in the Hoover Institution Archives, Stanford, can be found in Weiss, 'Polish Children's Home'.
250. Bożena Masojadówna-Piłacka in Piotrowski, *Polish Deportees*, 179. The huge hall could hold a thousand people and was used for festivities and theatre performances (Królikowski, 'Operation Polejump', 179).
251. Bożena Masojadówna-Piłacka in Piotrowski, *Polish Deportees*, 179–80.
252. The Polish exhibition was shown on twenty-eight occasions in fourteen South African towns, often as part of bigger wartime exhibitions (ibid., 180).
253. Królikowski, 'Operation Polejump', 156.
254. TNA: 61/685/14, p.1, Pennington for Ag. Chief Secretary to all Provincial Commissioners and relevant officials, 15.07.42.
255. EARA was led by Commissioner C.L. Bruton and his deputy E.B. Belcher.
256. The exact title and further responsibilities varied between the colonies and over time. In Kenya the title was first 'Director of Aliens and Internees', later changed to 'Director of Aliens, Internees and War Refugees'. In Tanganyika the responsibility switched in June 1943 from the 'Commissioner for Aliens and Internees' to the 'Director of Refugees' (TNA: 69 /787, p.208, Pennington, Director of Refugees to Burloyanis and Mavrides, 22.02.44).
257. TNA: 61/685/14, p.1, Pennington for Ag. Chief Secretary to all Provincial Commissioners and relevant officials, 15.07.42. TNA: 69/787, p.8, R.S. Hickson-Mahony, Labour Commissioner, DSM to Chief Secretary, DSM, 16.07.42.
258. Wójcik, 'Introduction to Chapter 6 Africa', 138.
259. TNA: K2/22474, p.8, Secretary of the East African Governors' Conference to Secretary of State and Chief Secretary, DSM, 04.12.42. The delegation consisted of thirty-seven officials (KNA: AH/1/51, p.22, A. Zawisza, Polish Consul General, Nairobi to Chief Secretary, 28.04.45).
260. At its height there were 8,011 pupils, 338 teachers and 20 instructors (Królikowski, 'Polacy w Afryce Wschodnie', 139).
261. TNA: 69/782/IV, p.817, J. Marynowski, New Arusha Hotel to District Commissioner, Arusha, 26.01.46.
262. KNA: AH/1/51, p.22, A. Zawisza, Polish Consul General, Nairobi to Chief Secretary, 28.04.45.
263. The consul in Dar es Salaam, for example, was regarded by the British officials as 'very unsuitable' for the post of Polish adviser and thus was not employed (TNA: K2 /22474, p.43, Director of Refugees, 31.07.45).
264. The 'Polski Komitet Obywatelski' was set up in Nairobi on 30 April 1946 (GP 26.05.46 'Nasze Stanowisko' by Chodzikiewicz). KNA: AH/1/51, p.101C, Prince E. Sapieha, Chairman of the Polish Civic Committee to Commissioner EARA, 25.07.46.
265. KNA: AH/1/51, p.96A, Memorandum of Polish Civic Committee to A. Creech-Jones, Under-Secretary of State for the Colonies, Nairobi, 22.07.46.
266. KNA: AH/1/51, p.101A, Bruton, EARA to all Directors of Refugees, 04.07.46.
267. Wójcik, 'Introduction to Chapter 6 Africa', 138. The Polish Red Cross in Nairobi was led by the former Polish foreign minister, Prince Eustachy Sapieha, who later became the head of the above-mentioned Polish Civic Committee.
268. TNA: 69 /787, p.175, Pennington, Director of Refugees to all Camp Commandants, 21.06.43.

269. The Polish newspaper *Nasz Przyjaciel* was at least partly financed by the American Polish community through WRS (NP Christmas 1947, 'Przewielebny Ksieze Dyrektorze!' by W. Słapa). Słapa was described by EARA commissioner Bruton as problematic, as he interfered with the refugee administration (MSS Afr. s. 1366/9, 'Rev. Father Wladislaw Slapa', n.d.).
270. KNA: AH/3/3, p.198, H.N. Gale, Personal Representative of the Director General, UNRRA to Foreign Office, London, 7.08.46.
271. Holborn, *International Refugee Organization*, 163. See also Chapter 2.
272. Wójcik, 'Introduction to Chapter 6 Africa', 137.
273. PRO: CO 822/133/1, 'War Refugees (Control and Expulsion) Ordinance 1946', Kenya, 12.03.46.
274. PISM: Kol 18/2, Conference of Directors of Refugees in East Africa, Nairobi, p.5, 17.–18.11.43.
275. PISM: Kol 18/2, 'Scheme for the Organisation of Polish Refugee Settlements in Africa', p.1, n.d.
276. When, for example, the Economic Control Board complained about illegal food purchases by the Poles, the director of refugees asked the camp commandant to issue an order prohibiting this and to explain the issue through the Polish camp officials (TNA: 5/28/1, Pennington, Director of Refugees to Camp Commandant Tengeru, 2.05.44).
277. TNA: 61/685/14, p.1, Pennington for Ag. Chief Secretary to all Provincial Commissioners and relevant officials, 15.07.42.
278. This was in the smaller camps of Kondoa and Kidugala (TNA: 69/782/IV, Pennington, for Director for Aliens and Internees to Camp Commandants Tengeru, Kondoa, Ifunda, 11.06.43).
279. MSS Afr. s. 116, 1, 'Camp Kondoa', report by Russel R. Johnston, American Red Cross, 27.01.44.
280. Kidugala's commandant Kazimierz Chodzikiewicz moved to Nairobi in May 1945 to work as the delegate for the Polish administration and later as Chief Polish Advisor (MSS Afr. s. 1366/9, p.27, 'Kazimierz Chodzikiewicz', personal summary by C.L. Bruton, EARA, n.d.). Captain Williams is mentioned as commandant of Kondoa in April 1947 (MSS Afr. s. 1366/9, J.P. Williams, Camp Commandant Kondoa to Pennington, Director of Refugees, DSM, 17.04.47). The Polish commandant of Kondoa, Dr Zamenhof, had by mid-1946 already been posted as medical officer to Kidugala camp (PRO: FO 371/57902, Chief Secretary EAGC to Under Secretary of State for the Colonies, London, 28.08.46).
281. PISM: Kol 18/2, 'Scheme for the Organisation of Polish Refugee Settlements in Africa', p.2, n.d.
282. Ibid.
283. EAS 27.06.46, 'The British Way', editorial.
284. KNA: CS/2/7/40, p.289/1, J. Macpherson, Treasury Chambers, London to Marston Logan, Colonial Office, June 1951.
285. KNA: AH/3/3, p.198, H.N. Gale, Personal Representative of the Director General, UNRRA to Foreign Office, London, 7.08.46. See also Woodbridge, *UNRRA*, Vol. II, 92–93.
286. TNA: 69/782/IV, p.850, Acting Director of Refugees, Tengeru to Member for Law and Order, DSM, 22.09.48. To be precise, it was first the Preparatory Commission of the International Refugee Organization (PCIRO) and from 20 August 1948 the IRO that were responsible. See Holborn, *International Refugee Organization*, 62, 68.

287. KNA: CA/12/23, p.17, Principal Immigration Officer to Member for Law and Order, Secretariat, 29.09.50. IRO: AJ/43/787/31/6, 'Disposal of Refugees Remaining in EA', Curtis, IRO Nairobi to IRO Mombasa, Director of Refugees Tanganyika, Camp Commandant Tengeru, Director of Refugees Uganda, 12.09.50.
288. EAS: 16.06.46, 'Polish Refugees' by Prince E. Sapieha.
289. My calculation from: MSS Afr. s. 1366/9, p.180, 'East African Refugee Administration. Distribution in Poland and Other Countries before the War', n.d.
290. Circa 1,500 went back to Poland under UNRRA arrangements (PRO: T 220/724, H.A. Curtis, Chief of Mission, IRO East Africa, Notes on Memorandum to the High Commission, 19.08.49) and a further 1,297 with the IRO (Holborn, *International Refugee Organization*, 362).
291. Kushner and Knox, *Refugees in an Age of Genocide*, 225.
292. Królikowski, 'Operation Polejump'.
293. Holborn, *International Refugee Organization*, 420. IRO: AJ/43/787/34/5, 'Rapport final sur l'Opération "Kenya"', IRO Nazargues, 12.07.48.
294. See Krolikowski, *Stolen Childhood*; Taylor, *Polish Orphans*.
295. Królikowski, 'Operation Polejump', 186. On the group, see Allbrook and Cattalini, *The General Langfitt Story*.
296. PRO: CO 822/145/5, p.37, 'Minutes of a Meeting held in the Home Office on the 21st March, 1950, to consider the Admission of further Displaced Persons into the United Kingdom', 21.03.50.
297. Ibid.
298. PRO: AST 18/115, National Assistance Board, The Warden, Ilford Park, Stover to Regional Controller, Ministry of Social Security, Bristol, 17.08.67.
299. Królikowski, 'Operation Polejump', 175. Królikowski puts the quota for Northern Rhodesia to 350, but this most likely includes the 92 Poles who married residents (IRO: AJ/43/790/55/2, 'Refugees Remaining in Africa', Curtis to IRO HQ, p.4, 9.02.49; Sandifort, 'World War Two', 54; Tembo, 'Strangers in Our Midst'). In one IRO document the 'Polish quota' for Southern Rhodesia is put at 200, although this was thought to include non-refugee Poles as well (IRO: AJ/43/652/45/2, Lush, IRO, Cairo to Huggins, Prime Minister SR, 24.06.48).
300. I will return to this issue in Chapter 2.
301. Bożena Masojadówna-Piłacka in Piotrowski, *Polish Deportees*, 181.
302. IRO representative Maurice Lush was convinced that South Africa needed white workers, and he hoped the country would accept half of the remaining Poles from the other colonies. In July 1948 he met Malan and his minister of interior, both of whom firmly rejected any ideas of Polish immigration (Lush, *A Life of Service*, 256). While the Smuts government had mainly encouraged British immigration, it was also open to other white immigrants in order to increase the white population vis-à-vis the black majority. The Malan government followed a narrower definition of the nation – one consisting of white Afrikaners only. The only immigrants partially acceptable for the nationalist government were German and Dutch. See Peberdy, *Selecting Immigrants*, 85–103; Henkes, 'Shifting Identifications'.
303. Królikowski, 'Operation Polejump', 187.
304. Interview with Edward Wojtowicz, Arusha, 20.04.2013. Wojtowicz passed away on 18 March 2015 and is buried at the Polish cemetery in Tengeru.
305. TNA: 471/999, p.4, Regional Assistant Director of Agriculture, Arusha to Provincial Commissioner, Chairman Natural Resources Committee, Northern Province, 26.07.50.
306. My sincerest thanks to Mariusz Lukasiewicz for bringing this fact to my attention.

Chapter 2

THE POSTWAR REFUGEE REGIME AND THE IMPERIAL ORDER OF THINGS

Starting in August 1946, the Poles in the African camps came under the care and protection of international refugee institutions set up by the United Nations. One of their representatives, Maurice Lush, argued for the employment of Poles in the proposed building of a military base in Kenya. In a 1947 confidential and personal letter to the IRO deputy executive secretary, Lush summed up the differences between their organization and the colonial administration: 'As an African administrator I can share the revulsion which they must feel at the impact of 7,000 white semi-skilled labour plus families! As an IRO official I have to press as hard as possible for it!'[1] Although Lush's attempts eventually failed, and no massive influx of semi-skilled Poles for permanent settlement occurred, it becomes clear that the IRO followed a different approach from the colonial administration. To show what exactly these differences were, and how the two sets of actors followed common principles, will be the aim of this chapter.

After sketching a brief history of the international organizations that emerged in the first half of the twentieth century to deal with subsequent refugee crises in Europe, I will show how these organizations (mainly focusing on the IRO) became responsible for the Polish refugees in Africa. In the second part I will enquire into the relation of the IRO representatives with the hosting colonial governments, and thus with colonial rule in general. There was a difference in the administrative approach signifying a new, rather social-bureaucratic and universalist outlook against the prevailing paternalistic approach of the colonial officials. While colonial administrators ruled different people differently, the activities of the new international organizations rested on the principle that all refugees had the same needs and were equal subjects of their social interventions. Despite these differences, the IRO officials took the imperial order for granted and operated under the basic assumption of racial differentiation. In the final part of this chapter I will relate these findings to a general understanding of the IRO as a Eurocentric organization, dealing exclusively with European refugees while ignoring others. The Polish refugees in Africa profited from this limitation, and although their voice was mostly ignored, they were nevertheless given preferential treatment.

During their long journey to Africa the Poles became refugees. Here, 'refugee' means the modern category that was established mainly in the postwar period and differed from earlier groups of people fleeing war and persecution.[2] While earlier refugees depended on their personal skills or the benevolence of individual rulers, the gradually emerging refugee regime universalized the assistance and established the category of 'refugee' in international law.[3] Despite their very specific trajectory, the Poles in Africa became part of this group of 'refugees' and were subject to the international organizations established to assist them. The Poles were thus situated at an important junction in the evolution of international refugee assistance. Their example shows the overlapping of the older logic of clearly circumscribed groups of refugees and the new universalized notion based on individual persecution. As a group they came under the care of the postwar refugee regime, with little regard to their individual eligibility. In order to understand the nature, scope and approaches of these institutions, let me briefly sketch the evolution of the international refugee regime.

The Emergence of the International Refugee Regime

The history of the 'modern refugee' started in the interwar period with the establishment of an international refugee regime.[4] In international relations theory, an international regime 'refers to the governing arrangements created by a group of countries to deal with a particular issue in world politics'. These arrangements 'reflect shared principles and norms, and have established rules and decision-making procedures'.[5] Despite the universalist rhetoric and ideology, it is important to note that the organizations were initially non-universal and had a clearly limited scope. The earlier interwar attempts were closely linked to the appointment of Fridtjof Nansen as the League of Nations high commissioner for refugees in 1921.[6] This institutionalization was a reaction to the upheavals of a European war that had displaced large numbers of people. As Claudena Skran shows, this first regime was successfully put to work by national governments because it had a very limited scope. Its initial organizations and legislation were only dealing with assistance for a clearly defined group of refugees from Russia.[7] These one million refugees were, on the one hand, seen as a burden for the hosting countries. On the other hand, a political obligation to help those who had fought against the Bolsheviks was felt, especially by the French and British governments, which had unsuccessfully supported them during the Civil War.[8] The extensive use of 'denationalization' measures by the Soviet Union led to the problem that many of them were stateless and as such were in need of a new internationally recognized status.[9] In the course of the interwar period, more refugee groups were gradually included under these arrangements.[10]

The first international refugee regime had a very clear European focus, as Europe was the continent where most refugees were being accommodated. The same holds true for the broadening of the refugee category after the Second World War.[11] Again, the institutions were temporary arrangements that were designed to deal exclusively with those people displaced by the war in Europe. The United Nations Relief and Rehabilitation Administration (UNRRA) was set up in November 1943 to deal with refugees and reconstruction in those parts of Europe that had been liberated by the Allies.[12] The initial impetus for this institution came out of the strategic consideration that uncontrolled refugee movements had the potential to severely hinder military operations. As Louise Holborn put it: 'It was basic for military success to control the refugees during combat operations'.[13] UNRRA's role was to follow the armed forces into Europe and take care of the displaced persons (DPs) there. Its main task was the repatriation of the 11 million non-Germans who found themselves outside their home-country; the largest number of staff caring for DPs was in Germany.[14] UNRRA was an organization that (although dominated by the United States)[15] included Western and Eastern nations alike, and existed thus in the brief period between the end of the Second World War and the beginning of the Cold War.[16] The Polish government-in-exile in London initially supported UNRRA's engagement in Poland as a commitment to Poland's integration with the West.[17] The Soviet membership in the organization and the cooperation with the communist government in Warsaw, however, led to deteriorating relations. Anticommunists criticized UNRRA for its efforts to repatriate the DPs and for strengthening the Warsaw government by supplying it with goods for redistribution.[18]

Apart from the repatriation of DPs, UNRRA aimed to help in the reconstruction of countries devastated by the war, and to help people to rebuild their lives. UNRRA had programmes in all the major war zones, but most of its resources by far went to Europe.[19] Although the most extensive single-country programme was in China, it was much smaller in relation to the devastated areas and numbers of suffering people than the activities in

Europe.[20] The UNRRA programme in Ethiopia, which had suffered under Italian occupation, was in turn one of the smallest. Only after a 'full-scale' programme had been started in Italy did Ethiopian officials successfully press for assistance, which materialized in the form of a small programme of medical training and agricultural support.[21]

UNRRA's successor, the International Refugee Organization (IRO), started operations in July 1947 and lasted until February 1952. The IRO took over many of the camps, responsibilities and even personnel from UNRRA,[22] but the main change was that the Soviet Union was not part of the IRO anymore.[23] The reason for this was the IRO's commitment to help refugees who opposed repatriation and to 'find new homes' for them elsewhere in the world through planned resettlement programmes.[24] By contrast, Soviet officials wanted to return all DPs to their home countries. As most of the refugees who refused to be repatriated came from communist-dominated countries, the communists were opposed to supporting them in staying abroad.[25] The main task for the IRO, like UNRRA, was to re-establish the displaced and thereby clear the refugee camps. But the IRO had more possibilities at hand. The organization's three means to achieve its aim were voluntary repatriation, resettlement to another country and local integration.[26] The IRO was largely Anglo-American dominated, with nearly 60 per cent of its budget coming from the US and nearly 20 per cent from the UK.[27] The composition of its staff partly reflected this dominance; the staff came mainly from the UK (33 per cent), the US (16 per cent) and France (14 per cent).[28] The IRO headquarters were located in Geneva, and most of its staff stationed in the three western zones of Germany, where over 80 per cent of the refugees who received care and maintenance from the organization were living.[29] In IRO's Middle East region (which included Africa and India) and the Far East there were only small missions dealing with comparably small numbers.[30] The IRO was a large international organization formed under US leadership by eighteen UN governments, and with a firm focus on operations in Europe.

In general, there was an increasing scope of activities on behalf of the subsequent refugee organizations. Nevertheless, they were all temporary and focused almost exclusively on European refugees. Even the 1951 Refugee Convention was only concerned with people who had been displaced by events in Europe that had occurred before 1951.[31] Only with the 1967 protocol was this temporal and geographical limitation lifted.

From Deportees to Refugees

In the following I want to clarify to what extent – or rather when – the Poles in Africa fell under the category of 'refugees'. Initially they did not flee their homes to escape persecution or war, but they were forcibly deported. So were they 'refugees'? Let me answer this question by recounting their history with reference to the categories in which they were placed by the relevant authorities. Thereby, I will not only sidestep a perennial debate within refugee studies (who is a refugee?) but I can also underline the practical, everyday relevance of different categorizations. To people on the move, categorization (or 'labelling') matters.[32]

In the beginning of their odyssey they were in the main simply Polish peasants, tradesmen, housewives, mothers or schoolchildren living in the multi-ethnic eastern part of interwar Poland. But at the moment of their deportation they became 'deportees' or exiles, with their Polish nationality being the main (but not only) reason for deportation. Brought to the Soviet interior, they were largely classified as 'anti-Soviet' or 'socially undesirable'.[33] With their release in June 1941 they lost their 'deportee' status, and as soon as they arrived in Iran they were described as 'evacuees'. Although the voyage across the Caspian Sea resembled current images of overcrowded refugee boats in the Mediterranean, these were planned and internationally coordinated operations (see Figure 2.1). The relocation of the Polish soldiers and civilians was in fact arranged by the NKVD.[34] In Iran they were mainly regarded as 'civilians', as their administration and the camp organization was in the hands of the British Army, and the military officials regarded the Poles who were not soldiers as an appendix to the Polish Army.[35] They came under the responsibility of the 'paramilitary'[36] Middle East Relief and Refugee Administration (MERRA), which had been established by the British government to deal with the Polish, Yugoslav and Greek refugees in

Figure 2.1. Ship with Polish soldiers and civilians arriving from the Soviet Union via the Caspian Sea at the port of Pahlevi, Iran, 1942. From Archiwum Fotografii Ośrodka KARTA, Signature: IS_SZUFLADA_BIURKOWA_2_STATEK_Z_KRASNOWODZKA, online.

the region.³⁷ As refugees, the Poles were consequently transferred to eastern Africa. In an *East African Standard* article that appeared before their arrival, the Poles were described as 'refugees' who had been removed by the Russians when Germany attacked Poland.³⁸ They were also described as 'refugees' in the colonial files, with the 'Director of Refugees' as the responsible colonial official. While they were referred to as 'evacuees' in a few British documents, the most common category was 'refugee'. The close connection of the two terms becomes apparent in the definition of 'war refugee' in the Tanganyika 'War Refugees (Control and Expulsion) Ordinance' of 1946:

> 'war refugee' means any person who has entered any part of East Africa during the war in pursuance of an arrangement made by any Government in East Africa for the reception of persons evacuated from war areas, and has been permitted to enter the Territory without observance of the Immigration laws.³⁹

Apart from the close connection of the legal definition of war refugee with this specific evacuated group, there is another aspect that is noteworthy here: the exemption of these refugees from the usual immigration legislation. This directly links the Tanganyika legislation with general understandings of refugees going back to the interwar international refugee regime. Skran says that the most important outcome of this regime 'was the establishment of the idea that refugees should be treated as a special category of migrant deserving preferential treatment'.⁴⁰ The Polish refugees having received the preferential treatment of being allowed in, the 1946 ordinance was especially designed to control and dispose of them after the end of the war. At least in Kenya, no sooner had the Poles arrived than its government made a plan to pass an ordinance after the war 'to get rid of all these people who had been admitted here temporarily during the present war'.⁴¹ Again parallels to the limited temporal scope of refugee assistance in the international refugee regime become apparent. The idea, at least until the beginning of the Cold War, was to give refugees a temporary shelter until the reasons for their flight were over.

While the initial categorization of the Poles as 'refugees' might have been made to cover up their deportation by the Soviet allies, with the end of the war the situation changed. As it became apparent that most of the Poles were unwilling to be repatriated, they became part of the larger group of DPs who found themselves in Europe after the war but were unwilling to return to their, by then, Soviet-dominated home countries. For the European DPs, the emerging 'Cold War came to the rescue', as Western governments were not willing to send back refugees to the communist side.⁴² The same held true for the Poles in Africa.

But let us go back to the days when the refugees were about to arrive in East Africa. How did the colonial administration prepare for the influx? What were the guiding experiences they had to care for the Poles?

Very much like refugee hosting in Europe, the techniques and procedures used were taken from the military sphere, especially regarding the establishment of camps.[43] The colonial administrators on the ground drew on experiences from the management of camps for Italian internees and prisoners of war. The initial planning of food rations, as well as the amount of labour needed for constructing Tengeru, were guided by the experiences from the Italian internee camp in Tabora.[44] The Southern Rhodesian camps were administered and operated by the army, and most of the British camp commandants in the other colonies were themselves former army officers.[45] In contrast to the interned 'enemy aliens' (Germans and Italians), however, the refugees were less restricted in their movement. Although they were generally obliged to live in the designated camps, the officials emphasized that they were allies and not enemies.[46] The Poles were related to the Polish army fighting with the British forces, and, therefore – in contrast to the enemy nationals who were always under suspicion of supporting the enemy – no further security measures were considered necessary. The close connection of the refugees with the military shows a parallel to the general strategic considerations regarding refugee assistance in Europe. While refugee assistance today is more connected to the humanitarian sphere, it was the close connection to the military that provided the impetus and guidelines for the establishment of camps.[47]

If we look for refugee legislation in East Africa, we find another group of 'refugees' that was already covered by a Kenyan Ordinance in 1938. They were war refugees as well, but they came from Ethiopia.[48] The 'Refugees Ordinance, 1938' was passed to control Ethiopians who had fled into Kenya's Northern Frontier District in 1936 and 1937.[49] Their control was stricter, resembling more an internment camp with barbed wire and military surveillance. The refugees were reluctantly accepted as they would, if turned back at the border, have faced torture or death by the Italians – a scenario that British officials could not reconcile with their self-identification as civilized rulers.[50] The main reason for the Kenyan reluctance was the British policy of non-involvement during the Italian attack on Ethiopia, but the fear that the influx of neighbouring peoples might cause unrest in Kenya's fragile north played a role as well.[51] Some pastoralists fleeing the fighting across the border were even disarmed and sent back to Ethiopia, as the Kenyan administration feared internal disturbances.[52] Although some of the Ethiopians in Kenya came under 'refugee' legislation, the Kenyan administration seem not to have taken these experiences as guidelines for the Poles who came later.

There were also a few hundred Jewish refugees from Central Europe present in East Africa who had fled Nazi persecution around 1938.[53] They were, however, not privileged by any special agreements when entering Kenya. Like other European immigrants who wanted to enter the colony, they had to prove that they possessed 'adequate financial resources' or had 'authentic contracts of suitable employment'.[54] Even if they had obtained a visa in Europe, but were found to have insufficient funds upon arrival, their entry was denied and they were turned back at the port of entry.[55] As the number of applications for entry into Kenya increased during 1938, a special board was set up to deal with Jews fleeing from persecution in Central Europe.[56] This did not, however, result in more permissions or preferential treatments – quite the contrary. The Kenyan Immigration Restriction Ordinance was even amended in late 1938 to give officials more power to keep 'undesirable persons' out, meaning primarily lower-class Jews.[57] There were several attempts by refugees or wealthy Jews from elsewhere to acquire land and settle groups of refugees ranging from a few dozen to several thousands. All of these schemes were rejected by the Kenyan authorities.[58] In the end only a tiny fraction of the over fifty thousand applications for entry into Kenya received between April 1938 and 1940 were approved.[59] Apart from the prevalent antisemitism of the Europeans in East Africa, there was also opposition to Jewish immigration from the Indian representatives in Kenya, who feared that it might strengthen racial discrimination against the Indian community.[60]

In contrast to the Ethiopian and Jewish refugees already present in East Africa, the mostly Christian Polish refugees were exempted from the normal immigration legislation and received preferential treatment. While the main reason was their close connection to the Polish army, it remains likely that their non-Jewishness and non-Africanness played a role in admitting them as well. There is no indication that the prior experiences with hosting the two refugee groups informed the colonial authorities in their treatment of the Poles. While the Ethiopians were mainly regarded as a local security problem, the Jews got no preferential treatment and were mostly denied access. By contrast, the Poles from Iran arrived under exceptional arrangements and later became internationally recognized 'refugees'.

UNRRA, IRO and the Refugees

The Poles were, for most of the time, under a dual Polish and colonial administration. When UNRRA took over financial responsibility in August 1946, this administrative set-up remained largely unchanged. Just as the British government was reimbursing the colonial governments before, it was now UNRRA that was paying the colonial administration for hosting the Poles.[61] For the British government this set-up was in fact quite welcome, and it pressed the organization to accept responsibility for the Poles.[62] It did, however, contribute substantially to the UNRRA budget anyway. What officials in Britain feared was the effect that the UNRRA takeover of administration would have on the Polish armed forces in Britain.[63] Like the Poles in Africa, most Polish soldiers were supporting the Polish government-in-exile in London and strongly opposing the communist government in Warsaw.[64] Apart from practical considerations, this might be the reason why UNRRA did not engage more directly with the refugee administration in Africa. The UNRRA Middle East Office in Cairo took over the responsibility for facilitating the voluntary repatriation of the refugees to Poland.[65] But only a small staff was temporarily sent to Nairobi.[66]

In preparation for the UNRRA takeover, Sam Jacobs, an UNRRA representative and Jewish US citizen, toured the camps in late 1944 to register the refugees. His tour was a disaster, and the Poles refused to cooperate and register, as they feared repatriation to Poland.[67] Tengeru's assistant camp commandant, Herbert Story, ascribed the problems during Jacobs' visit to his undiplomatic approach and to rumours among the Poles that he was a Soviet spy who was trying to send them back to Russia. These rumours were apparently initiated by Polish soldiers who had warned their relatives not to fill in the forms. Story described Jacobs as an 'American, very American, Jew', and cited Poles who had said they did not trust him because he was Jewish, with some even claiming to have seen him in Russia. One person fainted during the turmoil, and Story was surprised that Jacobs had managed to leave the meeting unscathed.[68] To understand the refugees' fierce resistance against registration, we have to consider their experiences before deportation. When the Soviet authorities took over eastern Poland, they started massive and repeated registrations to identify enemies of the new order. Being registered was a necessary precondition for being imprisoned or deported. Poles living under Soviet rule had learned: 'There was relative safety only in anonymity'.[69]

Jacobs, in turn, described the Polish staff unfavourably as antisemitic, anti-British and incompetent Polish nationalists. He closed a report about the situation at the Polish Children's Home in Oudtshoorn, South Africa, by citing a South African official: 'You cannot make a silk purse out of a Pole's ear'.[70] The quote, an adaptation of a well-known idiomatic expression, implied that the Poles were generally like something rather worthless that could not be changed into something refined and valuable. Jacobs described this as an apt summary of the conditions in the camp, referring to the incompetent Polish staff. It becomes clear that he not only accused individual Polish officials (which he also did at length) but that he understood the incompetency, immoral behaviour and fanaticism as being inherently Polish.

After Jacob's reports, UNRRA officials feared the consequences of taking over the Polish camps in East Africa. C.M. Pierce, director of the DP division in the UNRRA Balkan mission, shared Jacob's assessment and warned against an engagement with the Poles in Africa. The officials feared conflict between the anticommunist Polish refugees and staff, on the one hand, and the demands for repatriation by Soviet officials on the other. The Soviets were already members of UNRRA, and the Warsaw government was expected to join soon.[71] In a letter to the organization's headquarters in Washington, Pierce wrote:

> These Poles will form the nucleus of sizeable proportions, of reactionary and dissident political belief which may act as a threat to the security of the world. Therefore, it is highly advisable to approach this thing with all due caution and foresight. Unless it does so, UNRRA may well find it necessary to keep order with armed forces and machine guns.[72]

The refugees in turn regarded UNRRA with suspicion, and feared it would try to repatriate them by force. Furthermore, UNRRA was paying less per capita than the British government had spent before. With the takeover, some of the Polish staff, regarded as redundant, were dismissed, leaving them disgruntled.[73] The clearest example, however, of the refugees' distrust in UNRRA was the direct confrontation with a repatriation mission from Warsaw that was touring the African camps in June 1946. As part of the UNRRA repatriation programme, the communist Polish government had sent officials to Africa to convince the Poles to return to Poland.[74] Even before the arrival of the mission, strong feelings were aroused against them. In an article in the Polish refugee newspaper *Głos Polski*, titled 'Our standpoint', Kazimierz Chodzikiewicz emphasized that the representatives of the Polish refugees recognized only the London-based government as legitimate, and did not want to return under the 'current political circumstances'.[75] In the text he assured the refugees that the mission had no power to mingle in their administration, and all Poles who wanted to return had a free choice to do so. To keep things calm during the visit of the mission, the Polish representative on the Interim Treasury Committee in London sent a memorandum to all Polish officials responsible for the refugees to assure 'peaceful and proper behaviour'.[76] The Colonial Office instructed the chief secretaries of the hosting colonies to take any steps necessary to avoid 'unfortunate incidents'.[77] Tanganyika's director of refugees, Pennington, informed the provincial authorities and stated that, despite the fear of trouble, no police would accompany the mission. He explained that it would not be possible to control the situation if large numbers of refugees 'were "out" to make trouble'. Providing inadequate police protection would make a bad impression and be 'worse than useless'.[78]

As the officials had feared, some refugees were indeed out to make trouble. When the mission finally arrived in Tengeru, its members were greeted with hostility. Father Piotr Rogiński led a group of refugees who had put on rags and acted as if they were prisoners in a labour camp. In the end, tomatoes were thrown until the Warsaw mission officials fled the scene.[79] Rogiński was a prominent figure in the camp, and in the words of another Polish cleric, 'he was one of those Poles who, besides an ardent faith, had a firm attachment to the fatherland'.[80] One IRO official described him later rather negatively as 'somewhat unbalanced as a result of very harsh treatment in Russia'. For the IRO, Rogiński's open lobbying against repatriation was rather problematic.[81]

Problems with the UNRRA repatriation mission did not cease with the departure of the officials. On the international level, the Polish foreign minister sent a telegram from Warsaw to the UNRRA director general in July 1946. He urged UNRRA to speed up the repatriation of the Poles in the Middle East, India and Africa, reminding them of their obligations under Resolution 92.[82] This resolution referred to UNRRA's task to remove 'all obstacles to repatriation'.[83] This included the removal of unsuitable staff members who were obstructing repatriation – a right that UNRRA had reserved for itself when taking over responsibility for the Poles.[84]

The distrust in the organization on the part of the refugees continued. In February 1947, *Głos Polski* reported about the poor conditions under which a group of 152 Polish repatriates had to travel when moving from Uganda to the transit camp in Mombasa.[85] In this discouraging report, titled 'Cold, hungry and so far from home…', the author blamed UNRRA and a Warsaw official for the shortage of food, blankets and water on the train he met at the Nairobi station. He described it as a 'classic example' of the communist government's lack of interest in the fate of the returning Poles. In his description of the crowded conditions in third-class carriages attached to a freight train, he seemed to evoke memories of the deportations. Being crowded into cattle trucks was an incisive experience remembered vividly by the former deportees. However, in an article two weeks later, the editors had to admit that, although the conditions were as described, it was not UNRRA or Warsaw officials who were responsible but rather the British authorities in cooperation with the railway administration. As ties to the British administration were more vital for the Polish refugees, they did not really assign guilt to them but wrote instead about 'a series of misunderstandings' and emphasized the good relations with them.[86]

When the IRO took over responsibility for the refugees five months later, they inherited this negative image and initially met the same 'suspicious attitude' from the refugees.[87] Krolikowski confirms this Polish view of the IRO in his memoirs: 'none of us had confidence in that organization'.[88] This attitude changed only slowly, and some of the politically active nationalist Poles remained opposed to the IRO officials. They wanted to keep the Polish refugees together, and not return to Poland until the communist government had been overthrown. The IRO's approach of pushing the Poles into either resettlement, and thus integration into the prospective host countries, or repatriation into communist Poland did not appeal to them.

While the camp administration stayed the same under the IRO, this organization was more active and had more personnel on the ground. Roughly fifteen people were employed in the IRO office in Nairobi, of whom up to four were stationed in each of the camps that remained in October 1948 (Mombasa, Koja, Tengeru and Lusaka/Gatooma).[89] The IRO staff in East Africa reflected the general composition of IRO personnel, as they came from a range of countries with a predominance of British and American citizens.[90] The IRO was responsible for financing the camps, but its core task was to re-establish the refugees through repatriation, resettlement or local integration, and – to use the words of its Deputy Executive Secretary – to close the 'African chapter of a tragic human story'.[91]

While UNRRA had arranged repatriation only, the IRO officials had more options on offer to get the people out of the camps and into permanent residence. On the international diplomatic level, they tried to convince governments to accept more refugees for resettlement programmes. In regard to the current host countries they urged the governments to accept more of the refugees into permanent residency. And on the ground in the camps they worked to get the refugees 'movement-minded',[92] and to find individual solutions for them. The IRO officials in Africa showed no clearly stated preference for any of these 'durable solutions'; their main goal was to get the refugees off their books. The monthly reports and correspondence from the East Africa representative, Hubert Arnold Curtis, to the Geneva headquarters bear witness to this imperative. He proudly boasted about the numbers if resettlement operations were going successfully, and he was frustrated in those months when only minimal movements out of the camps had occurred.[93] The organization's priority can be illustrated by one of its charts from June 1948 showing the number of Poles in East Africa and their projected decline, as well as the approximate costs for maintaining them (see Figure 2.2).

In relation to the refugees, the IRO took a very clear stance against forceful repatriation. This was one of the chief differences from its predecessor UNRRA. While UNRRA had initially placed more emphasis on the sovereignty of states over their citizens and, in the first months after the war's end, had taken part in forced repatriations to the Soviet Union, this practice had already stopped when they took over responsibility for the Poles in Africa.[94]

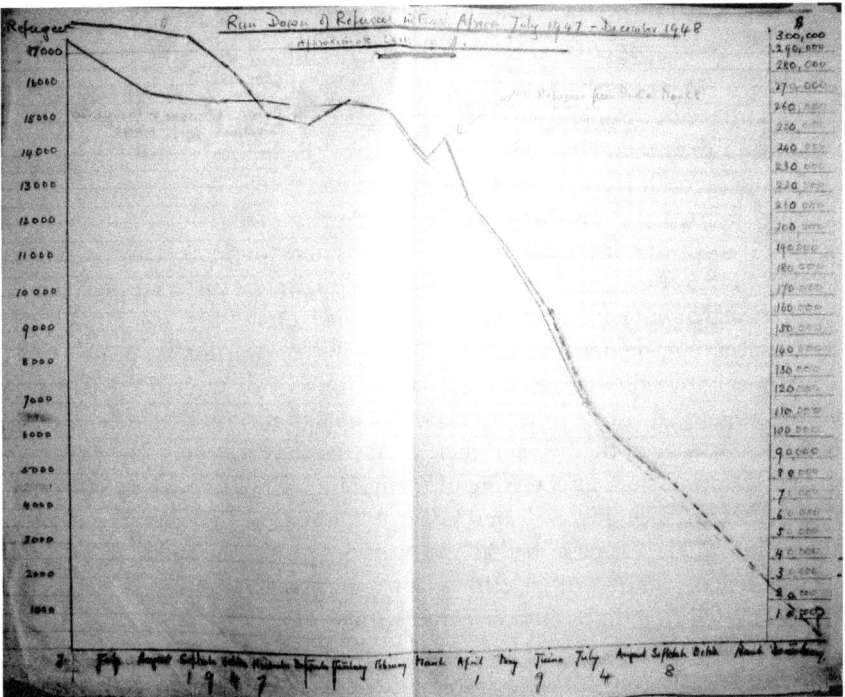

Figure 2.2. 'Run Down of Refugees in East Africa, July 1947–December 1948'. The line that starts higher represents the approximate costs in USD. The dashed line is only a projection from June 1948, and the process of emptying the camps was actually much slower. IRO: AJ/43/616/2/29, 'Summary of Deputy Executive Secretary's Tour in Turkey, Lebanon, Egypt, East Central and South Africa. May 30th – June 19th, 1948', Appendix A.

However, UNRRA's only solution on offer for the refugees was assistance in voluntary repatriation. Starting from the assumption that refugees did not enjoy the legal or political protection of a government, the IRO tried to give this protection to the eligible refugees. In this function it had some similarities with a 'diplomatic representation',[95] and accordingly, IRO officials enjoyed diplomatic privileges.[96] Eligibility was thus the criterion that decided if an individual would be protected by the IRO against forced repatriation or not.[97] The organization's East Africa representative, Curtis, made it clear: the IRO would not take part in the forced repatriation of an eligible refugee.[98]

In discussions about the 'eligibility' of certain individuals, it becomes apparent that protection by the IRO was not without conditions. In this regard not only the question of who would initially fall within the category, but also who should lose eligibility, is of interest. Illustrative of this point were the internal discussions about the withdrawal of eligibility of certain criminals between the IRO representative in East Africa and the IRO headquarters. As one paper from the headquarters pointed out, not every refugee lost IRO care and protection as soon as he or she got a criminal record.[99] Only hardened criminals, who were a threat not only to their host societies but also to their fellow refugees, were declared 'ineligible' and therewith lost the entitlement to IRO support and protection.[100]

How blurred the dividing line between petty and serious criminal was can be seen in the discussion between Curtis and Marie D. Lane, the chief of the Welfare Division at the Geneva headquarters. Curtis strongly urged her to declare two 'hardened criminals' who had 'established a reign of terror in the refugee settlement' ineligible.[101] Lane instead warned against this easy withdrawal after she had seen the criminal records of the two.[102] But after Curtis vehemently underlined his claim for ineligibility on the grounds of his better knowledge of the two and their character, she conceded. They thus lost their IRO protection, and a 'Note of Ineligibility' was given to them.

In other instances it was clearer: Gracjan L. lost all assistance without much discussion.[103] He was described as 'the most desperate criminal of all',[104] as he was sentenced, among other crimes, for attempted murder in Arusha after stabbing a fellow refugee thirteen times in the stomach.[105] Usually the dependents of the person who was declared ineligible faced the same consequences. In L.'s case, however, his wife and children remained under IRO care. The IRO underlined that the Tanganyika government could deport him if they wanted.[106] After serving his sentence (ten years hard labour) in a Tanganyikan prison, L. was able to remain in the country and was maintained by the British government until 1961.[107] He was one of the last Poles, and ended up unemployed in a boarding house in Dar es Salaam, seemingly an alcoholic.[108] The British government finally admitted him into the UK (although he spoke hardly any English) as the independent Tanganyika government wanted the last Poles removed.[109] In January 1962 he arrived in London by plane, but died in a road accident in Devon just two months later.[110] From his story it becomes clear that the withdrawal of eligibility by the IRO did not mean that a refugee would get deported immediately. Although there had seemingly been attempts to deport him to Poland or Russia, this was reportedly unsuccessful. He could rely for the rest of his life on the assistance of the British government; meanwhile his wife and children were resettled by the IRO in Australia.

Near the end of the IRO's lifespan, in early 1950, the practice of eligibility withdrawal came under scrutiny again. F.J. Lorriman, the IRO representative in Uganda, opposed the careless withdrawal after one woman became 'hysterical' upon learning of the IRO decision to declare her ineligible.[111] She was apparently a German ex-internee and about to get married to a Polish refugee.[112] Lorriman suggested stopping the declaration of ineligibility as the IRO was winding up anyway, but his superior Curtis refused, citing the IRO rules. According to him, she had wrecked her chances for resettling in Canada, and had refused to apply for Australia.[113] The German ex-internees in Uganda in need of assistance for resettling elsewhere were a group whose eligibility for IRO protection was under discussion. The 'Notes of Ineligibility' were furthermore issued not only to serious criminals, but also to those who had 'exploited the organization'.[114] Those declared ineligible had the right of appeal to the Review Board in the Geneva headquarters.[115] In the end, it seems from the evidence I have seen that none of the refugees were forcibly deported to either Poland or the Soviet Union.

IRO and the Imperial Order of Things

How did the new 'international' officials of the IRO relate to existing officials of the respective colonial governments? How did they fit into the still widespread colonial model of society? In the second half of this chapter we will examine whether the 'internationals' acted along completely new lines or whether they followed the general principles of the colonial representatives. After looking at differences in their approaches, I will then highlight their shared basic assumptions.

Top-Down Social Bureaucrats vs. Paternalistic Officials

From the moment the IRO took over the responsibility for the Polish refugees in Africa, the differences between the organization's representatives and colonial officials soon became apparent. While colonial officials, especially in Tanganyika, were proud to have established well-run camps for the Poles, IRO officials were surprised to see the comfortable living conditions there.

The IRO's main aim was to get the people out of the camps, and so their comfortable living conditions were regarded as a hindrance to achieving this. C. Stephan, the IRO representative in Tanganyika, described this after an early visit to Tengeru in 1947. In his report he summed up the views of the camp commandants by saying that they felt they had 'a "nice snug" camp together and nothing must disturb the administration'.[116] Stephan suggested instead a reduction of the per capita rate that the IRO was paying by 20 per cent. This was to be achieved through a reduction of food rations, a reduction in the amount of native labour employed in the camp, a reduction of paid Polish labour and the discontinuation of pocket money. Stephan supported his claim with the arguments that the refugees were receiving more calories than needed and that the employment of so many Poles was only to build up the morale of the refugees, which was not necessary anymore. All these reductions were meant to not only cut the IRO's expenses, but also to 'shake the apathy of the camp commandants and the refugees themselves'. Stephan further added that 'it may have to be done in the "hard" way in the end'.[117] In his opinion, the refugees were just too content with their life in the camps and therefore made no real efforts to be resettled elsewhere.

Like Stephan, Curtis praised the conditions in Tengeru and the good work of its commandant two years later, but he admitted that 'the old charge remains true, that it is not "movement-minded"'.[118] After criticism from a visiting resettlement mission from Canada, Curtis had to defend the conditions in Tengeru and the unenthusiastic response from the Poles to the idea of resettlement. He explained that the IRO were trying hard to get the people moved, but that the British officials, especially the commandants, were protecting their camp inhabitants against too much pressure. Curtis singled out the Tengeru commandant John Minnery and his assistant J.P. Williams as the main hindrances.[119] Long-time commandant Minnery was a 'devout Catholic' Scot who seems to have had a rather paternalistic and protective attitude toward his subordinate Poles.[120] A signed photograph of him with the dedication 'Poland will rise again' clearly illustrates his pro-Polish attitude.[121] He was praised by Tengeru's Polish inhabitants for his attitude as a 'friend of the Poles with a golden heart'.[122] After working for years on establishing a well-run settlement, he was described by Curtis as 'in effect mayor of [the] second largest white man's town in Tanganyika', which was 'built to endure'.[123]

Minnery's assistant Williams had asked a Canadian official, during a drinks party at the IRO representative's hut in Tengeru, why the organization was 'pestering' the Poles to go where they did not want to go.[124] Williams had earlier already criticized Curtis sharply for his proposal to reduce the standards of living in the camps: 'The document under review [Curtis's letter] exudes a lack of understanding of human nature and less still of the Slavic people who quickly answer to kindness; but Force even though called Levers simply makes them stubborn'.[125] As in colonial societies generally, these refugees were not considered as just a random collection of individuals, but as people with certain characteristics; and the colonial administrator who 'knew his people' was the person who had the authority to rule them. Outsiders coming into this little kingdom were an unwelcome intrusion.

There were, however, differences among the colonial officials as well, as one remark from the responsible government official in Kenya underlined: 'You will never get the Poles out of Tanganyika until you fire [the director of refugees] Pennington and [camp commandant] Jock Minnery'.[126] While the Kenyan stance towards the Poles was harsh, the Tanganyika officials cared more for the Poles. The IRO officials, in turn, brought unrest to Tanganyika with their emphasis on moving the refugees, who were, in Curtis's words, 'rotting so fast after six years in camp'.[127] To get them moving they wanted to cause 'upheaval' among them. They understood the refugees as mostly spoiled, 'having been "spoon-fed" for the past 5 years'.[128]

Very much like their IRO colleagues in Europe, they thereby followed a 'discourse of professional intervention' that depicted DPs as pathological.[129] From this point of view, the refugees or DPs had fallen victim to 'DP apathy', a concept that was rooted in psychological expertise.[130] Living without privacy in camps for long years and being provided with everything, the DPs had apparently lost all initiative and became completely passive.[131] Professional intervention from outside was needed in order to get the people moving and back into normal life again. Maurice Lush, the IRO representative for the Middle East, described the situation in East Africa in a report explaining that 'apathy and resistance of the refugee can only be overcome with decisive action'.[132] He saw the refugees in East Africa as victims of 'mental apathy and indecision, which needs shock treatment as a remedy'.[133] Lush described the older British commandants as 'sometimes perhaps a trifle too paternal'.[134] Curtis shared his opinion and wanted to make clear to the refugees that the 'IRO means business' and that the camps were not permanent institutions they could rely on.[135] The increasing pressure to close the camps was being felt by the Poles as well.[136]

So far, the situation of displaced Poles in Europe seemed to be comparable to those in Africa, but there were also differences. The main contrast was the relative comfort the Poles in Africa enjoyed in comparison with the poor living conditions in European DP camps. The refugees were well aware of this difference. Antoni Wierzbiński, the Polish-American priest in Tengeru, wrote in 1948: 'Our people are afraid to go to Europe, because if they are not selected by any mission, they would have to stay in camps in Italy or Germany where the conditions are simply inhuman'.[137] In the African camps conditions ranged considerably from Gatooma, which one cleric even described as 'a second Belsen', to Tengeru, characterized by an IRO official as 'verg[ing] on the luxurious'.[138] In July 1945 the Poles in Tengeru were able to donate considerable sums to their compatriots in the European DP camps.[139] This comparative convenience did not pass unnoticed with some less inclined colonial administrators. Stanley Walden, district commissioner of Iringa, noted in 1946 after he had taken stock of the supplies in nearby Ifunda camp: 'Considering the state of the world today, the Board is unanimous in the opinion that these people who are refugees might give up some of the luxury which they have had endowed upon them by Government during the past few years, and live more like their friends and allies are doing, in willing obedience and sufferance throughout the world'.[140]

As Holborn states in her book on the IRO, the Poles in Africa 'continued to live in favourable conditions in a European though colonial environment, 5,000 miles from European problems and unconcerned about their future'.[141] On average, the Poles in Africa were better off than their compatriots in Europe.

The often younger social bureaucrats of the IRO subsequently clashed with the older paternalistic colonial officials. Curtis, the IRO representative for the whole region, had just turned thirty when he got this prominent position.[142] Maurice Lush, who gave him this post, described him as 'a very fine educational official and "international"'.[143] Curtis had worked for UNRRA in Egypt before – a rather different background from that of the older colonial officials. Another example was Mollie Rule, who was exceptional as she was the only woman in the upper administrative layer of the Polish settlements.[144] She was the IRO representative in Tengeru and had some difficulties being accepted by the British commandant as his superior; for example, the camp commandant asked her to send her letters to the director of refugees through him, which she refused.[145] Her gender as well as her age might both have been reasons for this – although she had herself worked for the Southern Rhodesian government before joining the IRO.[146] The refugees, in turn, were using the tensions between the IRO and colonial officials to their advantage; as the IRO official Lush noted: 'Refugees undoubtedly play off the Commandant of the Camp against the IRO Representative, and vice versa'.[147] This was a sign of the differences between the two institutions and of the independent agency of the refugees.

The IRO staff followed an approach that I propose to call 'bureaucratic top-down social planning'.[148] For them, the refugees became numbers or cases, who did not really know what was best for them. The emerging class of international humanitarian workers developed and professionalized social-scientific expertise about 'the refugee', who thereby lost his historical specificity and served as a passive object of professional intervention.[149] As the historian Peter Gatrell has written about the international refugee regime of the postwar era: '[Refugees] were amalgamated into a category of persons to whom something was done by external institutions, including relief organizations that took the incapacity of the refugee for granted'.[150]

One telling example is the IRO opinion on the question of whether the Polish refugee representatives should be asked to write to their host governments about their own views and wishes for the solution of the refugee problem. In the minutes of an IRO meeting in Nairobi in January 1950 it was noted that they should not be asked, as the refugee representatives 'tended to talk about freedom and democracy, and send copies to Mrs Roosevelt'.[151] While they were not portrayed as passive in this quote, they were nevertheless seen as quite irrational and useless for the tangible task of getting them settled. In the efforts to push for solutions in the final months of the IRO's lifespan, the refugees and their representatives were not regarded as helpful allies. The IRO bureaucrats thought of themselves as the ones who knew what was best for the refugees, and acted accordingly.

While those Poles who were regarded as 'reasonable'[152] were given some subordinate power and voice, the IRO officials always started from the premise that they were the professional experts and should have the final say. However, the IRO statement went on to say: 'Suggestions from the refugees themselves might on the other hand be of assistance if they were sober and sensible in tone, and stressed the desire of the group to work and to fit into the economy of any country that would accept them'.[153] In other words, the refugees were only involved in the plans for their future if they submitted themselves to the interests of their prospective host governments. Their opinion was not asked for, but only their willingness to do whatever was demanded of them.

In Koja, the independent Polish Settlement Association was even closed down by the Ugandan IRO representative John Dillon.[154] The association was in contact with North American Catholic and Polish diaspora organizations, and lobbied for resettlement opportunities on that continent.[155] Dillon criticized them for a lack of cooperation with the IRO and other recognized Polish refugee organizations. He further argued that their futile efforts were only holding back the refugees from taking up the IRO's offers.[156] This distrust in the abilities and efforts of the refugees shows the IRO's top-down approach once again.

Apart from the conflicting approach towards the refugees, relations between the IRO and colonial officials were mainly cordial.[157] At least some of the IRO officials had worked in the colonial administration before, and the IRO's chief representative in the region, Curtis, despite his different background, seems to have become an integral part of white Kenyan society, and he stayed in the country until his death.[158] Maurice Stanley Lush, the IRO's chief of mission for the Middle East (and East and Central Africa) in Cairo, had been a high-ranking colonial official before.[159] During his first tour of the camps in the colonies for the IRO he often 'met old friends or was personally well known'. Kenya's governor Phillip Mitchell was an old friend, and the EARA deputy commissioner Belcher had earlier worked under him as head of the Italian refugee staff in Abyssinia.[160] The quotation from Lush that opened this chapter showed, however, that he clearly distinguished between the principles he followed as a colonial administrator and the ones guiding his work as an IRO official. In the former position he was committed to protect the order of colonial society against potentially transgressive 'semi-skilled whites'. In the latter position the principal aim was to settle the refugees, no matter where or how.

The Refugees in the Colonial Social Order

The basic assumption, shared by the IRO and colonial governments alike, was that the Poles formed part of the white population of the colonies. The following statement of the IRO official Arthur Rucker after his tour through East Africa can only be understood with reference to this assumption: 'E. African governments are prepared to accept refugees for resettlement in numbers which are high in proportion to the white populations of the countries concerned'.[161] The basis for the negotiations about the numbers of Polish refugees to be admitted into permanent local resettlement was the white population. So, although the 'Polish quota' was tiny in relation to the total population, it was regarded as high in relation to the white population.

The IRO tried to induce the imperial government in London and the colonial governments to accept more Polish refugees for resettlement. Although their imperative goal was to get the Poles out of the camps and into one of the 'permanent solutions', they realized that this could not be achieved through a change in colonial policies. In one IRO memorandum to the Kenya government, this acceptance of the colonial order became apparent: 'The International Refugee Organisation will not be party to the introduction of cheap European labour into Kenya. It is confident that the committee will wish that any Poles who are admitted shall enjoy normal European salary scales'.[162] The 'committee' mentioned here was a body that was set up in Kenya to decide about applications of Poles for permanent residence in the colony. The IRO clearly accepted the division of colonial societies with its inherent distinction between cheap (or 'unskilled') native labour and better paid (or 'skilled') European labour. It was a comforting signal to the Kenyan authorities and their colonial anxieties over the blurring of the social boundary. The political strength of the white Kenyan settler lobby was a further factor that made it necessary to underline the IRO's commitment to the colonial division of labour.

In the internal communication of the IRO, the position of the Poles on the margins of the European community was clearer. Curtis described their employment situation in an extensive report to the IRO headquarters in Geneva: 'In general, the Poles can make their best local contribution in marginal jobs – marginal in the sense that they are in the border area between jobs normally performed by Europeans and those normally performed by other races'.[163] The refugees who found employment in East Africa outside the camps worked in jobs that were 'comparatively unattractive to Europeans', for instance as housekeepers, receptionists or cooks in hotels and restaurants, or as clerks or storekeepers in the army. Other occupations that Curtis described as similarly unattractive and marginal were hairdressers, dressmakers and shop assistants ('a multi-racial field'). For nursemaids, the main competition was reportedly from Seychellois or Africans.[164] For Central Africa, Curtis explained, the situation was slightly different, as there existed a European working class. The working-class jobs that were performed by Indians in Kenya were, in Southern Rhodesia, often performed by white immigrants from South Africa.[165] This had the effect that employment opportunities for Polish refugees in this class were greater, but the competition from other marginal Europeans was tougher. As a result, fewer Poles worked in the hospitality sector, but more (mainly men) had the opportunity to work in the mining industry.[166] In both regions, most of the Poles who successfully entered the colonial economy found themselves on the edges of white society.

The special social position of the Poles was even more pronounced in regard to the deliberations about Polish agricultural settlements. While the Polish exile elites showed a marked interest in the establishment of a large-scale 'en bloc' agricultural settlement of Poles, the colonial authorities spoke out clearly against it.[167] In Curtis's view, many arguments made these plans unworkable, and he advised against them: apart from the land problematic and the fear of the establishment of a permanent Polish group, he regarded their form of agriculture as different. With the Polish cooperative farm in Tengeru, the refugees had already provided a successful example of an agricultural enterprise. The problem, Curtis noted, was that economically this farm could only support some thirty people at a European standard of living. If, however, they were to continue to live at a 'standard of living the Poles had been used to', considerably more people could be supported.[168] Following Curtis, this would mean the introduction of a third form of agriculture alongside African subsistence and European large-scale farming. He cited examples of other cooperative farming experiments of the time, like the Jewish kibbutzim and Russian collective farms, and hinted at ideas about the introduction of similar forms in the colonies.[169] The Polish cooperative farm was an economic model that was neither African nor classic colonial European. Accordingly, the Poles would, in this hypothetical scenario, occupy a third social position and not be at the lower end of the European group, but distinct from it. This permanent establishment of a third social group, however, was rejected by local governments, the Colonial Office in London and even Curtis himself. Nobody except the Polish elites in London and Nairobi, and maybe the refugees themselves, had an interest in the creation of a 'Little Poland' in Africa.

The strongest opposition to the permanent immigration of some of the Polish refugees came from the two territories that differed the most in their political, economic and social model: Uganda and Southern Rhodesia. How did their governments argue against the admittance of Poles? And how did the IRO officials try to change their attitude?

Uganda's reluctance to accept any number of Poles was regarded by Curtis as mainly a result of personal prejudice on the side of the Ugandan officials.[170] But Curtis clearly knew where the power lay in the imperial set-up. Instead of pushing the Ugandan government directly, he went to a higher administrative level in order to persuade them into accepting some Poles. He asked the IRO deputy director general, Arthur Rucker, to request the Colonial Office in London to push the Ugandan government to accept some Poles.[171] Rucker in turn asked one Foreign Office official in London, who had signalled a willingness to assist, to influence the Uganda government through the Colonial Office.[172] The Ugandan protectorate government had always argued that the country was not destined for European settlement at all.[173] The whole political and economic model for Uganda was based on indirect rule and the taxing of African agricultural production – not on white settlement. Allowing a large group of Poles in for permanent settlement would have met with opposition from the African elites, as the Poles would likely take some of the government jobs these elites were aiming for.[174]

The position of Southern Rhodesia was quite different, and the IRO officials therefore followed different paths in approaching them. Southern Rhodesia was a self-governing colony and, as such, could be approached directly. The colony had the largest white population in East and Central Africa, and this population was represented by its government. But European opinion rejected a permanent Polish settlement. The 'Polish quota' was merely two hundred, which was the lowest proportion in relation to the white population when compared to Northern Rhodesia, Kenya and Tanganyika. In order to increase this quota, the IRO official Lush argued that Southern Rhodesia, with its comparably large white population, was able to accommodate more of the Polish refugees.[175] Apparently being aware of the earlier Rhodesian opposition to accepting Jewish refugees, Lush was quick to underline that the Poles were '99 per cent Christian'.[176] But again, the IRO attempts proved futile. The minister of internal affairs and justice from Salisbury had already explained his reasons for opposing the permanent immigration of Polish refugees in an earlier letter to the IRO:

> In an open labour market they [the Polish refugees now in Southern Rhodesia] would come into competition with the indigenous African; would inevitably be reduced to his standard of living; and would have a most disastrous effect on the white living standards and on the economy of the Colony generally.[177]

In his view, the Poles would become poor whites if they were not subsidized. Owing to their lack of skills and understanding of the colonial division of society, they would be forced to live at a standard like that of the black population. This in turn would be a threat to the distinction between black and white, and thus to the basis of the colonial social order. He went on to explain:

> It is absolutely essential from a social point of view that the social difference between black and white should be maintained and that there should be no cohabitation between the two races. Unfortunately, experience has shown us that many of the Poles, in view of their general standard of life, are quite unable to appreciate this distinction, and for this reason are quite unsuited to settlement in this part of Africa.[178]

In contrast to Uganda, where large-scale white immigration was opposed by the government, the Southern Rhodesian officials were generally in favour of white settlement. In their eyes, the Poles were just not the right type of settler and constituted a serious threat to the high living standards and rule of the white minority.[179] But a related argumentation was forthcoming from the Ugandan government as well. While their main argument was the protection of the African population from foreign competitors, they also argued that the Poles were 'persons accustomed to a European standard of living' and thus required wages accordingly.[180] This argument came up in the discussion about the admittance of Polish refugees who were already in employment in Uganda. If the food and accommodation support from the IRO were to cease, their wages would only amount to 'starvation wages'.[181] The general reluctance to admit potentially poor whites into the colony was thus as strong in Uganda as in Southern Rhodesia.

As in Southern Rhodesia, many of the Poles in Uganda were employed at wages and in jobs that were not up to the European colonial standard. The jobs were somewhere in between those performed by the British and the Africans, resembling in parts those of Asian workers, and often described as 'semi-skilled'.[182] In Uganda some dozen worked at the Electricity Board,[183] and in Southern Rhodesia ninety Poles were employed in a textile factory at Gatooma.[184] Their employment at comparably low wages was only possible through the peculiar situation that their basic needs were already covered by the IRO (and previously by the UNRRA or the Imperial Government). If the Poles had become normal residents, this advantage would have ceased.[185] The risk this entailed was the blurring of the line between black and white. Although Uganda and Southern Rhodesia had the largest difference in the region in regard to white settlement, both shared this basic assumption.

Surprisingly, Kenya made an experimental exception to this rule. The Public Works Department in Nairobi employed a Polish 'working gang' that was paid at below European rates, but above Indian.[186] Their accommodation was to be built according to the same plan as that of Asian artisans as their wages could not support a European standard of housing.[187] It was the first and only European working gang of the department, and consisted of fifteen Polish men.[188] Their first task was to build a new control tower at Nairobi West airport, a building site that was mostly out of public view.[189] The background to this experiment was the shortage of artisans relative to the heavy demand for postwar construction work in Kenya. The IRO official Curtis connected this scheme to the emergence of a small European working class in Kenya at that time – or as he wrote, 'there are progressively more Europeans working with their hands'.[190] This trend, however, was not really widespread and the Polish 'working gang' remained a singular economic and social experiment. It seems they completed only this one building project.[191]

In conclusion it can be stated that the IRO officials, although having a different approach and aim, were clearly operating under the conditions of a colonial social order. While they tried manoeuvring these circumstances it was clear to them that they had to accept the colonial division of society and fit the Poles 'into the existing European communities in accordance with the immigration policies of the territories concerned'.[192] In these policies, Europeans were understood as destined to remain different from the Africans in terms of their social and economic position.

In her influential work on refugees, the anthropologist Liisa Malkki has brought to the forefront the importance of the 'national order of things' for a thorough understanding of refugees and their position in modern societies.[193] In her work she questions the 'taken-for-granted ways of thinking' about refugees in a world of nation-states,[194] and urges us instead to examine the 'displaced' refugee and the 'placed' nations as intrinsically connected. Refugees are seen as problematic, as they deviate from the supposedly stable world of nation-states. While completely agreeing with her understanding of placement and displacement, I have sought to show in this chapter that the world of the early postwar refugee regime was not entirely national. While it is largely true that most of the subjects and actors shaping the international refugee regime lived in nation-states in Europe, this is not the whole story.

At the end of the Second World War, large parts of the world were still part of what I will call the 'imperial order of things', in which nevertheless refugees lived and international organizations operated. To make the conceptual difference between nation and empire clear, let me cite Jane Burbank and Frederick Cooper: 'The nation-state proclaims the commonality of its people – even if the reality is more complicated – while the empire-state declares the non-equivalence of multiple populations'.[195] In the British colonies in Africa, this non-equivalence ran mainly along racially defined lines. The position of white refugees and the IRO officials in colonial societies shows the basic acceptance of the colonial division of society along the contested and socially constructed category of 'race'. The IRO bureaucrats argued generally along universalist lines, whereby every refugee was supposedly the same: a passive recipient to be provided with a standardized amount of food, clothing and shelter until he or she could be resettled. They calculated with numbers of calories, and classified refugees according to their skills and abilities, seemingly regardless of their race, nationality or religion. But operating in colonial societies and arguing with 'standards of living' that people were used to, the refugees under IRO care became racialized as well. In the end it was not only about the standardized 'refugee' who was regarded as a deviation from the national order and had to be firmly reconnected to 'place'. For resettlement into colonial societies, this place was racially structured; and the connection of the white population to the place was not always strong. Not all whites were 'rooted' in the African territories. In the colonial social order there were no standardized, average people, but only racially (and ethnically) defined groups of people. And these groups were thought to differ fundamentally in their basic needs. Refugees had to be inserted into one of these groups, and their racial categorization was generally paramount in determining which one.

This contradiction between the non-discriminating policy of the organizations and the existing discriminating labour policies on the ground became apparent in the personnel policy of UNRRA in China and the IRO in East Africa. UNRRA had generally two categories of staff: the international and better paid Class I staff and the locally hired Class II staff, paid according to locally prevailing wages, a system later taken over by the IRO.[196] In China this second class was further divided: resident Europeans were paid on average 30 per cent more than their Chinese colleagues.[197] UNRRA's historian George Woodbridge explained this difference with the need to compete with other employers in Shanghai, who paid more to the qualified Europeans, so that they could maintain their 'European standard of living'. According to him, 'this provoked complaints from the Chinese employees ... that the Administration was practising racial discrimination – as was, strictly speaking, the case'.[198] So despite UNRRA's intention not to discriminate 'on the grounds of sex, race, nationality or creed',[199] the circumstances forced them to accommodate. The same holds true for the IRO employment policy in Africa. The Nairobi representative explained that working conditions and rates of pay for local staff in East and Central Africa differed not only regionally but also according to their 'race' (European, Indian or African). He proposed to 'follow as closely as possible the comparable conditions of work for persons of those races in temporary Government employment in the particular territory concerned'.[200] Both organizations thus adapted to the colonial order of the labour market.

For Whites Only – Race and the International Refugee Regime

In this last section, I will connect my empirical findings with a general assessment of a central institution of the postwar international refugee regime – the IRO. Although the organization was guided by internationalist and humanitarian assumptions, it also operated in a world that was still to a large extent imperial. The politics of differentiation between racially defined groups therefore played an important role in the establishment of the international refugee regime, and its limitation to certain refugee groups was deliberate. As the IRO's historian Louise Holborn wrote, the organization's main success was the resettlement of more than one million refugees and DPs.[201] In the words of its last director general, it provided 'the most successful example of large-scale international cooperation for humanitarian purposes in history'.[202] One reason for the IRO's success in resettlement was that these refugees were white and therefore fitted well into the preferred criteria of the principal receiving countries. These countries were the white-dominated settler-colonial United States, Australia and Canada.[203] The migration of European refugees continued the model of white emigration to the 'new world', which had been one of the largest migration flows around the turn of the twentieth century.[204] Cohen has described the resettlement of European DPs accordingly as the 'final episode of the Great Atlantic Migration'. Postwar Australia pursued a massive immigration programme to tackle the Asian threat by increasing its white population.[205] No comparable efforts to resettle Asian or African refugees into Western countries has ever been made.[206] The unwanted refugees were first Jewish and later Asian and African – all regarded as 'not quite white' at their time of flight.[207] In the migration to Britain, European refugees were seen as a better alternative to black labour migrants from the Commonwealth.[208] The preference for Baltic refugees over those from Eastern or Southern Europe follows exactly the same line.[209] The Catholic Poles were thus located somewhere between the preferred North Europeans and the Jewish Poles.

While race, religion and nationality were not usually the official criteria for the admission of refugees, they mattered in practice. The visiting selection missions of the recipient countries had the power to pick out the ones they wanted. In preparation for the forthcoming Canadian selection mission to Lebanon, the IRO's Middle East chief, Lush, explained that the Canadians would have no problem with the Muslim faith of some Albanian refugees there, but they would not take them if they had 'oriental blood and lineage'.[210] When the Canadian selection mission was in Tengeru they allegedly declared that 'Jewish people would not be permitted'.[211] Turkey, in turn, offered resettlement opportunities for more than two thousand Muslim refugees, irrespective of their other personal characteristics.[212] In anticipation of antisemitic resentment, IRO officials also emphasized that the Poles in Africa were Christian and not Jewish, in order to 'sell' them to the receiving countries.²¹³ Lush even went as far as offering some Baltic or other nationals from amongst the European DPs in addition to the 'not very popular' Poles, if the British military would accept some thousands of them for the above-mentioned construction of a proposed military base in Kenya.²¹⁴ The IRO's additional offer was meant as an incentive, and illustrates the values attributed to different refugee groups under its care. But for the decision about the inclusion under the IRO's mandate, race was most important.

The exclusive focus of the IRO on white refugees and the white populations in colonial societies appeared in a report by Curtis from the IRO in Nairobi. He described the admission of Polish refugees for permanent settlement in the colonies as 'extremely generous'. Especially telling is his sentence: 'On any possible basis of comparison, their record stands among the leading countries of the world'.²¹⁵ He went on to explain that three of the territories had accepted so many refugees that they constituted more than 1 per cent of their white population, further arguing that if the West European countries and the United States would do the same, the refugee problem would be solved.²¹⁶ The idea that the non-white population could serve as a possible 'basis of comparison' was not even thinkable to him. Although their numbers appear on the same page, Curtis did not explain why he did not calculate the percentage of Polish refugees in relation to the total population of the concerned territories. Tanganyika, for example, accepted, with 2.7 per cent, the highest proportion of Polish refugees in relation to the European population; however, in relation to the whole population this amounted to a meagre 0.006 per cent.²¹⁷ It becomes apparent that as the IRO was a white organization for white refugees only, it was thinking about white host populations exclusively.

In a 2002 general overview of the emergence of the international refugee regime, Laura Barnett summed this up as follows:

> On a broader level, it is also important to note that the refugee regime has never been truly international until the last quarter century. 'International' organizations that developed to deal with the refugee problem focused exclusively on European and later Cold War issues. Refugees existed in other parts of the world, but these flows were generally ignored by a Eurocentric state system that concentrated on humanitarian action closer to home.²¹⁸

This was not only a geographical limitation or something referring to the just-ended war, but was one in which racism played a role.²¹⁹ The Polish refugees in Africa were clearly not 'close to home'. Nevertheless, they came under the IRO mandate. Among those who did not receive international care were the earlier Ethiopian refugees from the war with Italy, who were rather seen as a domestic problem in the British Empire.[220] Although African expatriates, humanitarians and anti-fascists in London lobbied for these refugees, they did not come under international protection.[221] In 1941, some of the Ethiopian refugees even fought with the British forces against the Italians in Abyssinia.[222] The fact that the Ethiopians were described as refugees at all might be related to the exceptional position of Ethiopia as an independent African member of the League of Nations. By contrast, colonized Africans who had been forced to flee their homes were never described as 'refugees'.[223] In East Africa, people had already fled their villages when they heard rumours of the starting war, because they remembered the forced conscriptions of the First World War.[224] They had good reasons for this, as conscription for the colonial economy was extended during the Second World War too. Apart from service in the armed forces, Africans had to work on white-owned plantations or even in the construction of some of the Polish refugee camps – an issue I will return in Chapter 5.

The largest number of refugees to be excluded in the postwar era, however, was found in Asia.[225] Millions of people had to flee following the partition of India and Pakistan in June 1947.[226] While the IRO did not help these refugees, the organization was nevertheless active in India at this time. Starting in July 1947, 4,250 Polish refugees in India received care and maintenance from the IRO.[227] Indian and IRO officials were aware of the connection between the two refugee groups. The IRO official Maurice Lush noted in retrospect that India took the line: 'either come here in force and deal with our seven million Indian refugees or remove your few thousand Europeans'.[228] The IRO took the latter decision and evacuated the Poles. As the situation after independence and partition was regarded as too dangerous, they were moved out of the country when the British troops withdrew in February 1948.[229] In March 1948, the last seven hundred of them arrived in East Africa under IRO arrangements.[230] The newly independent states had to cope with the partition refugees themselves.

The only larger group of non-European refugees to come under IRO care were 11,122 overseas Chinese, who were repatriated from Shanghai with IRO assistance.[231] The Chinese government had an interest in repatriating them to the South East Asian countries where they had lived before the war. However, they faced resistance from the respective governments. The IRO assistance for repatriation of this group was in turn partly 'a bargaining chip' that allowed the IRO to continue assisting the mostly Russian and Jewish refugees still in China.[232] The IRO made strong efforts to assist twenty-nine thousand Europeans after the communist revolution in October 1949, and resettled nearly twenty thousand of them.[233] Another European group in China bore some parallels to the Poles in Africa: 5,500 anticommunist White Russian refugees, who had originally fled to China after the Bolshevik revolution. They were transferred to a refugee camp in Samar, in the Philippines, and maintained there by the IRO.[234] As in Africa and India, IRO efforts in the Far East concentrated on the European refugees there. The IRO's successor, the UNHCR, focused again largely on resettling the remaining Europeans. The UNHCR responded much less readily to Chinese refugees in Hong Kong, taking for granted that Chinese refugees were unwelcome and even barred from most of the countries that had accepted European refugees.[235] Glen Peterson concludes that 'the early UNHCR was both a Cold War era institution and a colonial era institution'.[236]

So, despite the universalist rhetoric and the dedication to principles of non-discrimination, the humanitarian activities of the IRO and the early UNHCR were largely limited to European refugees and DPs. The privileged position of the Polish refugees in Africa shows that this limitation was based on racial and not regional categorizations. While the international refugee regime operated in Africa in the 1940s, its assistance was limited to the white refugees there. Only with the refugee movements during the independence war in Algeria did the international community (by then under the UNHCR) turn again to Africa, a continent that was to become the hotspot of the international refugee regime in the following decades.[237]

In this chapter I have analysed the members of the group as 'refugees', and traced their connection to and interaction with the organizations of the international refugee regime. In the next chapter I will shift my focus to another aspect of the group: their nationality. They were not just any white refugees, but came from a distinct region with a specific history. I will thus engage with the historiography of East Central Europe, and therein trace the discussions about (post-) colonial understandings of Poland's position vis-à-vis its neighbours. Just as the Poles in this chapter have been placed in the context of the emerging refugee regime, so they will be placed in the context of the debate around the reading of Polish history as 'colonial' history. The interaction of the Polish refugees with the hosting colonial societies will add a new dimension to this ongoing debate.

Notes

1. IRO: AJ/43/566, Maurice Lush, PCIRO Cairo to Sir Arthur Rucker, Deputy Executive Secretary, PCIRO Geneva, 2.10.47.
2. Malkki, 'Refugees and Exile', 498.
3. Until the nineteenth century, the term 'refugee' referred only to Protestant refugees from France. See Marrus, *The Unwanted*, 8.
4. Skran, *Refugees in Inter-War Europe*.
5. Ibid., 65.

6. Marrus, *The Unwanted*, 86–91.
7. Skran, *Refugees in Inter-War Europe*, 99–100.
8. Ibid., 89.
9. Goodwin-Gill, 'The Politics of Refugee Protection', 12.
10. Armenian, Greek, Bulgarian, Turkish, Assyrian, German and Saar refugees were added to the Russians; Skran, *Refugees in Inter-War Europe*, 85.
11. Matthew Frank and Jessica Reinisch propose to consider both postwar eras in Europe as one single 'Forty Years' Crisis' lasting from 1919 to 1959. See Frank and Reinisch, *Refugees in Europe*.
12. See Woodbridge, *UNRRA*. The organization thus predated the United Nations and only became part of it after the founding of the UN in 1945.
13. Holborn, *International Refugee Organization*, 18–19.
14. Reinisch, '"Auntie UNRRA" at the Crossroads', 73.
15. UNRRA had its headquarters in Washington, DC, received nearly three-quarters of its funding from the US (Woodbridge, *UNRRA*, vol. 1, 112.) and two-thirds of its international staff came from the US or UK (ibid., vol. 1, 244.).
16. Reinisch, '"Auntie UNRRA" at the Crossroads', 71.
17. Reinisch, 'We Shall Rebuild Anew a Powerful Nation', 475.
18. Ibid., 453; Marrus, *The Unwanted*, 323–24.
19. Reinisch, '"Auntie UNRRA" at the Crossroads', 73.
20. Millions of Chinese had fled their homes, and large parts of the country's infrastructure were destroyed under Japanese occupation. See Woodbridge, *UNRRA*, vol. 1, 371–72.
21. The UNRRA programme in Ethiopia was the smallest next to San Marino. See ibid., 334.
22. Woodbridge, *UNRRA*, vol. 1, 313. The reconstruction programmes of UNRRA were partly taken over by other UN agencies.
23. See Gatrell, *Making of the Modern Refugee*, 94–97.
24. Ibid., 108.
25. On anticommunism among European DPs, see Holian, 'Anticommunism in the Streets'.
26. Gatrell, *Making of the Modern Refugee*, 6–7.
27. Own calculation from 'Annex 5. Statement of contributions made by member governments' (Holborn, *International Refugee Organization*, 12), only taking in account the received contributions. The fiscal plan proposed a lower percentage of contributions from the US, but this was the actual amount contributed to the IRO expenses.
28. 'Annex 2', ibid., 100.
29. My calculation from July 1947, numbers from 'Annex 22', ibid., 238.
30. In the 'Middle East' region (i.e. East Africa, India, Egypt, Israel, Lebanon, Syria and Turkey) there were fewer than 4% of the total refugees under IRO care, while in the 'Far East' region (i.e. Shanghai and Philippines) there were little more than 1% (own calculations from ibid.).
31. United Nations General Assembly, '*Convention Relating to the Status of Refugees*', adopted 28.07.51. See also Gatrell, 'Putting Refugees in Their Place', 11; Malkki, 'Refugees and Exile', 501.
32. See Glasman, 'Seeing Like a Refugee Agency'; Zetter, 'Labelling Refugees'.
33. Sword, *Deportation and Exile*, 13.
34. Ibid., 65.
35. The British Secretary of State for Foreign Affairs used the terms 'civilian' and 'refugee' interchangeably in his memorandum regarding the situation in Persia (PRO: CAB

66/26/29: 'War Cabinet. Evacuation of Polish and Greek Refugees from Middle East', Memorandum by the Secretary of State for Foreign Affairs, 14.07.42).
36. It was theoretically a civilian organization, but most staff and supplies came from the British army (Woodbridge, *UNRRA*, vol. 2, 83).
37. Ibid., vol. 1, 21.
38. EAS 3.07.42, 'Polish Refugees from Persia'.
39. PRO: CO 822/133/1, 'War Refugees (Control and Expulsion) Ordinance 1946', passed in the Legislative Council on 7.03.46.
40. Skran, *Refugees in Inter-War Europe*, 261.
41. KNA: AH/3/3, p.1, H.E. Stacey, Crown Counsel for Attorney General to Chief Secretary, Nairobi, 06.01.43.
42. Gatrell, *Making of the Modern Refugee*, 97.
43. Kramer, 'Einleitung', 8; See also Malkki, 'Refugees and Exile', 499–500.
44. TNA: 61/685/14, p.1, Circular letter by Pennington, for Ag. Chief Secretary, DSM, 15.07.42; and TNA: 69 /787, p.8, R.S. Hickson-Mahony, Labour Commissioner, DSM to Chief Secretary, DSM, 16.07.42.
45. Wójcik, 'Introduction to Chapter 6 Africa', 137. However, at least one highly appreciated camp commandant (Herbert Story) was a Quaker and as such a 'conscientious objector' (TNA: 176 /87, p.7, Pennington to District Commissioner Iringa, 10.04.45). A visiting American Red Cross representative clearly recommended the Southern Rhodesian model of military administration for refugee camps (MSS Afr. s. 116, Report 'Camp Marandellas' by Russel R. Johnston, American Red Cross, 19.02.44).
46. EAS 28.07.42, 'Ready for Refugees' Reception – Tanganyika to Give Homes to 5,000 Poles', which follows the lines of the above-mentioned circular by Pennington.
47. Malkki, 'Refugees and Exile', 499.
48. Shadle, 'Reluctant Humanitarians'; Wilkin, 'Refugees and British Administrative Policy'. For a contemporary first-hand account, see Sequeira, 'Ethiopian Refugees in Kenya'.
49. *Kenya Gazette*, 2.08.1938, 'A Bill to Regularize the Residence in the Colony of Certain Refugees from Ethiopia', 998.
50. Shadle, 'Reluctant Humanitarians', 7.
51. Wilkin, 'Refugees and British Administrative Policy', 511.
52. Ibid., 514.
53. The movement began in October 1937 and lasted until May 1939 (KNA: BN/46/63/11, Member for Health and Local Government to Attorney General, 23.11.46).
54. KNA: BN/46/62/1, G. Pritchard Brown, Ag. Principle Immigration Officer, Nairobi to British Passport Control Officer, Vienna, 14.08.38.
55. E.g. the Austrian Jewish couple Arthur and Matilde Winter were sent back on the same vessel as they had only 160 pounds which was considered 'inadequate for immigrants to Kenya' (KNA: BN/46/62/51, Pritchard Brown to British Passport Control Officer, Vienna, 27.10.38).
56. KNA: BN/46/63/11, Member for Health and Local Government to Attorney General, 23.11.46.
57. Kennedy, *Islands of White*, 89.
58. KNA: BN/46/63/11, Member for Health and Local Government to Attorney General, 23.11.46.
59. PRO: CO 822/133/1, 'Aliens Legislation, Kenya', Minutes of a Discussion held at the Colonial Office, 27.06.47.

60. The Indian National Congress published a statement along these lines in the *Kenya Daily Mail* on 11.01.39 (cited in: KNA: BN/46/63/11, Member for Health and Local Government to Attorney General, 23.11.46).
61. KNA: AH/3/3/198, Humfrey N. Gale, Personal Representative of the Director General, UNRRA to Foreign Office, London, 07.08.46.
62. United Nations Archives, New York (hereafter UNA): S-1253-0000-0676: C.M. Pierce, Director Division on Displaced Persons, Balkan Mission to Fred Hoehler, DP Division UNRRA, Washington, 11.06.45. See also Taylor, *Polish Orphans*, 120.
63. PRO: FO 371/57780, Sgd. G.M.O. Day, War Office Liaison Staff (Poles) to War Office C.A. (D.P.), 17.01.46.
64. Sword, 'Their Prospects Will Not Be Bright', 369.
65. Woodbridge, *UNRRA*, vol. 2, 92.
66. The UNRRA staff in East Africa consisted apparently of a representative, an audit officer and a secretary (KNA: AH/3/3, p.55B, C.R. Lockhart, Chief Secretary EAGC to Emerson Holcomb, Director Repatriation Division, UNRRA, Cairo, 24.11.45).
67. Taylor, *Polish Orphans*, 109–14.
68. PRO: FO 371/51150, 'Copy of Report No. C.C.1. from Herbert Story', Friends Relief Service, London to American Friends Service Committee, Philadelphia, 3.02.45. Herbert Story was a Quaker, and he wrote the report for the Friends Relief Service headquarters in London. His report was copied by the British censorship as it contained criticism of an UNRRA official.
69. Gross, *Revolution from Abroad*, 200.
70. UNA: S-1253-0000-0713, Extract from a letter of Mr Jacobs to Mr Youdin, 7.05.45, attached to an undated report about the conditions in Oudtshoorn, p.8.
71. UNA: S-1253-0000-0676, Pierce, UNRRA Balkan Mission to Hoehler, UNRRA Washington, 11.06.45.
72. Ibid., 27.02.45.
73. Taylor, *Polish Orphans*, 121.
74. EAS 03.06.46, 'Polish Mission On Way To East Africa – Effort To Persuade Refugees To Return'.
75. GP 26.05.46, p.1, 'Nasze Stanowisko' by Kazimierz Chodzikiewicz.
76. KNA: AH/3/3, p.95A, Edward Raczyński to all Chief Polish Advisors (Nairobi, Tel Aviv, Beirut, Bombay, Johannesburg, Cape Town), 08.04.46.
77. KNA: AH/3/3, p.97A, Secretary of State, CO to Chief Secretaries Entebbe, DSM, Nairobi and Lusaka, 20.04.46.
78. TNA: 77/24/34, Pennington to Provincial Commissioners of Northern, Central and Southern Highlands Province, 2.05.46.
79. Zarzycki and Buczak-Zarzycka, *Kwaheri Africa*, 50.
80. Krolikowski, *Stolen Childhood*, 137. Rogiński (Roginski in the British files) had furthermore before been a military chaplain during the Polish-Bolshevik war and was described as a 'great patriot' (Królikowski, 'Operation Polejump', 175).
81. IRO: AJ/43/781, Curtis to Ag. Chief PCIRO, 'Mr. Harazin's report on Polish Camps in Tanganyika', 29.08.47.
82. UNA: S-1253-0000-0676, Wincenty Rzymowski, Minister Foreign Affairs, Warsaw to Fiorello LaGuardia, Director General UNRRA, 12.07.46.
83. Cited in IRO: AJ/43/787/33/3, T.T. Waddington, UNRRA Cairo to UNRRA Representative, Nairobi, 23.11.46.
84. UNA, S-1253-0000-0676, Director General UNRRA to Central Committee, 11.03.47. See also Taylor, *Polish Orphans*, 120.

85. GP 02.02.47, p.12, 'Chłodno, głodno i do domu daleko...'.
86. GP 16.02.47, p.10, 'Z Nairobi'.
87. IRO: AJ/43/781, H.A. Curtis, PCIRO East Africa and Rhodesia, Nairobi to PCIRO Middle East HQ, Cairo, 15.09.47.
88. Krolikowski, *Stolen Childhood*, 177.
89. IRO: AJ/43/616/2/29, M.S. Lush, Chief of Mission Middle East, IRO: Appendix A: 'Middle East staff as from October 1st 1948', 18.06.48.
90. According to IRO staff statistics, of the fifteen international staff members in East Africa, there were five from the UK, four from the US, two from Egypt and one from Canada, Denmark, Greece and New Zealand each (IRO: AJ/43/790/52/4, 'Statistical report on IRO personnel at 30th November 1948').
91. IRO: AJ/43/616/2/29, Arthur Rucker, Deputy Executive Secretary, IRO: Appendix F, 'Memorandum of present position of the IRO', 16.06.48.
92. IRO: AJ/43/787/31/31, H.A. Curtis, IRO Nairobi to M.S. Lush, Special Advisor on Middle East Affairs, London, 10.08.49.
93. IRO: AJ/43/781, 'Mission en Afrique Oriental. Rapports mensuels', June 1947 to March 1950.
94. Gatrell, 'Putting Refugees in Their Place', 4.
95. Holborn, *International Refugee Organization*, 311.
96. The respective governments in East and Central Africa, except Kenya, passed special legislation to extend diplomatic privileges to IRO officials (IRO: AJ/43/781, Monthly report for March 1949 by Curtis to IRO HQ, 4.04.49).
97. Holborn, *International Refugee Organization*, 314. The question of the eligibility of individual refugees in postwar Europe was also a major challenge to the field personnel. See Cohen, *In War's Wake*, 35.
98. IRO: AJ 787/31/11, H.A. Curtis to IRO Representative, Kampala, 06.04.50.
99. IRO: AJ/43/787/32/1, Marie D. Lane, Chief, Welfare Division, Health, Care and Maintenance Department, IRO Geneva, 24.05.49.
100. A list of six Polish refugees who were declared as ineligible: IRO: AJ 787/31/11, H.A. Curtis, Chief of Mission, IRO East Africa, Nairobi to EARA, Nairobi, 14.09.50.
101. IRO: AJ 787/32/1 A+B, Curtis to Director General, IRO HQ Geneva, 05.05.49
102. IRO: AJ 787/32/1 Marie D. Lane, IRO HQ Geneva to Curtis, IRO Nairobi 02.07.49.
103. IRO: AJ/43/787/31/11, Curtis, IRO Nairobi to IRO Representative for Tanganyika, Tengeru, 07.10.49. I have replaced the surname of some individuals with just its initial in order to protect their anonymity.
104. PRO: CO 822/146/1, Personal Summary, Gracjan L., attached to Beryl Hughes, Home Office to Dawson, Colonial Office, 9.11.50.
105. PRO: AST 18/115, R.M. Morris, Aliens Department, Home Office to C.N. Berry, National Assistance Board, London, 17.01.62.
106. IRO: AJ/43/787/31/11, H.A. Curtis, IRO Nairobi to IRO Representative for Tanganyika, Tengeru, 07.10.49.
107. PRO: AST 18/115, K.A. Woolverton, Colonial Office to D.E. Faulkner, Aliens Department, Home Office, 17.05.61.
108. PRO: AST 18/115, C.N. Berry, National Assistance Board to H.A. Saunders, NAB HQ 16.01.62.
109. PRO: AST 18/115, G.B. Pearce to Head, Home Office, London 07.09.61.
110. PRO: AST 18/115, H.A. Saunders, NAB to Rozalia L., Western Australia, 12.03.62.
111. IRO: AJ 787/32/5, F.J. Lorriman, IRO Representative Uganda to H.A. Curtis, IRO Nairobi, 19.01.50.

112. At least her name, Maria Werla, suggests this.
113. IRO: AJ/43/781, Monthly report for December 1949 by Curtis to IRO HQ, 6.01.50.
114. In one list of people declared ineligible, Curtis classified five as 'Criminals' and one (Jozef G.) as 'Exploitation of Organisation' (IRO: AJ/43/787/31/11, Curtis to Officer i/c EARA, Nairobi, 14.09.50). G. was a skilled mason, but a heavy drinker, who was supposedly involved in illicit distilling in Tengeru. He obtained a residence permit for Kenya to work for the Kenyan government in Nairobi in October 1949 (IRO: AJ/43/781, Monthly report for October 1949 by Curtis to IRO HQ, 31.10.49). Most likely he did not work to the satisfaction of his superiors there, and so had to return to Tengeru.
115. IRO: AJ/43/787/31/11, H.A. Curtis, IRO Nairobi to IRO Representative for Tanganyika, Tengeru, 07.10.49. On the IRO 'Review Board for Eligibility Appeals', see Cohen, *In War's Wake*, 41–44.
116. IRO: AJ/43/781, Monthly narrative report from Tanganyika office, C. Stephan, PCIRO Representative Tanganyika, 27.10.47 (received).
117. Ibid.
118. IRO: AJ/43/787/31/13, Curtis to M.S. Lush, Special Advisor on Middle East Affairs, c/o Chief of IRO London Office, 10.08.49.
119. Ibid.
120. IRO: AJ/43/781, Curtis to Ag. Chief PCIRO, 'Mr. Harazin's report on Polish Camps in Tanganyika', 29.08.47.
121. The photograph is available in the online collection of the Polish Institute and Sikorski Museum, at http://www.foto.karta.org.pl/przeglad-wynikow-wyszukiwania/?allword=Minnery&exactmatchword=&anyword=&nothiswords=&imageselected=74811. Last accessed 28 August 2019.
122. GP 2.12.45, 'Z Osiedli', p.10.
123. IRO: AJ/43/616/2/39, Telegram from [Curtis] Nairobi to [IRO HQ] Geneva, 22.07.49.
124. IRO: AJ/43/788/42/2, Curtis to Pennington, Director of Refugees, Tanganyika, 17.08.49.
125. MSS Afr. s. 1366/9, p.8, J.P. Williams, Camp Commandant Kondoa to Pennington, Director of Refugees, DSM, 17.04.47.
126. Curtis citing an informal remark by Neil Stewart, Director of Aliens and Internees, Kenya (IRO: AJ/43/781, Curtis to Ag. Chief PCIRO, 'Mr. Harazin's report on Polish Camps in Tanganyika', 29.08.47).
127. IRO: AJ/43/781, Monthly report for December 1948 by Curtis to IRO HQ, 4.01.49.
128. IRO Tanganyika representative Stephan's description of the refugees in Ifunda after interviews there (IRO: AJ/43/781, Report by C. Stephan, IRO Tanganyika, 15.12.47).
129. Gatrell and Baron, 'Violent Peacetime', 259. On the 'pathologization of uprootedness' see also Malkki, 'National Geographic', 32.
130. Gatrell, *Making of the Modern Refugee*, 104. See also Cohen, *In War's Wake*, 155.
131. Salvatici, 'Help the People to Help Themselves', 440.
132. IRO: AJ/43/790/55/2, 'Problems in East Africa', M.S. Lush to IRO HQ, 31.01.49.
133. IRO: AJ/43/790/55/2, 'Middle East Policy, Last Lap but One', operational memorandum by M.S. Lush, p.5, 15.07.48.
134. Lush, *A Life of Service*, 252.
135. IRO: AJ/43/781, Monthly report for October 1947 by Curtis to IRO HQ, 26.10.47.
136. Krolikowski, *Stolen Childhood*, 174.

137. Letter of Wierzbiński to Archbishop Tweedy of Hobart, Tasmania, written in November 1948, explaining why the refugees refused to go under IRO arrangements to Europe in order to meet resettlement selection missions there. Quoted from Allbrook and Cattalini, *The General Langfitt Story*, n.p.
138. IRO: AJ/43/790/55/2, M.S. Lush to Executive General PCIRO HQ, 27.11.47.
139. NP 30.06.45, 'Iskierki Polskie'. The Tengeru Poles collected 15,000 Shillings in just one day to support Polish DPs in Germany.
140. TNA: 176 /87, p.19, S.A. Walden, District Commissioner Iringa to Provincial Commissioner Southern Highlands Province, 'Emergency Board of Survey on Stores in Ifunda Camp', 28.05.46.
141. Holborn, *International Refugee Organization*, 420.
142. Hubert Arnold Curtis was born on 20 May 1917.
143. Lush, *A Life of Service*, 253.
144. At least one more woman, Jr. Commander D.M. Stewart, toured some camps for UNRRA as repatriation officer (MSS Afr. s. 1366/9, p.7, J.P. Williams, Camp Commandant Kondoa to Pennington, Director of Refugees, DSM, 17.04.47).
145. IRO: AJ/43/787/31/13, Curtis, IRO Nairobi to M.S. Lush, Special Advisor on Middle East Affairs, IRO London, 10.08.49.
146. IRO: AJ/43/616/2/29, 'Summary of Deputy Executive Secretary's Tour in Turkey, Lebanon, Egypt, East Central and South Africa. May 30th – June 19th, 1948', by Arthur Rucker, p.5.
147. IRO: AJ/43/790/57/1, M.S. Lush to IRO HQ, 14.02.49.
148. For a comparison between the more 'bottom-up' approach of the interwar refugee organizations and the postwar 'top-down' approach, see Easton-Calabria, 'From Bottom-Up to Top-Down'.
149. Cohen, *In War's Wake*, 77.
150. Gatrell, 'Putting Refugees in Their Place', 22.
151. IRO: AJ/43/790/57/1, 'Conference of I.R.O. representatives in East Africa – Minutes of Meeting held at Nairobi on 4th January, 1950', by H.A. Curtis, p.5, 4.01.50.
152. E.g. in the description of individual Polish officials (IRO: AJ/43/781, 'Mr. Harazin's report on Polish Camps in Tanganyika', attached to Curtis to Acting Chief PCIRO, 29.08.47).
153. IRO: AJ/43/790/57/1, 'Conference of I.R.O. representatives in East Africa – Minutes of Meeting held at Nairobi on 4th January, 1950', by H.A. Curtis, p.5, 4.01.50.
154. IRO: AJ/43/790/55/4, Dillon, IRO Uganda to Alicja Kisielnicka, PRS, Koja, 2.04.49. On this conflict see also Nowak, 'We Would Rather Drown Ourselves'.
155. IRO: AJ/43/790/55/4, Kisielnicka, Pienkowska et al., Settlement Association, Koja to Dillon, IRO Uganda, 27.04.49.
156. IRO: AJ/43/790/55/4, Dillon, IRO Uganda to Alicja Kisielnicka, PRS, Koja, 2.04.49.
157. IRO: AJ/43/781, Monthly report for March 1949 by Curtis to IRO HQ, 4.04.49.
158. IRO: AJ/43/787/33/3, H.A. Curtis, UNRRA Representative East Africa and Rhodesia to Commissioner EARA, 28.04.47. After a short appointment in London in 1951, he worked from 1952 until 1973 for the Kenyan Ministry of Education. In 1974 he renounced his UK citizenship and took on the Kenyan (PRO: HO 334/1643/54517). Together with Elspeth Huxley he later edited two books of Kenyan colonial nostalgia (Huxley and Curtis, *Pioneers' Scrapbook*; Curtis, *Memories of Kenya*). The *Kenya Gazette* announced his dead in Nairobi in 2003.

159. Lush had been, among other things, governor of the Sudan's Northern Province, and during the war was head of the military administration in Abyssinia, Madagascar and Tripolitania. See his autobiography, Lush, *A Life of Service*.
160. Lush, *A Life of Service*, 253.
161. IRO: AJ/43/616/2/29, 'Summary of Deputy Executive Secretary's Tour in Turkey, Lebanon, Egypt, East Central and South Africa. May 30th – June 19th, 1948', by Arthur Rucker, p.4.
162. IRO: AJ/43/790, IRO to Kenya Government, 'Memorandum on the proposed Admission of Polish Displaced Persons to Kenya', [ca. 1948] n.d.
163. IRO: AJ/43/790/55/2, 'Refugees Remaining in Africa', Curtis to IRO HQ, p.5, 9.02.49.
164. Ibid.
165. Kennedy, *Islands of White*, 52.
166. IRO: AJ/43/790/55/2, 'Refugees Remaining in Africa', Curtis to IRO HQ, p.5, 9.02.49.
167. See also Chapter 3.
168. IRO: AJ/43/790/55/2, 'Refugees Remaining in Africa', Curtis to IRO HQ, p.5, 9.02.49.
169. Ibid.
170. IRO: AJ/43/652/45/2, Curtis to IRO HQ, 7.03.49
171. Ibid.
172. IRO: AJ/43/652/45/2, Rucker to Wilkinson, Foreign Office, London, 15.06.49.
173. E.g. IRO: AJ/43/788/45/2, Wilkinson, FO, London to Arthur Rucker, IRO HQ 11.04.49.
174. For disputes between Uganda's government and its small settler population, see also Chapter 5.
175. IRO: AJ/43/652/45/2, Lush, IRO Cairo to Huggins, Prime Minister Southern Rhodesia, 24.06.48.
176. Ibid.
177. IRO: AJ/43/652/45/2, Office of the Minister of Internal Affairs and Justice, Salisbury, Southern Rhodesia to M.S. Lush, IRO Cairo, 4.12.47.
178. Ibid.
179. See Mlambo, 'Some Are More White'.
180. IRO: AJ/43/652/45/2, E.B. Boothby, Foreign Office, London to Rucker, IRO, 30.11.49.
181. Ibid.
182. In regard to possible employment opportunities for the Poles: IRO: AJ/43/566, Lush to Rucker, 2.10.47. And using the same terminology to describe Seychellois and Indian labour in another context: TNA: K1/26546, p.15B, C.R. Lockhart, Nairobi to G.E.J. Gent, CO, London, 27.07.44.
183. IRO: AJ/43/652/45/2, Curtis, IRO Nairobi to IRO HQ, Geneva, 1.06.49.
184. IRO: AJ/43/652/45/2, Office of the Minister of Internal Affairs and Justice, Salisbury to M.S. Lush, IRO Cairo, 4.12.47.
185. The pay levels of the Poles at the Gatooma textile factory were closer to African than to British Rhodesian wages (Tavuyanago, Muguti and Hlongwana, 'Victims', 963).
186. IRO: AJ/43/790/55/2, 'Refugees Remaining in Africa', Curtis to IRO HQ, p.2, 9.02.49.
187. IRO: AJ/43/788/45/2, 'PWD Scheme – Terms of Employment', Deputy Chief Secretary, Nairobi, 30.07.48.

188. IRO: AJ/43/781, Monthly report for April 1949 from Curtis to IRO HQ, p.2, 4.05.49.
189. IRO: AJ/43/781, Monthly report for October 1949 from Curtis to IRO HQ, p.5, 31.10.49.
190. IRO: AJ/43/790/55/2, 'Refugees Remaining in Africa', Curtis to IRO HQ, p.5, 9.02.49. A sociological study of a European community in the late 1940s comes to a comparable conclusion. See Sofer and Ross, 'Some Characteristics of an East African European Population'.
191. At least, I found no archival evidence of any other projects this group worked on.
192. IRO: AJ/43/790/55/2, 'Refugees Remaining in Africa', Curtis to IRO HQ, p.4, 9.02.49.
193. Malkki, 'National Geographic'.
194. Ibid., 3.
195. Burbank and Cooper, *Empires in World History*, 8.
196. Holborn, *International Refugee Organization*, 86.
197. Woodbridge, *UNRRA*, vol. 1, 241–42.
198. Ibid., vol. 1, 242.
199. Ibid.
200. IRO: AJ/43/790/52/4, 'Personnel Regulations – Local Employees', Curtis, IRO Nairobi to C.J. Wood, Special Assistant to the Director General, IRO HQ, 18.02.49.
201. Holborn, *International Refugee Organization*, 1. While Holborn wrote as an independent scholar, her book on the IRO was written under the auspices of the IRO Liquidation Board (Copeland, 'Louise W. Holborn Archives', 503).
202. Cited in Holborn, *International Refugee Organization*, 1.
203. The four countries receiving most refugees for resettlement through the IRO were: the USA 328,851; Australia 182,159; Israel 132,109; Canada 123,479 (numbers taken from 'Annex 40', ibid., 460). Israel constitutes a special case, as the resettlement of Jewish DPs was mainly conducted by Jewish voluntary organizations (ibid., 415).
204. McKeown, 'Global Migration, 1846–1940', 156. For the specific role of Polish labour migrants, see Morawska, 'Labor Migrations of Poles'. For the role of whiteness and the social position of East and South European migrants in the United States, see Barrett and Roediger, 'Inbetween Peoples'.
205. While Britons were the preferred immigrants, other whites were increasingly accepted in the postwar period. See Limnios-Sekeris, 'Australia and the Intergovernmental Committee', 191–93.
206. Cohen, *In War's Wake*, 125.
207. For the Jewish refugees or DPs, the situation had changed considerably from the closed doors they had found fleeing from Nazi persecution to the foundation of Israel and the massive movement there (see e.g. Wyman, *Abandonment of the Jews*; Safran, 'Jewish Diaspora'). On the change from antisemitic exclusion in the 1920s and 1930s to the gradual incorporation into the white race in the United States after the Second World War, see Brodkin, *How Jews Became White Folks*.
208. Wilson, 'Gender, Race and the Ideal Labour Force', 99.
209. New Zealand, Argentina and Chile clearly preferred Balts in their selection of European DPs (Holborn, *International Refugee Organization*, 401–4.) For the preference of Baltic women in the UK, see Dwyer and Bressey, *New Geographies of Race and Racism*, 56–57; Webster, 'Britain and the Refugees', 46.
210. IRO: AJ/43/790/55/2, Lush to D.C. Stephen, IRO Beirut, 9.06.49.

211. The World Jewish Congress cited this example as one out of many instances of racial and religious discrimination in the selection of immigrants (PRO: FO 371/87395-0003, 'Report of Declaration by World Jewish Congress Calling for Elimination of Selective Immigration as Practised by Many Countries', 10.01.50).
212. Holborn, *International Refugee Organization*, 388–89. Turkey's commitment to accept Muslim refugees has to be understood in the light of the importance of religion in the nation-building project of Turkey. The defining factor for the Greco-Turkish 'population exchange' of 1923 had been whether a person was Christian (=Greek) or Muslim (=Turkish). See Marrus, *The Unwanted*, 102.
213. E.g. Lush wrote of 'selling' the refugees to the territories (IRO: AJ/43/790/55/2, Lush to Executive General PCIRO, 27.11.47).
214. IRO: AJ/43/566, Lush, PCIRO Cairo to Brigadier G. Fanshawe, Director of Labour, Middle East Land Forces, 1.10.47.
215. IRO: AJ/43/790/55/2, 'Refugees Remaining in Africa', Curtis to IRO HQ, p.4, 9.02.49.
216. Ibid.
217. My calculation from the numbers in ibid.
218. Barnett, 'Global Governance', 255.
219. The emerging Cold War was another important factor for the preferential treatment of refugees from Eastern Europe (Gatrell, *Making of the Modern Refugee*, 97).
220. The Ethiopians in Kenya were not subject to any of the League of Nations efforts to help refugees. See Wilkin, 'Refugees and British Administrative Policy', 529.
221. Ibid., 524. See also Shadle, 'Reluctant Humanitarians', 7–8.
222. Killingray and Plaut, *Fighting for Britain*, 58.
223. See Glasman, 'Seeing Like a Refugee Agency', 343.
224. Killingray and Plaut, *Fighting for Britain*, 58.
225. The other excluded group of about the same size was the German expellees from East Central Europe. In contrast to other groups, this exclusion was a political decision not to help the former enemies. Their plight was regarded as a German national responsibility. See Gatrell, *Making of the Modern Refugee*, 94; Cohen, *In War's Wake*, 6; and as a starting point to the vast literature on the German expulsion, see Schulze, 'Forced Migration of German Populations'.
226. Oberoi, 'South Asia'; Gatrell, 'Putting Refugees in Their Place', 6–7.
227. As in Africa, this care consisted mainly of paying for the existing administration. Numbers from 'Annex 22', Holborn, *International Refugee Organization*, 238.
228. Lush, *A Life of Service*.
229. Holborn, *International Refugee Organization*, 418.
230. Lush explained that they 'have to be physically moved for political and security reasons' (IRO: AJ/43/566, Lush, PCIRO Cairo to Arthur Rucker, PCIRO HQ, 18.12.47). See also Taylor, *Polish Orphans*, 56.
231. 'Annex 17', Holborn, *International Refugee Organization*, 200.
232. Oyen, 'Right of Return', 565. Interestingly enough, the subsequent Chinese governments did not want to get rid of the refugees, but rather saw them as an asset to improve China's economic and political position in the region.
233. Peterson, 'Uneven Development', 3. The remaining refugees were assisted by UNHCR when it took over from the IRO. In IRO statistics, 'Europeans' appear as a separate category next to 'Overseas Chinese' in the Shanghai column ('Annex 17', Holborn, *International Refugee Organization*, 200–201).
234. Holborn, *International Refugee Organization*, 424–25; Oyen, 'Right of Return', 561, 567.

235. Peterson, 'Uneven Development', 15. For the institutional perspective on the same story, see Holborn, *Refugees: A Problem of Our Time*, vol. 1, 660–97.
236. Peterson, 'Uneven Development', 15.
237. Loescher, 'International Refugee Regime', 359–62. Newly independent Tunisia asked the UNHCR in 1957 to assist it with refugees from Algeria; see Ruthström-Ruin, *Beyond Europe*.

Chapter 3

COMPARING COLONIALISMS IN AFRICA AND POLAND

―⚬⚬⚬―

When comparing Polish refugees with their African neighbours, there are, at first sight, some similarities in the political and social situation of the two groups. Both were marginalized in their home countries and ruled by people who understood themselves as different from them. Before coming to Africa, most of the Polish refugees had lived in an area that was to become part of the Soviet Union and had been treated with hostility by Soviet officials. Poles who found themselves under Nazi-German occupation were racially oppressed as well. And there was the longer history of the partition period when Poles were ruled by neighbouring empires.

Since the turn of the millennium there has been a growing tendency in the literature to understand different periods of German as well as Russian/Soviet rule in Poland as forms of colonial domination.[1] Taking these claims as a starting point, the difference between colonized Africans and colonized Poles should, perhaps, not be that huge. Assuming that both groups were in a comparable situation, one might likewise assume that they realized this in their encounter in and around the refugee camps. This feeling of commonality might then, in turn, have resulted in acts of solidarity between actors of the two groups. The aim of this chapter is to see how far this happened on the ground, and how the empirical observations relate to different understandings of the postcolonial status of East and Central Europe.

The first section consists of a critical review of approaches to the understanding of Poland as a colony of Germany or (Soviet) Russia, closing with a brief comparison of the most successful movements against colonial rule – namely, nationalist ones – in Africa and Poland. In the second section, we will trace concrete acts of solidarity or discrimination in the interaction of Polish refugees and Africans during their stay there. In the conclusion, I will link the findings from my case to the general discussion of postcolonial understandings of Poland.

Point of Departure

When the Afro-American scholar, activist and writer W.E.B Du Bois was studying in Berlin in 1893, he had a conversation with fellow student Stanislaus Ritter von Estreicher from Kraków. Du Bois was surprised to hear that Poles were racially oppressed by German-speakers and that it was not only the oppression of black people by white people in the United States and Africa that formed the 'race problem'.[2] When he went to Poland, he encountered yet another aspect of racism. A cabman in a small Galician town directed him to a Jewish hotel where he started to learn about 'the Jewish problem'.[3] In a text published in 1952, Du Bois reflected upon this and his two subsequent visits to Poland, and argued that his experiences with the anti-Polish and, even more important, antisemitic forms of discrimination helped him to 'emerge from a certain social provincialism' and to broaden his understanding of the 'race problem'.[4]

Du Bois' learning process may serve as an illustration of the kinds of encounter I am looking for in this chapter. He saw the similarities of discrimination and realized that it is not only the colour of the skin that defines racism but that it is, as he wrote, 'a matter of cultural patterns, perverted teaching and human hate and prejudice'.[5] Did the Polish refugees gain comparable insights? They came from a situation of oppression by Germans and Soviets, and had experienced, through deportation and life in labour camps, very direct forms of oppression that were strongly connected to their social and political classification. How did they regard their situation vis-à-vis colonial society? And did acts of solidarity emerge out of the encounter? Or, to borrow Frantz Fanon's words, did the 'wretched of the earth' unite?

German, Soviet and British Colonialisms

We will first consider the growing body of literature that depicts German and Soviet rule in Poland as a form of colonialism. The idea behind this exercise is to question the assumption that the history of Poland can be understood by transplanting insights gained from the study of European colonialisms in other parts of the world. I will start briefly with German rule in 'the East' before scrutinizing the Soviet/Russian example.⁶ While the Poles who eventually came to Africa had had few direct experiences with the Nazis, it is safe to assume that they followed the news about the Nazi occupation of Poland and the brutal subjugation of its people.

German Colonialism in the East

As early as 1936, the London-based, Trinidad-born, anti-colonial activist and writer George Padmore compared British colonial rule in Kenya with Nazi rule in Germany. According to him, white settlers in Kenya showed 'racial arrogance' and 'fascist mentality' like the Nazis.⁷ Padmore also hinted at the continuity linking the brutality of colonial rule in German East Africa to the Nazi brutality against Jews and the political opposition in Germany in the mid-1930s.⁸ This argumentation was taken further by Aimé Césaire, who in 1955 claimed that the main problem Europeans had with Hitler was that, unlike the colonial powers, he committed atrocities against white and not black people.⁹ With the rise of postcolonial theory and global history, this line of thought has recently been taken up again.¹⁰

If we look at the Nazi-German occupation of Poland, there were quite a few direct personal continuations from the former colonial empire in Africa to the newly conquered East European countries. Indeed, they used a rhetoric that was inspired by the earlier colonial project.¹¹ David Furber is quite clear on this: 'the Nazi occupation of Poland was a colonialist project'.¹² German rule in 'the East' was, like colonialism elsewhere, the rule of a minority that understood itself as different from and superior to the local majority. German officials described the East in colonial terms as an empty land that had to be opened up and cultivated by racially superior people. The main difference from European colonialism in Africa was the relative geographical and cultural proximity, the lack of liberalism, the missing sense of being involved in a 'civilizing mission' and thus the extreme brutality.¹³

Like 'natives' in African colonies, Poles and other Slavs were perceived as racially inferior and incapable of civilizing the land.¹⁴ In the same vein, Kopp argues that Poland should be understood in postcolonial terms: colonial discourse constructs the essentialized Other as not only inferior but unable to change without foreign intervention.¹⁵ The German colonial discourse on the East can also be traced back to the partition period. Prussian-occupied Poland was imagined, like the North American frontier, as an area where the civilizing forces (Germans) fought against the savages (Slavs) to bring order from chaos.¹⁶ In a related context, Andre Gingrich has coined the term 'Frontier Orientalism' for Austrian descriptions of the perceived threat by the nearby 'Oriental' Turks, in contrast to orientalist depictions of faraway lands.¹⁷ According to historical and political circumstances the Oriental threat in Austria could be replaced by a general Muslim, Jewish or Slavic (especially Russian or Serb) menace. But what remains important to note here is the contested and fluctuating border towards the Other that had to be kept up discursively, and is best described as a frontier.¹⁸ The space behind the frontier is generally imagined as filled by less civilized people and as devoid of culture. In Turner's influential writings on North American history, the frontier is described as 'the meeting point between savagery and civilization'.¹⁹ Accordingly this line is not perceived as static, but as advancing the superior civilization into the savage lands – an idea that guided Nazi-German expansion to the East.²⁰

Understanding the German discourse on Poland (or 'the East') as a colonial discourse seems convincing, but this does not necessarily mean that the colonized subjects in Poland understood themselves as comparable to colonized people elsewhere.

Soviet Colonialism?

The experience of the Polish refugees who eventually landed on East Africa's shores was mainly dominated by the Soviet conquest and the history of Poland's eastern borderlands. We must therefore take a closer look at the understandings of Soviet Russian rule in Poland as a form of colonialism. In contrast to the German example, this seems less clear and is more contested in the literature.

Shortly after the Bolshevik revolution, socialists abroad described the Soviet Union as a model for the transformation of a colonial empire (the Tsarist Empire) into an egalitarian multinational state (the Soviet Union).²¹ George Padmore, mentioned above, took up this line of thought in a book he wrote in 1942, explaining the successful Soviet resistance against the Nazi attack by referring to the support of this new system from its formerly colonized peoples. He suggested that the lack of support for the British Empire on the part of its subject peoples against the Japanese attack in Asia was due to Britain's colonial domination.²² But this praise for the Soviet Union as an attractive alternative to colonialism was short lived – the disclosure of Stalin's atrocities put an end to this view.²³

A more critical understanding of the Soviet Union as a colonial empire gained momentum after its formal end in the 1990s. Frederick Cooper, for example, regards the Soviet Union as a form of imperialism.²⁴ In the same direction, David Moore argues that the post-Soviet world can be understood as postcolonial.²⁵ But Moore also points to the difference between Soviet-Russian rule in its Asian parts and its European parts. In the latter he sees a form of 'reverse-cultural colonization' that differs from the common (European) form of colonialism in that it is not accompanied by Othering of the colonized; indeed, the Russians were perceived to be inferior with regard to their civilizational stage.[26] While Ewa Thompson strongly argues for a postcolonial understanding of the Soviet domination of Poland, she admits that the Russians were not perceived as superior by the Poles.[27] She argues that this lack of respect for the colonial power distinguishes Soviet colonialism from British and French colonialisms.[28] Andrew Janos goes even further in his description of the peculiar nature of Soviet imperialism. He states that people from East Central Europe saw the Russians as 'charming primitives at best' and perceived the empire as 'a political entity in which the culturally inferior were ruling peoples of greater sophistication and civility'.[29] The efforts to provide legitimacy through the promotion of Russian high culture,[30] and the self-description as being further on the progressive path to communism, did not really convince anyone.[31] The discourse of civilizational superiority/inferiority, processes of Othering and – closely connected to them – racism as central to postcolonial understandings of colonial discourse do not lend much credibility to the interpretation of Poland as a Soviet colony.

From a postcolonial angle, different forms of colonialism have in common the fact that they are 'relations of domination that are enforced with physical, military, epistemological and ideological force, and were legitimized, for example, through discourses of "race" and "culture"'.[32] While Soviet domination in Poland was definitely one of military and physical force, it was not legitimized through discourses of race or culture. The class-based rhetoric paradoxically stressed instead the general equality of the members of the working class.

But what is even more important here is the fact that if the Poles were not regarded or driven to see themselves as inferior in the hegemonic discourse, then they had less reason to see themselves in the same category as the colonized Africans. If their culture was not devalued but 'just' oppressed, their national identity and self-perception as more European and thus more civilized than the barbaric, Asian Russians would not have been touched. Many of the Polish victims of the 1940 deportations perceived themselves as superior in terms of civilization to the people they encountered in the Soviet Union.[33] Although these deportees were completely powerless, their attitude towards Central Asians even resembled 'that of a colonial power towards its subject people'.[34] There is no need here to undertake a comparative analysis of the personal suffering of colonized Africans, Polish deportees or anyone else. What is at issue is what a hegemonic discourse does to one's self-understanding and thus one's relationship with, and behaviour towards, other people.

Colonial Kresy?

Arguing against the simple equation 'Poland = colony', Claudia Snochowska-Gonzales writes that postcolonial understandings of Poland are mainly formed in regard to Russian/Soviet domination, and have the political aim of painting the Polish nation as the innocent victim of aggression.[35] She points to some aspects of Poland's history, and present, that contradict this understanding of Poland as the colonized victim. The myth of the eastern borderlands ('*kresy wschodnie*') is the most important for my case, as most of the refugees came from this region. This myth is based on the assumption that Poland is the last bulwark of European civilization against the 'Asian' wilderness and its savage people.[36] As the 'real Pole' is understood as the bearer of civilization, Polonization of the eastern borderlands becomes colonization.[37] This perception re-echoes in the post-1990 boom of Polish literature on the 'kresy' and its centrality in Polish national discourse. Bogusław Bakuła criticizes this literature and its revision after 1990 from a postcolonial perspective, and sees strong currents of Othering in the descriptions of the non-Polish inhabitants of the 'kresy', and the ignorance of their perspectives.[38]

The perception of the Polish 'kresy' inhabitants as colonizers is also found in the memoirs of refugees who stayed in Africa. In narrating the story of a friend who had been deported from Równe district (now Rivne, Ukraine), Stefania Buczak-Zarzycka calls the region a 'colonial area'.[39] Her story starts in November 1939, when a Soviet plane dropped leaflets urging the Ukrainians: 'Arm yourselves with shovels and axes and destroy the Polish gentry and townsfolk'. This quote illustrates the entanglement of class and ethnicity in the region.[40] Most Polish settlers in the area were former soldiers of Piłsudski's Legion, and Buczak-Zarzycka describes them as 'colonialists'.[41] Mainly living separately from the rest of the population, these settlers shared some commonalities with colonial settlers. Her choice of terms must not be understood as an analytical reflection but tells us much about the everyday usage and self-perception of 'kresy' Poles. Mathew Kelly has described the self-understanding of Poles from the area in a way that resembles colonialist self-descriptions: 'Many [Polish kresy] settlers sincerely believed Polonization meant not cultural imperialism but progress, shining the light of a sophisticated European civilization on a primitive and impoverished people of indeterminate identity'.[42] This is an apt description of the civilizing mission – one of the central features of modern European colonialism.[43]

Originating from the 'kresy' mattered for the self-identification of Polish refugees in Africa. After the war, some refugees in the African camps formed associations that lobbied for a return of the eastern borderlands to the Polish state. They lamented the loss of the territories east of the Curzon Line, and sent letters to the United Nations condemning this border shift and the Soviet presence in Poland.[44]

With regard to perception and discourse, the picture that emerges is not one of a Polish colony with an imperial centre on each side, but rather a cascade of frontier regions from the west to the east. In the hegemonic discourse concerning civilizational stages (in the German-Polish case coupled with racial aspects) Germans were seen as superior to Poles, who in turn saw themselves as superior to Ukrainians and Russians. This cascade goes on if one looks at the Russian dominance in the east and south of the Soviet Union. Larry Wolff's study of the orientalist description of Eastern Europe in Enlightenment discourse points to the long history of this imagined geography. West European Enlightenment thinkers constructed Eastern Europe as simultaneously 'Europe, but not Europe'.[45] This 'demi-Orientalization'[46] put Eastern Europe not on the same level as the Orient, but somewhere 'between Europe and Asia, between civilization and barbarism'.[47]

Milica Bakić-Hayden argues in a related way with a focus on the Balkans. She has coined the term 'nesting orientalisms' to describe the discursive hierarchization of the Other in former Yugoslavia: 'In this pattern, Asia is more "East" or "other" than eastern Europe; within eastern Europe itself this gradation is reproduced with the Balkans perceived as most "eastern"; within the Balkans there are similarly constructed hierarchies'.[48] She shows that the ambiguous position of the Balkans on the margins of 'proper' Europe leads political actors to engage in discursive strategies that portray the eastern or southern neighbour as more oriental, thereby underlining claims of belonging to the West. In this argument, religion becomes an important factor, as Catholic groups distinguish themselves from the presumably less civilized Orthodox, who in turn look down upon the Muslim groups.[49] Thus religion is understood to be an indicator for the unchanging, essentialized group identities.

Tomasz Zarycki argues in an analogous manner for the larger region that in the zone between the Elbe River and Vladivostok the potential 'Eastness' leads actors to 'orientalize their eastern neighbours' in order to underline their own belonging to the West.[50] To be sure, this relation of superiority/inferiority is to be understood on a discursive level and does not imply that any culture, religion, society or language is better than another. It is, rather, a powerful legitimizing discourse of domination that is essential to modern colonialism. Attempts to change this discourse and establish an image of a progressive and superior Soviet Russia did not really succeed in Poland.

Polish Colonial Attempts

What further contradicts the description of Poland as a colony are the attempts that were made to turn Poland itself into a European colonial power in the interwar period, which was supported by a popular mass movement. This movement, organized as the Maritime and Colonial League, had its peak in popularity immediately before the outbreak of the Second World War.[51] Millions of Poles took part in the 'Colonial Days' held in April 1938 throughout the country.[52] These ambitions were supported by the general self-perception of Poland as a European power, for which colonies would provide raw materials and land for settlement. In the face of threats from Germany and the Soviet Union, these claims also had the psychological function of keeping morale high.[53] Mass mobilizations were intended to give more weight to the demands of Polish foreign policy spokesmen for a share of other colonial empires. One argument in the international arena was that the Polish territory and people had been part of the German Empire, and as such they should be entitled to a share of former German colonies, just as other European powers had received under a League of Nations mandate. All these attempts were unsuccessful, as the British foreign secretary simply refused to talk about it during the visit of his Polish counterpart; but it tells us something about the self-perception of the Polish nation vis-à-vis the colonized parts of the world. Poland wanted to be on an equal footing with the European colonial powers, and although it was not accepted as such, its position was in no sense comparable to that of a colonized country in Africa.

Related to this is the importance of racism for colonial rule in Africa. While the Nazis tried hard to classify and distinguish between different racially defined groups, this was much easier in parts of the world where the differences between ruler and ruled were more visible. The importance of visibility for control becomes obvious in the Nazi law that forced Jews to wear a yellow star. Christopher Fyfe has underlined the role of white rule as a system of control through his description of white skin as a 'uniform'.[54] Just as the uniform of the soldier or policeman signified that person's authority, so the white person in Africa was protected by his or her white skin. As Anthony Kirk-Green has written about the British colonial service in Africa, the 'bullet-proof waistcoat' of the white skin did not stop the bullet, but it deterred the other party from firing.[55] To be clearly recognizable, the difference had of course to be created and carefully maintained by segregation, the refusal to accept interracial relationships or whites who 'went native';[56] but the visibility of skin colour in itself lent a good deal of support to this system of rule.

Polish and African Nationalisms Compared

The most successful reaction against European colonial rule in Africa was the mobilization of the colonized in a nationalist movement that eventually took over the colonial state and transformed it into a national one. The visionary and practical power of the Pan-African movement should not be underestimated, but eventually it was the nationalists who dominated the independent African states to a great extent. In the Organization of African Unity, formed in 1963, there was consequently more emphasis on closer cooperation of nation-states than on the building of political entities that transcended the national frame.[57] Pan-Slavism in turn proved less attractive to Poles, as the movement was not useful in the fight against Russian domination. In the postwar era, African nationalist independence movements gained momentum, and among the Polish refugees too there was strong support for the nationalist cause. The former sought to create new nation-states on the territories of existing colonies; the latter wanted to re-establish a Polish nation-state that would be independent from both German and Soviet-Russian influence.

To what extent did these nationalist movements evince similarities that could have served as common ground for solidarity? To bring these two strands of nationalism[58] into one analytical frame, I will draw on a suggestion by Rogers Brubaker.[59] He criticizes the 'Manichean distinction' between 'civic' and 'ethnic' forms of nationalism (in short, there is no pure form of either one and the terms confuse normative and analytic aspects), and suggests a 'modest alternative':[60] the starting point in distinguishing between different forms of nationalism should be whether they are 'state-framed' or 'counter-state'. To get to grips with the disparate forms of nationalism, it makes a difference whether the nationalism in question is part of a nation-state or of a movement that opposes the existing political authority, be it national or imperial in character. Anti-colonial nationalist movements in Africa as well as Polish nationalism during the Second World War were both part of the 'counter-state' variety, as they were in opposition to the existing political system. Their main aim was to end rule from outside and to establish a sovereign and independent nation-state.

If one understands the German Reich and the Soviet Union as imperial forms, these nationalisms had the further commonality of being directed against empires. The main aim of both movements was the replacement of these imperial forms by sovereign nation-states. Furthermore, the boundaries of these territories were determined mainly by outside political powers. While this is quite clearly the case for African borders, which had mainly been negotiated in the capitals of the imperial states, it is equally true for Poland. In both cases the successful nationalists did not challenge these boundaries once in office.⁶¹ True, the Polish refugees from the eastern borderlands were not very content with the shifted Polish frontiers, as their places of origin ceased to be part of Poland after the Yalta Conference of 1945.⁶² Nevertheless, the postwar borders of Poland as well as of nearly all African nations were determined by external political powers, without consulting the national elites.⁶³

The main difference between Polish and African nationalists during and after the Second World War was the prior existence of Poland as a nation-state. While African nationalists connected their nations to earlier episodes in history as well, there were in most cases no political entities with borders similar to those of the post-independence nations. In early independent Tanganyika, the Maji Maji War against German colonial rule was utilized to unite the national population, despite the fact that it had affected only a part of the then colony.⁶⁴ Other post-independence nations were named after earlier, pre-colonial political entities from roughly the same region (e.g. Uganda, Zimbabwe). But these earlier political entities were not equivalent to the postcolonial nation-state in regard to territory, political system or population. Pre-colonial states were subdivided or merged in the territories of colonial states, and the post-independence consensus kept these territories unchanged.⁶⁵

The Polish refugees, for their part, had lived until their deportation in a nation-state – the Second Polish Republic (1918–1939). Although Poland's territorial borders had shifted repeatedly, their nationalism had not become 'counter-state' until shortly before they were deported. Polish 'counter-state' nationalism, however, had a longer history. Poland was divided from 1795 to 1918, and it was non-existent as a (nation-)state during this period. A reason for the resilience of Polish nationalism was, apart from the nation's long history (dating back to the tenth century), the delineation of an 'imagined community' by a common language and religion.⁶⁶ Although Poland was quite diverse in terms of language and religion until the Second World War, it was still relatively clear who was understood as belonging to the Polish nation proper (Polish-speaking Catholics) and who was not (Jews, Germans, Ukrainians and Belarusians).⁶⁷ Mass killings and population transfers during and after the war changed this structure considerably, and only traces of this multi-ethnicity were to be found in postwar Poland.⁶⁸ The war brought a linguistic and religious homogenization that had never before been seen in Poland, and one that is only rarely seen in today's independent African nations.⁶⁹

I touched upon one other important difference earlier when discussing Polish colonial attempts in the interwar period. This difference is related to global inequalities and strongly connected to the history of European colonialism. At the time when Poland's nationalism was not directed against a state but 'state-framed', its protagonists were striving to become a European power as well. And being a large European nation included, in their view, the entitlement to having colonies in Africa. By contrast, when African nationalisms became state-framed the option of acquiring colonial possessions overseas did not exist. Standing on the lowest rung in regard to globally organized racism, the anti-colonialists did not aim at becoming colonial rulers themselves.[70] Instead, they made the abolition of racial discrimination a global issue, and 'made the world over into a world of nation-states'.[71]

Compassion for the 'Wretched of the Earth'?

The Polish refugees who came to Africa were in no powerful position at all after going through the Soviet deportations, forced labour and the struggle for survival. But at the moment they entered into the colonial situation they wore the same 'uniform' of white skin as the British colonial officials or European settlers. Although their 'uniform' looked a lot more ragged in the beginning, it was still the uniform of privilege, and this uniform could not be taken off.[72] At the same time they could not take off their experiences of oppression, suffering, and being treated as second-class human beings. In the following section we will take a closer look at the way in which Polish refugees reacted to the colonial situation into which they had been incorporated. Did they broaden their 'provincialism', like Du Bois upon seeing the remnants of the Warsaw ghetto? Or did they take advantage of the possibility to be elevated from oppressed to privileged?

Solidary Poles

There are hints of a more egalitarian relationship between Poles and Africans in the reports of sexual relations and marriages between Polish women and Asian or African men. Although the main reason for the marriages may have been to gain residence status and financial support in a time of uncertainty, they nevertheless show an openness to crossing the societal boundaries of race. In colonial thinking, the transgression of these boundaries was regarded as especially problematic when it was white women who cohabited with black men. Most colonial officials regarded such relations with suspicion, and tried to prevent them.[73]

In the recollections of former refugees there are a few traces of anti-colonial solidarity. One example of clearly compassionate acts is found in the memoirs of Teresa Pławski, who had lived in Tengeru. She writes that African petty traders frequently sold fruits and vegetables in the camp without permission.

From time to time the camp police cracked down on them, beating and arresting them. To escape the police, the fugitives sometimes hid under the beds in the refugees' houses, as the Poles 'sympathized with the victims and always tried to help them'.[74]

Filomena Michałowska-Bykowska, who stayed in Ifunda, goes even further when describing the relationship with African camp-workers in her recollections: 'Initially they looked at us as if we occupied an inferior status position, but after a little while we got to know each other and our daily contacts became rather cordial'.[75] Such a statement was rather unthinkable in colonial discourse. The whole idea of whites being seen as inferior contradicted the colonial hierarchical logic. The colonial master may offer a cordial relationship to his servants, but this is a different form of cordiality, as he remains in the superior position. She goes on to explain the longing for relations of equality:

> Actually, the obligatory regimen of the settlement clearly forbade a display of friendship toward the natives, but having gone through the Siberian Gehenna we did not always understand the reason for this prohibition, and explained our behaviour by our felt need to treat everyone equally, no matter what the colour of their skin.[76]

She describes the contradictions between the colonial system (which in her case trickled down into the 'regimen of the settlement') and her humanitarian impulse after the experience of oppression in the Soviet Union. The bare fight for survival in Siberia seems to have been more decisive than the general oppression in occupied Poland.[77] But her story does not stop here. She explains that this general worldview manifested itself in donating clothes and blankets to poor African women and buying foodstuffs from Africans, although this was forbidden. She then goes on to describe an incident in which African robbers broke into a house at night, and the fear that this caused to her family and the other camp inhabitants. In the sequence of her narrative this could be understood as a lesson that one should not be too friendly to alien people. What is omitted here, however, is the relative wealth that the refugees enjoyed, without which they would have had no possibility of donating things. This relative wealth, coupled with the assumed wealth of whites generally, must have been a factor behind the night-time robbery.

Another form of interaction on equal footing took place between the outcasts and youngsters who came together for cock-fighting,[78] drinking locally brewed alcohol, and petty crime. The Catholic priest Lucjan Krolikowski described this in relation to problems with adolescents in the camps who were 'fraternizing recklessly … with native youngsters'. After learning some 'native swear words as a joke', their contacts became more serious and they engaged in unspecified deals in the marketplace.[79] In this regard, the adolescent refugees in Africa behaved like the adolescent DPs who stayed in German camps after the war, of whom Louise Holborn states that they 'tended to seek their recreation among the less desirable elements of the German community'.[80] While in both cases the more respectable parts of the refugee community did not engage much with the majority, the youths and outcasts seem to have been more open in this regard.

Illicit trading was, however, not limited to a few outcasts. In December 1944 in Tanganyika, a group of Polish refugees in a camp lorry on their way from Iringa town back to Ifunda settlement was stopped by police. In the lorry the police found large quantities of illegally purchased flour and sugar.[81] Owing to wartime shortages, the prices and quantities of these and other goods were strictly controlled.[82] The flour and sugar of the Polish refugees was confiscated and they were to be brought to court.[83] To get milder treatment they were asked to reveal the names of their (assumedly Indian) suppliers, but they refused to do so.[84] The director of refugees complained that this was due to the fact that the Indians 'posed as the real friends of the Poles', and had told them that it was only the British government that prevented them from getting their fair share of goods.[85] The cover-up of the Indian traders can be explained in pragmatic terms: the Poles wanted the goods, and denouncing their suppliers would hinder their further supply. Yet it also shows a considerable degree of distance from the colonial state. This reliance of the Poles on their own means, and their distrust of officials, is easily comprehensible, given that they had gone through situations in which officials had threatened their lives. Illicit trading had in many instances helped the deportees to survive. The feeling of belonging to a different nationality and their non-permanent status as refugees could be additional reasons behind this attitude. It was simply not *their* state.

A point that contradicts the equation of colonial rule and Soviet domination is that there were allegedly pro-Soviet communists among the refugees, who supported anti-colonial leanings within the African population. One example for these supposedly 'Soviet agents' was Helena Luczyc (born 1914), who lived until 1950 in Tengeru. According to British files, she had been a communist 'from 1923 [sic] to 1939', but she denied communist leanings in 1950.[86] She was described by the authorities as a 'notorious and dangerous character', and was refused immigration to the UK by the British Home Office. It was noted: 'She claims to have wide influence over the Masai and Meru tribes and to be preparing to lead them on a white massacre'.[87] This was coupled with accusations that she illegally sold home-brewed liquor and spread communist propaganda amongst the Africans in the region. This activity caused 'great perturbation' among colonial officials and African chiefs alike, who feared that Luczyc might convert their subjects to communism. The report closed with the assessment that she would be a security risk everywhere, but 'especially among the native population of East Africa'. It is not exactly clear what her activities and background were, but it seems that she had tried to stir up opposition against colonial rule. According to the British report, the other Polish refugees regarded her as Russian, as she came from the easternmost part of interwar Poland. By October 1950 she was reportedly married to an unspecified non-refugee resident, and objections against her residence in Tanganyika had been dropped.[88]

Another suspected communist among the Polish refugees was Bernard Masiuk. Apparently he was a Russian called Boris Afanasev, who had only posed as a Pole in order to get to East Africa.[89] Like Luczyc he was refused from immigration to the UK for 'security reasons'. In 1952, during an interview with the Tanganyika police in Tengeru, he 'constantly flourished a signet ring embossed with the hammer and sickle'.[90] Masiuk was described by the British officials as 'well behaved' and a 'good worker', who nevertheless repeatedly got into trouble with the Poles.[91] His Russian origin as well as his communist leanings seem to have been the reasons why he 'loathe[d] the Poles and refuse[d] to have anything to do with them'.[92] Even when about to be deported to Russia, he clearly spoke out in favour of the anti-colonial movement. He claimed that he 'wouldn't be very long away, as in a couple of years this country would belong to his brothers and that he would be back to help them win their fight'.[93]

Although the pro-communists were a tiny minority among the thousands of refugees, their anti-colonial stance clearly contradicts the equation of Soviet and British colonialism.[94] On a geopolitical level, the Soviet support for the independence movements can be explained as a strategy to weaken British rule. In the postwar period, officials in London were increasingly concerned about protests in the colonies, and especially from 1948 onwards they suspected a communist conspiracy behind virtually all large anti-colonial protests.[95] Yet the appeal of communism for anti-colonial activists could also be understood on ideological grounds. While European colonialists had the presumed superiority of whites at the core of their worldview, communism sided with the oppressed in capitalism and colonialism alike.

In the Colonizers' Camp

When the Poles arrived on the shores of East Africa, they carried, like every human being, cultural baggage with them. Like other Europeans, the Poles brought with them the images of Africa that were prevalent in contemporary Europe. This started with the fear of cannibals and savage people, remembered in many recollections, and which served to legitimize colonial rule.[96] In the memory narratives, this is usually followed by the sense of relief felt on their arrival upon realizing that Africans were in fact friendly and not as dangerous as expected.[97] Already in the Iranian transit camps, rumours and possibilities about future relocation were vividly discussed. Going to Africa seems to have been the least preferred option among the Poles. Fears of an unhealthy climate, wild animals and 'half-wild people' were widespread.[98] When the first group of five hundred Poles was ordered to get ready for the journey to Africa, their reluctance was so marked that the British military had to surround the camp in Tehran. Nevertheless, three hundred managed to escape, but were later persuaded through talks and lectures about Africa.[99]

Ideas about Africa came from a variety of sources. Little Stefania remembered the stories her grandmother had told her about a mythical land beyond the 'Seven Great Seas', where naked black people 'slept under the naked heaven'.[100] She further notes that she had read Henryk Sienkiewicz's novel *In Desert and Wilderness* ('W pustyni i w puszczy'), and therefore had a rather romantic notion of what Africa would be like.[101] This book was immensely popular, and Stefania was not the only refugee who had read it.[102] The book was available in the Polish shipping bookstore in Nairobi, and Sienkiewicz was reportedly one of the most popular authors in the Digglefold school library.[103] The literary scholar Anna Klobucka calls the novel 'the primary source of a Polish reader's awareness of Africa and its people'.[104]

In Desert and Wilderness is an adventure novel that was published in 1911 and set in the Sudan during the Mahdi rebellion (1881–85). The novel targeted young readers and featured as main characters a 14-year-old Polish boy (Staś) and a slightly younger English girl (Nel), who get kidnapped by Sudanese warriors.[105] The author Henryk Sienkiewicz was Poland's most influential nationalist writer and a Nobel Prize winner. He himself had travelled along the East African coast in 1890–91.[106] The whole story is quite Eurocentric and racist: Staś is portrayed as the superior and natural leader of the mainly speechless Africans, whom he saves from the Arab slavers. He stands clearly on the side of British colonialism against the Islamic rebels.[107] Klobucka states that 'Poles reading *In Desert and Wilderness* … sided … with a European explorer's and colonizer's viewpoint on Africa, rather than with the plight of its subjugated peoples'.[108] The close association of the Polish boy Staś with the English girl Nel makes this positioning quite obvious.

One scene of the novel is worth mentioning here: Staś fantasizes about how it would be if he were to come back to Africa, conquer some land there, 'civilize the natives, establish in that locality a new Poland or even start at the head of a drilled black host for the old Poland and defeat its subjugators'.[109] Although this is dismissed as a childish fantasy in the novel, it nevertheless is clearly the colonialist idea of taking and civilizing the land and its people, who are passively waiting to be ruled. The idea of forming a colonial army to fight for a European nation was interestingly enough later put into practice in both world wars.[110] An attempt to establish a surrogate Poland on African soil had already been made during the partition period. In 1882 Stefan Szolc-Rogoziński had travelled to Cameroon on a scientific expedition that had the clandestine political motive of finding a site for a Polish colony.[111] It must be remembered that *In Desert and Wilderness* was set in a time when there was no independent Polish nation-state. For the young Polish refugees there was not much fantasy needed to see parallels between the novel's main character and themselves.

As soon as the Polish refugees arrived in Africa, they felt the privileges of whiteness. During their deportation they had been locked up in cattle wagons, and after their release they had squeezed into any possible means of transportation. In stark contrast, in Africa they could travel in passenger carriages, often even in the first class.[112]

The Polish newspapers that were published in Nairobi are a good indicator of the self-positioning of the refugee elites.[113] While the colonized were described in rather paternalistic ways, commonalities with the British were emphasized. The marking of 11 November is a good illustration, being at the same time National Independence Day for the Poles and Remembrance Day for the Britons. Poles actively participated in Remembrance Day, underlining the 'Polish–British friendship'.[114] Further commonalities were emphasized through Polish handicraft exhibitions, music and theatre performances, which were used to showcase Polish abilities to the European community in the colonies.[115] Explanations of the Kraków 'lajkonik' celebrations in a Southern Rhodesian newspaper evoked the role of Poland as a bulwark of Europe. The celebrations thematized the invading Tartars and the Polish resistance to them.[116] The refugee elites transported an image of Poland as a West European nation fighting for the same camp as the British. This role, quite tangible in the current war, was presented in a longer historical context as well, where Poland fought for the Christian civilization of Europe against the barbarian threat from the East.

One interesting case from the British sources is the story of the K. family. Józef K. and his family were among the very last refugees who stayed in Tengeru. He was allegedly engaged in illicit distilling and selling of alcohol to Africans, and had some other convictions, one of which led to six months' imprisonment with hard labour for 'unlawful wounding'. He was therefore categorized as a criminal in the British files and thus not allowed to proceed to Britain.[117] K. must have been quite successful in his business, as he was in possession of a motorcycle[118] and stayed in the upscale Rex Hotel when visiting Dar es Salaam.[119] However, he neither spoke nor understood English.[120] Apparently he was better integrated into the non-British society networks. His illicit business contacts with Africans did not mean that he was anti-racist. When the nearby Greek school – to which the children of the last few

Polish refugees went after the Polish school had closed down – was closed as well, his son was sent to St. Joseph's Catholic School in Dar es Salaam. As soon as Mrs K. found out that this school was 'entirely African', she sent her husband there to get their son back.[121] Although they had desired to send their children to a Catholic school in Dar es Salaam or Thika, they seem to have expected these schools to have mainly European students.[122]

Responding to falling real wages, the 'Uganda Disturbances' were a series of strikes and riots throughout Uganda.[123] In January 1945, a precursor of the anti-colonial struggle manifested itself at the gates of Koja refugee camp. Strikers blocked the entrance and prevented a milk lorry from entering. Camp police started quarrelling with them until Kenyan troops from Kampala arrived and put down the riot by force, killing four protesters and injuring eleven.[124] The Polish residents of the camp did not actively engage in these events. The camp was seen as an institution of the colonial state and as such it was blockaded by the strikers. In this situation, although they were not seen as the target of protest, the Poles nevertheless belonged quite literally to the colonizers' camp.

Some Poles even tried to become colonizers in their own right. Reflecting earlier colonial attempts, Polish politicians in their London exile discussed the establishment of a Polish dominion in Africa.[125] They envisaged a territory where Polish refugees from Africa and DPs from Central Europe could concentrate. This Polish dominion was intended to be in one of the former German or Italian colonies in Africa.[126] While their ultimate goal was to return to a Poland free from Soviet influence, in the meantime they wanted to keep the Polish exile community together. General Władysław Anders, Commander of the Polish Second Corps, asked Winston Churchill as early as February 1945 to assure his soldiers, in the event of demobilization, of employment in Britain or alternatively a 'territory for colonization'.[127] But Polish military leaders and politicians in London were not the only ones to have such plans. In 1946 Major Francis John Bagshawe, a sympathetic Southern Rhodesian refugee official, proposed to settle some four hundred Polish families in a part of the colony.[128] He argued that there was plenty of room available in Rhodesia, but admitted that their material standards had to be lower than the usual 'standard of European living'. He proposed that the Poles should not be allowed to employ any 'native labour' due to the shortage of it. As the Poles were mainly from the 'peasant class', they would make good farmers themselves.

His proposal received an enthusiastic reply from the representatives of the Poles in Nairobi. They argued that his plan should be followed and extended to other colonies as well. The colonial governments, however, quickly dismissed these plans, and Bagshawe was removed from his post.[129] Three years later Sir Marston Logan of the Colonial Office reacted similarly to suggestions

Figure 3.1. Polish and African staff of the camp bakery in Koja, Uganda, 1944. From Archiwum Fotografii Ośrodka KARTA, Signature: OK_005183, online.

of mass settlement of Polish refugees from the IRO. Reportedly, he 'recoiled in horror on any suggestion that a large colony of Poles would remain indefinitely in some African territory'. He went on to explain that his office would 'put up a stiff fight' against any such plans if the local governments opposed them.[130] This clear rejection recalls the Polish attempts ten years earlier, when, in 1939, the Polish foreign minister's request to talk with his British counterpart about Poland's colonial claims had been similarly rejected.[131] In contrast to the earlier attempts, however, the postwar plans came from an even weaker political position and at a time when colonial rulers were struggling to gain renewed legitimacy. Calls for white settlement in Africa were untimely for Britain's postwar government. Although the repeated plans for establishing a Polish colony failed, they nevertheless reflect a general assumption that Poland was entitled to colonies.

The Limits of a Parallel: East Is *Not* South

In regard to my initial quest, we have seen that there were no big outpourings of solidarity from the Polish refugees towards their colonized African neighbours. The behaviour of the Poles seems to have been generally less discriminating towards Africans, but their basic assumption was that they were Europeans and, as such, supposedly superior. A photograph of the bakery staff in Koja, with its clear distinction between the Polish and African workers may serve to illustrate this hierarchization. With the exception of a few isolated, ideologically informed acts of Soviet-aligned communists, there was generally rather a humanitarian motivation. The reason for this humanitarian stance was to be found in the life-threatening experiences of deportation to and existence in the Siberian 'Gehenna'.

Concerning the general understanding of Poland *as* a colony, let me briefly turn to a person whose life and writings show some parallels to W.E.B. Du Bois, who served as the point of departure for this chapter. In one of the early texts arguing for the understanding of Poland as a Soviet/Russian colony, Clare Cavanagh portrayed Joseph Conrad, among other Polish writers, very much in the same way as I have portrayed Du Bois here. Conrad came with his experience of oppression (in Poland under Russian rule) to a situation in another part of the world (the Congo under Belgian rule), where he saw parallels, and spoke out against colonial domination. The anti-colonial stance of Conrad's *Heart of Darkness* has been widely acknowledged, and Cavanagh directly links this attitude to his experience of imperial domination by Poland's partition powers.[132] What she omits in her essay is the staunch critique by an African writer of the very same book. In an influential lecture in 1975, Chinua Achebe analysed the book and heavily criticized its racist depiction of Africans.[133] While Conrad is exposing the atrocities of Belgian rule in the Congo, he nevertheless portrays Africans as 'dehumanized' masses. As Achebe showed, no African individuals with voice or agency appear in the story.[134] We are left with the impression of an author who was both anti-imperial *and* racist.

Another Polish author who had travelled to colonial Africa was the above-mentioned Henryk Sienkiewicz. His self-positioning in the travelogue *Letters from Africa* is clearly pro-colonial and racist. Even in German East Africa, a colony that was ruled by the same power as the western part of Poland, he did not side with the colonized Africans – quite the contrary. He felt at ease in German company and described their administration in by and large positive terms.[135] Although he was a fierce critic of German rule in Poland, he did not transfer this critical stance to the African context. Sienkiewicz focused instead on the solidarity among the Europeans in Africa, transcending inner-European enmities.[136] And even when, in another context, he explicitly compared Poland's fate with that of an oppressed group of Africans, it was a white group – the Afrikaners in the South African War.[137]

For a general understanding of Polish history from a (post-)colonial perspective, the importance of racism and discourses of civilizational superiority must be recognized. To equate Poland with a colony would be to ignore the global dimension of colonialism and the central role of racism for European colonial rule in non-European parts of the world. East and Central Europe were signified by the discursive colonization of the neighbour further east, whereas in relation to the Global South, Central Europeans perceived themselves as part of the West. Asians and Africans were definitely regarded as more 'eastern' (that is, less civilized) than even the easternmost Europeans. In contrast to David Chioni Moore, who claimed that 'East is South',[138] I would say: East is *not* South.

The situation of Polish exiles was quite different from that of the African colonized, since the national elites understood themselves as part of the club of European powers. Poles were accepted Europeans, but the status of their nation-state had been questioned since the partition period. The West Europeanness of the Poles was questioned by many Europeans further to the west. The Polish interwar republic tried to be accepted as one of the great European powers but was relegated to the group of minor European states, despite its population size. Its repeated futile attempts to obtain colonies are the best illustration of this point. That the commonalities of oppression by a 'foreign' power did not translate into acts of solidarity on the part of the Poles is no surprise. When there was a Polish nation-state, its government wanted colonies as well. The struggle of Polish nationalists was a struggle to be accepted as a great European nation, as an accepted part of the West. And for some of them this meant an entitlement to colonial territory overseas. This is a perspective that anti-colonial nationalists in Africa never had.

Having discussed the national identification of the refugees in this chapter, I will focus on another socially relevant categorization in the next: the role of white women in colonial societies. I will thus take a closer look at the significance of the gendered composition of the group. To be clear, these two aspects, as well as their refugee status discussed in the previous chapter, are interrelated. Only for the sake of the structure and the connection to different strands of literature have I made this distinction.

Notes

This chapter deeply profited from comments made at the Academia Europaea Seminar 'Central Europe and Colonialism: Migrations, Knowledges, Perspectives, Commodities', held in Wrocław in September 2016.

1. For early contributions focusing mainly on Soviet/Russian domination, see Thompson, *Imperial Knowledge*; Moore, 'Is the Post- in Postcolonial the Post- in Post-Soviet?'; Cavanagh, 'Postcolonial Poland'.
2. The original text was published in 1952 under the title 'The Negro and the Warsaw Ghetto' in the magazine *Jewish Life*, reprinted in Du Bois, *Social Theory*, 45–46. For more discussion of the text and its relation to Holocaust studies, see Rothberg, 'W.E.B. Du Bois'.
3. Du Bois, *Social Theory*, 45.

4. Ibid., 46.
5. Ibid.
6. For the related discussion on the third partition power, the Austro-Hungarian Empire, see Feichtinger, Prutsch and Csáky, *Habsburg Postcolonial*.
7. Padmore, *How Britain Rules Africa*, 129–30.
8. Ibid., 58–60. Padmore's references to German colonial rule and fascism were left out of the German translation that appeared the same year (Padmore, *Afrika unter dem Joch der Weissen*). On this issue, see Polsgrove, *Ending British Rule in Africa*, 15–16. All of this is despite the fact that even Hitler compared German expansion in the East with the British Empire, and claimed in 1941: 'The Russian space is our India' (cited in Zimmerer, 'Birth of the Ostland', 202).
9. Cited in Furber, 'Near as Far in the Colonies', 543.
10. See Zimmerer, 'Birth of the Ostland'.
11. Madley, 'From Africa to Auschwitz', 450–57.
12. Furber, 'Near as Far in the Colonies', 542.
13. Ibid., 579.
14. Ibid., 564.
15. Kopp, 'Arguing the Case', 157.
16. This is best illustrated by the allegory that Frederick II evoked when he called the Slavs 'his Iroquois' (Wilson, 'Environmental Chauvinism', 27). See Kołos 'Wildness', for more examples of the 'Red Indian' metaphor in Prussian as well as Polish discourse of the positivist period. For notions of a civilizing mission in the First World War forestry discourse on the Polish Urwald, see Sunseri, 'Exploiting the Urwald', 322.
17. Gingrich, 'Nearby Frontier', 61.
18. Ibid.
19. Quoted from Turner's classic 1893 text on the centrality of the frontier in North American history (here cited from Turner and Faragher, *Rereading Frederick Jackson Turner*, 32).
20. Osterhammel, *Die Verwandlung der Welt*, 563. Although the expansion of the frontier was largely a topic until the nineteenth century, Osterhammel mentions Nazi-German expansion to the East as an example of its post-history.
21. Polsgrove, *Ending British Rule in Africa*, 62.
22. Padmore and Pizer, *How Russia Transformed Her Colonial Empire*.
23. In 1946, when the book was finally published, public opinion in the UK had already started to turn against the Soviet Union. Padmore's argument, which might have had some strength at the height of British–Soviet cooperation during the war, did not ring true at a time when Stalinist atrocities had come into public focus in the UK (Polsgrove, *Ending British Rule in Africa*, 85).
24. Cooper, *Colonialism in Question*, 156.
25. Moore, 'Is the Post- in Postcolonial the Post- in Post-Soviet?', 115.
26. Ibid., 121.
27. Thompson, 'Whose Discourse?'
28. Ibid., 6.
29. Janos, *East Central Europe*, 238.
30. Ibid., 221.
31. Ibid., 236. For the ambiguous outcome of Soviet efforts to legitimize westward expansion in 1939 as a 'civilizing mission', see Amar, 'Sovietization'. Moreover, the Russian Empire's attempts to achieve social and cultural hegemony were 'only marginally successful' in Poland (Mayblin, Piekut and Valentine, '"Other" Posts', 7).

32. My translation from German: 'Herrschaftsbeziehungen, die mit physischer, militärischer, epistemologischer und ideologischer Gewalt durchgesetzt und etwa über 'Rasse'- und 'Kultur'-Diskurse legitimiert wurden' (Castro Varela and Dhawan, *Postkoloniale Theorie*, 13).
33. Jolluck, *Exile and Identity*.
34. Ibid., 244.
35. Snochowska-Gonzalez, 'Post-Colonial Poland', 716.
36. Ibid., 717.
37. Ibid., 718.
38. Bakuła, 'Colonial and Postcolonial Aspects', n.p.
39. Zarzycki and Buczak-Zarzycka, *Kwaheri Africa*, 66.
40. For comparable examples of leaflets distributed during the Soviet invasion of Poland, see Gross, *Revolution from Abroad*, 35–36.
41. Zarzycki and Buczak-Zarzycka, *Kwaheri Africa*, 66.
42. Kelly, *Finding Poland*, 31.
43. It is one of the three features of modern colonialism in Osterhammel's definition of the term. See Osterhammel, *Kolonialismus*, 20.
44. The Association of the Eastern Borderland of the Polish Republic in Tengeru sent letters to delegates at the UN Assembly (NP 01.03.46, 'Protesty Zw. Ziem Wschodnich R.P. Tengeru do O.Z.N.'; GP 10.02.46 'Z Osiedli', p.12). In Koja, similar action was organized by another branch, formed in 1945 (NP 01.07.46, 'Zebranie Informacyjne Koła Zw. Ziem Wschodnich R.P. w Koji' by T. Zemoytel; PISM: Kol 174/3, 'Koło Związku Ziem Wschodnich Rz. P. w Koji', 16.11.46 by T. Zemoytel). In Masindi, a comparable organization was founded as early as February 1945 (NP 30.03.45, 'Pod znakiem obrony całości i niepodległości ojczyzny. Z Osiedla Masindi – Uganda' by Kornel Makuszyński).
45. Wolff, *Inventing Eastern Europe*, 7.
46. Ibid.
47. Citing Balzac in ibid., 357.
48. Bakić-Hayden, 'Nesting Orientalisms', 918.
49. Ibid., 923.
50. Cited here from Zarycki, 'Orientalism'. See also Zarycki, *Ideologies of Eastness*.
51. Hunczak, 'Polish Colonial Ambitions', 648. For the longer history of Polish involvement in the European colonial project, see Rhode, 'Zivilisierungsmissionen und Wissenschaft'.
52. Hunczak, 'Polish Colonial Ambitions', 653.
53. Ibid., 656.
54. Fyfe, 'Race', 21.
55. Kirk-Greene, 'The Thin White Line', 42.
56. See Stoler, 'Rethinking Colonial Categories'.
57. See Dodoo and Donkoh, 'Nationality and the Pan-African State', 155; Cooper, *Africa since 1940*, 81. On the attempts of Léopold Sédar Senghor and Aimé Césaire to transform the French Empire into a transcontinental, democratic federation, see Wilder, *Freedom Time*.
58. Of course, African nationalisms (as well as different strands of Polish nationalisms) have quite diverse histories.
59. Brubaker, 'Manichean Myth'.
60. Ibid., 67.
61. It is still one of the basic post-independence consensuses of African governments that the colonial boundaries should not be changed.

62. The bitter disappointment with the decision of the Allies to transfer the eastern part of Poland ('kresy') into the Soviet Union is a recurrent theme in recollections of Polish refugees in Africa. See Plawski, *Torn from the Homeland*, 151; Piotrowski, *Polish Deportees*, 153; Porajska, *From the Steppes*, 133.
63. Even the Soviet-aligned Lublin committee that formed the later Polish government did not take part in the Yalta Conference.
64. For a recent review of the literature on the Maji Maji War, see Greenstein, 'Making History'.
65. The Biafran attempt to establish a state that connects to pre-colonial entities, and its forceful crushing by the Nigerian state, is maybe the most prominent example.
66. For the importance of printed language in the emergence of nationalism, see Anderson, *Imagined Communities*, 36.
67. Gross, *Revolution from Abroad*, 4.
68. The Holocaust, the postwar expulsion of the Germans and the Polish–Ukrainian population transfers all contributed to this homogenization. For the latter, see Stadnik, 'Ukrainian–Polish Population Transfers'; Gousseff, 'Evacuation versus Repatriation'.
69. About a third of the Polish interwar population belonged to minorities. Somalia may serve as an exception to the rule, and shows that linguistic and religious homogeneity does not necessarily lead to a stable nation-state.
70. Notable exceptions can arguably be seen in the Moroccan rule in Western Sahara and the position of the Ethiopian Empire in regard to its neighbours. See Zunes and Mundy, *Western Sahara*; Reid, *Frontiers of Violence*.
71. Bright and Geyer, 'Regimes of World Order', 221.
72. Fyfe, 'Race', 21.
73. I will address this issue and the intersections of gender and race in colonial societies in more depth in Chapter 4.
74. Plawski, *Torn from the Homeland*, 144.
75. Filomena Michałowska-Bykowska in Piotrowski, *Polish Deportees*, 162.
76. Ibid.
77. As she was deported at the age of 12, this might not come as a surprise; see Urbanek, 'Z nieludzkiej ziemi'.
78. See, for example, Zarzycki and Buczak-Zarzycka, *Kwaheri Africa*, 37.
79. Krolikowski, *Stolen Childhood*, 110.
80. Holborn, *International Refugee Organization*, 234.
81. TNA: 176/87, p.6, S.A. Walden, District Commissioner Iringa to Camp Commandant Ifunda, 27.12.44.
82. Similar widespread illegal purchases were reported from Tengeru (TNA: 5/28/1, Representative Economic Control Board to The Secretary, Economic Control Board, DSM, 5.04.44).
83. TNA: 176/87, p.6, Pennington, Director of Refugees to Camp Commandant Ifunda, 9.01.45.
84. The British officials even urged a Polish government delegate who was about to visit the camp to press on the refugees to reveal the names, although it remains unclear if he succeeded (TNA: 176/87, p.6, Pennington, Director of Refugees to Camp Commandant Ifunda, 9.01.45).
85. Ibid.
86. PRO: CO 822/146/1, Personal Summary, Helena Luczyc, attached to Beryl Hughes, Home Office, London to Dawson, Colonial Office, 9.11.50. The year '1923' was most likely 1932, as she was a mere 9 years old in 1923.

87. Ibid.
88. PRO: CO 822/146/1, Pennington for Governor of Tanganyika to Secretary of State, Colonial Office, 28.10.50.
89. His background is not entirely clear, as he reportedly told a 'different story every time he [was] asked about himself' (TNA: 69/782, Campbell, Director of Refugees to Provincial Commissioner Northern Province, 16.10.52).
90. TNA: 69/782, Officer i/c Police, Usa River to Director of Refugees, DSM, 3.11.52.
91. PRO: CO 822/146/1, Personal Summary, Bernard Masiuk, attached to Beryl Hughes, Home Office, London to Dawson, Colonial Office, 9.11.50.
92. PRO: CO 822/350, Ag. Governor Tanganyika to Secretary of State, CO, London, 21.06.51.
93. Ibid. In February 1953, however, he was still under treatment for pulmonary tuberculosis in Moshi (TNA: 69/782, Specialist, Tuberculosis Hospital Kibongoto, Moshi to PC Northern Province, Arusha, 18.2.53).
94. See also Mayblin, Piekut and Valentine, '"Other" Posts', 3.
95. Furedi, *Colonial Wars*, 102.
96. Describing others as cannibals is a recurrent topic to depict the Other as savage. On the function of this discourse, see the classic, but controversial, Arens, *The Man-Eating Myth*.
97. See, for example, Plawski, *Torn from the Homeland*, 140; Zarzycki and Buczak-Zarzycka, *Kwaheri Africa*, 25; Diary of Krysia Maziarz, cited in Krolikowski, *Stolen Childhood*, 87.
98. Krolikowski, *Stolen Childhood*, 77.
99. Ibid.
100. Zarzycki and Buczak-Zarzycka, *Kwaheri Africa*, 2.
101. Ibid., 24.
102. Maria Dutkiewicz remembered that she had read the novel in Kazakhstan before coming to Africa (Niedźwiecka, 'Armia Andersa'). Another former refugee referred to it as well (Gabiniewicz, 'Dziećmi Andersa', 17), and Irena Sikorska wrote: 'Till now Africa existed only in my imagination, fed by books and films' (Sikorska, 'Irena Sikorska's Biography'). One scout leader referred to it in a speech (GP 2.12.45, 'Kronika Harcerska', p.11), and a travel report in the refugee newspaper was even titled 'Traces of "In Desert and Wilderness"' (GP 2.06.46, 'Sladami "W Pustyni i w Puszczy"', by H. Czarnocka, p.14).
103. GP 1.12.46, p.15; Zins, *Poles in Zambezi*, 78.
104. Klobucka, 'Desert', 248.
105. Ibid., 247.
106. Sienkiewicz had sailed along the East African coast up to Bagamoyo, but his journey inland was cut short by a disease. Shortly after his return he published a travel report, which was, however, less popular. See Uffelmann, 'Buren und Polen', 287–96.
107. For a postcolonial critique of the novel and its different translations, editions and cinematic versions, see Klobucka, 'Desert'.
108. Ibid., 247.
109. Cited in ibid., 251.
110. In fact, Staś's idea of using African colonial soldiers on the European battlefields was not absurd in the context of the time. The French general Charles Mangin proposed this in 1910 (Rössel, 'Die Front', 12). Consequently there were a considerable number of African soldiers in the French army in both world wars. See Killingray and Plaut, *Fighting for Britain*, 7.

111. Rhode, 'Zivilisierungsmissionen und Wissenschaft', 29.
112. Wróbel, 'Polskie Dominium', 21; Tomaszewski, 'Shade'. By contrast, at least one refugee group en route to Masindi travelled in the third class (MSS Afr. s. 705, Charles M.A. Gayer, Masindi, 14.09.42).
113. The Polish newspapers and the role of the refugee elites will be addressed in more depth in Chapter 5.
114. GP 21.10.45, 'Przed 11-tym Listopada' by Chodzikiewicz and Krajowski; GP 25.11.45, 'Z Osiedli'; GP 12.01.47 'Z Osiedli'.
115. The Polish exhibition in Kampala was attended by the international European elite of the capital (GP 12.01.47, 'Z Osiedli'). An exhibition in Tengeru school was reportedly popular among the 'English society' (GP 27.01.46, 'Z Osiedli').
116. This was part of a longer article explaining Polish traditions in the *Rhodesian Herald* in July 1943 (Zins, *Poles in Zambezi*, 74).
117. PRO: CO 822/146/1, Personal Summary, Josef K., attached to Beryl Hughes, Home Office, London to Dawson, Colonial Office, 9.11.50.
118. TNA: 69/782, Ag. Provincial Commissioner Northern Province to Director of Refugees, DSM, 24.12.52.
119. TNA: 69/782, Campbell to PC Northern Province, 26.09.52.
120. PRO: AST 18/115, The Warden, Stover to National Assistance Board, HQ 16.03.62.
121. TNA: 69/782, D.S. Troup to Director of Refugees, 18.09.52.
122. TNA: 69/782, D.S. Troup to Director of Refugees, 10.06.52.
123. Thompson, 'Colonialism in Crisis'.
124. Ibid., 607. For the perspective of one of the Ugandan workers on this incident see chapter 5.
125. Wróbel, 'Polskie Dominium'.
126. Ibid., 23.
127. Prażmowska, 'Polish Refugees as Military Potential', 230.
128. KNA: AH/1/51, p.96C, 'Poles as Rhodesian Settlers' by F.J. Bagshawe, Commandant Refugee Settlements, n.d. Major Francis John Edward Bagshawe (1877–1953) had served in the Matabele War, the Boer War and the First Wold War, and worked as provincial commissioner in Tanganyika until he retired to his Southern Rhodesian farm in 1937. Later he became director of refugees in Southern Rhodesia.
129. GP 29.09.46 'Z Osiedli'; KNA: AH/1/51, p.96A, Memorandum of Polish Civic Committee, Nairobi to A. Creech-Jones, Undersecretary of State for the Colonies, 22.07.46. See also Tavuyanago, Muguti and Hlongwana, 'Victims', 963. and Mlambo, 'Some Are More White', 156.
130. IRO: AJ/43/788/45/2, 'Discussions in London', Curtis, IRO Nairobi to Lush, IRO Cairo, 9.05.49.
131. Hunczak, 'Polish Colonial Ambitions', 655.
132. Cavanagh, 'Postcolonial Poland', 86.
133. Achebe, 'Image of Africa'. Cavanagh mentions in passing that the novel is 'controversial', and references some texts of the discussion on its 'alleged racism and sexism' in one footnote, but does not cite Achebe (Cavanagh, 'Postcolonial Poland', 85, fn.13.).
134. Only in two instances do Africans speak at all: to prove that they are cannibals and to announce the death of Kurtz (Achebe, 'Image of Africa', 1788).
135. Dirk Uffelmann detected some slight criticisms of German colonial rule in Sienkiewicz's writings, but assesses a generally positive relation of Sienkiewicz with the Germans and their rule (Uffelmann, 'Buren und Polen', 300–302).

136. According to Sienkiewicz, even Germans and French regarded themselves as brothers in Africa (ibid., 299).
137. Ibid., 307–9.
138. Moore, 'Is the Post- in Postcolonial the Post- in Post-Soviet?', 115.

Chapter 4

'AN INCREDIBLE POOL OF FEMININITY'

Gendering the Refugees

> One day … we saw big convoys of lorries, full of Europeans being transported to the station; mainly women, children and a few shabbily dressed old men.
> —Urmila Jhaveri, *Dancing with Destiny*[1]

As Urmila Jhaveri writes in her memoirs, the hungry and traumatized Europeans she observed arriving in Dar es Salaam in 1942 were mainly women and children. It was thus not only the poor state of their clothing and health or their different language that made them an exceptional sight for observers, but their gendered composition as well.

If we situate this case at the intersection of colonial history, gender and migration studies, there are some peculiarities to mention. Refugees in general and female refugees in particular are regarded as especially marginalized groups in a situation of increased vulnerability. The Polish refugee women, however, had a socially relevant identity aspect that was to their advantage: their whiteness. At the same time, they were not part of the ruling nation and had just gone through the humiliating experience of deportation and living in Soviet special settlements. Compared to the previous stations of their forced journey and the situation in war-ravaged Poland, they had 'stumbled into paradise', as some refugee children put it.[2] But in contrast to the carefree children, the Polish women had more worries about their unclear future and the highly unstable status of being refugees. They were restricted in their freedom of movement and dependent on the men in the Polish army as well as political decisions concerning their fate.

The central question of this chapter is the role that gender played during their stay in the African colonial societies. How were the refugee women regarded and treated by the colonial administrations? How did the male-dominated Polish administration treat them? And how did the women situate themselves and manoeuvre within this situation of privilege and constraint?

Early colonial societies were largely dominated by men. The first European colonizers were overwhelmingly male, and only with the establishment of a permanent presence of white settler communities did more women come to the colonies.[3] By the time the Polish refugees arrived in Africa, most settler societies had a nearly balanced gender ratio. This helped to sustain the white settler community and maintain its distance to the colonized. Intimate interracial relations were from the turn of the century more and more regarded as a problem for the respectability of the imperial project, and the resulting mixed population posed a classificatory problem.[4]

Reviewing the literature that could offer relevant insights into the Polish women's role and position, four possible interpretations are discernible. The literature on white women in British colonial societies focuses on two different segments of white female societies, and hence offers two interrelated interpretations of their gendered role. The first emerged out of a preoccupation with white women of the colonial elites. They were regarded as a privileged group, portrayed by some male scholars as villains, whose presence increased racial segregation and eventually became the reason for the loss of the British Empire.[5] In this view, the more open and integrated early colonial societies, where white men often lived in concubinage relations with black women, later came under attack by the white women following 'their' men and domesticating them. White women profited from their improved social position vis-à-vis the colonized, and misused their enhanced possibilities. Directed against this interpretation, some scholars have portrayed women as dependent on the white men but more capable of crossing racial boundaries.[6] This positive interpretation of their position has been rightly criticized for ignoring black women's perspectives and the racism of white women.[7] Consequently an interpretation of white women as profiting from whiteness while at the same time suffering under patriarchal control has emerged.[8] This strand of literature underlines the women's agency by highlighting their ideological labour in stabilizing colonial rule.[9]

A second strand of literature focuses on marginal white women. Following Ann Laura Stoler's emphasis on colonial boundary making, and the consequent focus on the importance of sexuality and reproduction, a new shift towards potentially transgressing white women emerged.[10] In contrast to the wives of colonial officials or settlers, these women were regarded as a threat to the colonial social order. White prostitutes seem to have been the most prominent example of such socially transgressing actors.[11] Their presence and independent agency provoked anxiety and activity in the colonial administration, as their 'immoral' behaviour undermined the proclaimed moral superiority of the white race.

To these two interpretations from the history of colonialism we can add two possible interpretations from Polish and migration history respectively. The first possibility derives from Polish historiography, and the gendered role of Polish women in particular. In this view, the *motherhood* of Polish women is regarded as central to the reproduction and preservation of the nation. Katherine Jolluck has pointed to the importance of the idea of patriotic and selfless motherhood for the self-identification of the Polish women who had been deported to the Soviet Union.[12] In the national image of '*Matka Polka*' (Polish Mother), the women's patriotic task was to preserve the Polish nation under foreign rule through the raising of Polish children, nursing their national identity and resisting the intrusion of alien influences.[13] While men's role was the heroic fight to liberate the nation, '[w]omen's Polishness called for purity, selflessness and fostering unity among the collective'.[14] In this view, intimate contacts with anyone outside the nationally defined group represented an unwanted deviation or even a betrayal of the nation. Underlining the central role of women in nationalism, Nira Yuval-Davis states: 'it is women – and not (just?) the bureaucracy and intellectuals – who reproduce nations, biologically, culturally and symbolically'.[15] In this understanding, women have once again the role of stabilizing the community – but this time it is the Polish and not the colonial community.[16]

Another frame for understanding this group of female refugees comes from migration studies. Following intersectional approaches, non-white refugee women are seen as victims of 'multiple discrimination'.[17] Piling up marginalized categorizations (e.g. female, black, non-citizen), they are regarded as the ultimate victims and therefore in need of special protection by international legislation and organizations. At the same time, the dislocation of refugees from one social context to another opens up opportunities to actively renegotiate gender roles.[18] Refugee women are not mere victims, but can actively improve their social position and profit from dislocation by widening their possibilities. They are thus historical actors in their own right.

The role of the Polish women can thus be interpreted in three different but interrelated frames: as *stabilizers*, as a transgressive *threat* and as *actors* making the most of their situation. These interpretations underlie the structure of this chapter.

First of all, important for the female role as *stabilizer of the community* is a general dependency on men. This leads us to ask which community they should stabilize. When regarded as part of the colonial settler society, they would serve to stabilize and become part of it. The interpretation in a Polish national frame would instead see them as '*Matka Polka*' of the exiled Polish nation, whose main task would be to raise children in Polish ways. From a male perspective, this boils down to asking: to whom did the Polish women and their reproductive capacity rightfully belong – to the Polish nation or the British settler community?

In a second section I will focus on incidents and opinions that point to the role of the Polish women as a *threat to the colonial order*. Relationships between Polish women and men who were neither British nor Polish were regarded as especially dangerous if they transgressed the social boundaries of race. Relationships with other Europeans or Asians are an interesting point, as the male opinions were less clear-cut. Where was the line drawn, through which means and by whom? And how were the boundaries enforced?

The third section will look at the opportunities that the involuntary dislocation brought to women for changing prescribed gender roles. The focus is here on the *independent agency* and perspective of the refugee women themselves. How did they deal with the new situation? To what extent did racial privilege, the social turmoil of the war and the resulting occupational opportunities give these women the chance to renegotiate their social position? How did they navigate and defy constraining social structures?

Female Camps with Male Leaders

The British government was hosting the Polish refugees because it had an interest in the Polish army fighting with the Allies against Nazi Germany. This strategic rationale was already clearly gendered: while Polish men were fighting with British men against Germany, their women and children had to be taken care of. Only 11 per cent of the Polish refugees in East and Central Africa were men, and they were mainly of advanced age or unfit for military service.[19] The vast majority of refugees consisted of women (47 per cent) and children (36 per cent) and some youth (6 per cent).[20] Consequently, the camps were described as an 'incredible pool of femininity' with a 'motherly' atmosphere, and thus stood in contrast to the male-dominated public world of the European colonizers.[21]

While the camp inhabitants were mainly women, the Polish and British administrators were almost exclusively men. One of the few exceptions was the post of the 'Women Supervisor' in Tengeru, filled by the wife of the British quartermaster or the wife of the camp commandant.[22] Their task remains unclear, but they were definitely not considered to be as important as their husbands. While the individual qualities of possible camp commandants were discussed, the role of the women supervisors was not a topic in the files. The women supervisors' work was also paid considerably less than that of their husbands.²³ Apart from this there was, as mentioned earlier, only one female IRO official in a senior administrative position.

British women were mainly active in the reception of the refugees. It was mainly through the women-dominated welfare organizations that they helped the refugees at the beginning.²⁴ Some women were part of the delegations escorting the first groups of refugees from the port in Tanga to Tengeru camp.²⁵ White women in Dar es Salaam and Nairobi assisted the refugees upon their arrival.²⁶ The welfare of children and women was seen as a task for women, whereas the overall responsibility and power lay in the hands of male administrators with military ranks, clearly reflecting the gendered roles of 'caring' women and 'protecting' men.

All responsible colonial officials (camp commandants and directors of refugees) were men. Although the Colonial Service began recruiting women in 1937, their numbers remained tiny.²⁷ The Polish delegation in Nairobi and the internal organization of the camps were likewise dominated by men. The Polish camp leaders and their subordinate group leaders were overwhelmingly male; only the head of the orphanage in Tengeru was a woman.²⁸ And while many Polish teachers were women, the headmasters of the schools were largely men.²⁹ It was not only the British but also the Polish patriarchal order that was reflected in the division of labour and distribution of power.

Figure 4.1. Group of Polish children and teachers in front of their school in Tengeru, Tanganyika, 1945. From Archiwum Fotografii Ośrodka KARTA, Signature: FOK_0010_0002_0001_013, online.

Depending on the Men in the Army

The preferential treatment of the Polish refugees was closely linked to the Polish soldiers who fought alongside the British against the Germans. As the refugees were largely women and children, while the soldiers were predominantly male, this relationship was also a gendered one.[30] While the 'martial masculinity' of the 'gallant fighters' in the Polish army set them on a par with their British 'brothers in arms', the female refugees had to be protected.[31] Throughout the war years, the colonial public was reminded of the Polish contribution to the war effort through newspaper reports about the heroic Polish soldiers.[32] British officials in East Africa argued accordingly that the refugees were the 'very deserving families of our gallant Polish allies'.[33] It was not only the direct family relationship of the father fighting in the army and the mother and children staying in the camp, but also mediated through their belonging to one nationally defined group. In September 1943, the Southern Rhodesian government declared itself willing to accept 'Polish refugee women and children'.[34] Although a few men came as well, the group was generally perceived as female.

Apart from this general dependence, there was also a direct financial connection to the male relatives in the army through the sending of remittances by the soldiers to camp inmates. On top of that, the Polish government paid extra allowances to families of Polish soldiers.[35] Without relatives in the army the refugees received only general allowances and, if they had a job, an income from that work. Hence the refugees who had a relative in the army were financially better off than the ones without. The social stratification within the refugee camp and its connection to the male family member is captured in Barbara Porajska's autobiography. She describes the moment when her father joined her and her mother in Masindi camp: their position dramatically improved because of his post as chief of the camp police and as a lecturer in the school. The whole family moved to a better house in the 'Street of Masters' – as she called the area where the camp elite lived – and could even employ an African servant.[36]

The postal service proved another important link to the Polish soldiers on the European battlefields. The correspondence, however, was not just limited to relatives. Some Polish orphans also wrote to soldiers in the army and received parcels from them. Father Krolikowski complained that some of them were painting a bleak picture of conditions in the African camps in order to get presents from the soldiers.[37] Maria Romanko, who stayed at the Polish school for girls in Digglefold, recalled that the only male contacts they had were pen pals in the Polish army. According to her, it was 'considered a patriotic duty to correspond with them', and some of the correspondence led to marriages later on.[38] *Głos Polski*, the Polish newspaper from Nairobi, was sent to the soldiers as well, and described by its editors as 'contact between us and our army'.[39] In the camps people gathered around the radio to hear news from the front lines, further strengthening the close bond between the refugees and 'their' army.

At the end of the war, the difference between those with and those without relatives in the army became even more relevant. The Polish soldiers eventually had the opportunity to settle in Britain and their relatives could move there as well.[40] The refugees without relatives in the army feared repatriation to Poland, although the colonial authorities insisted that they would never forcefully repatriate anyone. In the end they were admitted as well, but in the meantime they had lived in uncertainty. Some women followed Polish men already living abroad, again depending on their marital status for gaining access. This connection between marriage and residential status becomes clear in the case of a Polish woman who applied for permission to go to Canada and marry her fiancé, who was already living there. The Canadian authorities granted admission under the condition that she signed a declaration guaranteeing that they would marry within thirty days of arrival.[41]

Although the agency and their status as European allies protected the women from arbitrary actions on the part of the colonial authorities, they remained highly dependent on others. On a general level, this dependency was on the Polish army as a whole. On a personal level, individual relations with men in the army or elsewhere defined their status. This dependency was the necessary precondition for the gendered role of women as the stabilizing core of the community. Let us look at the two identity groups and how their male leadership tried to keep women under their control.

Reproducing the Polish Nation in Exile

The reproductive capacity of women lay at the core of the idea of Polish national resilience. The Polish history of resistance to foreign domination served as a guiding interpretative frame for the gendered roles in the national struggle. While the men fought against foreign oppressors, the women protected the domestic sphere as '*Matka Polka*' against the intrusion of non-Polish influences, and they reproduced the next generations of Poles.[42] Women's ability to give birth to children put them at the centre of the national community, as only through them the future of the nation could be saved. Going back to the emigration after the failed November 1830 uprising and its rich cultural production, Polish national discourse regarded the diaspora as responsible for continuing the struggle for Poland from abroad.[43] This narrative provided an interpretative frame for the appropriate behaviour of Polish refugee women.

But there were also practical concerns about the ascribed ability of single mothers to handle their adolescent children. Polish men complained about the absence of patriarchal authority, not only with regard to the women in the camp but also regarding their children. Apart from the many orphans in the camps, most of the children in families had no father either. One of the few Polish men, the priest Krolikowski, wrote about some unruly adolescents in the unstable camp situation: 'The situation was made worse by the fact that every home was fatherless. Women were in the majority; if there were any men at all, most of them were sick or very old'.[44] The lack of stability and perspective for the refugees was, in his view, worsened by the fact that the single mothers struggled to bring up their children and discipline them sufficiently: 'A father's authority might have remained firm, but in such abnormal conditions, mothers could do little with their adolescents'.[45] The priest commented on the absence of men in the schools as well, where most teachers were women whom he regarded as incapable of disciplining the boys.[46]

One answer to the perceived inability of single women to discipline their children was the boy scout and girl guide movements, which flourished in the camps.[47] Most of the refugee children were in these groups and they became an important part of organized camp life. Krolikowski describes it as an excellent means of education that could restore the inner harmony and balance of the youngsters.[48] The scouting movement with its uniforms, internal hierarchies and strong emphasis on the community was closely linked to the military.[49] In Koja settlement the scouting organizations were set up with instructors from the Polish army.[50] Scouting in the camps was a means to keep young people busy with orderly, disciplined activities, and to promote Catholic values and Polishness. As one refugee recalled her scouting experience in Masindi: 'The organization strengthens friendships and engrains in our young hearts our love of God and our country'.[51]

Scouting was part of a larger project of the Polish administration to create a Polish milieu within the camps. Other Polish institutions were the school and church, which became a priority after the initial organization of the necessities of life. Delegates of several Polish ministries in Nairobi controlled the schools, the church, welfare and social activities, and created, together with the camp inmates, a 'Little Poland'.[52] Wróbel calls the camps 'small oases of Polishness' that could not be found in war-torn Europe.[53] Through newspapers, church activities, cultural groups and events, the Polish community was recreated in exile. As many refugees spoke no other language than Polish, this communal feeling was further strengthened. The close bond to the nation was kept alive through public commemoration of the common suffering through foreign oppression and deportation, assigning the refugees to 'the historic ranks of Polish exiles'.[54]

The long history of the partition period and Polish national resistance served as a guiding principle, giving to Polish women the task of reproducing the nation and raising Polish children. With institutional support from the Polish administration, the women created Polish surroundings within the camps. But as we will see, not all refugee women conformed to their allocated role.

Becoming Part of Settler Society

While Polish administrators saw the women and their children as part of their nationally defined exile community, rightfully belonging to the Polish men in the army, some British settlers had their own interest in them. Marrying British men was for some refugee women a means to evade the uncertainty of their status and join the settler society.[55] One refugee woman married the British commandant of Bwana Mkubwa camp,[56] and some quite young women married British citizens as well.[57] Although there is no evidence of why they got married, it remains clear that women took on the citizenship of their husbands. One refugee from the Southern Rhodesian camp of Rongai put it plainly in 1947: 'I would rather desert my fianc[é] than return to Poland. I have no wish to return home. I will marry an Englishman'.[58] Marrying an Englishman was for her not a romantic idea, but the best way to tackle the lingering threat of being sent back to Poland. In the end, over two hundred Polish women married non-Polish men and therewith gained residence.[59]

For white men in the colonies, the large group of young single white women proved attractive. Only one in ten women lived together with her husband in the camps.[60] Their perceived availability for settlers is intrinsic to a request by John Olivier from Kisumu, Kenya. He asked a refugee official for a housekeeper, aged under twenty years, whom he intended to marry if he succeeded in divorcing his wife.[61] The East African IRO representative noted in his final report that in Southern Rhodesia local prospectors used to write to the camp commandants proposing marriage to any suitable girl who was prepared to share their life. He further notes: 'These proposals were posted without comment on the camp noticeboard, and a number of successful cases of local resettlement followed'.[62] For the IRO this was a welcome way to reduce the number of refugees under its care. For colonial officials it led to an increase in the white settler population, as the women's status was dependent on that of their husbands. Marrying British men, they thus became part of the British population.

Two other cases illustrate, however, that marriage to a British resident was not always an easy way to a secure status. Janina Christie (née Leszwa) had married a British citizen, but later found out that he had already been married to another woman. Christie's marriage was nullified, raising the danger her losing her British citizenship.[63] A comparable story happened to Tekla Marczuk, who in 1950 wanted to marry a British employee of the Uganda Electricity Board. She had no living relatives and a 'crippled leg', thus reducing her prospects for resettlement abroad. Enquiries by colonial officials having found that both were 'respectable people', Marczuk got permission to leave the camp and she lived with her prospective husband for a year, despite him not yet being divorced from his wife, who had left him earlier. When his wife unexpectedly returned with the couple's two children, she threw Marczuk out of the house. As the refugee camps in Uganda had already been closed by then, the Ugandan governor enquired in London if the eighth-month-pregnant Marczuk could get a visa for the UK.[64] In both the above cases, the women's residential status was clearly dependent on their marriage to the British men.

The position of European children in colonial societies needs some explanation here. Like women, they were regarded as especially vulnerable to influences from the colonized and thus 'social contamination'.[65] The children of European colonial officials and settlers were, if possible, sent to Britain for schooling to reduce this influence.[66] In the Rhodesias, where many settlers could not afford British boarding schools, their children were educated in segregated European schools or sent to boarding schools in South Africa. The Polish children in turn went to Polish schools in the camps or in the specially set up Polish school settlements for further education in Digglefold (for Central Africa) or Rusape (for East Africa). On this point, the Polish authorities' interest in keeping the children Polish coincided well with the British interest in maintaining the distance between white children and the colonized.

To sum up, the Polish refugees found themselves in a situation of dependency that had a gendered aspect. The whole refugee group depended generally on the Polish army and its contribution to the Allied war effort. As this army consisted largely of male soldiers and the refugees were mainly women, female dependency on men already existed (either directly through family relations and/or more indirectly through national categorization). Without the Polish soldiers, the refugees would not have been able to enjoy the hospitality of the British Empire. Most women retained their strong bond to the Polish nation and later became part of the Polish diaspora in Britain (and elsewhere), fulfilling the prescribed female role as custodians of the community in exile. They created, together with the male-dominated Polish administration, a Polish milieu in the camps that was rather successful in raising the refugee children in Polish ways. After the war, many women joined their husbands or else married Polish men in order to be able to settle

Figure 4.2. Group of refugee women in the hills above Koja camp, Uganda, 1948. From Archiwum Fotografii Ośrodka KARTA, Signature: FOK_0009_0002_0001_035, online.

abroad. Some other women married settlers with a permanent residential status, in order to be able to stay where they were. These relations were regarded as unproblematic by the colonial administration, as their whiteness gave them the potential to become British. As a woman's citizenship status and relation to the nation was dependent on the status of her husband, the refugee women could become part of settler society. Yet they entered into an unequal relationship, as their residence permits depended on those of their husbands. If it worked out well, they accepted the name of their husbands, blended into settler society and disappeared from the files.

Transgressing the Boundaries of Whiteness

The stabilizing role of women for nationally as well as racially defined groups necessarily comes with a downside. As white women in colonial societies occupied a central position in the reproduction of the settler community, they were at the same time a threat to the community if they transgressed its boundaries. As Ann Laura Stoler notes, 'control over sexuality and reproduction [was] at the core of defining colonial privilege and its boundaries'.[67] A strong interest in the 'sexual interface of the colonial encounter' has always been shown by participants, observers and critics of the colonial project alike.[68] Consequently the control of the sexuality of this large group of white women was of concern to male administrators in the colonies. Taking a closer look at sexual relations between Polish refugees and people who were neither British nor Polish helps us to see where these lines were drawn. It also shows that the perceived boundaries of respectable sexual relations depended on the gender of those involved as well as on the position of the assessing officials.

Controlling the Sexuality of the 'Polish Girls'

In 1946, Ifunda's camp commandant M.R. Douglass and district commissioner Stanley Walden from the nearby town of Iringa had a revealing conflict over the suitability of partners for the Polish women. Walden accused Douglass, besides gross mismanagement of the camp, of being obsessed with preventing relations between Polish women and Italian men.[69] According to Walden, Douglass had convinced the police to send an Italian internee, who had been released on parole in order to work in Iringa, back to the internment camp in Tabora. Douglass's reason was the Italian's intimate relationship with a Polish woman, who intended to marry him. He accused the woman of being a known prostitute, and pointed out that the Italian man was already married and had children.[70]

Douglass is portrayed in Walden's letters as a man who saw himself responsible for controlling the sexual contacts of 'his' Polish women with other men. Walden wrote that the quartermaster of the camp, who was Douglass's brother-in-law, was reported to have said to one 'perfectly respectable' government official that 'he could have all the girls he wanted' when he visited the camp. At the same time Douglass was allegedly allowing the Polish women to attend parties at a Greek farmer's house.[71] By contrast, a visiting American Red Cross representative spoke highly of Douglass, whom he portrayed as the 'presiding figure in the village' and a 'sincere and kindly man, a retired army major and humanist, full of an abiding love for small children and stray cats'. Like a benevolent leader, Douglass inspected the camp every morning with his 'safari car', taking 'gabbling, laughing youngsters' for a ride and greeting the adults in Polish, which he had learned in order to converse with his subjects.[72] Douglass was clearly the paternal leader of the camp.

Evidently, both Walden and Douglass saw it as the responsibility of the British camp commandant to control the refugee women and their relationships with any men who were outside their nationally defined group. Relationships with Polish or British men were not an issue for the officials. The accusation of letting 'the Polish girls'[73] attend parties outside the camp derived from the same understanding as the attempts to put an end to relations between Polish women and Italian men. The seeming sexual availability of young refugee women for camp officials has some parallels to the situation in German DP camps, about which one former official wrote that the lives of some colleagues were characterized by an 'excess of alcohol and the easy comfort of sex'.[74]

Luckily for the historian, Walden was quite 'outspoken on paper',[75] and raised a point that was not mentioned as directly by most other officials. In a confidential letter to the commissioner of Tanganyika Police he wrote: 'If there is going to be any question of sexual intercourse with the Poles I should say that it would be better that it should be with white men rather than with Indians and Africans as is at present the case'.[76]

This implies that there was a noticeable amount of sexual intercourse between Polish women and Asian and African men. There seems to have been no need for Walden to explain why interracial sexual relations were undesirable (we will return to this issue). Since he included the Polish women as well as the Italian men in the group of whites, race seems to have been more important than national categorizations for him. Walden was more critical towards Greek men. For Douglass, the Italians were the more dubious group – maybe because they had been enemy aliens before – but again, the sexuality of the Polish women was seen as something that had to be controlled by men who were 'non-contested whites'.[77]

Greeks and Italians shared a social position on the fringes of the settler society. British prejudices about their supposedly Mediterranean temperament and lasciviousness might play a role as well. The presence of both communities in Tanganyika went back to the German colonial period, consisting mainly of impoverished peasants who had initially come as railway contractors.[78] While a few Greeks became rich after the transition to British rule,[79] the majority of them remained rather marginal, working on farms or owning small shops.[80] There were more cases of Polish–Italian relationships, perhaps due to their comparable social position and their common faith, but also to the fact that the Poles were mainly women, while most Italians were men. All Italians were interned at the outbreak of the war, and there were furthermore camps for Italian POWs from the war in Ethiopia.

Some cases from the files may serve to highlight the ambivalent racial position that some officials ascribed to Italian men. In Southern Rhodesia, two Polish women escaped with Italian men to the neighbouring Portuguese colony of Mozambique, only to be returned after a month through the British consul.[81] A Swiss farmer who employed Italian parolees and Polish women near Tengeru had to assure the British authorities that he had accommodated them at a fair distance from each other and that he prevented any 'social intercourse'.[82] The Kenyan official Reginald Caldwell complained at length about refugees and their conduct in Nairobi, citing some individual cases.

Among others, he mentioned one Polish woman who intended to marry an Italian called Eulisse Conti, adding: 'If Mr Conti is going to entertain her in the Oriental rather than the British way of life, the grave social problems so frequently referred to will surely materialize'.[83] When, during the war, Italian POWs were released on parole to take up employment in Kenya, there were concerns that they might pose a threat to lone white women.[84] While there were no such concerns about a threat posed by single British men, the Italians' position on the edge of white society becomes apparent. It seemed uncertain if they were leading 'oriental' or 'British' lives; their behaviour was more important than any physical characteristics.

At the Kenyan school settlement Rongai, concerns over Polish–Italian contacts were pronounced as well. The camp had been built by Italian POWs in late 1944, and some of them were accommodated next to it. In April 1945, Karol Sander, the Polish leader of the settlement, informed Camp Commandant Williams about what he had experienced during his nightly inspection of the settlement.[85] Sander found some Italians standing at the windows and talking to the Polish women inside. As soon as they noticed him, they all ran away, and neither he nor the camp policemen could catch them. Some weeks later, Williams sent an angry letter to Sander complaining about the 'regrettable tendency towards fraternizing with the Italian Evacuees' and ordered him to instruct the Poles to stop any interaction with the Italians.[86] Although it was already two weeks after the war had ended in Europe, Williams surprisingly reminded him that the Italians belonged to one of the Axis nations. Months later, Polish officials from Nairobi came for an inspection of Rongai and recommended the removal of nine Polish women (and their sons), who had been in constant and close contact with Italians. Without detailing the form of 'contacts', the officials suggested that all Italian workers should leave the camp, as they 'would cause constantly some troubles with the female refugees, which have a very bad influence on the school-youth'.[87] They proposed to replace the Italian workers with Polish specialists.

The Gendered Problem of Miscegenation

White women and poor whites were the categories of people that defined and threatened the boundaries of (male) European prestige and control.[88] In colonial settler societies, women were seen as the carriers of white culture and thus had to be protected by white men. As Stoler puts it, 'as white women were made custodians of a distinct cultural and moral community, the protection of their honour became an issue with which all European men could agree and affirm their unity rather than their differences'.[89]

The other side of the stabilizing role of white women as custodians of the community was the 'black peril' discourse that surfaced in Britain and the Empire in the interwar period. Going back to the participation of black soldiers in the First World War, relationships of black men with white women were perceived as a sexual danger which connoted a political danger for white hegemony.[90] In the settler societies of Southern Rhodesia and Kenya, the fear that black men might rape white women was one of the chief anxieties, in spite of the virtual absence of actual cases.[91] This prevalent fear served to close the ranks and foster solidarity within the settler communities. To keep the perceived danger in check, elaborate social boundaries between Europeans and Africans were drawn and kept up. White newcomers who were unfamiliar with these rules were regarded by some as a threat, and therefore blamed for a supposed increase in black peril cases.[92] It was thus not only the fear of the colonized men that lay behind the 'black peril' scare but also the threat that white women might damage white prestige and the assumed moral superiority. The 'black peril' helped to keep the distance between colonizer and colonized, and served as an argument to keep independent white women under control.

At the same time, it would be short-sighted to assume the same role for the Polish women as seems to have held true for British women in the colonies. The discrimination against non-British whites in Southern Rhodesia and the British protest against the allegedly favourable treatment of Poles and Italians vis-à-vis 'Britishers' in Tanganyika point to such a differentiation.[93] Around the turn of the century, concerns had been voiced about British motherhood and the falling birth rate in Britain. The fear was that other whites would fill the places in the British Empire unless national reproduction gained momentum.[94] To tackle this threat, one imperial philanthropist even started a scheme in the interwar period to send British children to Southern Rhodesia.[95] Thus whites of other nationalities were regarded not only as part of the same racial group but also as belonging to potentially competing nations. The Polish refugees were perceived as being members of the same race but another nationality.

Before the arrival of the Polish refugees there was some discussion in Southern Rhodesia as to whether to fence in Marandellas camp. One International Red Cross representative argued for the erection of a fence, and explicitly referred to the loose sexual morals of East European women and the possibility that they might have intercourse with African men.[96] The same concern was addressed in Northern Rhodesia by the Lusaka Women's Institute, led by the wife of a Methodist minister. Some Polish women in Lusaka camp, it was believed, not only provided sexual services to white soldiers, but openly solicited African men.[97] In a related way, the executive council of the Federation of Women's Institutes of Southern Rhodesia complained about the lack of a fence around Marandellas, arguing in a memorandum that the refugees were women from the 'peasant class' and therefore 'they have not had the opportunity to sublimate, through intellectual interests, certain natural instincts'.[98] The perceived danger was averted by the eviction of the Africans who had been living next to the Polish camp.

Sexual promiscuity was seen not only as a character trait of East European women, but also of Africans and the lower classes in Britain. Contemporary British observers explained this as an effect of 'overcrowding' in African villages as well as in European city slums.[99] Allegedly, having a whole family sharing one room would lead to unconstrained sexuality. The women who formed the welfare organizations were almost exclusively from the British upper class, and their concern over the Polish women's sexuality was clearly class-based. While the stated reason for the fence was the prevention of intercourse between Polish women and African men, some have also suggested that white women feared contacts of these unrestrained lower-class women with their own men.[100] Either way, it was the combination of low class background, whiteness and femininity that made them suspicious.

The white women's agitation was related to the 'black peril' panic in yet another sense. The federation warned against the 'effect upon the Natives of seeing white women and children living under these conditions', and the consequent 'bad effect on our prestige'.[101] In Northern Rhodesia as well, women's organizations argued that the immoral behaviour of the Polish women might be 'undermining the respect due by Africans to all European women'.[102] Behind these concerns was the fear that the lowering of white women's prestige through some of them might directly threaten the security of all white women. The underlying assumption was that the sexual appetite of black men could only be held in check through strict adherence to social and physical distance. If marginal white women lowered this distance, all white women were supposedly in danger of sexual molestation by black men.[103] Although the actual danger of sexual assault was low, 'the anxiety itself was real enough', and it seems to have driven the women of Marandellas to demand stronger segregation of the Polish women.[104]

From a male colonial perspective, the Polish women were problematic in related but different ways. Their allegedly unconstrained sexuality and lack of distance vis-à-vis the colonized posed a general threat to the difference between white and black, and thus to the core of colonial hierarchization. As white women were regarded as the carriers of white culture, the issue of sexual relations between white women and black men posed a larger threat to the image of white superiority than relations between white men and black women. In the logic of patriarchy, *taking* the women of the other is something different from having one's women *taken* by other men. Women as the symbolic embodiment of the national boundary were also seen as the weakest point in the defence of it.[105] According to Fischer-Tiné, 'women were generally regarded as the weakest link in the coloniser's chain and had accordingly to be protected by diligently isolating them from the "degrading" contacts with native society'.[106]

Sexual relations between male colonizers and colonized women had, at the time of the European conquest, been regarded as a natural necessity. Until the mid-nineteenth century, British administrators in India argued that such relations helped to keep the men virile and heterosexual in the absence of white women.[107] In West Africa before formal colonial rule, relations between European men and African women formed an integral feature of economic and political networks.[108] These relations became problematized only with the gradual formalization of colonial rule and the emergence of a mixed-race community that threatened to blur the boundaries between black and white. As discourses do not tend to disappear at once, and late colonial society was still dominated by men, there was still a perceived difference between interracial sexual contacts, depending on the gendered composition of the population involved. White women who had sexual contacts with African men were considered as degenerate, unnatural or insane.[109] In Southern Rhodesia, the cohabitation of white women with black men was outlawed as early as 1903. By contrast, the attempts by Rhodesian women's organizations to pass similar legislation for the opposite case (white men and black women) were repeatedly repelled by the male-dominated Legislative Council.[110]

As Wendy Webster points out, there was a gradual shift in British self-perceptions that developed around the period of the Second World War.[111] The colonial world before the war was generally represented as a masculine domain of conquest, adventure and bravery, where European men filled the 'virgin land'.[112] In the postwar era, this self-perception changed and the images of empire were dominated by notions of a besieged, domestic world threatened by black men, in the colonies as well as in Britain.[113] The threat of miscegenation that allegedly undermined British identity was described in a gendered form where the relationships between black men and white women were seen as the prime problem.[114] There still existed thus the gendered evaluation of miscegenation observed already in colonial India in the early twentieth century: 'the fear that the colonized could sexually "possess" white women'.[115]

A contrasting case, in which a Polish man and an African woman had sex, may serve to highlight the importance of the gendered composition of interracial relationships. In 1952, when there were only a handful of Poles remaining in Tanganyika in the former camp of Tengeru, the chief conservation officer, who was now in charge of the institution set up on the premises, complained that he had found a Polish man in an 'intimate relationship with the wife of one of our field mechanics'.[116] He used this as an argument to press for the removal of the last Poles from the area, seeing the problem mainly as one that could damage relations between the men involved. He went on: 'I am not concerned with the morals of the refugees in any way, but such incidents, when my own staff are involved, cause a great deal of trouble and of course do not further an amiable racial relationship between the males concerned, however amiable the relationship between the opposite sexes may have been'.[117]

The officer explained, apparently with regret, that he could not accuse the Polish man of anything more than being inside closed premises after 6 PM without the permission of the owner. What remains remarkable is that a relationship between a man and a woman only became an issue because it disturbed the relations between the men and thus affected the smooth operation of the Soil Department. As there were no white women involved, this incident did not really threaten the moral integrity of the white community. It was, rather, a nuisance for the already difficult 'racial relationship' – a hint at the growing anti-colonial movement in East Africa.

Relations between Polish women and African men were seen as a bigger problem. In February 1944 two Polish women were sent from the Ugandan camp Koja to Makindu because they had had sex with African policemen. The camp commandant described their act as having a bad effect on the local Africans.[118] In the surroundings of Koja there was even a rumour that children from relationships between refugee women and African workers had been killed in the camp hospital.[119] While it is not clear what actually happened, it remains to be noted that there are strikingly few descendants of intimate Polish–African relationships.[120] Rennie Bere, camp commandant of Koja in 1943, noted in retrospect: 'Some of the girls had affairs with local Africans. But not many; and I cannot recollect a single case of either an illegitimate half-caste baby or of venereal disease'.[121] Bere's connection of 'illegitimate half-caste' babies and venereal disease speaks volumes. Afro-European children were pseudo-scientifically dismissed as degenerate and inheriting the worst of both parents.[122] Around the refugee camps, the perceived threat of a sizeable mixed population seems to have been avoided – a population whose existence posed a threat to 'the Manichean categories of ruler and ruled'.[123]

The refugee women were nevertheless in everyday contact with African men. Not only could the Poles freely move around the vicinity of the camps, but numerous Africans were employed in the camps as well. They did most of the hard, manual labour that was not seen as suitable for Europeans, and women in particular.[124] There was a clear conflict between the aims of racial segregation, the gendered division of labour and the need for cheap African workers. To limit the possibilities of interaction between (male) African workers and (female) Polish refugees, the movement of the former into the camp was controlled by the British administration.

At the time of their arrival, the refugees had often lived alongside the Africans who were still engaged in building the camps. In Kidugala in January 1943, for example, there was one African worker for every two refugees.[125] Later the same year the governor of Tanganyika visited some camps in the region and decided to exert firmer control over the movement of African workers.[126] The director of refugees ordered all camp commandants to tell their respective district commissioner the number of workers they needed and to issue passes for them. These measures were enforced by camp police stationed at the gates and checking all people entering. Although the above-mentioned examples show that there were always loopholes, the colonial government took efforts to control the women in the camps.

Polish–African relationships were a matter of concern not only to the colonial officials, but to Polish officials as well. In October 1944 the Polish authorities requested the Tanganyika government to pass legislation that marriage without prior consent from the Polish consul would be invalid. The stated reason for the proposal was 'the desire to do everything possible to prevent ill-considered marriages between Polish refugee women and persons of non-European descent, and also between such women and European residents of the territory who were known to the local British authorities to be persons of bad character and/or to possess insufficient means to maintain a wife and family'.[127]

While the proposed legislation was aiming to control Polish–African marriages, it becomes apparent that the Polish officials also considered marriages with other non-Europeans to be undesirable, and they actively tried to prevent them. In the case of marriages with European residents, they were only concerned if the prospective husband was known to be undesirable or poor. In any case, the Polish authorities wanted to have a say. While most territories passed legislation that required the local officials to seek consent from the Polish consul, the Tanganyika government was not allowed by the Colonial Office to follow suit.[128] Marriages involving Polish refugees were to be performed by Polish chaplains in the camp chapels only.[129] The Tanganyika authorities found another way to prevent undesired marriages. They advised the marriage officers (and ministers of religion) to request that the refugees obtain consent from the Polish consul. The officers were not legally in a position to hinder the conduct of otherwise lawful marriages, but the government official was confident that the refugees would follow the consul's advice.[130] The Polish administration thus secured an important way to intervene in the process.

The strategy apparently proved successful in neighbouring Kenya too. Roman Królikowksi, former Polish liaison officer in Nairobi, noted that in 1960 there were about sixty Polish women married to other Europeans (English, Italian or Greek). 'Fortunately there are no Negro husbands', he added.¹³¹ As the refugee population was overwhelmingly female, it remains open to speculation as to how the Polish officials would have reacted if Polish men had wanted to marry non-European women.

Apart from Africans and Europeans there were also Asian men in the colonial territories, especially in East Africa, who occupied an 'in-between' position socially. Relationships of Polish women with Indian, Seychellois or Muslim men were frowned upon by both British and Polish officials. Many Asians occupied a better socio-economic position than Africans. The Indian community could draw on long-established trade networks, and they had improved their economic position in the interwar period. In Tanganyika Indians worked in trade or the British civil service, or had taken over plantations from expelled German settlers.¹³² There were apparently some marriages of Polish women to wealthy Indian plantation owners in Tanganyika, especially after the war had ended.¹³³ One Polish woman in 1948 married an Indian 'in spite of every effort to dissuade her', as the governor noted.¹³⁴ In Southern Rhodesia two Polish women who were in relationships with Indian men were also included in the list of twelve 'undesirables' recommended for eventual deportation.¹³⁵ While their relationships were not the sole reason for their inclusion in the 'undesirable' category, this fact served as a further argument against them.

In October 1948, Genowefa Najman, a Polish refugee woman from Koja, converted to Islam in order to be able to marry 'a British subject of Muhammadan religion, Mr Muhamed Jusaf of Jinja'.¹³⁶ To conduct the marriage she converted on the day she married him, and changed her name to Nargis Mohamed. Through this move she gained the right to stay in Uganda, although she would have had the opportunity to go with the other Poles to the UK under the 'Operation Polejump' scheme. Her motives are not entirely clear, but she was the mother of an 'illegitimate' daughter, born in Koja in 1945. Less than one month before her marriage she was ordered to proceed through the Mombasa transit camp to Britain.¹³⁷ The hurried conversion and marriage seem to have been because she preferred to stay with her husband in Uganda instead of going as a single mother to an unknown country.¹³⁸ The colonial officials involved showed some unease concerning Genowefa's decision, as she had to personally show a document proving the legality of her marriage to the Ugandan director of refugees. For the religiously defined national group of Poles, she was however lost.

People from the Seychelles occupied a social position in East Africa that had some similarities with that of other Asians, but was less clear-cut. Their labour position was discussed in correspondence about the possible immigration of Seychellois to Tanganyika. Just like Indians, their labour was described by colonial officials as mainly 'semi-skilled'.¹³⁹ In a letter to the governor of the Seychelles, a Tanganyikan official explained that Seychellois men worked mainly as drivers or mechanics, while the women were mainly children's nurses or seamstresses. The official warned that Seychellois girls in Tanganyika were prone to prostitution if they were not proficient in English.[140]

The dislike for relationships between Polish women and Seychellois men becomes apparent in letters by Kenyan official Reginald Caldwell, who complained that the conduct of Anna Wosinska, a Polish girl employed by a Seychellois family in Nairobi, caused 'anxiety to the Polish Office'.[141] He described Wosinska as having a 'a bad influence over other girls employed in the neighbourhood'. Although her employers were satisfied with her conduct, Caldwell ordered her back to Tengeru camp, where her mother was living, 'supported by the fact that she now wishes to marry a Seychellois'. He went on: 'I understand her employer sees no reason why she should not, because he is a white Seychellois, whatever that may be'. Caldwell's dislike of Seychellois men and his perception of them as 'not quite white' is obvious. Nevertheless, Wosinska succeeded in marrying before she was sent back to Tengeru, leaving the Kenyan officials to note that nothing more could be done.[142] The ambiguous position of Seychellois immigrants becomes palpable in the qualification of one Seychellois employer as 'definitely dark' in a letter that was advising against her employment of a Polish woman.[143] In another instance, Caldwell succeeded in preventing the marriage of a Polish woman in Nairobi to a certain Mr Ayub, who had been charged with the murder of a European police officer. He noted that, 'after motherly advice from a Polish Office lady, she returned to camp'.[144] The opposition to relationships with Asians was supposedly shared by Polish elites as well: Caldwell wrote that 'the few cultured Poles' in Nairobi sympathized with his view that the unruly Polish girls had to be controlled.[145]

Prostitution

In the eyes of some colonial officials, one of the most dangerous groups among the Polish refugees were women who worked as prostitutes with African customers. In 1944 there was a series of incidents in Northern Rhodesia that finally led to the establishment of an isolated 'segregation camp' in Katambora. As shown earlier, the camp did not work out as expected, but the argumentation for its establishment is revealing.[146] Northern Rhodesia's governor Waddington explained the reason for setting up the camp in a confidential telegram to the Colonial Office in London.[147] He described a series of incidents in the refugee camp Bwana Mkubwa that made it necessary to isolate some of the 'unruly elements' among the Poles. He reported an 'affray' in the camp, in the course of which several people were stabbed, some criminals arrested, and four of them were sent to Kenya. But the most serious problem Waddington singled out was that some women who were practising prostitution with African men: 'One of the chief problems at the moment is the control of a number of prostitutes who were included among the evacuees. The suspicion that they were plying their trade among Africans has recently been confirmed. This is a very serious matter and might have most unpleasant repercussions.'[148]

The emphasis and dramatization of the sexual contact with Africans shows that it was considered as not only an issue of sexual morality, but as a threat to the race-based colonial order of society. This was not the only incident of prostitution among the Polish refugees. In Tanganyika another woman, described as a 'known prostitute', was 'associating with Italians, Asians and Africans' around Tengeru.[149] She was fined and imprisoned in the camp before being moved to another camp in Ifunda. In Kenya, some Polish women from Mombasa transit camp were reportedly active in prostitution with African men in the town.[150] Their behaviour led one Czech resident of Mombasa to send a complaint about five Polish women to the camp administration, arguing: 'As I am also a foreigner I feel it to be my duty to stop such degradation of European women freely prostituting themselves to Arabs, Indians and even natives, and destroying the last reputation of the Polish and foreign element in this country'.[151] Especially the public form of their prostitution concerned the writer.

Women classified as prostitutes were placed under the category of 'undesirables' in a report on the last remaining refugees and their migration prospects.[152] In a similar list from Southern Rhodesia, seven out of twelve 'undesirable' refugees were described as prostitutes.[153] Although their numbers were tiny in relation to the overall group of refugees, their activities were seen as problematic from the authorities' point of view. Prostitution of white women with black men in a colonial setting can be understood as a 'double transgression of gender as well as racial norms'.[154] These women were transgressing not only the boundaries of race, but of accepted gender roles as well. They did not stay in the domestic sphere, but acted against the standards of respectability.[155] Colonial administrators feared that this could damage the image of the supposedly morally superior Europeans in the eyes of the colonized.[156]

A strategy to deal with the moral threat of prostitution was the labelling of women as 'professional prostitutes', thereby externalizing them. This, and further descriptions of the Poles as generally different from the British, were attempted answers to the problem. Attributing their immoral practices to the generally loose sexual morals of East European women or the class of professional prostitutes left the moral superiority of the British intact. How accurate the description of women as 'professional' was remains unclear. It may well be that women who engaged in casual sexual relations with black men were called prostitutes in an attempt to distinguish them from the other women in the camps. According to Lwanga-Lunyiigo, the official assumption in Uganda was that every white woman having sex with a black man had to necessarily be a prostitute.[157] Apart from this, white prostitution in Southern Rhodesia had been practised earlier by non-British whites, coming mostly from Germany, France and Portugal. In light of the strong sexual imbalance, this measure helped to keep miscegenation in check without harming British national prestige.[158]

In Southern Rhodesia, one camp commandant argued that the Polish women should not work outside the camp, as they were unsophisticated and could get into trouble if meeting 'undesirable persons'.[159] The authorities further seem to have attempted to prevent young Polish women from being exploited or drifting into prostitution. In Iringa, the proprietor of the White House Inn was not allowed to employ a Polish woman as housekeeper. She was regarded as too young by the authorities and so he was instead ordered to replace her with another, more mature and experienced woman.[160] It is not clear what lay behind this order: it may have been an attempt to prevent a young woman from exploitation, or to restrict her attempts to make an independent living, or both.

As we have seen, relationships between Polish women and African men were unwanted by both Polish and colonial authorities. Relationships with Indian, Muslim or Seychellois men were unwanted as well, but less clearly contested. Sharing some similarities with the position of Italians, the ambivalent position of Seychellois made further clarification necessary. While in the case of the Italian man mentioned earlier these qualifications were in regard to his 'way of life', in regard to Seychellois the question of skin colour was mentioned. For Europeans in general, the only problem was poor men of 'bad character'. The abhorrence of interracial relationships was shared by Polish and colonial officials alike. In contrast to men on the fringes of whiteness, African men could not qualify as respectable partners for the women.

Another aspect of these cases is described by Will Jackson in his study on 'loose women' in colonial Kenya in the same period. While sexual relations between white women and black men were legally outlawed, Jackson shows that such instances were not taken to court, but rather tackled discretely. Especially after the Second World War, open racism was discredited and the colonial rhetoric shifted to development, welfare and 'multiracial partnership'.[161] While Kenyan settler society still disapproved of interracial relationships, these cases were not dealt with as openly as before. The most important means to bring women into line was the social pressure to conform exerted by neighbours, relatives and institutions. In Jackson's study, the white women were discretely sent to Britain or taken to a mental hospital so as to not cause a public scandal.

A public scandal that did rock the whole empire in 1948 was the marriage of Ruth Williams, a British woman, to Seretse Khama, heir to the kingship of the Bangwato in Bechuanaland Protectorate.[162] While liberals in London and many Africans supported the marriage, the neighbouring South African government, white settlers and some traditional leaders in Bechuanaland opposed this union vehemently. The fear of repercussions on the British relationship with the South African Union, but also the danger of alienating settlers in Southern Rhodesia and Kenya, induced the British government to ban Seretse from entering the protectorate. In discussions around the marriage it became apparent that, while the postwar period saw a gradual shift towards non-discrimination, this was met by vehement opposition to interracial relationships from settlers. In 1948 the newly elected nationalist government of South Africa implemented the infamous apartheid policy. This development was closely watched by many settlers in the British colonies. As David Anderson noted for the 1950s, the rise of anti-colonial movements saw a similar rise in white power.[163]

Transgressive refugee women could be discretely controlled. Officials tried to dissuade the women concerned, making it necessary for them to seek permission to marry from Polish officials. Living in supervised refugee camps further helped to keep deviant women in check. The attempted establishment of the Katambora segregation camp in a remotely situated area, and without much publicity, was another attempt to keep 'dangerous' women out of sight.

Dislocation as Opportunity: 'The Inferior Sex with the Superior Race'

As Margret Strobel has put it, white women in the British Empire were from the dominant viewpoint 'the inferior sex with the superior race'.[164] White women were in an ambivalent situation of dependency and power. Anne McClintock writes: 'The rationed privileges of race all too often put white women in positions of decided – if borrowed – power, not only over colonized women but also over colonized men'.[165] Moving to the colonies offered some white women the possibility to break out of the subordinate role in their patriarchal home societies and to lead a more independent, adventurous and unconventional life.[166] Yet while this might hold true for British upper-class women in the colonies, the position of the Polish refugee women was less clear. Although they were generally categorized as European and white, their nationality, lower-class background and non-permanent refugee status complicated the picture.

Like all white people in a colonial society based on racial differentiation, Polish women also enjoyed some privileges. They profited from what Harald

Fischer-Tiné has termed the 'racial dividend':[167] even the most marginalized whites profit from the fact that they are potentially regarded as white in a society based on racial differentiation, and thus enjoy at least some privileges vis-à-vis the black population. The Polish refugees were furthermore seen as allies during the war, and were thus treated better than the interned 'enemy aliens'.[168] They were relatively well accommodated, and lived according to standards that reinforced the difference between white and black, as the living conditions in the camps were generally better than those of many Africans outside.[169]

Moreover, the Polish women had gone through harsh conditions in the Soviet interior, usually without husbands, and those who survived must have been empowered and hardened by this experience. They did not easily fit the model of the subordinate woman cherished in patriarchal imagination. Like the women practising prostitution, they seemed to be self-confident individuals who could make their own way without husbands. Albeit unintended, these women threatened to undermine the patriarchal and racial order of their hosting colonial societies.

An example of the anxiety this caused colonial officials is found in a letter from Dr MacQuillan, the Medical Officer of Health in Arusha. He complained that a group of fifty Polish refugees from Tengeru had invaded the premises of a private European swimming club at the nearby Lake Duluti.[170] Although a printed notice in Polish had been put up that forbade their entry, they went for a swim. He wrote that 'one woman "gate crasher" was quite aggressively vocal in defence of her trespass upon private premises', evoking images of dangerous and self-confident Polish women. This incident is part of a longer letter, in which he complains about the health risk that the Polish refugees posed to the people living near the camp, and especially in Arusha town. He describes the Poles as lacking an awareness of public health and thus constituting a danger, especially for the European children who frequented the swimming club. MacQuillan's depiction of unruly, dirty and disease-carrying peasant women puts their respectability in question, and points rather to a class-based division.

In Northern Rhodesia, British officials looked critically at Polish women doing manual labour. One official explained the problem as follows: 'The sight of a European woman doing hard manual work such as hoeing gardens, carrying sacks of potatoes on their backs, etc. will be detrimental to the position of all European women'.[171] One Tanganyika official described the Polish women as 'strong', although he doubted there would be builders or tradesmen among them.[172] Hard-working women, including those who made bricks and pushed heavy wheelbarrows for the building of the Polish church in Masindi,[173] like the above-mentioned 'gate crasher', all defied the notion of weak women in need of male assistance.

In their Soviet exile the Polish women had been forced to work in traditionally male occupations like timber logging. These experiences of hard work without male company, horrible though they may have been, strengthened the survivors and may well have given them confidence in their self-reliance. As Janina Milek recalled after her resettlement from Tengeru to Australia: 'I could do all the work that a man could do'.[174] Milek had worked hard in Siberia and wanted to work in railway building in Australia, but despite her intentions she only found employment as a domestic worker. Like many other women in postwar Europe, she was ordered back into the domestic sphere in the Australia of the 1950s.

The image of the strong Polish woman relates to the way in which the gendered division of labour changed during both world wars.[175] For some of the female refugees, the special conditions during the war created new employment opportunities. About six hundred Polish refugees from the Middle East and Africa went to the UK to join the Women's Auxiliary Air Force.[176] During both world wars, many women moved out of the domestic sphere and started working in jobs that had been considered male domains in peacetime. Nevertheless, women's work continued to be regarded as inferior to men's work.[177] In Kenya, the British military had asked the East African Refugee Authority in 1943 if they could provide refugees to set up a 'Women's Auxiliary Squad' at the Royal Air Force (RAF) base in Nairobi.[178] Over eighty young Polish women between eighteen and twenty-five years old were recruited, and lived on a camp at the military base.[179] They had English lessons first, and then learned mechanics, communications, administration and typewriting later on. They were paid according to British military rates, which were comparatively high, and afterwards some found employment in clerical jobs in the military. About thirty of the Polish women married British airmen.[180] The group of young women must have been an attraction to the male soldiers at the RAF base, many of whom had been having sexual relations with African prostitutes.[181]

As in Nairobi, 130 young Polish women worked in the Southern Rhodesian Women's Auxiliary Air Service at the RAF stations in Thornhill and Heany.[182] In 1943 a 'Committee for the Employment of Polish Women Evacuees' was set up in order to release 'manpower for the front line'. Its task was to bring Polish women into employment in the air force and army canteens, radio communications and other military-related jobs.[183] During the war the colony was used as a training ground for the air force, resulting in an influx of thousands of military personnel. As these white men were 'unfamiliar with the strict rules that governed racial relations', many of them entered into relationships with African women, thereby causing concern to the established settler society.[184] The Northern Rhodesia director of refugees, Stewart Gore-Browne, preferred 'regular liaisons' between white soldiers and Polish women from the nearby camp to the 'troubles [that] might follow miscegenation'; yet such liaisons were criticized by a local white women's organization as 'prostitution'.[185] While the main reason for the Polish women's employment in the military camps was their much needed contribution to the war effort, it had the side effect of redirecting the white men's sexual desires towards white women, and this was unofficially welcomed.

Apart from making a direct contribution to the war effort, the Polish refugees worked in other fields as well. After an initial phase when the camps were being set up and their internal administration was staffed by Polish and other workers, some refugees were made available for the job market outside the camps. Prospective employers had to apply to British officials for permission. The authorities then checked the suitability of the employer, and the Polish camp leader had the task of picking the right candidate from among those refugees willing to be employed.[186] In a press communiqué that announced the availability of Polish and Greek refugees for employment, it was mentioned that they were mainly women and children and thus the preferred employment would be as 'nursemaids'.[187] As the male refugees were few, old and/or unfit, and were furthermore needed for the staffing of the camps, one official in Tanganyika stated that there were no refugees available for employment in male jobs, such as that of 'estate assistant'.[188]

Although not as clearly linked as the military jobs, employment as 'nursemaids' had a background in the war conditions as well. As early as 1942, calls were made by Kenyan settlers to be allowed to employ European refugee women on white-owned farms. One writer to the *East African Standard* complained that some settler women were alone on their farms, as their men were serving in the army, while many refugee families were sitting idle. He proposed that refugee daughters past school age should help in settler households, and that refugee sons should fight in the army.[189] In the other colonies as well, Polish women were sought by European families for domestic work in their households.[190] In Kenya, many young Polish women were employed as 'nanny-companions' in European households. The term suggests that they were not only supposed to nurse the children but to provide the settler women with company as well.

Behind these suggestions lurked most probably the idea, once again, of white women being especially vulnerable to the threat of black men. Placing another white woman on a farm was maybe not considered as safe as the presence of a white man, but it could help a bit – safeguarding against the assumed danger posed by black men and against too close an interaction with black servants. The change in attitude from wartime to the postwar era becomes clear in a 1947 letter of Reginald Caldwell, the Kenyan Director of Aliens, Internees and War Refugees.[191] He explained that the idea of admitting Polish women into Kenya from the camps in Uganda and Tanganyika had been good during wartime, when the men were in the army and thus European women were alone on the farms. But according to Caldwell, these exceptional conditions had long passed, and although he still received many applications for Polish nannies, he had ceased to issue permissions to enter Kenya.[192] He furthermore complained that the Polish women were 'infiltrating' Nairobi after their employment on European farms had ended.

During the war, Polish nannies had also seemed to counteract the prevalent fear of a bad influence and medical threat posed by black nannies. In the interwar period there was an ongoing discussion in Kenya's settler society about the need to regulate the employment of African 'ayahs' (nannies) to minimize the threat of sexual crime at the hands of domestic servants, and the transmission of diseases to European children.[193] During the war years, the fact that more European women were working outside the home for the war effort, led some in their community to fear that the close contact between black nannies and white children could lead to 'social rottenness' in the next generation.[194] The cheap white labour force of Polish women was a welcome answer to this threat – giving settler women the possibility to contribute to the war economy while safeguarding their children at home. When the men returned after the war, however, the women were expected to return to the domestic sphere.

In Northern Rhodesia the situation was comparable. Domestic servants in the colony were mainly African men, but there was a strong demand for white women servants as well.[195] But Polish women in Northern Rhodesia had a reputation for loose sexual mores and a willingness to perform hard manual labour.[196] In the memoirs of a former Northern Rhodesian district officer, the connection between domestic work and the social advancement of his wife becomes apparent. He remembered that she 'was able to get a Polish nanny from a refugee camp and was then able to get herself a job as … a business manager'.[197] She herself reminisced that she had felt free, as someone was looking after her small child.[198] As elsewhere in the world, the domestic work by migrant women opened up possibilities for more privileged women to enter into the male-dominated labour world.[199]

Even in the subordinate role of domestic worker, Polish women enjoyed some privileges of whiteness. One refugee woman who had worked in European households in Southern Rhodesia remembered: 'Having black servants to do the housework, I did not have to perform physical tasks. My role was to supervise'.[200] Although she was not happy with her employment and considered it degrading and lonely, she was, due to the colonial division of labour, clearly in a commanding position.

Thus, young Polish women provided an answer to some of the social and labour problems of colonial settler societies. As nannies they helped to reduce the influence of Africans on the lives of European children and lone women. For the military the women served not only in vital auxiliary tasks to keep the war machine running, but at times also as preferential partners for white soldiers. These young women became a problem, however, when they moved away from the confines of a respectable European household or military barracks. The fact that some women independently moved to Nairobi or married against the will of Polish and colonial officials alike shows their initiative and determination to go their own ways. They profited from the gendered and racialized division of labour and society, but some also made choices that contradicted the colonial social order. Having gone through hardships, these women opened up possibilities that led them far away from their pre-deportation role as peasant wives in peripheral eastern Poland.

But the racially differentiated labour market also put constraints on the possibilities of employment for whites. While the Poles were valued as cheap labour by some employers, others feared the blurring of social boundaries and the creation of a poor white population. The willingness of some Poles to take jobs below the 'European standard' was seen as a problem by some British officials in Southern Rhodesia.[201] In a 1950 meeting in London concerning the future of Polish refugees in East Africa and Lebanon, one Colonial Office official pointed out that some of them might find employment in the UK, as they were 'unemployable for racial reasons in East Africa or Lebanon'.[202] Europeans in the colonies could not work under conditions that were regarded as perfectly normal in Europe. For the Polish refugee the privilege of whiteness at the same time limited the options for residence. While this policy enabled some Poles to avoid menial jobs, it also prevented many from finding any employment at all. The 'three-D' sector ('dirty, dangerous, demeaning')[203] that often provides a niche for labour migrants was closed to white refugees in colonial societies.

Some three hundred Polish women also gained permanent residence through marriage to local men. Although these marriages must be seen in the light of general dependency and inequality, the women nevertheless made choices and opened up opportunities for themselves. As Doris Lessing wrote about Southern Rhodesia in her novel *Landlocked*: 'After all, this was a country where women could pick and choose'.[204] The IRO was aware that some women only married to gain residency, and it tried to prevent this.[205] But it did not succeed in preventing marriages of convenience completely. Mr Rubin from Kenya reportedly complained about 'matrimonial difficulties' with his Polish wife, claiming that he had married only to facilitate her entry into the colony. When his sister-in-law wanted to join the couple, he was against it. The Kenyan official Caldwell remarked that Rubin would go insane if she succeeded in moving in.[206] Such women were no passive victims of patriarchal control.

Gendering the Refugees • 159

Figure 4.3. Young Polish women and Ugandan men on a boat trip on Lake Victoria next to Koja camp, Uganda, 1943. From Archiwum Fotografii Ośrodka KARTA, Signature: OK_1836_039, online.

Even in the supervised and disciplinary space of the camp, young Polish women created uncontrolled and unsupervised spaces. One of them remembered there was strong competition among the girls for the few teenage boys in the camp. The main street in Masindi settlement, known as 'Do whatever you like' street at night, served as a meeting place for sweethearts, because the supervision of the priests and teachers did not reach there.[207] In Digglefold the absence of boys led the girls to dance with each other on Sunday afternoons, thereby creating their own spaces of exchange and entertainment without conforming to ascribed gender roles.[208]

Not only 'Womenandchildren'

Discussing the relationship between gender, nation and war, Nira Yuval-Davis writes: 'Wars are seen to be fought for the sake of the "womenandchildren", and the fighting men are comforted and reassured by the knowledge that "their women" are keeping the hearth fires going and are waiting for them to come home'.[209] The one-word phrase 'womenandchildren' was coined by Cynthia Enloe and describes an understanding of women and children as passive, indistinguishable victims.[210] The Polish refugee women were not waiting at home, but the British government and the Polish government-in-exile in London evidently saw the necessity of providing them with a safe wartime home in order to keep up the morale of the Polish soldiers. It was furthermore necessary to assure the Polish soldiers that these women were still 'their' women.

As shown above, Polish refugee women were in a situation of dependency vis-à-vis their male relatives and compatriots. The colonial administration would never have hosted them if it had not been for Britain's interest in the Polish soldiers fighting with the Allies against Nazi Germany. On a conceptual level, the construction of women as dependents of men is part of gendered discourses of national belonging. Women are central to the reproduction of any community (symbolically, but also physically through bearing children). This central role in the construction of nations makes women stabilizers of communities. In our case, however, the position of the Polish women is not entirely clear. For the male-dominated Polish administration the women were – owing to their Polishness – clearly part of the nation-in-exile. On the other hand, for white settlers, these women could – owing to their whiteness – potentially become part of their community.

The central role of women in the construction of the male-dominated community made these women potentially dangerous if they did not fulfil that role. Women who crossed the social boundaries of race caused concern to Polish and British officials alike. For the Poles, their transgression robbed the Polish nation-in-exile of some members; for the colonial administration they damaged the image and prestige of the white population. While relationships of white men with black women were unwanted, the opposite combination was considered far worse. As white women were central to the stability of the community, their conduct had to be controlled. White settler women likewise condemned relations between Polish women and African men, as these threatened their distanced and superior position vis-à-vis the colonized. But Polish refugee women were also actors in their own right.

Understood as actors and not mere victims or objects of male interest, the Polish refugee women were strong and independent, and made the most of their involuntary journey. They cared for their children, took up such employment as circumstances offered, and travelled around half of the globe. While most Polish women eventually married Polish men or reunited with their husbands, a few chose to marry men who were neither Polish nor British. Either to gain access to residency or because of affection, they deliberately chose to ignore their prescribed roles.

The gender composition of the Polish refugee community set it apart from the male-dominated colonial community. Although there were nearly as many white women as white men in late colonial societies, the public sphere was dominated by men. In the perspective of the colonizers, white women were the custodians of white culture and had to be protected against the threat of black men. Protecting the women was at the same time protecting their own identity: 'The management of sexuality, parenting, and morality was at the heart of the late imperial project'.[211]

For the British authorities it was a matter of taking care of, and protecting, the women and children of the allied men who were fighting in the war. But to do that involved controlling and manifesting gender differences and hierarchies. As in all patriarchal societies, the protection and control of women went hand in hand. Against the background of a racially structured hierarchical society that was feeling more and more besieged, this protection/control was even more important.

To tackle the threat that the huge number of white women posed to the image of white moral superiority, the British administrators followed two strategies. First and foremost was the seclusion of the Polish refugees in camps and the attempt to minimize their interaction with the colonized, although this was restricted by the fact that they were regarded as allies and thus enjoyed some freedom. They were controlled through male camp authorities and sanctioned if they crossed the boundaries of race. Secondly, there was the strategy of externalizing the Poles in general, but specifically in certain problematic segments, such as women who entered interracial relationships or worked as prostitutes. To understand the Poles as 'other' (and inferior) left the image of the distinct and superior 'British race' intact.

Isolating the Poles completely was not viable, however. As in all colonial societies, a complete segregation was economically impossible. African labour was as essential to the running of the colonial economy as to the running of the refugee camps. In contrast to the British settler households, the difference between other European inhabitants and African workers was easier to maintain in the controlled and organized environment of the camp. Its hierarchical organization, labour supervision and entrance controls on African workers helped to reduce intimacy between white and black. The creation of a separate Polish milieu was largely successful. For women who had arrived with images of a wild and dangerous continent in their mind, the creation of a Polish community was reassuring. After what had been experienced in the Soviet Union, the more familiar surroundings of Polish settlements in Africa were not only enforced by the administrators, but deliberately created by many of the women.

Following these last three chapters on different socially relevant aspects of the refugee group, the next chapter will consider three perspectives on the Poles' position within their hosting colonial societies: the perspective of the British administrators and settlers, Polish self-identifications, and African perspectives on the refugees.

Notes

1. Jhaveri was born in 1931 on Pemba Island, and grew up in Dar es Salaam. Her parents had arrived in the 1920s from Gujarat.
2. Taylor, *Polish Orphans*, 55.
3. For the Southern Rhodesian example, see Kennedy, *Islands of White*, 36, 178; Mlambo, *History of Zimbabwe*, 81.
4. See Ray, 'Interracial Sex', 10; Stoler, 'Making Empire Respectable', 651; Hyam, 'Concubinage'.
5. For examples and a critique of this view, see Callaway, *Gender, Culture and Empire*, 3–4; Strobel, *European Women*, 1–2.
6. See Callaway, *Gender, Culture and Empire*.
7. Haggis, 'Gendering Colonialism'.
8. Strobel, *European Women*; McClintock, *Imperial Leather*, 6.
9. See Callan and Ardener, *The Incorporated Wife*. This discussion is taken up for a contemporary example by Fechter, 'Gender, Empire, Global Capitalism'.
10. Stoler, 'Rethinking Colonial Categories'.
11. See Levine, 'Venereal Disease, Prostitution'; Tambe, 'The Elusive Ingénue'.
12. Jolluck, *Exile and Identity*, 140.
13. Blobaum, 'The "Woman Question"', 814; Burrell, 'Male and Female Polishness', 76; Fidelis, 'Equality through Protection', 308.
14. Jolluck, *Exile and Identity*, 285.
15. Yuval-Davis, *Gender and Nation*, 2.
16. On the nexus of motherhood, nation and empire in the British example, see Davin, 'Imperialism and Motherhood'.
17. Pittaway and Bartolomei, 'Refugees, Race, and Gender'.
18. For an overview of gender in migration studies, see Donato et al., 'A Glass Half Full?' For a review of historical perspectives on the same issue, see Sinke, 'Gender and Migration'.
19. Nearly half of the men were over 50 years old (MSS Afr. s. 1366/9, p.181, 'East African Refugee Administration. Camp Total for all East African Territories', n.d. [1945]).
20. My calculation from numbers at the end of 1944 in PISM: Kol 18/2, 'Stan liczbowy Uchodzcow Polskich w Afryce na 31.XII.1944'.
21. Both quotes are from interviews with former refugees. Cited in Allbrook and Cattalini, *The General Langfitt Story*, n.p.; and Burrell, 'Male and Female Polishness', 76.
22. TNA: 69/782/IV, Pennington, for Director for Aliens and Internees to Camp Commandants Tengeru, Kondoa, Ifunda, 11.06.43; TNA: W3/31299, p.10, Winnington-Ingram for Commissioner of Aliens and Internees to Chief Secretary, DSM, 3.05.43.
23. The Tengeru Women Supervisor earned 240 pounds a year (TNA: W3/31299, p.1, 3.05.43). The camp commandant of the much smaller Rongai settlement got 720 pounds a year (KNA: AH/1/49, p.32B, 'Rongai detailed Estimates for 1945' attached to Ag. Director of Aliens and Internees to Chief Secretary, 21.04.45). The Director of War Evacuees and Refugees in Northern Rhodesia got 1,000 pounds a year (Rotberg, *Black Heart*, 236). And even a quartermaster in Northern Rhodesia received at least 360 pounds (KNA: AH/20/145 p.1, Director of Refugees, Lusaka to Commissioner EARA, 04.11.44).
24. They collected, for example, toys for the Polish children (TNA 69/782/4, Elsa Bonavia, Chairman Women's Service League, Tanga to Camp Commandant, Tengeru, 27.10.42).

25. TNA 69/782/1, p.31, Voucher, transport escort of Polish refugees from Tanga, 24.12.42.
26. Macoun, *Wrong Place, Right Time*, 21. MSS Afr. s. 705, 'Welcome to Polish refugees', newspaper clippings of Charles M.A. Gayer, date and title of publication missing [most likely *East African Standard* in 1942].
27. Levine, *The British Empire*, 149. For male domination in the Southern Rhodesian administration, see McCulloch, *Black Peril, White Virtue*, 86. For Nigeria, see Callaway, *Gender, Culture and Empire*.
28. TNA: 69/782/4, Camp Commandant Tengeru to Provincial Commissioner, Arusha, 13.06.45.
29. I have no complete statistics of the Polish school headmasters. In the documents I only came across one female 'head teacher' in Koja (NP 1.07.46, p.17, 'Treci Maja w Koji' by J.W.).
30. This does not imply that Polish women played no role in the fight against Nazi Germany. But for the strategists the most important issue was the male soldiers. For the predominantly female Polish Auxiliary Air Force and the Polish Independent Women's Battalion, see Cottam in Cook, *Women and War*, 473–76. Some young single women had entered the Polish army already during its reformation in the Soviet Union (Chappell and Milek, *Persian Blanket*, 128).
31. For the British context, see Webster, 'Britain and the Refugees', 36.
32. See Zins, *Poles in Zambezi*, 73; EAS 17.08.42, 'Powerful Polish Army'.
33. EAS 03.07.42, 'Polish Refugees from Persia', p.14.
34. Cited in Zins, *Poles in Zambezi*, 67.
35. TNA: W3/ 31798, p.3, F.A. Montague, Ag. Chief Secretary to the Government to the Editor, East African Standard, 31.12.43.
36. Porajska, *From the Steppes*, 121.
37. Krolikowski, *Stolen Childhood*, 115.
38. Romanko, 'From Russian Gulag', Chapter IX, n.p.
39. GP 14.10.45 'Z Osiedli', p.10.
40. For the discussion on the admittance of Polish ex-soldiers to the UK after the war, see Sword, 'Their Prospects Will Not Be Bright', 368–71.
41. TNA K2/38647, p.7, J.W. O'Brien, for Ag. Undersecretary of State for External Affairs, Ottawa, Canada to Secretary Tanganyika, 3.12.48.
42. Burrell, 'Male and Female Polishness', 76.
43. Jaroszyńska-Kirchmann, *Exile Mission*, 1. See also chapter 5.
44. Krolikowski, *Stolen Childhood*, 108.
45. Ibid. Another Polish official argued instead that the discipline problems with the youth in Rongai stemmed from the school's focus on intellectual education, and a consequent lack of vocational training (NP 15.09.47, 'O Problemach Wychowawczych na Uchodztwie slow kilka' by Jerzy Dolega-Kowalewski).
46. Krolikowski, *Stolen Childhood*, 114.
47. Wójcik, 'Introduction to Chapter 6 Africa', 139; TNA: 69/782/IV, 'History of Tengeru Camp' written by Miss Jowitt, attached to a letter of Camp Commandant Tengeru to EARA Nairobi, 6.11.43.
48. Krolikowski, *Stolen Childhood*, 126.
49. Generally the scouting organizations around the world differ very much in outlook, content and aims. During the war the Polish scouts (most prominently the Gray Ranks or 'Szary Szeregi') took over an important role in the armed resistance against the German occupation. For an interesting analysis of the African scouting

movement in a British colonial setting, see Parsons, *Race, Resistance, and the Boy Scout Movement*.
50. Teresa Rogińska-Slomińska in Piotrowski, *Polish Deportees*, 148.
51. Porajska, *From the Steppes*, 126.
52. From a psychological viewpoint, this community building in 'Little Poland' further served to emotionally stabilize the traumatized refugees (Evert, 'War Experiences', 381).
53. Wróbel, *Uchodźcy polscy*, 152.
54. Burrell, *Moving Lives*, 51.
55. Porajska, *From the Steppes*, 131.
56. Irena Paszkiewiczówna married Shannon Grills, the commandant of Bwana Mkubwa camp (PISM: Kol 147/11, 'Kronika – Afryka Rodezja Północna – Polskie osiedla uchodźce', n.d.).
57. 17-year-old Jadwiga Kuklis is an obvious example (TNA 69/782/IV, p.860, Camp Commandant, Tengeru to PC Northern, 31.08.49).
58. Quoted in Tavuyanago, Muguti and Hlongwana, 'Victims', 962.
59. According to an IRO report from early 1949, 276 Poles were 'resettled by marriage' in the following territories (without specifying more about the couples): Kenya 4; Uganda 53; Tanganyika 76; Northern Rhodesia 92; Southern Rhodesia 51 (IRO: AJ/43/790/55/2, 'Refugees Remaining in Africa', Curtis to IRO HQ, p.4, 9.02.49). According to Królikowski, two hundred Polish women married foreigners, while Holborn writes of over three hundred (Królikowski, 'Operation Polejump', 186; Holborn, *International Refugee Organization*, 421).
60. While more than half of the women were married, less than one thousand lived together with their husband in the camps (own calculation from MSS Afr. s. 1366/9, p.181, 'East African Refugee Administration. Camp Total for all East African Territories', n.d. [1945]).
61. IRO: AJ/43/790/55/2, R. Caldwell, Director of Aliens and Internees to Curtis, IRO Nairobi, p.3, 15.04.48.
62. Final report of IRO East Africa representative Curtis, cited in Lush, *A Life of Service*, 256.
63. The final outcome of this case is not found in the records (PRO: CO 822/146/1, Personal Summary, Janina Christie, attached to Beryl Hughes, Home Office, London to Dawson, Colonial Office, 9.11.50).
64. PRO: CO 822/350, Governor Uganda to Secretary of State for the Colonies, London, 9.07.51.
65. Stoler, 'Rethinking Colonial Categories', 149.
66. Ibid., 150; Kennedy, *Islands of White*, 116.
67. Stoler, 'Rethinking Colonial Categories', 154.
68. Stoler, 'Carnal Knowledge', 53.
69. TNA: 176/87, p.12, S.A. Walden, DC Iringa to PC Southern Highlands Province, Mbeya, 13.04.46.
70. TNA: 176/87, p.12C, J. Matheson, for Commissioner of Police, Intelligence and Security Bureau, DSM to Messrs Unga Ltd., Iringa, 26.03.46; C.E. Hallam, Branch Manager, Unga Ltd., Iringa to DC Iringa, 3.04.46.
71. TNA: 176/87, p.12, Walden, DC Iringa to PC Southern Highlands Province, Mbeya, 13.04.46.
72. MSS Afr. s. 116, Report 'Camp Ifunda' by Russel R. Johnston, American Red Cross, 27.01.44.

73. TNA: 176/87, p.12B, Walden, DC Iringa to Lt. Col. N. Stewart, Ag. Commissioner of Police, DSM, 18.02.46.
74. Warach, *Hope*, 153–54.
75. TNA: 176/87, p.18, PC Southern Highlands Province, Mbeya to Pennington, Director of Refugees, DSM, 2.05.46.
76. TNA: 176/87, p.12B, Walden, DC Iringa to Lt. Col. N. Stewart, Ag. Commissioner of Police, DSM, 18.02.46.
77. I borrowed the term from Vargas, 'Off White'.
78. Iliffe, *Modern History of Tanganyika*, 142.
79. Ibid., 264.
80. Their marginal position is apparent in the unfavourable portrayal of them by a British settler in Tanganyika (Reid, *Tanganyika without Prejudice*, 142f). The position of Greek shopkeepers in Northern and Southern Rhodesia seems to have been comparable to Asians (Shurmer-Smith, *Remnants of Empire*, 52, 54f; Shutt, *Manners Make a Nation*, 11.).
81. MSS Afr. s. 1366/9, p.137, 'Undesirable Polish Refugees', Camp Commandant Marandellas to Director of Refugees, Salisbury, 15.01.47.
82. TNA: 69 /782/3, p.15, District Commissioner Arusha to Camp Commandant Tengeru, 12.08.43.
83. IRO: AJ/43/790/55/2, R. Caldwell, Director of Aliens and Internees to Curtis, IRO Nairobi, p.2, 15.04.48.
84. Fedorowich and Moore, *British Empire*, 51.
85. PRO: ED 128/107, Karol Sander, Polish Camp Leader Rongai to E.R.C. Williams, Camp Commandant Rongai, 5.04.45.
86. PRO: ED 128/107, E.R.C. Williams, Camp Commandant Rongai to Karol Sander, Polish Camp Leader Rongai, 21.05.45.
87. PRO: ED 128/107, Seweryn Szczepanski, Chief Polish Educational Adviser and K. Chodzikiewicz, Ag. Chief Polish Adviser, 27.09.45.
88. Stoler, 'Rethinking Colonial Categories', 139. I will address the 'poor white' issue in more detail in Chapter 5.
89. Ibid., 149.
90. Bland, 'White Women and Men of Colour', 32.
91. Kennedy, *Islands of White*, 138. For the history of black peril scares in Southern Rhodesia, see also McCulloch, *Black Peril, White Virtue*.
92. Kennedy, *Islands of White*, 141.
93. TNA: W3 /31798 p.1A, 'Ex-Service' Arusha to the Editor, East African Standard, Nairobi, forwarded to Chief Secretary, DSM on 1.12.43.
94. Davin, 'Imperialism and Motherhood', 10.
95. Boucher, 'Limits of Potential'. The scheme was supposed to alleviate child poverty in Britain and, at the same time, to ensure British demographic domination in the Empire.
96. Tavuyanago, Muguti and Hlongwana, 'Victims', 959.
97. Hansen, *Distant Companions*, 146.
98. Cited in Hodder-Williams, *White Farmers in Rhodesia*, 160–61.
99. Reid, *Tanganyika without Prejudice*, 216.
100. Tavuyanago, Muguti and Hlongwana, 'Victims', 959.
101. Zins, *Poles in Zambezi*, 69, cited from footnote 11.
102. Hansen, *Distant Companions*, 146.
103. Kennedy, *Islands of White*, 141. See also Kufakurinani, *Elasticity in Domesticity*, 176.

104. Kennedy, *Islands of White*, 138.
105. McClintock, *Imperial Leather*, 354.
106. Fischer-Tiné, *Low and Licentious Europeans*, 2.
107. Strobel, *European Women*, 3. See also Stoler, *Carnal Knowledge*, 2; Levine, *British Empire*, 151.
108. Ray, *Crossing the Color Line*, 37.
109. The 1915 Brundell Report in Southern Rhodesia 'concluded that white women who had sexual relations with Africans were either prostitutes, indiscreet and careless, or simply nymphomaniacs'. See Kufakurinani, *Elasticity in Domesticity*, 173–75.
110. Kennedy, *Islands of White*, 171.
111. Webster, 'There'll Always Be an England'.
112. For the race and gender dimensions of the 'myth of the empty land', see McClintock, *Imperial Leather*, 30–31.
113. Webster, 'There'll Always Be an England', 561.
114. Ibid., 559.
115. Fischer-Tiné, *Low and Licentious Europeans*, 212.
116. TNA: 69/782, Chief Soil Conservation Officer, Soil Conservation Service, Department of Agriculture, Tengeru to Troup, Provincial Commissioner Arusha, 18.09.52.
117. Ibid.
118. Lwanga-Lunyiigo, 'Uganda's Long Connection', 11.
119. Interviews with Edward Sinabulya and Mukeera Kasule, former African workers in the camp, Koja, Uganda, April 2013. I will come back to this rumour in more detail in Chapter 5.
120. The only people I heard about during my field research in the area of the three biggest camps were two descendants of a Polish–African relationship in Tengeru, one rich African transport company owner from Masindi, who was said to have married two Polish women, and one Polish woman who reportedly married an African man and moved to Kampala.
121. MSS Afr s. 1652, p.1, 'A Polish Interlude in Africa – 1943–1944. A Personal Account of the Polish Refugee Settlements Established in Uganda during the War Years', by Rennie Bere, November 1978.
122. E.g. in the report on mixed-race children in Liverpool: Christian, 'The Fletcher Report 1930'; Bland, 'White Women and Men of Colour', 33. See generally, Stoler, 'Rethinking Colonial Categories', 199.
123. Stoler, 'Sexual Affronts', 226.
124. The Polish officials made the point that, although agreeing with the principle that native labour should be reduced, certain work had to be performed by Africans as the Poles were mainly women and children (PISM: Kol 18/2, Conference of Directors of Refugees in East Africa, Nairobi, p.3, 17.–18.11.44).
125. There were 778 Polish refugees and 368 Africans working in the construction and maintenance of the camp on 15 January 1943. See MSS Afr. s. 1378, Box 2, file 8, Report 'Kidugalla [sic] Polish Refugee Camp as seen on 15.01.43' by Bertram Wilkin, Senior Medical Officer, p.11.
126. TNA: 69/782/IV, Pennington, Director of Refugees, DSM to Camp Commandants Tengeru, Kondoa, Ifunda, Kidugala, Kigoma, Morogoro, 11.09.43.
127. TNA: 176/87, p.2, Pennington for Chief Secretary to All Provincial Commissioners in Tanganyika, 25.10.44.
128. PISM: Kol 18/2, 'Conference of the Directors of Refugees in East Africa', p.3, 6.–8.11.44. It remains unclear why the Colonial Office did not approve the legislation. A reason could be Tanganyika's special legal status under UN Trusteeship.

129. PISM: Kol 18/2, Conference of Directors of Refugees in East Africa, Nairobi, p.6, 17.–18.11.44.
130. TNA: 176 /87, p.2, Pennington for Chief Secretary to All Provincial Commissioners in Tanganyika, 25.10.44.
131. Królikowski, 'Uhuru', 90.
132. Iliffe, *Modern History of Tanganyika*, 263f.
133. Plawski, *Torn from the Homeland*, 152.
134. PRO: CO 822/350, p.5, Ag. Governor Tanganyika to Secretary of State for the Colonies, London, 21.6.51.
135. Both women were furthermore categorized as prostitutes. Reportedly, one was 'contemplating marriage with an Indian' and the other 'had an Indian sweetheart' (MSS Afr. s. 1366/9, p.137, 'Undesirable Polish Refugees', Camp Commandant Marandellas to Director of Refugees, Salisbury, 15.01.47).
136. International Tracing Service, Digital Archive, Bad Arolsen (hereafter ITS): 3.2.1.6/81342892, Zeznanie/Statement by Genowefa Najman/ Nargis Mohamed, Koja 8.11.48.
137. ITS: 3.2.1.6/81342887, E.B. Belcher, EARA to Camp Commandant Koja, 14.09.48.
138. It is not known if her husband was the father of the child, or what his social background was. The town of Jinja is about 90 km from Koja. There is a certain 'Yusaf Mohammed' in the records of Asians expelled from Uganda in 1972, who owned a plot on Main Street in Jinja (see Byerley, 'Becoming Jinja', 41). This might be a hint that Genowefa's husband could have been a wealthy Asian.
139. TNA: K1/26546, p.15B, C.R. Lockhart, Nairobi to G.E.J. Gent, CO, 27.07.44. One 'coloured Seychellois' woman, married to a British man, worked in the office of the International Refugee Organization in Mombasa, but it remains unclear what her job was (Zarzycki and Buczak-Zarzycka, *Kwaheri Africa*, 59).
140. TNA: K1/26546, p.5, D.M. Kennedy, Governor's Deputy, DSM to Governor, Mahe, Seychelles, 18.02.39.
141. KNA: AH/1/51, p.112, Caldwell, Ag. Director of Aliens and Internees and War Refugees, Nairobi to Chief Secretary, Nairobi, 08.10.47.
142. KNA: AH/1/51, p.122, W.N.B. Loudon, Deputy Chief Secretary, Nairobi to Caldwell, 20.11.47.
143. KNA: AH/1/51, p.175, Superintendent of Police i/c Immigration Department to Member for Law and Order, Secretariat, Nairobi, 12.03.48.
144. KNA: AH/1/51, p.112, Caldwell, Ag. Director of Aliens and Internees and War Refugees, Nairobi to Chief Secretary, Nairobi, 08.10.47.
145. Ibid.
146. For more details on the difficulties in running the camp, see Chapter 1.
147. PRO: CO 795/132/4, p 63, Ag. Governor Lusaka to Secretary of State, 28.02.44.
148. Ibid.
149. TNA: 176 /87, p.12C, C.E. Hallam, Branch Manager, Unga Limited to DC Iringa, 3.04.46.
150. Luise White writes that it was 'common knowledge' that Polish women from the transit camp were practising prostitution with Africans, and without arrests or censure (White, *Comforts of Home*, 190).
151. MSS Afr. s. 1366/9, p.132, V. Kozeny (Czech), Mombasa to Camp Commandant, English Point, Nyali, 26.11.46.
152. The other members of the undesirable group were 'habitual drunkards', and both together numbered seven in mid-1950 (PRO: CO 822/145/5, 'Report of the British

Mission to East Africa on Polish Refugees', by T.W.E. Roche, Chief Immigration Officer, p.3, 6.07.50).
153. The others on the list were three suspected communists, one 'agitator' and one drunkard (MSS Afr. s. 1366/9, p.137, 'Undesirable Polish Refugees', Camp Commandant Marandellas to Director of Refugees, Salisbury, 15.01.47).
154. Fischer-Tiné, *Low and Licentious Europeans*, 152.
155. Anne McClintock notes: 'Prostitutes visibly transgressed the middle-class boundary between private and public, paid work and unpaid work, and in consequence were figured as "white Negroes" inhabiting anachronistic space' (McClintock, *Imperial Leather*, 56).
156. See Fischer-Tiné, *Low and Licentious Europeans*, 186–232. Although set in another time and place of the British Empire, the chapter on European prostitutes in India is insightful for the role of this group in a colonial setting.
157. Lwanga-Lunyiigo, 'Uganda's Long Connection', 11.
158. Kennedy, *Islands of White*, 178. For the same argumentation in regard to colonial Bombay, see Tambe, 'The Elusive Ingénue', 164.
159. Marandellas Camp Commandant Breithaupt in 1943, cited in Tavuyanago, Muguti and Hlongwana, 'Victims', 961.
160. TNA: 24 /80/37 Vol.III, p.730, E.K. Biggs, Camp Commandant Ifunda to The Proprietor, White House Inn, Iringa, 7.11.47.
161. Jackson, 'Dangers to the Colony', n.p. Kirk-Green also observes a shift in British colonial policy from 'trusteeship' to 'partnership' after the mid-1940s. See Kirk-Greene, 'Colonial Administration', 284.
162. Williams, *Colour Bar*; Hyam, 'Political Consequences of Seretse Khama'.
163. Anderson, *Histories of the Hanged*, 3.
164. Strobel, *European Women*, xi.
165. McClintock, *Imperial Leather*, 6.
166. van Tol, 'The Women of Kenya Speak', 433.
167. He developed the term from the concept of the 'patriarchal dividend', which describes the privileging of marginalized men resulting from hegemonic masculinity (Fischer-Tiné, *Low and Licentious Europeans*, 238–40).
168. TNA: W3/31798, p.3., F.A. Montague, Ag. Chief Secretary, DSM to the Editor, East African Standard, 31.12.43. However, even the Italian prisoners of war in Kenya seem to have profited from the 'racial dividend', as they were reportedly treated above the standard of the Geneva Convention (White, *Comforts of Home*, 151). After the British victory in Ethiopia, African soldiers complained that Italian POWs were living better than them (Parsons, 'Military Experiences of Ordinary Africans', 7).
169. Taylor, *Polish Orphans*, 86.
170. TNA 69/782/IV, p.774, Dr MacQuillan, Medical Officer of Health, Arusha to Senior Medical Officer Northern Province, Moshi, 14.01.44.
171. Confidential letter about the Polish refugees by the provincial commissioner of Central Province to the chief secretary in Lusaka in July 1943. Cited from Hansen, *Distant Companions*, 146.
172. MSS Afr. s. 1378, Box 2, file 3, Report 'Tengeru Camp as seen on 22.12.42', by Bertram Wilkin, p.35.
173. See the photograph in Wojciechowska, *Waiting to Be Heard*, 224.
174. Chappell and Milek, *Persian Blanket*, 197.
175. Bland, 'White Women and Men of Colour', 30–31. See generally, Higonnet et al., *Behind the Lines*.

176. EAS 03.04.44, '600 Polish Women Join W.A.A.F.'. Nearly half a million women served in the three women's auxiliary services in Britain. See Stone, 'Creating a (Gendered?) Military Identity', 606.
177. Higonnet and Higonnet, 'Double Helix'. Kufakurinani argues in regard to Southern Rhodesia that the domestic sphere was expanded during wartime; see Kufakurinani, *Elasticity in Domesticity*.
178. Królikowski, 'Operation Polejump', 163.
179. KNA: AH/1/51, p.61, J.S. Coney, for Director of Aliens and Internees, Nairobi to Chief Secretary, Nairobi, 08.09.45.
180. Ibid.
181. White, *Comforts of Home*, 162.
182. Zins, *Poles in Zambezi*, 82. At least one Polish woman reportedly worked as a mechanic for the air force (PRO: CO 822/146/1, Personal Summary, Zofia Demian, attached to Beryl Hughes, Home Office, London to Dawson, Colonial Office, 9.11.50).
183. Rupiah, 'History of the Establishment of Internment Camps', 147.
184. Kennedy, *Islands of White*, 179. See also Shutt, *Manners Make a Nation*, 84.
185. Rotberg, *Black Heart*, 237.
186. TNA: 77/24/28, p.13, Winnington-Ingram for Commissioner for Aliens and Internees, DSM to Camp Commandants Tengeru, Kondoa, Ifunda, Kidugala, 3.03.43.
187. Ibid.
188. TNA 69/782/3, p.6, Pennington for Commissioner for Aliens and Internees, DSM to Provincial Commissioner Northern, 13.10.42.
189. EAS 10.07.42, 'Refugees', by John Williams, Kitale.
190. In Tanganyika there were a number of applications from European families to employ Polish women in their households (e.g. TNA: 69/782/3, p.11, Lotte Kaufmann, Oldeani to PC Northern, 6.12.42; and TNA 26/60, p.68, Director of Refugees to Camp Commandant, Morogoro, 21.07.44). The Polish consul and the Department of War Evacuees in Southern Rhodesia received fifty requests for Polish women to work on farms, and in crèches and private homes in the first months after their arrival (Zins, *Poles in Zambezi*, 81).
191. KNA: AH/1/51, p.112/1, Caldwell, Ag. Director of Aliens and Internees and War Refugees, Nairobi to Commissioner East African Refugee Authority, 23.09.47.
192. KNA: AH/1/51, p.112, Caldwell to Chief Secretary, Nairobi, 08.10.47.
193. van Tol, 'The Women of Kenya Speak', 445.
194. EAS 02.07.44, 'Ayahs' by 'Old Resident' and 'Father', both from Nairobi. For the same anxiety in other colonial contexts, see Stoler, 'Carnal Knowledge', 89.
195. One observer noted in the late 1930s that 'European nannies were about as scarce as ice in the Sahara – and about as expensive'. Cited in Hansen, *Distant Companions*, 144.
196. Ibid., 146.
197. Coe and Greenall, *Kaunda's Gaoler*, 69.
198. Cited in Hansen, *Distant Companions*, 145.
199. For an overview, see Harzig, 'Domestics of the World'.
200. Romanko, 'From Russian Gulag', n.p.
201. Rupiah, 'History of the Establishment of Internment Camps', 151.
202. PRO: CO 822/145/5, Notes of a meeting held in the Treasury, 16.02.50. In the UK most resettled Poles worked as unskilled labourers in low-paid jobs, disregarding their former status. See Kushner and Knox, *Refugees in an Age of Genocide*, 226.
203. Hoerder, 'Migration Research in Global Perspective', 82.
204. Lessing, *Landlocked*, 140.

205. IRO: AJ/43/790/55/2, IRO to Kenya Government, 'Memorandum on the Proposed Admission of Polish Displaced Persons to Kenya', p.2, n.d.
206. IRO: AJ/43/790/55/2, Caldwell, Director of Aliens and Internees to Curtis, IRO Nairobi, p.3, 15.04.48.
207. Porajska, *From the Steppes*, 130.
208. Romanko, 'From Russian Gulag', n.p.
209. Yuval-Davis, *Gender and Nation*, 111.
210. See Enloe, *Bananas, Beaches and Bases*.
211. Stoler, 'Sexual Affronts', 226.

Chapter 5

POLISH REFUGEES AS PART OF COLONIAL SOCIETY

British Perspectives on the Refugees: Peasants out of Place

On Sunday evening there was a strange scene on Nairobi railway station – strange that is to Kenya, though not Europe, or even Britain. As dusk fell and the lamps were lit, a long, bright train drew in and faces peered from the windows; round faces, rather anxious and unsmiling as though wondering 'What next?' And the women and little girls wore handkerchiefs on their heads, tied peasant-style over their hair and knotted under their chins.[1]

This quote from a Kenyan newspaper article captures the impression the Poles made on the white settler population upon their arrival in Nairobi. The refugees were not only a reminder of the ongoing war and misery in Europe, but it was plain to see that they were different from the British residents in the colony. It was not only their anxiety and fearful looks, but also the 'peasant-style' kerchiefs on their heads that made their difference obvious. Sociologist Stuart Hall describes English identity as a strongly centred vantage point from which everyone else is placed in relation. 'And the thing which is wonderful about English identity is that it didn't only place the colonized Other, it placed everybody else'.[2] Taking the 'strange scene' on Nairobi station and Hall's general notion as starting points, this chapter will enquire how British colonial administrators and settlers regarded and thus placed the Polish refugees in their respective colonial societies. It attempts to exemplify Hall's notion in concrete empirical settings, and thereby get a more nuanced picture of the complex realities of life in colonial East and Central Africa.

In order to trace the social position of Polish refugees in the British colonies we need, first of all, to clarify the different social situations in the respective colonies. The six countries that hosted Polish refugees followed a broad range of models of colonial statehood, and had accordingly differing social structures. In answering the question of where the Poles were socially positioned, the extent and character of the European community concerned is of paramount importance.

The Uganda Protectorate is one extreme in the continuum, marked by indirect rule and the near absence of a European settler population. It consisted of five African kingdoms, and the colonial administration controlled only the upper layers of the state. Occupying a rather marginal position in the British Empire, the European population in the protectorate was just under 2,000 in 1935/36, rising to about 2,500 in 1948/49.[3] By contrast, the Polish refugee population stood at nearly 7,000. Uganda was not generally seen as a place for large-scale white settlement. The small European community, however, had considerable influence on the (limited) decision-making power of the Ugandan government.[4]

Tanganyika and Northern Rhodesia formed the middle ground in regard to white settlement. Following the defeat of the Germans in the First World War, Tanganyika Territory was administered by Britain, first under a League of Nations mandate, and then from 1946 as a United Nations trust territory. It had a small European population, numbering 8,200 in 1931 but growing to circa 20,000 by 1958.[5] Compared to the other East African colonies, Tanganyika's white population was the most cosmopolitan, with non-British Europeans constituting more than one-third.[6] This was due to the earlier German settlement as well as the fact that trusteeship status did not allow any discrimination against nationals of other League members.[7] Alongside the Poles, Tanganyika hosted some 500 Greek refugees and 3,000 Italian POWs during the war.[8] Apart from this there was a long-established, economically vital and growing Asian population in all three East African territories.

Northern Rhodesia had a slightly larger European population than Tanganyika, growing from nearly 14,000 in 1931 to over 37,000 by 1951. Initially not destined for white settlement, the discovery of copper led to the growth of white immigration, partly from Britain, but mainly from South Africa.[9] The economic importance of the mining industry of the Copperbelt was a feature that set the colonial economy apart from Tanganyika, which was predominantly agricultural. Just as the settler community in Tanganyika stood in the shadow of the more numerous Kenyan settlers, so did Northern Rhodesia's whites look to Southern Rhodesia. Tanganyika's and Northern

Rhodesia's settler communities were only marginally involved in decision making, but they tried to increase their position and become more like their bigger neighbours. In this regard the Central African territories of Nyasaland and the Rhodesias show some parallels to the East African territories of Uganda, Tanganyika and Kenya.[10] In both regions discussions about amalgamation were ongoing, with settlers mainly arguing for a closer union to increase their political position and to counter demands for stronger African participation.[11]

Kenya and Southern Rhodesia were the 'classic' settler colonies of the British Empire in Africa. Both were economically and politically dominated by white settler populations, and had a certain degree of political independence. Southern Rhodesia was a self-governing colony whose status nearly paralleled that of a dominion.[12] Kenya, by contrast, was under the supervision of the Colonial Office in London, but the settlers nevertheless had a strong voice that was heard in Nairobi as well as in London. While Kenya's European population stood at 21,000 in 1939, Southern Rhodesia's was with 63,000 about three times as numerous.[13] As Dane Kennedy makes clear in his comparative study of the two communities, both developed distinctive settler cultures that put a strong emphasis on guarding the social boundaries with the African population. Both communities 'shared essentially the same perceptions of the African climate and people, the same anxieties about physical and racial security, the same pressures for social conformity and ethnic aloofness'.[14] While Kenya's settler community was mainly a rural, hierarchical society dominated by the 'gentlemanly stratum', its larger Southern Rhodesian counterpart had the image of a more egalitarian white society consisting of less affluent whites.[15] By 1960, three years before Kenyan independence, the European population in Kenya had risen to 61,000;[16] meanwhile in Southern Rhodesia it was already 223,000 in the same year.[17] The latter had followed a path different from the other colonies. Despite the refusal to accept larger numbers of Poles, it encouraged other European immigration with 17,000 white immigrants entering in 1948 alone.[18]

The Union of South Africa was at the other extreme in the continuum of colonial models. It was an independent dominion in the Commonwealth, with a huge and – more than in the two above-mentioned settler colonies – politically divided white population. It was a country where white identities were contested, and the numerically stronger Afrikaner community formed an important antipode to the English.[19] As the Union government admitted a mere five hundred Polish refugee children, I will only focus on its model character for the other settler communities. The Union, with its clear commitment to white settlement and rule, had an important role in the thinking of white settlers in the other colonies. For settlers in the Rhodesias this was very pronounced, as many of them came from South Africa, but East African whites too looked to the Union as a model for a stronger white community.[20] Many of Kenya's white settlers had strong ties with South Africa, and the successful participation of the South African army in the East African campaign of the Second World War consolidated the Union's image in the region even further.[21]

The 'Poor White' Problem

South African concerns about, and policies tackling, the 'poor white problem' were closely followed in the other colonies. In South Africa, the existence of an impoverished Afrikaner population went back to the nineteenth century, but only with the 1932 report of the Carnegie Commission on the Poor White Problem did it become a topic of public debate.[22] Poor whites posed a threat to the boundaries of race, and were regarded as potentially politically dangerous when in close contact with the urban 'coloured' proletariat.[23] In the postwar era this threat became closely associated with the fear of a spread of communist ideas. Consequently, policies that privileged white workers helped to keep the perceived problem at bay and increased the material and social distance between black and white.

Settlers and colonial administrators in Kenya and Southern Rhodesia were well aware of these discussions and policies, and tried to safeguard their societies against the emergence of a poor white stratum.[24] The Kenyan government kept most poor whites out of the colony through immigration restrictions. The Southern Rhodesian government, in turn, started various programmes to improve their condition, as many of the poor whites were locally born.[25] In both colonies the '"poor white problem" ... was one of the central bogies of colonial society'.[26] The policy of lifting poor whites out of poverty was reflected in the governments' treatment of the Polish refugees. One British observer described the improvement in the conditions of the Polish refugees: 'They arrived in Africa in a pitiful condition, with few clothes and no shoes, half-starved and weak from their travels, but some months in Nairobi built them up, and they reached Marandellas in February in much better shape'.[27]

Colonial administrators in Tanganyika and Northern Rhodesia were likewise aware of this issue. In regard to the Polish refugees, Tanganyika officials were 'gravely concerned with the "poor white" problem' that the remainder of them presented.[28] The Northern Rhodesian governor had earlier argued against the admittance of Jewish refugees, as this could produce a 'class of poor whites'.[29] For Ugandan officials the question was apparently less important, as they were against any form of large-scale white settlement.

For what follows it is important to bear in mind that local circumstances varied widely. The socio-economic and political situation in a settlement like Masindi in the middle of the Budongo forest was very different from the conditions in Lusaka Camp, with the centre of the new capital within walking distance. Nevertheless, the colonial administrations as well as the European populations in all the colonies did at least share some common ground. The sources that I draw upon in this chapter point to the fact that they were part of imperial networks. This is obvious for colonial officials who communicated with London as well as each other, met at conferences and were sometimes transferred from one colony to another.[30] But the interested settler population as well knew what was going on in the other colonies. The *East African Standard* was published in Nairobi, but read in both northern Tanganyika and Kenya, as correspondence from the readers testifies. Developments in other colonies were closely followed, and the Union of South African was a focal point of interest for European settlers in East and Central Africa.

The Perspective of the Colonial Administration

'In short, with very few exceptions, everyone wants to see the last of the Poles'.[31] With these words the British immigration officer, Thomas W.E. Roche, summed up the attitude of the colonial authorities in Tanganyika in a 1950 report. The other governments shared this view. When the Polish

Figure 5.1. Group of Polish and African farmworkers at the Polish pig farm in Koja, Uganda, 1944. From Archiwum Fotografii Ośrodka KARTA, Signature: OK_005192, online.

refugees had arrived some eight years earlier, the mood had been more welcoming. Although officials were not really happy with the influx of these European refugees, they nevertheless saw it as a necessary contribution to the 'Commonwealth war effort'.[32] Through articles in the newspapers they painted a positive picture of the Poles as 'the most loyal of our allies and very pro-British'.[33] The first editorial on the Poles in the *East African Standard* – although pointing to the lack of alternatives and the importance for the war effort – noted: 'The arrival of these refugees, who will come in their thousands, will create for us in East Africa further complicated problems'.[34] The problems anticipated were not specified in the editorial, but this chapter will show what caused a deterioration in relations and how the British administration in the different colonies regarded the Poles in view of their social position within the respective colonial societies.

Guests Who Have Overstayed Their Welcome

One of the decisive events in regard to the Polish refugee sojourn in East and Central Africa was the realization after the end of the war that Poland would be Soviet-dominated and its eastern border shifted westwards. As the eastern part of the country – where most of the refugees came from – was to be incorporated in the Soviet Union, it was clear to many of them that they would not return. They were stuck in the colonies, and the initial plan to host them 'for the "duration"' and provide 'wartime homes' had become obsolete.[35] So, what was to be done with them?

Shortly after the war, the East African Governors' Conference met and agreed on a memorandum to send to the Secretary of State for the Colonies in London. The governors, fearing that the Poles might try to stay in their colonies permanently, underlined their united stance against permanent residency:

> It was also AGREED that a firm line should be taken regarding the dispersal of foreigners already in the Territories, with particular reference to Polish refugees, and that it should be made quite clear to the Secretary of State that on no account should these people be permitted to remain in East Africa.[36]

In the memorandum the governors put forward two arguments: the loss of British dominance within the European population, and the impediment to the development of Africans. They wrote: 'If the immigration of foreigners was allowed to continue on a large scale, the inevitable result would be that the European community in East Africa would cease to be predominantly British and the development of the Africans would be impeded'.[37]

The first argument was found as well in the Southern Rhodesian restrictions upon European immigrants who were not 'of British stock'.[38] While the main anxiety of the Rhodesian settler community was related to the threat from the African majority, there was nevertheless concern about being outnumbered by non-British settlers. This concern was directed mainly against domination from Afrikaners, but it also applied to Jewish and other European immigrants.[39] While the postwar era witnessed a large influx of European immigrants into the country, legislation was passed to assure that most of them were British, thus preserving the 'Little England' in Central Africa.[40] The argument was not only about nationality, but also about class, as the problematized others were usually of a lower class. In this regard, colonial anxiety regarding poor whites and the nationally argued fear of losing British dominance coincided.

In Kenya and Tanganyika, the main competitors – after most of the Germans had been interned during the war – were Indians. In Tanganyika they had profited economically from the transfer of power from German to British hands, taking over some plantations and clerical jobs in the administration. As Tanganyika was a Mandate Territory, Indians could furthermore not be barred from immigration and were no longer categorized as 'natives'.[41] The numerically strong Polish refugee community added to the prevailing feeling of being besieged by foreigners. One Nairobi resident remarked in a letter to the *East African Standard* in 1944: 'It seems likely to me that Nairobi as it is at present constituted (or a large part of it) will be entirely occupied by Indians and refugees'.[42]

The other argument in the memorandum seems to reflect a general shift in colonial postwar policy that put African development (at least rhetorically) to the forefront. The role of the British administration was presented as leading and protecting Africans on a progressive development path to modernity and eventual self-government. While the settlers in the colonies wanted more immigrants of their kind, the Colonial Office was instead arguing for an increased immigration of technical experts who could modernize the colonial economy and teach Africans new 'scientific' agricultural methods. The refugees were not this kind of expert, and settling a large group of lower-class whites would have contradicted the argumentation for African welfare. In Kenyan settler circles, which partly overlapped with the administration, the Colonial Office was loathed for its lack of support for further European settlement. Reasons for this shift in policy derived from the increasing de-legitimitization of colonial rule. As Frederick Cooper argues, after the end of the war the British Empire was physically and morally weak and had to find new ways of re-legitimating colonial rule.[43] On the one hand, open racism had been discredited through the Holocaust and the Allies' insistence on racial equality; on the other, it was clear that the colonies had helped to save the metropole during the war. The appeal of the Soviet model posed another threat, and finally the independence of India put the normality of imperial rule into question.[44] The British response was an increasing emphasis on economic development and the gradual preparation of the colonies for self-governance. The Colonial Office's aim in the postwar period was the creation of viable and friendly successor states.[45] In this delicate political situation the colonial governments had no interest in white settlers who were neither experts nor British.

The increasing impatience with the refugees is also discernible in the notes of Kenya's director of manpower. In July 1945 he wrote that he was getting applications from refugees for assistance in obtaining employment. He was disgruntled on two grounds: 'In the first place, employers are not anxious to take them on, and secondly I, at heart, have in fact no real wish to find them jobs when, as nearly always applies, it means one job less for British ex-servicemen'.[46] He enquired what the plans were regarding the 'refugee problem' and suggested that they were not only taking jobs but also accommodation away from Britons. He closed by urging the Kenyan administration to get rid of them: 'Surely now is the time for these people to return to their home countries and get in on the ground floor of reorganisation of business and everything else. But unless the Kenya Government gives them the word "go" they will be quite content, and in fact eager, to stay in Kenya to the detriment of the British, and I feel sure to the African in the long run'.[47] While he cited African interests as well, his main interest clearly lay in safeguarding jobs for British ex-servicemen in Kenya.

In late 1947, senior IRO official Maurice Lush summed up the view of the different governments after a tour through the camps and all seven capitals. Having consulted the governments, he underlined their different statuses and summed up: 'Only in one respect was there unanimity on the part of all governments. This was the strong desire to be quit of all refugees as soon as possible and to absorb the minimum number into the economy of the territory'.[48] He explained that the colonial governments saw the removal of the refugees as the ultimate responsibility of the British government. Reminiscent of current attitudes in refugee hosting nations, he added that the governments did not lack sympathy with the refugees as long as they were outside their territories. They saw the refugees as 'guests who have now long overstayed their welcome'.[49]

There was hence the general perception of being besieged by others, be they Indian merchants, Afrikaners, Jewish or East European refugees. While this might sound familiar to current day political observers, there were, however, reasons that were more specific to the colonial situation and that differed from anti-refugee sentiments elsewhere.

The Second World War and the End of Empire

The period of the refugees' sojourn in the British Empire was a time when colonial rule was coming under increasing pressure from within and without. The two postwar superpowers, the United States and especially the Soviet Union, had officially anti-colonial ideologies.[50] Britain was severely weakened from the war, and the very concept of a colonial empire was increasingly under pressure. Although the promised 'self-determination' of the 1941 Atlantic charter was quickly limited to European nations by Churchill, colonial rule was put into question.[51] While colonial empires had been a fact of political life in 1940, ten years later their normality and future was in doubt.[52] For independence movements in Africa the war meant a watershed.

These developments impacted on the empire's room for manoeuvre. After the war, the Colonial Office compiled a report about the possibilities of permanent settlement for European displaced persons in the British Empire. The findings were disillusioning. In West Africa, the report declared, local opposition to European immigration 'would certainly be strong and might lead to serious disorder'. For East and Central Africa it was likewise assessed that even in the event of small-scale European settlement there was the 'likelihood of political trouble, particularly from Africans'.[53] The contradictions to the expressed colonial policy were further explained: 'It would be difficult to reconcile the transplanting of a European peasant economy on any substantial scale to tropical Africa with the advance towards African self-government'.[54]

It became clear that there was no space for large-scale settlement of European refugees in the empire. The growing African nationalist mobilization in the postwar era showed colonial politicians their limits. The Kenya government was likewise afraid that, if the 'hard core' of criminals and medical cases were to remain in the colony, this was 'likely to exacerbate the already difficult racial relations'.[55] The political situation in Kenya was already volatile, and the administration did not want any further trouble. For colonial administrators in London and Nairobi the era of large-scale white settlement was over.

No other development made it clearer that colonial rule was coming to a close than the advent of Indian independence in 1947. The last Polish refugees in Kolhapur were directly affected by the end of British rule there. When British troops withdrew from India in February 1948, the remaining Poles were evacuated as well. While some of them went to the French zone of Germany, the majority were transferred to another part of the shrinking empire. Nearly seven hundred of them joined their compatriots in Koja.[56] The Polish refugees thereby incidentally followed the new concentration on the African part of the British Empire in the postwar period.

To re-legitimate imperial rule, the British government increased investment and started development projects, conceived explicitly in the interests of the colonized. While large-scale alienation of land and the establishment of European farms was not an option for the colonial administration, there was nevertheless an increase in the flow of European immigrants to most colonies. But as noted earlier, these were specialized technical experts commanding development projects supposedly in the interest of African welfare, and not European settler farmers let alone peasants. The development projects brought growing numbers of Europeans temporarily to the African colonies. As Alison Smith notes, the sojourn of the Poles and Italians 'formed a precedent for the various large contingents of European skilled manual workers'.[57]

In Tanganyika, for example, the – notoriously unsuccessful – groundnut scheme brought an influx of skilled European manual workers.[58] Some of them followed directly in the footsteps of the Poles. In Ifunda, the groundnut scheme employees of the Overseas Food Corporation (OFC) moved into the houses from which the Poles had just moved out.[59] In the short period of overlap, the camp commandant complained about the unruly OFC employees, as they had moved into an empty ward of the hospital while six Polish patients were still living there. As the OFC employees were enjoying their time with loud gramophone music and drinking parties, the camp commandant threw them out for 'ungentlemanly' and 'disgusting' behaviour.[60] It seems that the OFC staff represented a new type of settler, who clashed with the established norms of respectable European behaviour.

In Tengeru, in turn, the new administration complained about the few remaining Poles. The Game Department and the soil conservation officer took over the premises to establish a natural resources school for Africans.[61] When the new administrators moved in, the last eleven Polish refugee families were still living in part of the camp. The soil conservation officer as well as the principal of the school repeatedly complained about the Poles' bad behaviour, and pressed for their removal.[62] They were afraid the example of this group of petty criminals and undesirables would affect the conduct of their African pupils.

Other Polish settlements were used for colonial development projects as well. The governmental Nyabyeya Forestry School moved into the premises of Masindi settlement after the Poles had left.[63] The Southern Rhodesian refugee and internment camps were placed under a committee, to which government departments and local authorities could apply.[64] With the departure of the Poles, the colonies received buildings and land which they put to use for their new development policies. While there had been no room for any large-scale colony of Poles, the material remains of the Polish refugee sojourn were, however, useful in meeting the empire's need for re-legitimation. The

Tanganyika director of refugees clearly argued for the removal of the Poles from Tengeru by emphasizing the need of premises for educational purposes for Africans. In 1949 he declared his theoretical willingness to host the remaining 'hard core' of the last one thousand Poles (although it remains unclear if he really meant his offer), but explained that Tengeru was needed for other projects.[65] While the special conditions of war had brought the Poles to Africa, the postwar era with its growing anti-colonial movements made the colonial administration eager to get rid of this awkward population segment.

Government Attitudes in Kenya and Southern Rhodesia

The attitude of the administration in the settler colonies of Kenya and Southern Rhodesia towards the permanent settlement of Polish refugees needs some explanation. The Kenyan and – more clearly – the Southern Rhodesia government were generally committed to white settlement, yet both were unwilling to allow a large group of Poles to settle permanently in their territories. Why were these settler colonies not happy with the influx of more whites?

Kennedy has made the differences between these two countries clear in his comparative study. While Kenya was in India's orbit, Southern Rhodesia had been in the orbit of South Africa.[66] Kennedy refers mainly to the currency, penal code, bureaucratic structure and personnel, but he points to the importance of the Afrikaner and Indian populations as well. Poor Afrikaner immigrants filled socio-economic niches in Southern Rhodesia comparable to those filled by poor Indian immigrants in East Africa.[67] These same niches of semi- or unskilled labour were the ones where the Poles could have fitted in. One British woman in Kenya, for example, applied for permission to employ four Polish artisans, to which the Kenyan official replied that the work could well be done by an Indian contractor, albeit at a higher cost.[68] The governments were thus rather reluctant to admit Poles permanently. Only limited numbers of Poles were allowed to take up residency under closely supervised schemes, like the Polish working gang of the Kenyan Public Works Department mentioned above.[69]

Kenya had earlier been unwilling to admit Poles even for the duration of the war. The memories of the war with Italy in Ethiopia were still fresh in people's minds, and the colony was an important military hub itself. There were furthermore already over 58,000 Italian prisoners of war in the colony in December 1942.[70] The Kenyan government established only a small school settlement in Rongai and the transit camps in Makindu and later in Mombasa. An additional factor informing this decision may have been the earlier resistance against mass settlement plans for Jewish refugees.

After warding off most of the Jews, it would have been quite a turnaround to suddenly host large groups of Poles. Individual Poles were, however, admitted to work in Kenya in response to wartime labour needs. After the war, the administration made efforts to get rid of them again, insisting that the Poles' home was in the camps in Uganda and Tanganyika.

The few Poles who permanently settled in Kenya had experienced, according to the IRO representative Curtis, some problems with adjusting to their new society. Curtis argued that this was due to the 'multiracial composition of Kenya's population and the almost complete absence of what might be called a European working class'.[71] In June 1950 he proposed the establishment of a welfare committee to assist the settled Poles, without explaining the nature of their problems. In his view, the Poles in Central Africa experienced fewer problems and hence needed no special assistance. While Central Africa was 'multiracial' as well, there existed apparently a white working class into which they could integrate.

The Southern Rhodesian government had initially admitted some Poles, but after the war it adopted the toughest policy towards the Poles. There was again a difference between wartime and the postwar era. The Southern Rhodesian refugee official Bagshawe was one of the most pro-Polish officials, and he even advanced a plan to settle some of them permanently. After his plans were published in 1946, however, he was dismissed and the hitherto excellent living conditions for the Poles deteriorated.[72] In January 1947 the government closed the Polish camps and transferred their inmates to Gatooma, where sanitary and housing conditions were much worse.[73] Bagshawe's welcoming attitude was thwarted by other officials, who were clearly opposed to any permanent Polish settlement. Most Southern Rhodesian officials regarded the Poles as an inferior type of white settler, who would push down European wages and thus blur the boundary between black and white.[74]

As Alois Mlambo shows, Southern Rhodesian immigration policy became generally directed against non-British whites in the first half of the twentieth century.[75] In 1944 the Southern Rhodesian minister of defence assured Rhodesians that postwar immigration to the country would be predominantly British. Amid loud applause he said to an audience of soldiers: 'I am keen that at least 80 per cent of immigration should be from British stock; we want to build up Southern Rhodesia as part of the British Empire'.[76] In the *Rhodesian Herald*, concerns about a loss of the British character of the colony were voiced, and the government introduced quotas on non-British immigration.[77] The fear of losing both the British character of the settler community and the difference between white and black led to harsh restrictions on white immigration. To some imperialists, the only suitable whites for the empire were those of British stock.[78] The Poles became, in the words of Tavuyanago,

Muguti and Hlongwana, 'victims of the [Southern] Rhodesian immigration policy'.[79]

Northern Rhodesia

Northern Rhodesia formed a kind of middle ground with regard to both hosting of refugees and permanent settlement after the war. The most important political issue in Northern Rhodesia, especially after the war, was the question of amalgamation with Southern Rhodesia and, closely connected to it, the role of white settlement. Pushing for white settlement and the amalgamation was Roy Welensky, a railway union leader who was to become prime minister of the Federation of Rhodesia and Nyasaland in 1956. Welensky, who was himself of mixed Jewish-Lithuanian and Afrikaner descent, but clearly pro-British, said in 1948:

> I am going to do everything in my power to bring more Europeans into Northern Rhodesia. I don't care where they will come from, Great Britain, Holland, Germany, South Africa, Australia, America – it doesn't matter a damn – just let them have a white skin and be willing to work. The very day we have 100,000 in the country we will demand Dominion status![80]

Welensky, like other proponents of white settlement and federation of the Rhodesias, had the aim of achieving dominion status with a predominantly white political constituency. Although he claimed that the nationality of the whites did not matter, Welensky did not include any East or South European countries in his statement. Maybe they were not white enough for him. In immigration practice there was a clear preference for British settlers.

The initial acceptance of the Poles had been more or less dictated by London and the war conditions. But as soon as the Poles arrived, the first government official responsible for them started to get annoyed. Stewart Gore-Browne, the director of war evacuees and camps from 1942 until mid-1944, developed a strong antipathy towards the Poles.[81] The first arrivals were the five hundred middle-class Poles from the Cyprus group. According to Gore-Browne, these 'town-dwellers' were not made for the pioneer conditions in the colony and they complained constantly about the conditions.[82] He was further annoyed by their elitist class-consciousness and the antisemitic tendencies that marked controversies among them. The Poles from Iran, who followed, had mainly a peasant background, but Gore-Browne still found them 'impossible'.[83] Apart from repeated disputes and brawls among them, he was disappointed by their ungrateful behaviour. As he wrote: 'They get free issues of clothing from Red X and, if they think their neighbour's issue is better than their own, they will tear up their own clothes or throw them at the donor's head'.[84]

Despite Gore-Browne's dislike for the Poles, Northern Rhodesia accepted quite a number of them as permanent settlers in the end. A quarter of the one thousand Polish applicants for permanent residence were granted the right to stay. The lucky ones were mainly Poles who were already in permanent employment or were trained artisans.[85] In comparison with the total white population in the colony, Northern Rhodesia accepted nearly as many Poles as Tanganyika: the Polish quota constituted 1.6 per cent of the total white population in Northern Rhodesia and 2 per cent in Tanganyika.[86] The two colonies with a medium-sized white population seem to have been the most welcoming in regard to permanently settled Polish residents.

Uganda – Administration and Settler Disputes

Uganda had played a central role in the refugee hosting, but had no sizeable settler population. As one Foreign Office official explained to the IRO, European settlement was very strictly controlled.[87] After the IRO and some of the few 'unofficial' Europeans (those who were not employed in public service) in Uganda had urged the government to accept more Poles, the government saw the need to explain its view in the country's leading newspaper. Early in 1949, the Ugandan government published a statement in the *Uganda Herald* that was posted in Koja settlement as well. It was announced as a reaction to 'misconceptions regarding the position of the Polish refugees', and stated:

> Opportunities for European settlement in the Protectorate are extremely limited. In the interests of the African population it has been the policy of the Protectorate Government for many years to restrict the opportunities open to non-natives with regard to the ownership of land, and to occupations which are, or will shortly be, capable of being carried on by Africans.[88]

This was a clear stance of the Uganda government on the path towards African self-government and the gradual replacement of Europeans on the labour market. The communiqué was a direct reaction to readers' letters, which had spoken out in favour of permanently settling at least those Poles who had found employment in Uganda.[89] One supporter of permanent Polish settlement was F.J. Gorton, who owned a farm ten miles from Koja settlement and – being an old scout himself – had earlier helped the Polish scouts.[90] Gorton argued that Britain had an obligation towards the Poles, who had fought for it during the war. He further claimed: 'The consensus of unofficial opinion is in favour of their being allowed to stay'. Another writer supported Gorton's opinion, but criticized him for his naivety in expecting anything good from the government.[91] The few white settlers in Uganda, it seems, would have been happy to get some addition to their ranks, whilst the government was more interested in protecting African interests.

From the end of the Second World War, British colonial rule was in serious doubt in Uganda. As Gardner Thompson writes, 'the war period exposed the essential and abiding boundaries of British power'.[92] The Ugandan colonial state had always been weak, but during the war it had seriously overstretched its possibilities, and Ugandans were becoming less inclined to support it any longer. While they had willingly supported the war effort, by the end of the war 'Ugandans found Britain unable or unwilling to reciprocate their loyalty'.[93] The 1945 strikes and riots had taken the colonial state by surprise, and its harsh reaction had exposed its limited means.[94] The Uganda Protectorate was indirectly ruled, and it relied especially on cooperation with the Ganda elite. After the war had exposed the state's inability to control rising prices and offer employment opportunities to returning African soldiers, colonial rule was seriously questioned.[95] It would not have been wise to further alienate Ugandans by giving government jobs or land to the Poles.

Another reason mentioned in the government statement was fear of the creation of a permanent Polish community in Uganda. As the Poles were de facto stateless and the IRO opportunity of resettlement was about to fade, any Poles admitted, even temporarily, could eventually become permanent settlers.[96] While the Uganda government argued that this was to the disadvantage of Africans, another reasoning may also have lain behind this stance: the British model for the protectorate envisaged the employment of colonial administrators for their working life, after which they were to retire to their home country. A permanent Polish community would have been a further potential competitor for British dominance – like the Afrikaners in South Africa. The Polish community would have combined a mass of semi-skilled workers, a vocal intellectual elite and distinct sociocultural institutions. As such it would have had the potential to challenge the British administrators, who were mostly posted for some years and then retired elsewhere. Thus, in addition to Africans and Indians, another competitor would have threatened British control in Uganda.

While the small white settler community opposed the tough stance of the Uganda government towards permanent Polish settlement in the protectorate, their demands did not change official policy. Although British settlers generally had some influence on the government's decision making, this demand was firmly rejected.[97] The personal relations between official and unofficial British people in Uganda were cordial, as they formed a small community. They were neighbours, met for sundowners and played bridge or golf together.[98] In the postwar period, however, the government slowly grasped that the situation had become increasingly volatile and the government had not much to offer to address the population's grievances. As cooperation with the Ugandans was becoming increasingly difficult, settlers lost influence on the government. The communiqué against Polish settlement has to be seen in this context.

White Criminals in Colonial Societies

One small group among the refugees whom no one wanted to have in the country were those who had been convicted of illicit activities. The British Home Office refused them entry to Britain, no potential resettlement country was interested, and the local colonial authorities were eager to get rid of them. Those refused ranged from petty to professional criminals. The most serious criminal cases were murders and a series of jewel robberies in Northern Rhodesia. The authorities suspected a Polish criminal trio in Southern Rhodesia to be behind this series.[99] According to one official, it was common knowledge among the Polish refugees that even before leaving Poland the three were 'thieving their way through life'.[100] The other side of the spectrum consisted of petty criminals who were convicted after brawls, knife fights or for more minor offences as 'unlawful assembly', 'being outside permitted limit'[101] or 'being drunk and disorderly'.[102]

But it was not only crime as such that posed a problem. Pennington, the director of refugees in Tanganyika, stressed the difference between a colonial and a European country: 'A European with criminal tendencies is a much greater menace in a predominantly native territory than in a European country'.[103] Why did Pennington make this distinction? A report about the situation of the last Polish refugees in Tengeru in 1950 offers a clue. The visiting Home Office official, T.W.E. Roche, explained the situation as follows:

> The continuous existence of a matter of thirty European criminal family individuals would, of course, be a great danger to the large native population of Tanganyika; the bad influence of white criminals is wholly disproportionate to their numbers. Normally the gaols of the Territory do not contain more than a handful of Europeans.[104]

Roche's assessment – made after one month in Tanganyika and informed by interviews with the relevant colonial officials – was, in the first place, a paternalistic plea for the protection of the colonized. While in his statement the whites were the bad guys, they were nevertheless much more powerful than their African victims. Secondly, Roche mentioned the 'bad influence' that white criminals exerted without specifying on whom. Given the colonial belief that Africans were eager to copy Europeans and easy to manipulate, it seems likely that he was referring to the danger that criminal whites might induce Africans to follow their example. But Roche's last sentence is noteworthy: there were usually only a few Europeans convicted in the colonies. Apart from the low total numbers of Europeans, this was due to the selective immigration policies that permitted only Europeans with sufficient means into the colonies. Furthermore, biases in the legal system as well as solidarity among Europeans led to there being relatively few convictions.

The anonymous Polish authors of the Northern Rhodesian *Kronika* were rather amused by the mild treatment that Polish criminals received, and explained that the colony was completely unprepared for an influx of European criminals. They argued that Northern Rhodesia's whites were a decent and unproblematic element, as they had material means and assured jobs. Mocking the mild treatment of the Poles, the authors observed that white criminals were treated 'like gentlemen'. This is illustrated in the *Kronika* with the anecdote of one Pole in a detention cell of the Lusaka magistrate who had been arrested for stabbing. Reportedly, his lunch had come from the first-class Grand Hotel in town. He complained about the food and threatened to go on hunger strike if he could not get his lunch from the other first-class hotel in town, which he preferred – a demand to which the authorities gave way.[105] The two hotels were the only ones in town catering to Europeans.

White criminals presented colonial societies with a twofold problem. On the one hand, they were damaging the image of white moral superiority, as white criminals clearly exposed the lack of it. On the other hand, colonial rule functioned through solidarity within the white population. The moment that whites were caught assaulting and robbing other whites, this common bond and mutual trust among them was damaged. While Europeans expected to meet some liars and thieves in their encounters with Africans, there was a stronger trust in the law-abidance of Europeans. White criminals therefore posed a threat to the very heart of colonial rule.

Settler Perspectives on the Refugees

Although there was some overlap and intense interaction between European settlers and colonial officials, the two groups had at times diverging interests. The above-mentioned example from Uganda is a case in point. Likewise for Kenya's settlers, who were known for their highly critical stance towards officials, colonial administrators were only 'tourists' who stayed for some years in Kenya and did not really understand the situation on the ground.[106] Let us therefore trace various settler perspectives on the Polish refugees, and show how they differed from attitudes of the administration, between the colonies and within the communities.

In Tanganyika, the initial call by the administration to welcome the Polish refugees was met by the British settlers and mainly the women's welfare organizations. Donations of clothes, money and toys, especially for the orphans in Tanganyika, were made mainly in the year of their arrival. In 1942 the provincial commissioner in Arusha even opened a bank account (the 'Polish Refugees Benefit Fund') after he had received some contributions.[107] After the initial generosity, there followed the collections from the Victory Day festivities in Arusha.[108] Following this event, however, the account was closed. In the Tanganyika town of Mbeya, a comparable account was opened in 1942 but it was 'dormant' from January 1943 onwards.[109] Reflecting growing impatience in the administration, the end of the war brought the wish to resume what was 'normal' and have the refugees return to their homes. The settlers' generosity ceased.

Poles as In-Between Group

The intermediate position of the Poles from the settler viewpoint becomes apparent in the autobiography of the British social scientist John Barnes. Barnes had done anthropological field research close to Fort Jameson, Northern Rhodesia, at the time the Polish refugees were there. He described the Poles' ambiguous social position as follows: 'These Poles presented a problem for the racial stratification system. They were undeniably Europeans ... But these Poles were peasants, and were earning their living in the town doing menial jobs usually performed by Africans'.[110]

Barnes explained the treatment of the Poles by British settlers with an illuminating anecdote. One day he was sitting with some white men on the veranda having a drink before lunch. When an African woman servant passed by and entered the house there was no reaction by the white men at all, and the conversation went on uninterrupted. Next, a Polish woman servant entered the house. This time the conversation was interrupted shortly; the men shifted uneasily in their seats, but did not greet her. When, finally, a white woman who was not Polish passed the men, they stood up and exchanged greetings with her.[111]

The ignorance of domestic servants is described by Karen Hansen as the 'paradox of conspicuous presence and social invisibility'.[112] While domestic servants necessarily share physical space with their employers, they do not share social space, and social interaction is usually reduced to the minimum. In Hansen's work on domestic service in Zambia (and Northern Rhodesia) she points to the centrality of difference between employers and servants. Hansen asserts that domestic service, especially if the servants live in the same household, 'can only operate smoothly in situations where servants and employers are considered different from each other. These differences are constructed and informed by essentialist notions of race, culture, sexuality and class'.[113]

In Barnes's anecdote, the men clearly saw the African woman as different: she was of another race, culture, gender and class. The non-Polish white woman was, by contrast, clearly part of their social group. It was the Polish servant who caused unease. Being a domestic servant, she was ignored as a social being, and the inherent inequality of domestic service points to the importance of class for differentiation. In a European setting her position would have been completely unproblematic, as she would clearly have been considered lower-class and culturally different. The unease was caused by the colonial situation with its strong link between class and race. In Northern Rhodesia white domestic servants were rare, and there was no pattern at hand for the construction of social difference. The unease came from the discrepancy between, on the one hand, the expected positioning of white women as part of the white group, and the exclusion of domestic servants from this group on the other. The Polish servant was not part of the same social group as the white men on the veranda, but nor was she completely invisible.

A second anecdote in Barnes's autobiography shows that it was not only the occupational position as domestics that defined the Poles' position in Northern Rhodesian society. One day he went to a second-class shopping area in Fort Jameson to buy maize. As he arrived, the Indian vendor greeted him in Polish, as he seemingly expected any white men buying there to be Polish.[114] Other white men would go shopping in the better shops or send their employees. While Poles were, by their outer appearance, part of the colonizing group, their socio-economic position put them on the lowest rungs of the white social ladder.

Another British social scientist described Polish refugees in Ifunda in comparable terms. The anthropologist Peter Worsley worked in the linguistic unit of the groundnut programme that was accommodated in the former Polish refugee camp in Tanganyika's southern highlands. In his autobiography he noted:

> It was extra-ordinary, in colonial times, to see Europeans, hundreds of Poles, many with blonde hair and 'Slavic' cheekbones, trading their meagre possessions, mainly European clothing, such as karakul hats, for a few shillings to the local Africans, for there was little to distinguish either side in economic terms.[115]

Although there was quite a difference between the economic situations of Poles and Africans, Worsley's observation is interesting. He underlines the racial belonging of the Poles to the white group, while pointing to their economic equivalence to and interaction with Africans. This points again to their closeness to 'poor whites', whose problem was their crossing of the racially defined social boundary between black and white. But the Poles' position within the hosting colonial societies was not a simple in-betweenness. There were more issues at play from the settler point of view.

Poles as Competitors

Even before the Poles arrived, there existed a general anti-refugee attitude among Kenyan settlers, which was articulated by Evelyn Brodhurst-Hill in her 1936 book *So this is Kenya!* Being herself a settler wife, she mainly argued against the administrations in Nairobi and London alike, who were letting down the European settlers.[116] But she also attacked another issue of her time. She saw it as a problem that some naive philanthropists wanted 'to make Kenya the dumping ground for yet another distressed minority or misunderstood section of the earth's teeming millions'.[117] She spoke out clearly against Jewish immigrants, doubting their persecution in Germany, but as she spoke out against other refugees as well, it is not clear if her opposition was motivated by antisemitism. Brodhurst-Hill instead accused the 'theorists' (liberal politicians) of ignoring 'the point of view of the settler, who is not in favour of the introduction of "poor whites" into a "black country"'.[118] She further explained that they were townspeople who could never become successful farmers. At the same time, she criticized earlier plans for the immigration of Czech-Slovakians or 'another mixed bag of European peasants'.[119] Her elaborations show that there was a generally anti-refugee sentiment among Kenyan whites.

Not surprisingly, the Poles were not welcomed by all settlers. Towards the end of 1943, an anonymous British ex-serviceman from Arusha wrote a letter to the editor of the *East African Standard*. Signing himself 'Ex-Service', he complained bitterly about the 'petting and pampering of refugees and foreigners' (meaning Jews, Poles and Italians) in the East African territories. Of the Poles from Tengeru he wrote:

> We have heard heart-rendering stories about their pitiable plight when they came here a year or so ago. Now, any day of the week one may walk into any shop in the town and the betting is that you will find it full of Poles buying all sorts of articles, mostly cloth, at prices that ordinary folk cannot pay.[120]

'Ex-Service' further accused Poles and Italian POWs of employing domestic servants at higher wages than usual, leaving the British settlers without personnel. He thereby argued along nationalist lines and regarded the foreigners as dangerous competitors for jobs, goods and personnel. To 'Ex-Service', the problem was the liberality of the colonial government, which helped foreigners more than its own nationals. Dramatically he urged the British settler population to stir itself up, because otherwise there would be no

British settlers in East Africa at the end of the war: 'Settlement will have been accomplished by our guests, mostly German Jews'.

The two categories 'Germans' and 'Jews' need to be distinguished. Northern Tanganyika had been a major focus of German settlement until the First World War. After their initial expulsion, many German settlers returned after Germany joined the League of Nations in 1926. During the war, the German threat to British rule in the colony was a constant leitmotif. In Dar es Salaam, trenches were dug around schools and public places, windows were shuttered and lights switched off at night.[121] A major emergency exercise in late 1942 reminded East Africans of the imminent danger. The scenario was a naval invasion supported by sabotage from German fifth columnists within Kenya.[122] Another reminder about the threat the Germans posed to British rule in East Africa was the discovery of a secret 'Hitler Shrine' on the premises of the Berlin mission next to Dar es Salaam harbour. According to the *East African Standard* it had been the secret meeting place of German Nazis before they were interned.[123] Fear of a German re-seizure of power in Tanganyika was further fuelled by the resurgence of the colonial revisionist movement in Germany in the 1930s.[124]

The other aspect of the statement of 'Ex-Service' was the Jewishness of the proposed settlers. Antisemitism was also a reason for the objections to Jewish immigration before the war and later voices against Jewish refugees in Kenya. In July 1942, a British Kenyan complained about idle refugees who were not supporting the British war effort.[125] His complaint was met by protest letters from Jewish refugees, who explained that they were willing to contribute but, as 'enemy aliens', were not being allowed to.[126] In the *East African Standard* columns, individual Jewish refugees were a bigger topic than the Poles in the camps, perhaps because of their more recognizable presence.

Interestingly, the letter by 'Ex-Service' was not published but sent to the Tanganyika government, which wrote an extensive response. Maybe the topic was too controversial during the war years, and the need for a united front against Germany too important. This changed with the end of the war.

An *East African Standard* editorial in June 1946 addressed the fear of 'alien dilution' if the Poles were to be allowed to stay permanently. Although the author sympathetically explained the reasons for the Poles' reluctance to go home, he nevertheless urged: 'They cannot be absorbed in the East African Community. They are too numerous; they would not fit into the economic and social framework; many are women and children with no resources and none on whom to depend'.[127] The Poles were thus at the same time a competitor who would threaten British dominance, and an inferior, uneconomic class that did not fit into the economic or social framework of the East African colonies. This framework referred most likely to the colonial socio-economic order of Kenya, as signified by rich white landowners and cheap African labour. The cheap Polish (as well as Italian) labour force was a welcome addition during the war, when many young British men were serving in the armed forces.[128] After the war, unskilled, lower-class Poles without capital no longer had a place in the East African colonial economy. The housing crisis in Nairobi added further to the resentment against foreigners.

Elspeth Huxley offers another interesting perspective on the Poles living in Masindi camp. Having grown up in Kenya, she was one of the best-known writers and proponents of white settlement in the colony. During a trip through East Africa she called at Masindi settlement. Her travelogue offers a Kenyan settler perspective on Poles in Uganda:

> It is a curious experience to find yourself, within a few miles of the Budongo forest, driving past little gardens where sturdy-looking European peasant women are getting in the washing, and through groups of flaxen-haired, pale-skinned children strolling home from school. The cottages are mud-built in native style, and it was strange to see white faces instead of black ones peering out of the doorways.[129]

In her description, the Poles, apart from their outer appearance, resemble Africans more than Europeans. The deviation from her expectations becomes apparent in her 'strange' feelings. She further describes them as privileged through British taxpayers' money, and fortunate in comparison to other East Europeans. According to her, 'the cutting of all their peasant roots had robbed them of the sap for independence'.[130] She thereby appeals to general anti-refugee as well as anti-Polish resentment. Another aspect is the class distinction she makes: while Europeans in agriculture in East Africa were called 'farmers' or 'planters', these 'peasants' were closer to Africans. As C. Olley from Salisbury wrote in *The New Rhodesia* newspaper: 'The Poles are a bunch of peasants whose skill and efficiency is little above the native'.[131] These peasants, some of them living in African-style housing, were causing strange feelings, as they did not fit into colonial society categories.

Richard Hodder-Williams argued comparably in his historical study of white farmers in Marandellas district. He mentions that the refugees were almost entirely peasants and therefore a farm was set up for them. 'But being peasants created problems.'[132] Some of the Poles wanted to send their children to government schools to have them away from the other peasants in the camp, but this was refused by local officials. Most likely these were the children of the few upper-class Poles, pointing to a class division among the refugees to which I will return in the next subchapter. Hodder-Williams went on: 'On the other hand, [white] villagers were concerned to isolate them, especially from possible contact with blacks'.[133] From a white settler perspective, the Polish peasants in Marandellas needed to be kept out of sight of Africans. This assessment reflects another aspect of the treatment of poor whites, namely isolation.

Conclusion

The initial distribution of the Poles was dictated by the obligation to contribute to the war effort. The colonies that had so far made the smallest direct contribution and had the weakest political voice were obliged to host most of the refugees: Tanganyika and Uganda. The middle ground in the wartime hosting fell to the Rhodesias; while Northern Rhodesia had less say in the decision making, Southern Rhodesia's decision was made directly in response to the Polish government's appeal. The reluctance of Kenya to host any sizeable number was justified with reference to its military importance, but the dislike by Kenyan settlers of lower-class whites and the established policy of keeping less affluent whites out may have informed this decision.

Another question was the acceptance of Poles as permanent settlers after the war. While all governments wanted to get rid of the Poles, small numbers of them were accepted. The 'Polish quotas' that the different governments agreed to accept differed considerably. The least willing to accept Poles was Uganda. The political turmoil it was experiencing, the colony's dependence on African elites and the general policy of the Colonial Office all prohibited the extension of white settlement. The classic settler colonies of Southern Rhodesia and Kenya were comparatively unwilling to allow any substantial number of Poles into their colonies. Although their governments – and, even more, their settler communities – were willing to accept white immigrants, they had a strong preference for those from Britain. The most welcoming were Northern Rhodesia and Tanganyika. While admittance was modest here in regard to the overall population, it was substantial in regard to the white community.

What could have been the reasons for this pattern? The Kenyan and Southern Rhodesian settler societies were already so big that the threat of political division loomed. In the face of growing opposition from the colonized population, the ranks had to be closed. A large group of Poles might, on the one hand, be a possible competitor for political domination. Afrikaners in Southern Rhodesia and Indians in Kenya already constituted groups with the potential to threaten British dominance, and it was unclear with whom the Poles would side, or whether they would be a possible contender in their own right. On the other hand, most Poles were peasants, lacking substantial capital. There was a prevalent fear among administrators and settlers that they could become a 'poor white problem', dealing a blow to white prestige – all of this in a situation in which wartime conditions had already put in question the idea of permanent white superiority.

The last group of remaining Poles, who were firmly described as 'poor white', were unwanted by any country.[134] Criminals, prostitutes and refugees with communist leanings were the ones causing the greatest concern to the authorities. Criminals threatened not only the image of white moral superiority but also the social cohesion of the white community. The assurance that T.H. Preston, the head of the Middle East Relief and Refugee Administration, gave to East Africans in 1942 might have sounded ironic in their ears eight years later: 'I don't think that you will regret having had these Poles'.[135]

It was, however, not only the criminals who were unwanted, but the Polish group as a whole that was generally regarded as subaltern whites by the British settlers and administrators. As Kennedy notes about the 'poor white problem': poverty per se was not the main problem. The main issue was them being contented with this poor way of life or failing to maintain standards, which was essentially a question of 'character, in the public school sense of the term'.[136] The majority of the Poles were of 'the peasant type',[137] and therefore worlds apart from the character building of British public schools. To borrow the words from a sociological study from the 1940s, they were not 'clubbable' – that is, not socio-economically fit to join the European clubs.[138] According to Dipesh Chakrabarty, the term 'peasant' can be understood in the Indian context as a 'shorthand for all the seemingly nonmodern, rural, nonsecular relationships and life practices'.[139] Following the geographer Tim Cresswell, 'being out of place' indicates a violation of the expected behaviour in a given social space. This expected behaviour is no universal norm, but is linked to the individual's position in the social structure.[140] Building on Mary Douglas's classic book *Purity and Danger*, things or people that are out of place are generally considered as dirty and thus dangerous.[141] For our case this can be illustrated by two examples: African peasants were as much 'in place' in African colonial societies as were European administrators or farmers employing African workers. Polish peasants were in turn 'in place' in the Polish countryside. But what contradicted and unsettled the order of the colonial social space was *white* peasants, who were simply 'out of place'.

In the next subchapter we will see that the Polish refugees positioned themselves differently. I will first 'unbox' the Polish refugee group and expose their inner class divisions. Furthermore, we have already outlined the gendered differences among the Poles. Despite these divisions and their politically weak refugee status, they drew on the Polish exile tradition to create a diaspora that had some, albeit limited, agency in the process.

Polish Self-Perceptions: European Allies in Exile

'What kind of roof will we find there in this mysterious Africa, we homeless wanderers?'

With these words, Anna Suchnicka described her feelings upon arrival in Tanga port.[142] Like most other refugees she was in a mix of curiosity, anxiety and fear. Most of them had come from the Polish periphery and had never before travelled abroad. Another former refugee remembers in her memoir: 'What was Africa anyway? We knew nothing of what it would be like'.[143] A closer look into Polish sources and recollections shows, however, that some Poles had had an idea of colonial Africa and their likely social position in it. Others learned fast to adapt to the new conditions. However, the social position of the Poles that is discernible from British colonial sources was not the same as the position in which they apparently saw and portrayed themselves. Polish sources and recollections give in part a contrasting view of the refugees' place in society. I will highlight these differences and thereby try to provide a fuller picture of this particular group, and will also aim to add another facet to the history of colonial societies in general.

In analogy to the previous subchapter, which differentiated between various British perspectives on the Poles, this subchapter will first of all differentiate between the group of Poles, mainly drawing on their own sources. In the moment of displacement, all migrants find themselves in new social settings, where they have to orient themselves anew. But the Poles did not arrive with bare hands. On the one hand they brought their own experiences, norms, values and historical narratives. On the other, they possessed visible aspects of identity that guided the reactions of the hosting populations – the most obvious being their race, gender and age. Other less visible aspects influenced their experience as well, like class, religion, their status as refugees and their link to the Polish army.

Following Brubaker and Cooper's critique of the term 'identity' and their more precise analytical alternatives, this subchapter is mainly about the self-identification or social positioning within these new social circumstances.[144] Rather than dealing with categorizations from outside, it focuses on people's own understanding of their place in society. Another analytical aspect that is usually subsumed under the misleading term 'identity' is the sense of belonging to a distinctive bounded group – described as commonality, connectedness or groupness.[145] The majority of refugees shared common geographical origins, language, religion and experiences. Communal living in camps under a distinctive Polish internal administration and in a Polish milieu furthermore strengthened this bond between the camp inhabitants. Taking all this into account, I will try to answer the seemingly straightforward question:

Where did the Polish refugees see themselves in the social stratification of colonial societies?

Polish Newspapers and Recollections

To answer this question, a turn towards sources produced by the Poles themselves is necessary. This part is based on two genres: first, there are contemporary Polish newspapers published by and for the Polish refugees, and secondly, published recollections by former refugees themselves. Two newspapers are analysed here. *Głos Polski* (The Polish Voice) was published weekly by the Polish Press Fund in Nairobi from October 1945 onwards.[146] The second newspaper used here is *Nasz Przyjaciel* (Our Friend), a fortnightly published by the Roman Catholic chief chaplain, Władysław Słapa, in Nairobi. Both newspapers contained reports on everyday activities in the Polish settlements as well as world news, with a special focus on the situation in Poland. While the first was more secular, the second paid special attention to religious life and issues. Both were dominated by the refugee elites (former government officials and priests respectively), and although constituting the bulk of the refugee population, women rarely published articles in either.

This absence of the 'average' refugee voice in the newspapers is partly balanced by the second type of source, written recollections. Although here again it was the more educated who wrote books, there are also examples of works published by people with a peasant background,[147] as well as collections of interviews and recollections where the individual backgrounds are not disclosed.[148] Furthermore, most of the published recollections are from people who were rather young during their stay in Africa, reflecting the high proportion of children and youths in the refugee population. A general problem with memory literature is that it is as much shaped by the circumstances at the time and place of writing as by the historical events described. A critical approach to both source genres and their perspectives is thus necessary.

Unpacking the Refugee Group

The Polish refugee group was not a homogeneous entity. In order to get closer to a more differentiated picture of Polish self-understandings, there is a need to distinguish, although the available sources limit this endeavour. Class, religion and nationality need to be taken into account.[149] But unclear categorizations, shifting denominations and fuzzy boundaries between the categories were more common than might be expected. There were furthermore individuals among the refugees who, although categorized as Poles, are better described as cosmopolitan actors with an individual agenda. Here we

Figure 5.2. Church celebration, probably Corpus Christ in Masindi, Uganda, 1944. The Bible passage on the banner translates as 'But take heart! I have overcome the world' (John 16:33). From Archiwum Fotografii Ośrodka KARTA, Signature: OK_1836_045, online.

will unpack the group by highlighting its general divisions, and afterwards introduce some individuals who defied the seemingly clear categories.

Class Divisions

Early one morning in February 1943 a ship with Polish refugees arrived in Beira port. The exhausted group embarked on a train and made their way up to Northern Rhodesia. In the course of their journey they had a stopover in Livingstone. After marvelling at the Victoria Falls, the group proceeded to a large hotel next to the train station. Inside they were welcomed by some Poles who had earlier fled the country and now resided in the hotel. They had prepared tea and sandwiches for their newly arrived compatriots. The friendly hosts were, however, disappointed at the sight of the newcomers. As one of the newly arrived refugees remembers the encounter: 'I sensed … that they thought that "big fishes" from Poland were coming. Most of them were very nice but some did not appear happy to see us, the lowest class, out of Russia'.[150]

As this anecdote of the friendly but disappointing encounter illustrates, class was an aspect that clearly distinguished the refugees. The Poles who resided in the comfortable hotel were most likely part of the 'Cyprus group': about five hundred Poles who were closely related to the Polish government and had fled from Poland via Romania and Cyprus to Northern Rhodesia. As Henryk Zins writes about them: 'These were people that represented a higher professional and cultural standard'.[151] They were mainly accommodated in hotels along the railway line, and filled many posts in the Polish administration of the camps. The colonial official in Northern Rhodesia, Gore-Browne, remarked: 'Their class consciousness is something one has to see to believe'.[152] In contrast to them, most of the Poles who came through Russia had a lower-class background, being mainly peasants. The first fault line among the Poles thus ran between the upper-class elites and the majority with a peasant background.

Religion and the Edges of the Refugee Community

Another aspect was religion. While the vast majority of refugees were Roman Catholics, there was a minority of Jews and Orthodox Christians among them. The few Orthodox and Jewish graves at the Polish cemetery in Tengeru bear witness to their presence.

Soon after the Poles had arrived in Africa, some Jewish inhabitants of Nairobi heard about antisemitism and discrimination in the refugee camps. Concerned about the situation, they joined together with the South African Jewish community and sent a representative on a tour through the camps. Arthur Abrahams went from Cape Town to Nairobi, and in September 1943 he set out to visit the East African camps to assess the situation. He reported that Tengeru was home to the biggest Jewish community among the camps, numbering thirty-seven, followed by Masindi with twenty-six, Koja with twenty and Ifunda with nine. Abrahams concluded that the Jews were, in contrast to his expectations, quite happy and content to be where they were – an understandable attitude in view of the conditions in Europe under Nazi rule. The Jewish community in Nairobi further helped the Jewish Poles in the camps with the building of the Tengeru synagogue, the supply of Matzo and the resettlement of six Jewish orphans to Palestine.[153]

Some reports about antisemitism among the refugees stand in stark contrast to Abraham's positive assessment. Rennie Bere, the British commandant of Koja, vividly described one incident in his recollections: 'I do not know how it started, but two or three hundred extremely tough-looking peasant women, armed with picks and shovels and axes, went rampaging round the settlement shouting "Juda! Juda! Makowski Juda!" and demanding Michael's blood'.[154] According to Bere, a rumour had spread among the refugees that the Polish camp official Michał Makowski was a Jew, although he was not. Other reports add to this assessment of antisemitism among the refugees.

One unnamed UNRRA representative accused several of the Polish staff in the South African children's camp at Oudtshoorn of antisemitic attacks against the only Polish Jew in the settlement, the hospital doctor. According to the report, the doctor was finally removed and went to Palestine to evade further harassment.[155] British authorities in London were also warned about antisemitic tendencies in the East African camps. In late 1944, the Foreign Office enquired whether some former members of the Polish government could be secretly brought from Romania to East Africa. British diplomats in Bucharest feared that the group of about eighty was in danger from the Soviet authorities, who had just taken over control of the country.[156] The major concern of the Colonial Office was whether they were Jewish. According to the officials there had already been trouble with the 'few refugees of Jewish extraction' who were among the many 'peasants from Eastern Poland'.[157]

The contested issue of antisemitism among the Polish refugees remains unclear from this scant evidence. It is also possible that officials had other reasons to paint a bleak picture of the Poles. The Colonial Office wanted to prevent a further influx of Poles who might become permanent settlers 'through the backdoor'.[158] The background of the unnamed UNRRA official, in turn, is completely unknown. Bere wrote of his experience of the antisemitic incident at Koja in hindsight, over forty years later. While there seems to have been antisemitism among at least some sections of the refugees, we cannot know for sure how prevalent this attitude was. It is instead quite clear that the Polish national community in the camps and beyond defined itself as a religious community as well.[159] The Catholic Church was usually the unquestioned centre of the settlements, most obviously in Koja, where the whole street grid ran towards the main church. I will later return to the central role of Catholicism.

Information about Orthodox refugees is even harder to come by. Only in Tengeru was an Orthodox church erected just outside the camp, with support from local Greek farmers.[160] The main reason for this is again the close connection of Catholicism and Polishness. Reportedly, many of the Orthodox refugees had been Polish citizens of Ukrainian or Belarusian nationality before the deportations, who had declared themselves Polish to get out of the Soviet Union. The fluidity of religious categories becomes apparent in another UNRRA report from Oudtshoorn. Therein it was explained that twelve of the settlement inhabitants had formerly been Russian Orthodox, but had converted to Catholicism.[161] According to the IRO repatriation officer Franciszek Harazin, there were about one thousand Ukrainians and Belarusians among the Polish refugees in June/July 1947 in Tanganyika alone. At the same time, a Polish official estimated there were about seven hundred in Uganda and a further three hundred in Northern Rhodesia, adding up to about two thousand Ukrainians and Belarusians in all of East Africa.[162] Based on these estimates, the IRO's Curtis explained that it was difficult to know the exact numbers as many of them had changed their names in order to be able to leave Russia.[163] 'Ukrainian carrie[d] a certain social stigma' in the settlements, he added. He went on that the Ukrainians and Belarusians had five years to learn the Polish language and 'enter "Roman Catholic" instead of "Orthodox" in all registration forms'. According to Harazin, Poles in Kondoa settlement even formed a minority with 300 of the 435 inhabitants described by him as 'not Polish'.[164]

Harazin's figures need to be treated with caution, as it is uncertain what his intention was or how he came to his estimates. His task was to encourage and facilitate repatriation, and those identified by him as Ukrainians and Belarusians may well have been Polish citizens of Ukrainian or Belarusian nationality before the war. The Polish Consulate in Nairobi itself stated it was difficult to determine exactly the nationality and religion of the refugees.[165] The British officials communication with the refugees relied largely on Polish officials and interpreters, and often did not really grasp the internal dynamics and cleavages within the refugee group.[166] Historian Jerzy Grzybowski estimates there were about two thousand Orthodox Belarusians among the whole group of civilian evacuees from the Soviet Union, of whom over four hundred stayed in Tengeru camp later.[167]

Either way, there are two remarkable aspects of Harazin's report and the reaction to it. First of all, the uncertain numbers in the categories of Poles, Ukrainians and Belarusians reflect the pre-war situation in eastern Poland. The region was highly diverse, and despite nationalist attempts to create clear-cut national categories the situation on the ground was complicated.[168] In interwar Poland, a Polish citizen was not necessarily a Polish national (which means ethnically Polish) – an issue that was hard to grasp for many Western officials.[169] As Lynne Taylor shows, the determination of the nationality of East European DPs was a confusing and often inconsistent exercise for military and international officials in Europe as well.[170] Furthermore, while there were identifiable groups, there were also people who did not fit neatly into one national (that is ethnic) category. Attempts at 'Polonization' or 'Russification' remind us that people also changed categories by adopting the socially favourable language, religion and thus categorization. The wartime upheaval and chaos in the Soviet Union further added to the possibilities of changing national categories. After the Sikorski–Maiski Agreement and the amnesty, becoming Polish turned into a means to escape the dangerous and repressive situation in the Soviet Union. A second aspect is the negligible impact of Harazin's report. Although the report was widely, albeit confidentially, circulated among IRO and colonial officials alike, this did not result in noticeable reactions or any change in policies. In the British files the group is invariably called 'Polish', and the issue of nationality is never problematized.

The emerging Cold War might explain why there were no mass deportations to the Soviet Union, and all the refugees were, with very few exceptions, officially treated as Poles.

One case to illustrate this is Anna Assen-Ajmer. According to a British file she was accused of being communist by the Polish camp leader in Tengeru and by 'Free Polish' sources in London. Because of these allegations she was refused entry into Britain on security grounds. The reasons for the accusations and the 'antipathy felt towards her in the camp' were supposedly due to her being Belarusian. Nevertheless, she was categorized as Polish and the Tanganyika government made no efforts to deport her to Soviet Byelorussia. Assen-Ajmer was further described as a 'slightly eccentric' woman, fluent in French. Her siblings lived in Casablanca, and she had good prospects of joining them there.[171] She might thus also serve as an example of those refugees who did not neatly fit into any of the national categories but rather navigated the changing and sometimes conflicting categorizations of the postwar period with her personal transnational network.

Cosmopolitan Individuals

Karol Szustek is a striking case. Although included in the Polish refugee group, judging from his British file, he was neither Polish nor a refugee. He spoke no Polish and had never been to Russia. The file categorized him as 'Austrian Jew, of Hungarian extraction'.[172] Szustek had been a Jewish bookseller and publisher in Vienna when Germany annexed Austria. He managed to escape via Romania to India, and subsequently set up a business in Bombay. His business collapsed in 1949, leaving him stranded in Bombay in his late fifties. Somehow he must have heard of the institutional arrangements for Polish refugees, and according to his British file 'he threw himself on the mercy of the International Refugee Organization, who took him to Tanganyika. Since then he has done nothing'. While Szustek went to India and Tanganyika, his wife worked as a domestic help for a Hungarian family in Zurich. Szustek had application forms for obtaining a visa to Switzerland, but did not fill them out as he regarded it difficult to set up a business there. He stated: 'I would rather go to the United Kingdom and get my wife to join me there'. The British selection team refused him entry. To them, only the IRO was responsible for this man, whom one immigration officer described as 'an insufferable type'.[173] By October 1950 he had left Tanganyika for Austria.[174]

For transnational individuals like Szustek, who had no real home country after the end of the war, the assistance of international institutions offered the possibility of finding a place to stay. It is impossible to assess how many more cleverly 'wangled'[175] their way into the supposedly homogeneous group of Polish refugees. The upheavals of war, deportation and flight created a chaotic situation that was difficult to survey. Furthermore, the refugees came from a region where it was unclear who was a citizen of which state and a member of which ethnic, linguistic or religious group. While the majority of refugees seem to have been Polish-speaking Catholics, there was a substantial minority of others.

But even some of those who were unmistakably Poles (by nationality *and* citizenship) followed a trajectory that had nothing to do with that of the majority of the other refugees in Africa. A prominent case is that of Wacław Korabiewicz (1903–94). He was a widely travelled poet, doctor, journalist and ethnographic collector, who served as a Polish refugee official as well. Before the war he had already travelled through Greece, Turkey and India, and worked as a ship's doctor. The outbreak of the war caught him on board a ship; he was interned in Stockholm and later travelled to Brazil. From 1943 to 1946 he served in Lusaka as deputy delegate of the Polish government-in-exile.[176] Korabiewicz, also called 'Kilometre',[177] was admired by some of the young Poles, but he was opposed by Polish clerics as he was advising the youth on the 'principle of free thinking'.[178] After his service as a refugee official, he collected ethnographic items for the King George V Memorial Museum in Dar es Salaam, and worked as a doctor in a local hospital. During his travels he acquired a good knowledge of Kiswahili, and 'established numerous contacts with Africans'.[179]

These contacts and his supposedly 'cordial' relations with the communist government in Warsaw worried the Tanganyikan government.[180] They feared that his communist leanings in combination with his contacts with Africans could cause political trouble in the colony. In late 1950 local officials therefore made efforts to get rid of him. But Korabiewicz refused to go to Poland, claiming his life would be in danger there. British officials were not so sure about this, but could not deport him either. Pennington tried in vain to convince British officials to accept Korabiewicz, as he would be a 'greater menace in Tanganyika than in the United Kingdom'.[181] After this request was declined, Tanganyikan officials even asked the Colonial Office to pay him the ship passage to India. Korabiewicz had an Indian visa and contacts in Delhi, and was willing to leave if his travel fare were paid. But he had other conditions as well: he wanted a guarantee of re-entry into Tanganyika should he be unable to get a permanent residence permit in India. The governor's deputy admitted that this arrangement would be 'kind of a gamble', but he feared that otherwise they would never get rid of him.[182] By the time this arrangement was accepted some months later, Korabiewicz had changed his mind and planned instead to work as a doctor on a sisal estate in Tasmania.[183]

One year later he was still in Tanganyika.[184] Not until 1954 was he expelled from Tanganyika, after he had sent ethnographic objects to Poland without permission.[185] His post in the Polish refugee administration suggests an affiliation with the Polish government-in-exile and thus anticommunist convictions. But his books were published in communist Poland; he collaborated with its institutions and returned – after another sojourn in Ethiopia – to Poland in 1958. Korabiewicz seems to have been a cosmopolitan traveller who kept his links to Poland despite his passion to travel. When asked who he was, he used to reply: 'I am a vagabond'.[186] His post in the Polish refugee administration was just one of the many possibilities he found to earn a living somewhere in the world.

Another prominent Pole who might have shared some convictions with Korabiewicz was Dr Julian Zamenhof. He was a nephew of the Esperanto inventor Ludwik Zamenhof, and grew up in a Polish Jewish upper-class humanist family.[187] He often visited his uncle, who hosted Esperantists from around the world, and made a strong impression. Julian Zamenhof was less interested in Esperanto than the rest of his family and was described as a pacifist and democrat.[188] He studied in Warsaw and Paris, became a surgeon and married the ophthalmologist Olga Nietupska.[189] In Tanganyika he worked as medical officer in Kidugala and Ifunda, and even rose to the rank of camp commandant in Kondoa.[190] This exceptional position enabled him to become part of white society, as testified by the fact that he and his wife were privately hosted by Captain MacDonald after Ifunda camp was closed. Reportedly, Zamenhof felt it dishonourable to go as a normal refugee to Tengeru, and preferred to stay with his friend until he was resettled to Britain.[191] In contrast to Korabiewicz, he was clearly accepted by the colonial upper class. Later he worked as a general practitioner in Swindon – despite his specialist training in surgery – until his death in 1961.[192]

In February 1946 the secretary of state for foreign affairs, Ernest Bevin, addressed the general problem of categorization in the House of Commons. Since many of the Polish ex-soldiers in Britain had come from territories that now belonged to the Soviet Union, he asked: 'Have they to be returned to Poland? Have they to be returned to the East of the Curzon Line?'[193] Behind this was the open question of the national categorization as Polish. Was it the place of birth, the self-identification as Polish ('nationality') or the citizenship? The Polish government in Warsaw clarified this issue only in November 1946 by explaining that all Polish *nationals* from east of the Curzon Line were welcome in the new Poland.[194] Polish citizens of Ukrainian nationality from the same region, however, were regarded as Soviet citizens.[195] In regard to the Polish refugees in Africa, British officials seem to have followed a pragmatic mixture instead. They accepted the vast majority of them and, as far as I know, none of the refugees went to the Soviet Union. Although the colonial administration was aware (at least since the Harazin report) that many of the Polish refugees were Polish citizens of Ukrainian or Belarusian nationality, the most important aspect here was their connection to the Polish army – an army whose members were not only ethnic Poles but included some Polish civilians of Belarusian nationality.[196] After all, the morale of the Polish soldiers had been the most important rationale behind the decision to host the refugees. As the Cold War developed, it led to a generally more generous acceptance of refugees from communist countries.

Refugees as Diasporic Players

Having demonstrated that the Polish refugee group was diverse, I will address the majority and the elites of this group as historical actors in their own right. The Polish refugees drew on three interrelated resources for their ability to influence decision making: first, the long history of Polish exile activity; second, connections with the worldwide Polish diaspora; and third, their self-categorization as European allies on a par with the British. These resources were put into action in resisting plans by the colonial administration, the British government and international organizations alike.

Poland has a long history of producing and mobilizing national sentiment and culture under foreign domination and in exile. This history goes back, at least, to the refugees from the failed November 1830 uprising who settled

Figure 5.3. Parade of Polish refugees, presumably on the occasion of 3 May, Polish Constitution Day, Tengeru, Tanganyika, 1948. From Archiwum Fotografii Ośrodka KARTA, Signature: OK_005153, online.

in Paris (the émigrés of the 'Wielka Emigracja').[197] The cultural production of this émigré community has formed an integral part of the Polish national canon ever since. When fate threw the Poles into remote camps on the African periphery, they arrived with an interpretative frame and practices that provided guidance. Reproducing Polish culture, language and religion became an aim that gave the '*tułaczy*' (wanderers) a task and a meaning. In Polish newspapers, public meetings and cultural activities in the camps, the tradition of the Polish diaspora was maintained and recreated.

Some examples may serve to illustrate this. The theatre group in Koja staged plays by Adam Mickiewicz;[198] and in Ifunda, a lecture about the author was held.[199] Mickiewicz was the most famous poet of the 'Wielka Emigracja' and a central author of Polish romanticism. Lectures on Polish history and the common celebrations of national holidays further strengthened the bond to the 'fatherland'.[200] The Polish girl guide group in Digglefold was named after Emilia Plater, the best-known female heroine of the failed November uprising.[201] The garden in front of the administrative block in Tengeru contained a trimmed hedge spelling 'Poland 1942' to commemorate the refugees' arrival.[202] The institutional creation of a Polish milieu in the settlements served to sustain this bond to the nation and the social cohesion of the group.[203]

Another way to recreate the Polish community in the settlements was the communal eating of Polish food. Based on interviews with former refugees, Monica Janowski argues that Polish 'foodways' were central in the performance of 'Polishness' in exile.[204] According to one former refugee, who had stayed in Tengeru, the Poles never ate African cooked food, but put efforts into maintaining their Polishness through the preparation of Polish 'proper' food.[205] The scepticism towards African food is also apparent in one story from Karanga prison, near Moshi in Tanzania. According to Gerald Mkindi, there were once some Polish prisoners who refused to eat the food provided. Apparently a Polish variety of beans was brought to feed them, of which the cook took some home. They are still cultivated in the area, and called 'Polish beans'.[206]

In late 1946 an anonymous author raised the question in *Głos Polski* of whether to return to Poland or to continue wandering around. The author argued against a return under the prevailing conditions of Soviet oppression. He further countered fears that the Poles would fall prey to 'denationalization' when settling elsewhere. To him, Polish history provided evidence for the ability of Poles to keep their national identity in exile. He further cited the American Polonia's commitment to the Polish cause as a proof of the importance of staying in exile.[207] This argument leads us to the second resource the Polish refugees drew upon to construct their diasporic identity: the link to other Polish diaspora organizations.

The most important nodes in the Polish diaspora network were the government-in-exile in London and Polonia organizations in the United States.[208] The link to the government is obvious, as the Polish camp administration was part of the administrative machine of this government until its de-recognition. Afterwards the administrative posts were still largely filled by the same personnel. Polish organizations in Africa were fast to declare their full support for the London government-in-exile in 1945.[209] Some senior Polish officials in Africa were representatives of the international Polish diaspora organization Światpol, which was set up by the interwar Polish government to strengthen the link between diaspora and motherland. The stated aim of Światpol was to stimulate national unity and keep up national culture among Poles abroad.[210] Many of the refugee officials had been members of the Polish government before the war, so their support came as no surprise.

American Polonia organizations supported the refugees during their entire sojourn in Africa, sending clothes and shoes. The donations were sometimes even too generous, resulting in unused surplus gifts, such as half a ton of tooth-cleaning powder or ten thousand pairs of children's shoes.[211] *Nasz Przyjaciel*, the Catholic newspaper published in Nairobi, got financial support from American Catholic organizations.[212] In Tengeru, two of the priests were Polish-American, and the first social centre was also sponsored by the American YMCA.[213] The Poles in the camps were consequently full of praise for the American Poles. In May 1945 in Uganda, the inhabitants of Masindi settlement paid homage to the American Polonia at a public meeting organized by the local 'Association of the Eastern Borderlands'.[214] At a comparable meeting, Koja's inhabitants praised the American Poles for their 'titanic fight for the "Polish Question"'.[215] Gratitude was thus expressed not only for the material assistance but also for support in the common struggle against Soviet domination in Poland. American Polonia activists understood themselves after the war as a kind of successor to the Paris émigrés. From a distance they vocally supported the struggle for freedom in the Polish homeland.[216]

Contacts to compatriots in the United States and Canada were also utilized by the Poles in the camps to gain access to these countries. Poles in Koja, for example, refused to return to Poland, because they argued that they were working out plans with American and Canadian diaspora organizations to move there.[217] Others corresponded individually with relatives abroad, such as an uncle in New York or an aunt in Argentina.[218] Especially in the postwar era, the Poles used their diaspora networks to find a place somewhere in the world. IRO official Curtis summarized the efforts of the refugees in 1949: while the 'average refugee in the camps still pins his hopes on America', the 'Polish intelligentsia in Nairobi still pin their hopes on the United Kingdom'.[219] Curtis's assessment confirms the two most important nodes in the global Polonia network for the Poles in Africa and the class differentiation of the refugee group outlined previously.

Communal living under camp conditions was a further factor that helped to create and recreate the feeling of belonging among the camp inhabitants. As Liisa Malkki shows in her study of Hutu refugees from Burundi in 1980s Tanzania, living in camps strengthened their self-identification with the group and recreated a sense of belonging to a diaspora that would eventually return to the home country. Other refugees, who had lived independently in towns, crafted their identities rather pragmatically in response to everyday challenges.[220] As Malkki notes, camp refugees were 'identifying themselves as a people in exile' and thereby responded to their exclusion from the national order through creating another, purer nation in the camp.[221] The grouping according to nationality in DP camps in postwar Germany had a comparable effect.[222]

This understanding of the camps as a permanent and nationally Polish settlement is also apparent in the terminology used by the Polish administration. In contrast to the British administration, which underlined the temporary character of the Poles' sojourn through the consistent use of 'camp', the Polish administration and newspapers wrote of '*osiedle*' (which translates roughly as 'settlement'). The Polish term for camp ('*obóz*') was used only for concentration and DP camps in Europe, and the Kenya transit camps of Makindu and Mombasa. And this was not confined to the administration. The former refugee Barbara Porajska remembers that upon arrival the refugees gave names to the different 'villages' of Masindi and erased the word 'camp' from their vocabulary, explaining: 'We have had enough of camp life'.[223] The best illustration of the difference between the British and Polish perceptions of the situation is the contrast between the titles of the British 'Camp Commandant' and the Polish 'Settlement Leader' (*Kierownik Osiedla*). While the former ran a temporary camp, the latter led a seemingly stable residential community of exiles.

Encampment of nationally defined groups can strengthen their feelings of belonging together, and this can be put to use as a common ground for organizing protest and resistance. As Hilton has shown in regard to Polish and Latvian DPs in postwar Europe: 'DPs' cultural nationalism provided them with both purpose and agency, to act within the world of political nations from which they were displaced'.[224] Despite their dependent and weak position, the Polish refugees in Africa had some success in protesting against decisions by British colonial and international officials.

Polish Refugee Resistance

The most obvious case in point is the refugees' resistance against forced deportation to Poland. Especially in the postwar period, repeated proposals to deport unwanted Poles back to their home country were made by the administration. In 1950 the acting governor in Uganda strongly warned against the careless deportation of petty criminals or drunkards to Poland. He urged other officials to consider that many refugees regarded an order to return to Poland as 'tantamount to a sentence of death'. As proof, he cited two cases that had made him realize the severity of this prevalent fear: when told about the possibility of deportation, one refugee tried to commit suicide, while another died of a heart attack after drinking large amounts of mixed alcohol.[225] In Tanganyika, two mothers threatened to kill their children if they were to be sent to Poland.[226] Apart from these threats, many refugees refused to fill in the necessary forms of the communist authorities, thus hindering the issuing of Polish passports and causing trouble to the British administration. In the end, it seems, hardly anyone was forcibly deported to Poland. While the association with the Polish ex-soldiers in Britain and the emerging Cold War may have been the decisive factors influencing the British decision to admit most of the Poles to Britain, their active resistance to returning to Poland was certainly a contributing factor.

Other examples show the refugees' agency in less decisive issues. In 1944 the refugee administration planned to establish a central Polish secondary school for children from the East African camps in Rongai in Kenya. The transfer of Polish orphans to Rongai posed no problem to this plan, but the relocation of children who were living together with their parents in Ugandan camps was met with resistance. The Polish consul received a petition against relocation, signed by 126 parents from Koja.[227] After this concerted action, the commissioner of the East African Refugee Administration had to concede: 'The idea of placing a secondary school at Rongai has been abandoned owing to the reluctance of the parents to be parted from their children'.[228] After their experience of deportation – often coupled with the separation of family members – the Polish parents were reluctant to let their children go. Their resistance was successful and Rongai was established on a smaller scale for the orphaned children only.

In another instance, the Poles in the camps fought with the support of the government-in-exile, Canadian Catholics and the Vatican to resettle the last group of orphans from Tengeru to Canada. The communist government in Poland claimed that the children rightfully belonged 'home' in Poland. The resistance against this plan caused a diplomatic row in 1949.[229] When the children had a stopover in Italy, fears were aroused that they might be sent to Poland. Consequently, an angry crowd of Poles invaded the house of the IRO representative in Tengeru. As the IRO was responsible for the transfer operation, the Nairobi representative of the organization was fast to ask the organization's Geneva headquarters for an assurance that the orphans would not be forcibly sent to Poland.[230] It remains unclear what the decisive factor was in the finally successful resettlement to Canada, but the efforts of the refugees themselves showed their potential for independent action.

On other occasions, however, their resistance was less successful. When the Southern Rhodesian government decided to concentrate all remaining refugees in Gatooma, Polish officials protested vehemently. A joint inspection by British and Polish officials came to the conclusion that the conditions were absolutely unsatisfactory, and Władysław Kadow, the Polish deputy commander of Marandellas settlement, stated that the sanitary and health conditions 'resemble a pigsty'.[231] The Apostolic Delegate even compared Gatooma to a German concentration camp.[232] Nevertheless, all the refugees in Southern Rhodesia were moved to Gatooma. The unhealthy conditions and reduced rations led to undernourishment and the spread of disease among the Poles. After several reports and inspections, the Rhodesian official, who was blamed for deliberately creating these bad conditions, was at least removed from his post and conditions improved slightly.[233]

These few examples shall suffice to show that the Polish refugees could, despite their divisions and sometimes differing views, act politically and influence some of the decision making regarding their living conditions and futures. The long tradition of Polish exile and connections to the global Polish diaspora helped to keep the bonds between its group members. The self-description as Polish 'exiles' offered a stronger position than the representation as 'refugees', who are generally considered as helpless, voiceless and passive victims of greater forces.[234] This example shows once more that the construction of refugees as victims without agency distorts the history of refugees. Although restrained in their decisions, refugees have always been active in influencing their fate. The Poles used their self-conception as exiles and their strong 'groupness' as a common ground from which to struggle politically to improve their situation.

European Allies

There was another resource that helped these refugees as well: their whiteness. While they had not been white in Poland, they became white upon entering the colonial situation. Before the deportations, other categories had mattered more. Being Polish, Ukrainian, Belarusian, Catholic, Orthodox, Jewish, peasant, landowner, intelligentsia, male or female – these were the important aspects defining roles and opportunities in society. In the colonial situation, these categories did not vanish, but being white mattered increasingly. In comparison with their compatriots suffering under German oppression and warfare, and even in relation to Polish DPs in Germany, the Poles in Africa fared well. On a visit to Tengeru in 1949, one Canadian IRO official was surprised about the comfortable circumstances in which the Polish refugees lived. He had worked in European DP camps before, and in his report he contrasted the 'Polish party' in Tengeru with the 'extreme misery' in which Polish DPs were living in Germany.[235] After the war, the refugees were even able to make collections on behalf of their compatriot DPs in Europe.[236] The *East African Standard* described the Polish refugees as 'among the more fortunate' compared to other refugees in Europe.[237]

This description is confirmed by recollections of the refugees themselves. After their stay in Africa, most looked back on a time of uncertainty but also of establishing a normal life after the horrible experiences of deportation, forced labour and escape. It was an interlude in the personal odyssey that was mostly followed by permanent resettlement in some other place. The time in the African camps, especially for the children, was an exotic adventure. One refugee remembered that she was astonished about the generous supply of food in Lusaka camp: 'The war is so bad, how can they give us so much meat?'[238] One former inhabitant of Tengeru remembered: 'we had all the amenities of a small town'.[239] And a Polish official reported that this camp resembled a modestly organized vacation camp. He further explained that conditions in Tengeru were worse than in Poznań province but better than the conditions under which peasants were living in the eastern borderlands or central Poland.[240] The region where the refugees came from was one of the poorest in Poland, and at least in some of the African camps many enjoyed an improved material standard of living.[241]

After their years of suffering following deportation to the Soviet Union, it was in the African settlements that the refugees found security and welfare provision. The poem by Anna Suchnicka quoted at the beginning of this subchapter goes on: 'Freedom of prayer, study. Freedom of work, word, thought. Dressed, fed, cured, does anyone ask for more?'[242] The Poles received housing, food, clothing and monthly allowances. On top of that, African workers did most of the hard manual labour.[243] Initially the refugees were supposed to do three hours' voluntary work in the settlements daily, but this was not enforced.[244] Some got permission to work in paid jobs inside and later outside the settlements, but they always had a place where they could return to and be maintained. One Kenyan official even complained that this knowledge eliminated their 'spirit of determination to succeed' in their jobs.[245]

Hence, although migration to Africa was not what the Polish refugees had wanted, in the end they found themselves in a position where they profited from colonial society, simply through belonging to the 'superior' group of Europeans. As one refugee, who was a child during the time in Africa, put it much later: 'I learned to be a racist. For no reason other than being white, I could travel first class on the train while native Africans could not'.[246] Especially in contrast to their previous experiences of violence and suffering in the Soviet Union, there remained a largely positive remembrance. As one former refugee put it, remembering her departure from Mombasa to Australia: 'I hadn't imagined that I would one day [bid] farewell [to] this Dark Continent which had so generously opened its arms to shelter us during those war years'.[247]

The Polish refugee newspapers show that many Poles arrived with contemporary European images of Africa and ideas of European superiority. One travel report of a journey through Sudan, published in *Głos Polski*, may serve as an illustration. The Polish refugee author contrasts the living conditions of the natives ('like thousands of years ago') with the modern colonial luxury of the ship in which she was travelling on the River Nile.[248] Sitting in the European dining room, she was clearly part of the colonial upper class.

The Polish elites, mainly former members of the pre-war establishment, fostered a self-conception as part of a suppressed but, in terms of civilization, superior European nation. In a speech on Polish Constitution Day, Consul Aleksander Zawisza lectured the Southern Rhodesian public about the long liberal democratic tradition of Poland, explaining that Poland had at times even overtaken other European countries in its development.[249] Similarly, in an interview with the *East African Standard*, Henryk Strasburger, a visiting delegate from the London government-in-exile, underlined Poland's West Europeanness. He explained to the British audience: 'The Poles really belong to Western Europe – we have what is called Roman culture'.[250]

From Polish sources it becomes apparent that the British perspective of 'looking down' on the Poles was not shared by them. As shown earlier, the Polish refugee elites understood themselves in Africa as being closer to the colonizers than the colonized.[251] They underlined that their status as European allies put them on an equal footing with the British. The Digglefold girl guides planted a flowerbed featuring the Polish and English coats of arms next to the scout lily.[252] In front of the camp's administrative buildings, Polish flags were flying next to those of the British – at least symbolically the two nations were equal.[253] One article about Masindi stated emphatically: 'Here flies the Polish flag'.[254] Drawing on their specific national tradition, global diaspora connections and underlining their Europeanness, the Poles influenced decision making about themselves. This clearly contrasts with the picture from British sources, where the Poles are described as an inferior social group in need of welfare and control.

Polish–African Entanglements in Church and Housing

The issues raised in the Polish newspapers from Nairobi furthermore reflect what seemed important to the refugees. First, the building styles of the refugee houses showed the social effects that ensued from the material structures provided by the colonial authorities. Second, the church buildings provide an example of where Polish initiative and creative adaptation of building techniques resulted in a mixture of Polish and African churches. And third, the religious life of the Poles was a field not covered in British sources but it was prominent in the Polish ones, illuminating the diverse relations between Polish and other Catholics. The agenda setting in the Polish newspapers thereby shows the independent agency of the Polish refugees.

Housing the Poles

Although it might seem a rather technical issue, the materiality of the settlements and its differing perceptions can shed some light on the social position of the refugees in relation to the hosting colonial societies. Before the refugees' arrival in Tengeru, the Tanganyikan government in Dar es Salaam ordered the erection of '1,200 Rondavel Type Huts'.[255] Two Greek constructors were contracted to build the houses, which were eventually completed by thousands of African workers under the leadership of the Public Works Department.[256] The government's decision to build round rather than rectangular houses was criticized by the medical officer, Bertram Wilkin, and the district commissioner in nearby Arusha.[257] Wilkin was highly critical of the quality of work of the contractors, and generally preferred the Public Works Department to do the building. He further criticized the round houses as follows: 'Because household furniture is rectangular, round huts do not accommodate [it] so well as squared buildings of equal floor area'.[258] While this argumentation against the unfitting layout does not really convince, his general dislike of the low quality of the houses is obvious. An implicit association of round dwellings with Africans, and these in turn with unhealthy conditions, may have been another reason. On other occasions the medical officer was equally sceptical about Africans entering the camps, and regarded them as carriers of disease.[259] In response to Wilkin's criticism, a meeting of Polish and British authorities in Dar es Salaam came to the conclusion that rondavels should be sufficient, as the costs for rectangular houses would be too high.[260] While keeping costs low was a priority, it is still striking why some colonial officials, who were otherwise obsessed with keeping up the difference between white and black, were willing to build houses perceived to be 'African'.

But how did the inhabitants perceive their dwellings? In the Polish sources, round houses were clearly associated with Africans. In one article in *Nasz Przyjaciel* the author jumps to the incorrect generalization that 'all Negro houses, far and wide in Africa, are round with a pointed roof'.[261] Another author, describing Tengeru in the same newspaper, mentions the 'peculiar huts – as in Poland, but round'.[262] The reaction of the refugees on arrival in Tengeru is described in a report on the first year of the camp: 'There were some who at first sight looked askance at these living quarters, telling themselves that these could never be homes'.²⁶³ By contrast, in one article on the Polish settlement of Rusape it was emphasized that the houses there were not 'beehives' but 'good-looking small houses'.²⁶⁴ In the same vein, in another article on the small Northern Rhodesian settlement of Fort Jameson, one inhabitant praised the conditions there by pointing out that the houses 'look completely different from the Negro houses one meets in other Polish settlements'.²⁶⁵ The perceived inferiority of round houses was also apparent by the fact that the Tengeru camp authorities (both British and Polish) were housed in bigger and rectangular houses.²⁶⁶ Through the lens of housing, the ordinary refugee seemed to be on a par with the Africans. This is reflected in recollections of former refugees, describing Tengeru as resembling an African village.²⁶⁷

There was generally some variability in the housing in the different settlements. While the standard house in Tengeru was a single round structure, in Masindi it consisted of two attached round houses.²⁶⁸ In Koja the houses were small rectangular cottages, resembling more the Polish peasant home. One refugee from Marandellas remembers that they were 'housed in traditional African huts made from clay, with straw roofs and no windows'.²⁶⁹ The low standard in comparison to European colonial architecture was defended by one British official with the words: 'My instructions were to build a temporary camp and not a model village'.²⁷⁰ Whatever the intentions were, the social effect of the material structures was an image of the Poles as being different from the British. This perception was shared by Poles and British alike, although the Poles did their best to distinguish their settlements from African ones. In the descriptions of settlements with rectangular houses, this feature was underlined. Furthermore, the inhabitants emphasized the Polish character through decorations with national symbols, names, trimmed hedges and flower gardens.

Polish–African Church Buildings

A building of high symbolic importance for each settlement was the church. The erection of it was completely left to the Poles, and sometimes supported by international religious organizations. The colonial sources do not mention any of these activities, as the authorities were neither involved nor interested in them. As most refugees were firm adherents of Catholicism, there was a room in every settlement in which to celebrate Holy Mass. Although communal rooms were used at first, it did not take long before the Polish community started building churches in most settlements. In Tengeru, building the church in stone had already started within the first year after arrival.²⁷¹ The design of the churches, like the housing, followed patterns that were partly Polish and partly African. The church in Rusape settlement, Southern Rhodesia, had the most outstanding design. It consisted of three round houses that were connected with covered porches. In an article in the Catholic newspaper, the author praised the Polish priest: 'He has just created a new style of church in Africa'.[272] Significantly, it is the Polish man who was praised as innovator. In this case too, the design evolved out of financial constraints rather than transcultural interest, but a creative adaptation of local building techniques was nevertheless involved in building this church.

The church in Tengeru was described in recollections as having been 'designed along the African, not the European model'.[273] Although its rectangular design with a gable roof is not as extraordinary as the Rusape one, it clearly differed from the churches of Poland. The parish priest understood the building as a 'memorial' to commemorate the Poles' stay in Tanganyika and a means of 'spreading the faith among the blacks'.[274]

In contrast to these churches, two shrines, built in Marandellas settlement, were described as being built 'according to the pattern of Polish roadside chapels'.[275] The church in Masindi also resembled the Polish model more closely. It is a rather impressive structure in Romanesque style, and is still standing today (see Figure 3.1). Construction started in 1943, with strong involvement of the refugee community, who produced the bricks. On 1 November 1945, it was consecrated by the Bishop of Uganda. In an article about this ceremony the church is described as 'a votive offering to God's gratitude for the miraculous salvation from Soviet Russia'.[276] The large inscription above the main door emphasizes its national Polish character: 'Polonia Semper Fidelis' (which roughly translates as 'Always Faithful to Poland'), and the national coat of arms, the Polish eagle, is hanging above the inscription. As the term 'Polonia' was also used as a name for the Polish diaspora, the inscription could equally be interpreted as a commitment of the Polish exiles to the nation. Next to the main door there is another inscription, explaining that the church was built by 'the Poles in exile on the way to their liberated homeland'. What is interesting about this inscription is the fact that it was engraved in four different languages: English, Polish, Latin and Runyoro. This underlines the internationality of the church and the settlement, which was controlled by British administrators, inhabited by Polish, Roman Catholic refugees and built, maintained and surrounded by African workers in the kingdom of Bunyoro.[277]

The examples of church-building activities show that these were not simply Polish churches built for the Poles by themselves. Their design rather reflected the intermingling of Polish and different African building styles. They were mainly used by the Polish community of the settlements, but were also meant to stay and be used by other Catholics after the departure of the Poles. The Polish authors wrote with a certain pride about their creative adaptation of

African techniques and designs. They thereby elevated themselves above the local Africans, while at the same time appreciating their skills. British sources, by contrast, remained silent about these building activities.

The Common Catholic Faith

As we have seen, Catholicism played a central role in the daily lives of most Polish refugees. Religious activities do not feature in the British sources, whereas one Polish newspaper was almost entirely devoted to religious issues. Coming from a religious community, their faith may well have been strengthened through their experiences of deportation, loss of relatives, and suffering in the Siberian 'Gehenna'. While religious affiliation can be a strong barrier because of group formations and identifications, it can also serve as a bridge across social divides, especially in colonial society. Whereas only a few British officials and settlers were Catholic (a counterexample is the earlier mentioned Tengeru camp commandant and 'friend of the Poles', John Minnery), the refugees shared a common denomination with three other groups: Polish missionaries, Italians, and African Catholics.

The most obvious connection the refugees had was to the few Polish missionaries already present at the time of their arrival. The first priest in Abercorn was a Polish missionary who had already worked in Africa for fifteen years, was fluent in some African languages and was delighted to meet his compatriots.[278] Upon arrival in Tengeru, the refugees were surprised to find out that 'Polish nuns had preceded us here'.[279] A Polish sister from the Kilema mission station had rushed to Tengeru to receive them there, and later the refugees repeatedly made the sixty-mile journey to visit her mission.[280] In Kasisi, close to Lusaka, there were further Polish missionaries. One of them was the Jesuit Adam Kozłowiecki, a survivor of the Auschwitz and Dachau concentration camps, who had been sent to Northern Rhodesia in 1946 and later became Archbishop of Lusaka.[281] In a Polish refugee newspaper report about a visit to Kasisi, the author especially praised the work of the Polish sisters.[282] She particularly mentioned that the sisters spent such a long time away from their home country and were taking care of African orphans. At the end of the visit the children sang Polish songs, fascinating the author because they sounded like Polish children.[283] Through their compatriot missionaries, the refugees not only came into contact with African Catholics but were also influenced by the missionary view on Africa.

The common faith also led to strong connections with Italians. In the Polish settlement of Kondoa, the role of the parish priest was filled by an Italian missionary who had learnt Polish to communicate with his flock.[284] In Ifunda the first priest was also an Italian from a nearby mission.[285] The common religious affiliation may also have been a factor behind the numerous Italian–Polish intimate relationships.[286] Italians and Poles were closely connected not only through their position as non-British whites but through their common faith as well.

One article in the Catholic Polish refugee paper gives an indication of how African Catholics were perceived by the Poles. In December 1946, Jerzy Dołęga-Kowalewski, a refugee from eastern Poland, wrote an article entitled 'Black Saints' about the history of Ugandan Catholicism and the Uganda martyrs.[287] By sketching the history and political system of the Buganda kingdom, and drawing comparisons to European history, he acknowledged that there had been an independent political system in Uganda before colonialism. He narrated the history of a group of Ganda Catholics who had been executed in the 1880s and beatified by the Pope in 1920, known as the Uganda Martyrs. While acknowledging their sacrifice, the author goes on: 'European culture, the pride of the white people, gave to the Negro what is the most important – Christ's teaching'.[288] Thus although describing African agency, he still looked at it from what he considered a superior vantage point. He could be proud because it was white European culture that had brought the right kind of belief to Africa.

This paternalistic perspective is even more apparent in an article the same author had published two weeks earlier. The title, 'Such big black children…', is telling in this regard.[289] In the article he recounts anecdotes of the Hungarian adventurer and anthropologist Emil Torday from the latter's time in the Belgian Congo. Dołęga-Kowalewski concludes by referring to his own experience among Africans, stating that they are 'for the time being, big black children', but that if one (implicitly referring to the white man) puts in some work and 'heart', they will benefit from it.[290] This is colonial paternalism par excellence, and resonated well with nineteenth-century visions of a 'civilizing mission'. In contrast to the biological racism that denies the colonized Other any possibility for improvement, such cultural racism acknowledges the theoretical capacity of the Other to reach one's own supposedly superior status.

This perception of belonging to a superior European Christian civilization is also found in a speech held at a public meeting in Koja settlement. The speaker describes the 'distinctive and healthy Polish culture stemming from the trunk of Western European civilization, Christianity and its idea of democracy'.[291] Polish culture was thus at the same time part of Western Europe but also a distinguishable entity. The close association of 'Western European' civilization with Christianity and democracy again makes it clear that the Poles felt themselves to be part of the superior European group. This perception can also be seen in the establishment of a separate YMCA centre for Africans in Kidugala settlement. While there were activities at the Polish YMCA in nearly every settlement,[292] Kidugala was the only

Polish settlement where a YMCA centre for Africans was established.[293] In the newspapers we can trace the establishment of a little school in what was called the 'Negro Club Room', in which a course in needlework was held for African women.[294] From the set-up of the centre it is clear that it was a place where Africans could learn from Poles, and not the other way around. The Poles thereby bore greater resemblance to missionaries than to war refugees.

In published recollections written years after the authors' experiences in African refugee settlements, there emerges a picture that differs from contemporary Polish sources. The authors put more emphasis on a relatively equal relationship between Polish and African Catholics. One former refugee writes of close cooperation between the parishes at the Polish settlement of Bwana Mkubwa and the African Catholics in the nearby town of Ndola.[295] The former refugee Maria Romanko even recounts that, together with other pupils of the Polish school settlement Oudtshoorn, she sometimes went to the mission church in town and deliberately joined the black congregation there 'to give an example to white South Africans'.[296] This statement in her memoirs has to be understood in the context of having been written much later, mainly for children and grandchildren in Canada. However, it is conceivable that there was interaction between Catholics across the racial divide.

The contrast between contemporary newspaper sources and the memory literature can be explained from two perspectives. Let us begin with the historical circumstances of the writing itself. While the newspapers were produced and printed in a colonial society in which racial differentiation was a basic principle of the social order, the memoirs were written at a time when colonialism was a thing of the past and largely de-legitimized. Furthermore, the newspapers were produced at a time when the Poles were in a precarious position. They had no country to which they could return. This was especially true in the postwar period. When the communist government in Poland was internationally recognized, the anti-communist Polish refugees became dependent on the goodwill of others. In this situation it would have been of the utmost importance to underline their qualifications for immigration, and therefore their (West) Europeanness.

A second reason for the contrast is the social position of the authors. While the people writing in newspapers were mainly part of the Polish nationalist pre-war elite, and were closely connected to the government-in-exile in London, the authors of the memory literature came from more diverse social backgrounds. The prominent writers for the newspapers were men, while the vast majority of refugees were women and children. The perspective of the memory literature is thus closer to the average refugee's perspective, but further away from the historical circumstances.

Conclusion

The examples show the value of a multi-perspective approach and the use of sources from the diaspora alongside the colonial archives. While the round houses built for the refugees in Tengeru and Masindi were regarded by both British and Poles as signs of Africanness, the Polish inhabitants from other settlements stressed that their houses were different. The Poles living in 'African' houses did their best to underline how they differed from Africans by planting 'European' gardens. Lush flowerbeds, trimmed hedges and cottage gardens had a reassuring function. The church buildings and the practice of Catholicism formed, in turn, a field that did not appear in the British sources, but was of importance to the everyday life of the refugees. Both the buildings and the practice were left under the control of Polish and international religious organizations, and were thus far more prominent topics in the Polish sources. While the church buildings reflect the varying adaptation of African styles, the religious practices as well as the writing about them show the perceived Polish commonality with, as well as superiority over, the Africans. In the view of the Poles, they brought their faith from Europe to the Africans, and thus helped them.

The Polish newspapers generally paint a picture that differs from the British placement of the Poles on the fringes of the white community. Rarely writing about Africans, and if at all, then in a rather colonialist perspective, the Poles portrayed themselves as members of a European allied nation on a par with the British. While some African features were appreciated and adapted (as in church design), this was done from the vantage point of superiority. Polish memory literature instead portrays a more egalitarian relationship. This may be credited to the time and societies in which the authors wrote, but it may also have been due to their social position, as the authors of memoirs happened to be more representative of the average refugee than the elite male authors of the newspaper articles. The small anecdotes of friendship and exchange with African neighbours and workers were either unknown to the elites or not considered desirable subjects for public mention.

The self-identification that can be traced in these Polish sources shows some similarities with a missionary outlook. The authors understood themselves as European and in possession of superior knowledge, but were friendly and willing to share something with Africans. One former refugee sketched the impression they allegedly made on the Africans: 'The natives considered us friendly whites, capable of physical labour'.[297] The Polish refugees were, furthermore, in contact with some of the few Polish (and Italian) missionaries already present in Africa before their arrival. Henryk Zins's book about the history of Poles in present-day Zimbabwe and Zambia is indicative in this regard. While the first part is mainly about Polish missionary activities, the second part recounts the story of the Polish refugees.[298] It is quite likely that the missionaries conveyed their view of Africa to their compatriots. For the refugees, spreading the (European) faith gave their involuntary sojourn some purpose.

The class division within the Polish refugee group was further complicated by religious and ethnic diversity, and some refugees had followed trajectories different from those outlined in Chapter 1. Although only few of them are mentioned in the sources, it is likely that more passed unnoticed. Nevertheless, the group was predominantly Polish-speaking and Catholic. The most important reason for the hospitality of the colonial governments, albeit at times reluctant, was the link of the refugees to the Polish army and their Europeanness. Informed by the Poles' sense of belonging to a long tradition of Polish exiles and supported by encampment, the majority of the Poles followed their own agenda. Through refusals to fill in forms, protests, letters and suicide threats, they were able to exercise a degree of influence upon the decision making of the colonial administration as well as international organizations. The self-perception of an exile community that rightfully belonged to the European club of nations gave these demands further weight.

Having looked at British perspectives on the Poles and their social location on the edges of whiteness, and then at the refugees' understanding of their own place in the host societies, we will now trace African perspectives. From interviews with former camp workers and neighbours, and through some traces in the sources and secondary literature, another assessment of the refugee group will emerge.

African Perspectives on the Refugees: Approachable Whites

> 'I saw them in Arusha. They were very white. You could see that they could not live in hot countries … They were brought to another, colder country.'[299]

Sitting in his office in Dar es Salaam, Luhende had to think twice to remember this long-gone incident from his childhood, but then the memory came back vividly. As a ten-year-old boy he had heard there was a big group of whites in the area and had gone to see them. He and some of his friends had wanted to ask the whites for money, but upon seeing the Poles he realized that these were people with problems of their own. Unable to stand the African heat, they had been brought to cooler places and not settled permanently. For the African boys their whiteness was initially a marker of the Poles' privileged position. Seeing them in a rather destitute condition did not make their whiteness less important, but was rather a marker for their being out of place. In contrast to other white settlers they were regarded as incapable of adapting to tropical conditions. Taking Luhende's qualification of the Polish refugees' whiteness as a starting point, I propose to follow the calls by scholars to trace whiteness in particular local and historically situated contexts.[300] I will not, however, limit the inquiry to race but look at any aspects that were deemed important by Africans living and working close to the Poles: their socio-economic position as powerless refugees, their role as employers of African workers, the common religious practice and the influx of the large group as a potential threat. These contradictory aspects mattered to the people who had been in contact with the Poles.

Most of the Africans who lived near places where the refugee camps were set up had never seen any Poles before. People had heard about the war in Europe, but most did not know much about the situation in Poland or the arduous journey that had brought the refugees to Africa. It must have been strange to see a large group of distressed whites arrive in remote corners of the African countryside. They were brought to a variety of places. Some small camps were built attached to already existing mission stations like Morogoro and Kondoa. The bigger camps were set up as separate places in rather isolated locations. In Uganda, the place for Masindi settlement was cut out of the forest, and Koja settlement was built on a peninsula on Lake Victoria. Despite the peripheral settings, there were always African neighbours who were already living there. On top of this, the settlements attracted people from the area around who came to work there. Africans built the houses, worked as guards or porters and supplied the settlements with food and firewood. The settlements changed the economy of the surrounding region and brought into contact people who would otherwise never have met.

The aim of this subchapter is to trace the perspective of the African neighbours and workers. These strange newcomers shared their skin colour and some privileges with the British colonizers as well as other European settlers, but at the same time they lived under restrictions and were by no means in housing of a colonial 'European standard'. Most of the Poles would never have moved to Africa if the fate of war and deportation had not brought them there. Far from wanting to build up a business or administer an empire, they mostly dreamt of returning to their peasant homes in Poland. They did not arrive with capital or an English public school education, but with the experience of fighting for survival in the special settlements of the Soviet interior. What impressions did these encounters make on their hosts? What did they leave behind apart from cemeteries, churches and other material structures?

The African neighbours and workers lived in colonial societies characterized by white minority rule, but in the everyday lives of most people Europeans played no role. Especially in Uganda, where two of the biggest

Polish settlements were set up, many Africans had never actually met one of the colonizers.³⁰¹ Colonial rule was passed down through the hierarchical structures of indirect rule, although the ideology of white superiority played an important role.

Some Methodological Remarks

A common problem when writing colonial history in Africa is the lack of written sources from the African point of view. The same holds true here. While Polish refugees, British colonial administrators and settlers left behind a range of written sources, the African neighbours, workers, friends and onlookers did not write about the Poles.³⁰² To trace African perspectives on the Polish refugees I therefore set out to conduct interviews with people who remembered their stay.

Nine interviews were conducted in April 2013 in the vicinity of the three biggest Polish settlements: Tengeru (Tanzania), Koja and Masindi/Nyabyeya (both Uganda).³⁰³ To find the informants, I relied on three people who fulfilled the role of caretaker for the Polish cemetery in each of these places.³⁰⁴ They led me to interview partners – and translated in some contexts – and I recorded interviews with these three as well, in which they provided valuable second-hand information as well as telling me about contemporary issues regarding the memorial complex evolving around the cemeteries. I also went to Morogoro and asked my way around the mission premises in Bigwa. One small and short-lived Polish camp had been attached to the mission. My efforts, however, were fruitless as no one had heard of the Poles. This failed attempt may serve to clarify the importance of the caretakers and of material remains like the cemeteries.

The most revealing interviews were the two I conducted in Koja. Both men had worked in the Polish camp and had, despite their age, vivid memories of the Poles. Of the four interviews in Nyabyeya, only two informants had first-hand memories of the refugees, and so the other two conversations were less productive, one having arrived after the Poles had gone, and the other having no clear memories. In Tengeru I was only able to do one interview, which was with a person who had come after the Poles had already left. Here, the best source was the expert interview with the caretaker, who, apart from his close involvement in the memorial activities, was himself the son of the former caretaker, who had worked in the camp.

In addition to these interviews, I had earlier asked three elderly people in Dar es Salaam about the Polish refugees during interviews for my diploma thesis in 2009. Their short remarks gave some further insight into the impression the Poles had made. One important limitation of the interviews is that all my informants were men. The only interview with a woman (in Nyabyeya) was unfortunately not fruitful. The interviews thus cover exclusively male perspectives. One of the interview partners of 2009 has already died and one man in Koja was on his deathbed at the time I wanted to interview him. This points to the urgency of the interviews as well as the problems facing oral history studies for the late colonial period in Africa.

On top of these practical issues there are some methodological limitations in using these interviews as sources alongside written ones. First of all, there is the social situation of the interview itself.[305] In contrast to written sources, where there is no direct interaction between the writer and the researcher, the informants answer questions in reaction to the social presence of the interviewer.[306] They tend to give information that seems suitable and socially desired by their counterpart. As most informants expected me to be Polish (why else would I be interested in the refugees?), any praise for my supposed compatriots should be seen against this background. My positionality as a white researcher might likewise have encouraged my informants to speak well about 'my people', be they refugees or colonizers.

Furthermore, as Jan Vansina has put it in regard to oral traditions: 'They are the representation of the past in the present. One cannot deny either the past or the present in them'.[307] I would add to this observation that the time in between the point of interest in the past and the present of the interview forms another aspect of all recorded statements. The experiences of colonial rule, independence and postcolonial developments are important issues to consider. When the British colonizers are described in rather negative terms, this may reflect the everyday experience of colonial rule as much as the postcolonial national narrative. The ascription of special knowledge and skills to the Poles might be because current educational institutions like the Forestry College in Nyabyeya and the Agricultural College in Tengeru are housed on the premises of the former Polish camps.[308] The importance of Catholicism, attributed to the Polish refugees by some informants in Nyabyeya, may also have been exaggerated due to the fact that the interviewees were strongly involved in activities around the church that was built by the refugees, and that they stayed in close contact with Polish missionaries after the refugees had left. Apart from descendants of the refugees, Polish clergymen are the people who seem most interested in the story of the refugees.[309] These examples show that a critical approach towards the statements in the interviews is necessary.

Despite all the limitations, the interviews offered a unique opportunity to trace African perspectives on the Polish refugees. Interviews are the only way to bring up issues and interpretations that were of no interest to the administrative elites, but that mattered to the people on the ground. In the colonial sources about the Polish camps, Africans appear only as wanted labourers, or as unwanted intruders who had to be controlled. Asking some of them directly offered a glimpse into their sense-making during this episode. Explaining why the Poles came, what they did and how they interacted with others complements and at times contradicts the conclusions one might draw from Polish and British sources. Furthermore, the stories told by the informants about the Poles add facts and facets to the diverse encounters and the everyday life in and around the Polish settlements. Limited as they are, the interviews offer valuable insights into the structure of late colonial society in East Africa, and the place of the Poles therein. Wherever possible I have drawn on other sources that give an idea of African perspectives in order to broaden the empirical base.[310] There remains, however, a regional focus on Uganda and northern Tanzania in this subchapter.

I have structured the categorizations of the Polish refugees from the interviews and other sources in analogy to the colonial dualism. Firstly, the Poles are described as equal partners, either in friendships, romantic relationships, religion or in suffering under the British colonizers. In the second subchapter, I gather statements in which the Poles are described as part of the colonizer's camp: as materially privileged, employers or even a threat. I then try to pull these diverging descriptions together and to sketch the social position of the Polish refugees as seen and remembered from African perspectives.

Figure 5.4. A group of Polish and African fieldworkers, probably in Tengeru, Tanganyika. From the collection of Katarzyna Oko, courtesy of Fatimah and Amena Amer.

Poles on an Equal Footing

A recurring topic in the interviews was the description of a generally unproblematic relationship between Polish refugees and African workers. As John Onega of Nyabyeya put it repeatedly, 'they lived here nicely'.[311] He emphasized that there were no problems or strife among the Poles, or between them and the Ugandans. Onega insisted that Africans loved them and that 'people cried a lot when they left'.[312] This praise of the Poles was not shared by all informants, but a generally positive memory ran through all statements. Teresa Tiko, for example, also claimed that there were no problems, and nor was there any quarrelling.[313] As cautioned earlier, to take this simple assessment as an accurate description of the historical situation would be shortsighted. However, the generally positive memory makes it quite unlikely that it was a quarrelsome time for those involved. In most cases, the Poles got along well with their neighbours.

The only written primary source from an African perspective I can draw upon is a short article in the Luganda newspaper *Matalisi*, published shortly after the Poles' arrival in Uganda in October 1942,[314] in which the Polish refugees are described under four headings: first, they are 'extremely strong in build'; secondly, 'they do not practise discrimination'; thirdly, their language is 'nice sounding but extremely difficult to write'; and fourthly, there is 'a rumour that they are contented with life in Uganda and do not intend to go back to their country'.[315]

The second point is the most interesting here. The writer felt a need to mention non-discrimination, suggesting that he found this exceptional. One must assume that he had the British or other Europeans in mind. We might leave it at this, and link this harmonious account with one former refugee's assessment of the African viewpoint concerning the Poles in Kondoa: 'Those who lived here were good people. They gave food to our children and were on friendly terms with the whole village'.[316] But this may be too simple.

Poles as Refugees

Self-evident as it may look today, it was not always clear that the Poles would have to leave. Some of the Polish officials, as well as sympathetic British settlers and colonial officials, indeed made efforts to settle them permanently after the war. Furthermore, many African neighbours and camp workers were not well informed about the group at the time of their arrival. In Abercorn, one African worker remembered that he and others were asked by the local district commissioner to cut grass for the roofs of the camp houses without knowing who would eventually sleep under them. Only when the Poles arrived did he realize who it was for.[317] For Edward Sinabulya it seemed clear, in retrospect, that they were only sojourners in Koja; as he put it in the interview, 'The houses were not permanent. They were temporary houses'. He knew that it was only for the duration of the war, and added: 'As soon as the war ends, these people will go back'. Sinabulya described the semi-permanent buildings, concluding that the British as well as the local community knew that they were not meant to stay on as permanent settlers.[318]

Sinabulya described the Poles as refugees and thus placed them in the longer history of refugee hosting in Uganda. When talking about the restrictions that governed the life of the Poles he made the analogy to current refugee camps, and argued that 'if you are a refugee and you are in a refugee camp you don't so much go out as you could have wished and they have to control you somehow'.[319] Experiences with refugees and camps have been a feature of Ugandan life ever since the Poles arrived. In 1955, only four years after the last Polish camp in Uganda was closed, eighty thousand refugees from the Sudanese Civil War arrived in northern Uganda, and in 1959 more refugees came from Rwanda into south-western Uganda.[320] At the time of its independence in 1962, Uganda was already host to over a hundred thousand refugees from neighbouring countries.[321] Many more have fled to and from Uganda since then. In Sinabulya's description, the Poles are not a special privileged group, but refugees from war, like others that followed.

Polish Women as Partners

Another issue that points to an understanding of the Poles as 'normal' people are references to intimate relations between Polish women and African men. Having touched upon this already, I now wish to highlight the meaning these relationships had for the African men working and living around the camps. To the interviewees, the absence of Polish men made it obvious that intimate relationships between Polish women and African men were bound to develop. Only a few, however, resulted in official marriages. Simon Joseph, the caretaker of Tengeru cemetery, knew of only one Polish woman who had married an African, Anna Karaiskos, and she lived in the region until her death in 2003. One of her daughters was still in Arusha and the other children lived in South Africa and the United Kingdom.[322] Otwia Filimon of Nyabyeya remembered a certain Kasigwa, a rich African from the nearby town of Hoima, who had married two Polish women.[323] Kasigwa had owned several buses and lorries, and was, according to the informant, the only one to have married Polish women from Nyabyeya. Sitting on a bench in the Polish church for the interview, Filimon, a devout Catholic, dismissed this relationship in sharp tones. He said repeatedly 'evil spirit' when talking about Kasigwa – perhaps it was the polygamous arrangement or a dislike of the man's personality, or maybe to express disapproval of interracial relationships.

Apart from marriages there were also less formal intimate relationships between African men and Polish women. Both informants in Koja remembered that there had been clandestine meetings of Polish women and African men in the hills next to the camp. Sinabulya mentioned that some men went there to have sex with the girls – mainly the watchmen who stayed overnight rather than the workers, who had to leave the camp in the afternoon. He also mentioned that some babies had come out of these affairs, but, according to a rumour he had heard, they were all killed in the camp hospital.[324] Mukeera Kasule confirmed Sinabulya's observations, and described them in more detail. According to him, the arrangements for the night-time meetings were made during work in a secret language.[325] They talked about 'lukluk' to avoid the discovery of their meetings by Polish and British authorities alike. Those involved knew that they would not go through the main gate but would meet later in the hills. According to Kasule, news of the strangling of babies born from these intimate meetings was passed on to the Africans through other Poles, who might say: 'Ya, we know you blacks; you pass here and here and come and impregnate our girls – but things are not good, because the kid has been killed'.[326]

But how to interpret the rumours of the baby killings? Following Luise White, the question should not necessarily be whether this rumour was true or not, but rather, what it meant to the people who told and heard it.[327] While the descriptions portray the Polish women as equal partners, they were not just like any other potential sexual partner. The romantic meetings in the hills were clearly perceived as something forbidden. The officials who tried to prevent such meetings were not only British but also older Poles. There seems to have been a rift between the young Polish refugees trying to enjoy their time and the older ones, who were keener on sustaining the respectability of 'their girls'. The rumours of the baby killings are a clear expression that these were unwanted relationships. While official policy and law did not interfere with these sexual encounters, social pressure was prevalent.

Powerless Prisoners

All interviews touched upon a comparison of the Poles with the British. Patrick Kunambi, with whom I talked in Dar es Salaam, remembered the Poles who lived in Morogoro camp. He described the difference between the two groups as follows: while the Englishman does not like to mix with other people, the Poles were, by contrast, normal, ordinary people who got used to the people living there.[328] British arrogance, aloofness and social segregation seem to have made a big difference in the perception of the two groups.

Edward Sinabulya described the relationship in a similar manner: 'The British were very proud. Nobody could come near them, they resented the

Blacks so much. On the other hand, the Poles were receiving the Blacks, they received them with both hands'. He ascribed this difference to the Poles' status as refugees living in camps. To him the Poles were 'like prisoners' and as such they felt inferior to the British, which could be the reason why 'they came so much with the Blacks'. The British were the bosses and supervisors of everything and everybody in the camp: 'They had their special quarters; their special houses in which they slept'.[329]

Likewise, the other informant in Koja, Mukeera Kasule, told me that 'the British were like the leaders who stayed up in their quarters and they were in their own class. They were so above that it was not easy to reach them. So they didn't mix at all'.[330] Again, the British kept their distance, whereas the Poles were in everyday contact. For Otwia Filimon in Nyabyeya, the distance between Africans and the British was so great that they hardly even mattered. To him it was the Polish refugees who built and lived in the camp, while the British were living in the capital Kampala and just passed by without any impact.[331]

In comparison with the British, the Poles were perceived as poor and powerless, as in the remarks by Luhende, mentioned in the opening of this subchapter. The expectation that whites must be rich was contradicted by their destitute appearance. It was, furthermore, clear to most interviewed that they had been brought and sustained by the British and were not moving of their own free will. As John Onega told me, 'They had no power in it. They were not asked'.[332] This perceived powerlessness is maybe the strongest contrast to the powerful British colonial officials. The low socio-economic position of the Poles is further underlined by the fact that some Ugandans organized a boxing tournament to collect donations for the refugees.[333] According to Carol Summers, this event stood in line with other fundraising events organized by Ugandans to support the Commonwealth war effort, and consequently to improve their situation vis-à-vis the colonial administration. This wartime hope quickly faded after the war, leading to widespread discontent, strikes and riots.

In Abercorn, Damson Chizu Simpungwe remembered that the Poles had asked Africans who came into the camp to teach them how to make handles for shovels, hoes, picks and axes. African residents further taught the Poles how to eat grasshoppers and to catch birds with a sling, and told them which fruits to eat.[334] It was the Africans who taught the refugees their superior knowledge.

The powerless appearance of the Poles is confirmed in the memoirs of Urmila Jhaveri, an Indian Tanzanian, who grew up in Dar es Salaam. She saw lorries full of Europeans passing through the town: 'These unfortunate prisoners seemed hungry and traumatized'.[335] People in Dar es Salaam were wondering where these poor people had come from; she wrote: 'It was whispered that these prisoners were Italians, Hungarians, Jews, Poles and even some Germans. Nobody seemed to know from where they had been herded or [to] where they were being sent'. Only after some weeks was it revealed that they were Polish.

Likewise, Edward Sinabulya said that in Koja 'there were a lot of restrictions ... many people here confused them with prisoners'.[336] He added that the refugees in the camp were guarded by Kenyan, Ugandan and Polish watchmen. While these feature in Polish and British sources as those who protected the Poles from (African) intruders, from an outside perspective this carefully watched over and partly fenced in camp must have looked like a detention camp. This categorization of the Poles as 'prisoners' was not, however, shared by other informants. Otwia Filimon described the Poles of Nyabyeya as freely moving around and often going to other towns nearby.[337] Sinabulya explained the reasons for the British isolation of the Poles as follows: 'The Africans were nearing independence, they were starting to have independence thoughts, so the British feared that these Polish could be so intelligent as to start advising these people what to do. So that's why they tried as much as possible to keep them away, so that they [did not] mix'.[338]

There are two points here that I would like to highlight. First, the Poles seemed to have useful knowledge for a nationalist independence movement; and second, in the emerging independence conflict, they were positioned on the side of the colonized, not the colonizer. The Polish refugees appear as would-be collaborators of Uganda's emerging nationalist movement, but prevented by the British from contributing to the struggle. Given the background of foreign rule during Poland's partition period up to the Soviet-dominated postwar situation, this assessment is not altogether surprising.

The fear of an anticolonial influence from the Poles (especially from the few communists among them) was indeed present within the colonial administration in neighbouring Tanganyika. The situation around Tengeru was starting to get politically volatile in the 1940s. The north-east of Tanganyika was the most prosperous region of the territory, but was also the area where European pressure was felt the most. Around Mount Meru, where Tengeru camp was located, there was a long-standing farming community of Afrikaner and other settlers. In 1948 the report of a government land commission, headed by Judge Wilson, proposed to remove Meru peasants from two farms (both only about 30 kilometres from Tengeru) in order to create a homogeneous block of European settlement between Meru and Kilimanjaro. While Wilson's plan received approval from one Meru chief, it was met with fierce resistance from many other Meru factions.[339] The conflict – known as the Meru Land Case – culminated in the forced removal of Meru peasants in 1951, and a consequent discussion in the UN Trusteeship Council in New York.[340] While organized around 'tribal' associations, the whole conflict set a precedent for the evolving independence struggle, as the mass action against the evictions and the discussion in an international arena brought much attention to the case. The British fear of communist influence was later underpinned by a Soviet resolution in the Trusteeship Council calling for the restoration of the land to the Meru.[341]

Amid growing postwar opposition against colonial rule, the Poles were a further complicating factor for the colonial administration. Permanently settling this large group of whites would have met with strong opposition from the increasingly organized local residents. Despite Sinabulya's suggestion, however, there are no traces of actual Polish attempts to support the independence movement.[342]

The living conditions of the Polish refugees were not, of course, static. Sinabulya explained that there was a gradual improvement in their material situation. He remembered that upon arrival in Koja they had 'just bare hands'. He observed: 'When they came, they came with totally nothing. But after some time here they became rich'.[343] This observation is confirmed in the written sources. The wretched impression the Poles made upon arrival soon gave way to reports about their improved health and spending power. The rags were soon exchanged for donated, bought or self-produced clothes and pith helmets – the obligatory headdress of whites in Africa. Lifting the poor whites to a certain material standard seems to have worked out well. Overlooking the financial basis for this recovery, some of the interviewees – and former refugees as well – ascribed the recovery of the Poles solely to their own efforts and abilities.

Poles as Fellow Catholics

In the religious arena a lot of interaction took place. Two of the cemetery caretakers underlined the connection between the Poles and Catholicism. Ochau Paito Caesar of Nyabyeya explained that the reason for their coming to Uganda was the strength of Catholicism there.[344] Caesar, who is active in the Polish-built Catholic church, emphasized Polish religiosity as a reason for his admiration. Yet, if the reason for bringing the Poles to this part of Uganda had been the common faith with the hosting population, the obvious region for settlement would have been Buddu, the early centre of Buganda Catholicism.[345] Neither Nyabyeya nor Koja were especially known for their Catholic predominance. Professor Lwanga-Lunyiigo suggests that the colonial administration might have isolated the Poles out of fear that they might help Ugandan Catholics and thereby improve their position in comparison to Anglicans.[346] The special role of the Poles' faith was also highlighted by Simon Joseph, the caretaker in Tengeru; it was, he said, the Poles who brought Catholicism to the Arumeru region, where before there had been only the Lutheran denomination.[347] Both explications must be considered in the light of the fact that the informants had not met the Polish refugees when they lived in the camps, but are now in close contact with former refugees, their descendants and Polish clergymen. It thus seems that interpretations of this history have been influenced by later developments, and may have well been strengthened by the still existing Polish church of Nyabyeya.

Yet even those Nyabyeya informants with first-hand experience confirmed the importance of religious activities as a field of encounter. Two of them remembered that after the church was built in Nyabyeya many people came; it was always packed, and the Poles prayed a lot.[348] Mukeera Kasule added that when one of the refugees died in Koja, work would come to a standstill, and everyone – African workers and Poles alike – would take part in the burial ceremony (apparently Poles did not attend African burials, but a Polish burial was nevertheless an occasion for them to come together with the Africans). The persistent material existence of the Polish cemeteries no doubt enhances the remembrance of this facet.

In descriptions of the religious commonality, the Poles play a special role. They either brought the faith or were inspiring examples of the right sort of religiosity. Their position in the religious encounter was not one on an equal footing, but rather comparable to a teacher–pupil relationship. They thereby followed in the footsteps of Christian missionaries, who in Uganda formed a quarter of the white population.[349] The missionaries were particularly influential through the schools they established. As shown above, some of the Polish clergymen understood themselves as missionaries as well. While the common faith facilitated interaction between Poles and Africans, this did not necessarily happen on an equal footing.

Poles as European Masters

Here I will draw together oral accounts that, in contrast to the aforementioned examples, understood the Poles as belonging to the white part of colonial society. Owing to the colour of their skin, Polish refugees were generally described as whites. As one old man in the streets of Tengeru said briefly, 'They were whites'.[350] Obvious as this may seem, my initial vignette may serve as a reminder that whiteness is not always or everywhere the same. To Luhende, the Poles were *too white* for the African heat and as such out of place.

John Onega recalled with some admiration that the Poles in Nyabyeya lived separately from the Africans and in a much nicer way.[351] Simpungwe remembered that the Poles in Abercorn had a machine to grind millet and therefore had much finer flour than the people living around, who did the grinding with stones.³⁵² The Poles' privileged material situation made an impression on Otwia Filimon as well. He described them as 'good people', because they supported him materially by giving money for food and soap. He worked for the Polish church in Nyabyeya, and the Poles thus provided him with a job and an income.³⁵³ As mentioned earlier, the Poles were the only white people who mattered to him: 'Poles, Europeans, very good people'.³⁵⁴ Using the terms interchangeably reveals that, in his experience of the colonial period, the nationality of the Europeans was Polish and not British.

Edward Sinabulya remembered the story of the Buganda riots that reached the gates of Koja camp in 1945 mentioned earlier in Chapter 3.³⁵⁵ It all started, he told me, when one man from Kampala came to Koja by bicycle and encouraged the workers to strike. As workers were already discontented with their low pay of only twelve shillings a month, they stopped working and gathered at the gate. To cope with the crowd, the English camp commandant brought Masai soldiers with machine guns from Kenya. When the Indian-owned milk lorry arrived on its daily rounds, workers blocked the gate and some started to empty the churns. The commandant ordered his Kenyan soldiers to shoot at the protesters. According to Sinabulya, the Kenyans were at first reluctant to shoot and thus fired only in the air, but the commandant forced them to shoot directly, leaving six protesters dead. In this way, the protest was put down and the rioters scattered. Later, when the situation had cooled down, the British told the workers to come and negotiate with them. Sinabulya said that he was a coward and did not go, but all who went were arrested. As a result of the strike the salary was later raised to fourteen shillings.³⁵⁶

What does Sinabulya's story tell us about the Polish refugees and their position in regard to colonial society? While the Poles themselves played no active part in the conflict, their settlement was seen as an institution of the colonial state. The Poles were not the target of the riot, but cutting off their supplies was a means of confronting the colonial government. For the African workers, the camp was a site of employment. Their employer was the colonial state, and confronted as such. During the war Ugandans had supported the war effort and felt entitled to an improved status, but the British administration had disappointed them by treating them as subordinate clients.³⁵⁷ Organizing popular mass action against their employer, the Ugandan government workers successfully improved their economic situation, but exposed the brutality and helplessness of the Ugandan central government.³⁵⁸ The reliance on Kenyan troops to put down the protests illustrated the limits of Uganda's government, and awoke fears of a closer union, dominated by the Kenyan settlers.

The main reason for the protests in Koja was not antagonism towards the Poles, but rather the role of the camps as sites of employment. Rising prices had led to falling real wages, causing widespread discontent among the workers.[359] While the camp workers were paid by the British government, the refugees were in most cases their direct superiors. There were also many non-European employers in the colonies, but hardly any Europeans who did not employ Africans. The Polish settlement leader in Kidugala rightly explained to the Poles that farming in Tanganyika meant making use of the African labour force.[360] The resulting role of the Polish refugees as employers is thus the focus of the following pages.

Poles as Employers

Even before the Poles arrived in eastern Africa they had already changed the socio-economic structure of some places. The proposed building sites for the big refugee settlements in Tengeru, Nyabyeya and Koja became workplaces for thousands of people. In the construction of Tengeru alone, around four thousand workers were employed.[361] The labour commissioner in Dar es Salaam became concerned about the high demand for African labour, fearing that this might worsen the existing difficulties in obtaining labour for work on the northern plantations. His proposed solution was to recruit labourers from other parts of Tanganyika, where they were not needed for essential industries.[362] The construction of the camps had to be finished very fast, so as an incentive to work under high pressure, Wahehe workers in Ifunda were issued with 'beer and meat on what would by ordinary standards be a lavish scale'.[363] The construction of Nyabyeya camp attracted roughly two thousand workers from many places in the region.[364] According to Nyabyeya's British commandant, the Public Works Department complained that they could not get any workers for their projects as working conditions in the refugee settlement were better.[365] In Koja a further one thousand workers were employed in the construction, and others from the northern Acholi region were recruited as guards for the settlement.[366] In the settlements most of the hard labour was done by Africans, and the settlement elites (both Polish and British) employed domestic servants as well.

For African workers, the refugees were employers like other members of the elites. Some left their former jobs working for European masters to work in the Polish camps, like Simon Joseph's father, who had worked for a German settler near Tengeru until the latter was interned at the outbreak of the war.[367] Several colleagues did the same. Hundreds more came from other parts of Tanganyika to work in Tengeru. Nyabyeya had already been a diverse community before the arrival of the refugees, because an Indian-owned sawmill attracted many workers. John Onega, for example, came as a young man from Nebbi district in north-west Uganda to carry timber for the sawmill, and later started working as a porter at the Polish camp.[368]

Nyabyeya's diversity still manifests itself today in the use of Kiswahili as lingua franca, because none of the twenty-six linguistic groups is dominant.³⁶⁹ In Koja, eight of the twenty-three workers arrested after the riot in 1945 were immigrant labourers from Rwanda.³⁷⁰ The Polish settlements thus became places of employment and encounter for a diverse range of Africans, not unlike other industrial, agricultural or administrative centres. For workers who switched from Indian or German employers, the Poles' social position had some similarities to that of the former.

Although the Tanganyika chief secretary emphasized that Polish refugees in Tengeru were not allowed to employ African servants, he admitted that the government could not prevent those with sufficient income from doing so.³⁷¹ Hence, the Polish camp elite employed African servants, like other members of their class. We can trace one African servant in the recollections of Barbara Porajska, who had stayed in Nyabyeya settlement as a child. She remembers, that with the arrival of her father, who became chief of the Polish camp police, her family became part of the 'elite of the camp'.³⁷² They moved to the section of the settlement where the British commandant and those Poles working as administrators, doctors, teachers or priests were living. Part of this elite position was the employment of a domestic servant – a so-called 'boy' (but aged about 20) named Farasico, who lived in a nearby village.³⁷³ Porajska explained the relation between them as follows: 'From the very first day, Farasico, [my sister] Ala and I become very good friends. But Farasico knows he has to keep his distance; we, the white race, are the masters, and though we smile at him and try to talk to him, he never enters the hut without permission'.³⁷⁴ The two girls were by the colour of their skin, as well as their social status, part of the ruling group. Porajska was surprised that Farasico learnt Polish quickly, while her efforts to learn Kiswahili were rather half-hearted.³⁷⁵ She goes on to explain that they were too friendly to their 'boy' and 'spoiled' him. This discourse of colonial masters stands in contrast to the initial description of friendship.

Mukeera Kasule himself worked in Koja as a domestic servant in Polish homes, splitting firewood and washing clothes. He remembered the Poles as being very well mannered, and unlike the British, Poles ate together with Africans, and after work sometimes gave them some extra money.³⁷⁶ Taking into account the importance of food for maintaining and performing the community, this communal eating is remarkable. Domestic servants are usually not allowed a place at the employer's table. It was most likely 'Polish' food that was served and not African. The power to define the situation was still in the hands of the Poles, but they seem to have been less distanced and more open than the British.³⁷⁷

Another observation Porajska made was that Farasico seemed rather arrogant towards the African workers who performed menial jobs around the settlement, such as digging soil or cutting grass.[378] She contrasts his healthy, prosperous appearance with their poor and ragged look. This makes it necessary to look for differentiation within the workforce.

Differentiation within the Workforce

While the Poles were generally regarded as employers by African camp workers, this workforce was not homogeneous. Edward Sinabulya remembered two cleavages. First, there was the difference between the ordinary workers or porters, like him, who did their job and then moved out immediately, and the specialized workers, who stayed longer in the camp, working in the hospital or administration. Secondly, there was the difference between those local people who were working voluntarily, and a diverse group of tax defaulters who had been brought to Koja to work their debt off. The latter slept 'like prisoners' in a huge hall and left after they had finished their time.[379]

While there was no mass conscription in Uganda, Tanganyika's population experienced vastly extended regimentation during the war years.[380] Settlers in Kenya, Northern and Southern Rhodesia conscripted labour for work on their farms as well.[381] Conscription was thus not limited to the army but indeed was more common in other industries. Especially the conscription of labour for plantations in Tanganyika caused great discontent, and was described in retrospect as 'close to temporary enslavement'[382] and 'the most traumatic intervention, both for the Africans and the administration itself'.[383] The massive public discontent over these forced measures nearly led to a revolt, and conscription was only discontinued at the insistence of the British government in 1946.

For Tengeru, the provincial commissioner of the Northern Province found it impossible to obtain all the labour needed for construction locally. He therefore asked the Tanganyika government to send him eight hundred conscripted labourers for three months from the Central Province, which the director of manpower allowed.[384] Another nine hundred conscripts from the Western Province, four hundred from Moshi and one hundred from Arusha worked alongside five hundred voluntary workers from Kigoma.[385] In June 1943, when Tengeru was already occupied by the Poles, at least one hundred further conscript workers were sent in two transports from Moshi.[386] For more than one year, the construction of the camp went hand in hand with the refugees moving in.[387]

The forced work of tax defaulters and conscripted labour for the construction of camps for people who had themselves been forced labourers is a little ironic in itself. While I have found no certain information on the working conditions on these building sites, the circumstances for conscript labourers on the plantations were described as much worse than for conscripts in the army. Westcott notes for Tanganyika: 'Those in the army waxed fat and returned healthy; those on the estates grew thin and went home debilitated by disease'.[388] As mentioned above, working conditions in the camps were reportedly better, so it seems safe to assume that conditions for the Poles in the Soviet interior had been much harsher than those for Africans in the construction of their camps in Tanganyika.

Mukeera Kasule mentioned another difference within the workforce around Koja camp: Baganda and Acholi were the dominating 'tribes' and both had their own bars according to their preferred taste (banana beer for Baganda and millet beer for Acholi). However, according to him the division was not very strict, as either group could visit the other bar if they liked. Asked if the Poles joined them as well, he said that they were not allowed out in the evenings.[389] Apart from this restriction, one gains the impression of a multicultural setting, where every community had its own institutions, but members were nevertheless free to join the others. For Tengeru, Simon Joseph paints a strong difference between the African workers, who were living close to and on an equal footing with the Poles, and the African neighbours, who were not allowed into camp and stayed completely apart.[390]

Poles as Customers

The Poles were not only employers but customers as well. While their consumption of foodstuffs was seen with scepticism by other Europeans (as it led to rising prices, especially during the food shortages of the war period),[391] Indian traders and African producers welcomed the new marketing opportunity. To give some idea of the quantities involved, Baboo's Milk House – an Indian trader from Moshi – supplied the nearly four thousand Polish refugees of Tengeru with milk and more than forty thousand eggs every month.[392] At that time the Polish settlement was apparently their largest single customer.[393] The Indian shopkeepers in Arusha were reportedly 'doing a big trade' with the Polish buyers, who visited them daily by bus from Tengeru.[394] Other Indian traders were accused of selling controlled products to Poles on the black market.[395]

Apart from the big trading firms, African producers sold fresh products directly to the Poles. To control the market activities and reduce the 'indiscriminate wanderings of the refugees on the roads and in the native reserve', a 'native marketplace' was set up on the outskirts of Tengeru camp.[396] Mukeera Kasule remembered that there was a market just inside Koja camp, next to the gate. It consisted of thirty stalls from which Africans sold eggs, chicken and other foodstuffs. He further mentioned that sometimes Poles sold their own products to Africans as well.[397] Edward Sinabulya's father was a fisherman and sold fish to the refugees, although, according to him, this was not allowed.[398] Otwia Filimon mentioned that people outside Nyabyeya camp cultivated a lot of European potatoes and cabbages, which they delivered and sold to the Poles.[399]

As most Poles had come from rural areas, many started the cultivation of vegetables and kept animals for their own supply. Sinabulya remembered that the Poles grew not only European vegetables, but cassava as well. In Tengeru by 1944 the whole potato supply of nearly twenty-five tons per month was produced by a cooperative farm run by Polish refugees.[400] This farm was leased by the Polish consul with the aim of making the camps self-supporting, at least in fresh vegetables.[401] According to one informant, the refugees in Tengeru were supplied with flower and vegetable seeds from Kenya.[402] The story of the 'Polish beans', mentioned earlier, points in the same direction. The Poles wanted not only to take over the food supply, but to substitute it with 'European' or even 'Polish' food.

Despite the Polish production efforts, the camps remained a major sales market for traders, farmers and peasants in the region. Their role as customers seems to have had the furthest-ranging effect in the rural areas surrounding the camps. In one interview in Nyabyeya, the only specific story the informant had heard about the Poles was that they had bought chickens, eggs and vegetables.[403]

Poles as a Threat

In contrast to the positive memories concerning the Polish refugees, one of Sinabulya's stories stands out. He recounted the killing of an African driver by a certain Joseph, a Polish refugee from Koja. It all happened after a traffic accident, in which the camp truck, loaded with refugees on their way to Kampala, overturned, leaving one of them dead. When the African driver came back to Koja, Joseph started kicking him until he died. According to Sinabulya, Joseph was never put on trial for the killing, but the incident was just taken as something normal.[404] The Koja caretaker Edward Wakiku added that he had heard several stories about this man, who was known for his brutality and used to beat up Poles and Africans alike. According to Wakiku he slept at the British quarters and was given some responsibility to watch over the camp and terrorize the Poles as well.[405] I did not find any written evidence for this incident in the files, but this is not the main interest here.[406] What is revealing is that Sinabulya described it as 'normal' that a Pole had killed an African and was not convicted for it. Despite the official legislation, the Poles appear to have stood above the law.

In contrast to this description of a seemingly lawless situation in Koja, Mukeera Kasule described a dual system of courts and prisons. If a quarrel between Africans and Poles happened, both were arrested and placed in their respective prisons, the Poles inside camp and the Africans outside. Kasule remembered that some of the Polish men liked to get drunk on gin, and fighting often broke out between them. While some Poles appear in these descriptions as rather quarrelsome, there seems to have been a 'separate but equal' system to enforce the law.

A general fear of white people is evoked in Simon Joseph's description of the reaction of Africans living next to Tengeru camp. He recounted that they were afraid and ran away when the refugees walked to the nearby village, wondering why these people, upon arrival so white, had become so red.[407]

In the 1950s and 1960s, the anthropologist John Beattie was researching spirit medium cults in Bunyoro, collecting items for an extensive list of spirits that might possess a person. While the older and positive *cwezi* spirits remained constant, the list of evil *mbandwa* spirits included more recent additions.[408] Among these were the spirits of tanks (*kifaru*) and aeroplanes (*ndege*) as well as Europeanness (*njungu*) and Polishness (*mpolandi*). Being possessed did not mean that the person was possessed by Poles, tanks or Europeans, but rather by the general force or power through which the Poles, tanks or Europeans were what they were.[409] Two aspects of this incorporation of Polishness are noteworthy here. First of all, Polishness is not the same as Europeanness. The spirits that make Europeans European are not the same as those that make Poles Polish. European nationalists would maybe speak in a comparable manner to a specific *Volksgeist* inherent to each nation. While it remains open how this force was characterized, there was evidently a striking difference between Poles and other whites. A second aspect is the negative connotation of Polishness, contradicting the generally positive assessment in the interviews.

Beattie explained the incorporation of the Poles by referring to the fears that the massive influx of foreigners to Nyabyeya had caused among local residents. According to Beattie, local people feared that these newcomers might try to eliminate them in order to take away their land. Reportedly, the Mukama (king) of Bunyoro often visited the camp and showed a genuine interest in the Poles, who were impressed by his 'old-fashioned dignity'.[410] After the British conquest there was widespread discontent in Bunyoro with the fact that some of the kingdom's best land had been incorporated into neighbouring Buganda. Bunyoro had been severely weakened by this and experienced population decline throughout the whole colonial era. Presumably, the ongoing campaign for the return of the 'lost counties' from Ganda rule informed concerns about the Polish newcomers.[411] Apart from these local specificities, it remains quite plausible that a large influx of foreigners did cause concern to local residents, as often happens today when a refugee camp is established in Europe. Seen through the lens of *mbandwa*

Figure 5.5. Drawing of the Mukama of Bunyoro by visiting painter Feliks Topolski, Masindi, Uganda. From: Topolski and Collis, *Three Continents*. Copyright: The Estate of Feliks Topolski.

spirits in Bunyoro, the Polish refugees were a threat, but a different one from the other Europeans.

Some evidence from British files hints at a comparable fear among African elites in northern Tanganyika. The British mission sent to enquire into the situation of the last Polish refugees in 1950 spoke with two chiefs in the area around Tengeru. The results were summed up as follows: 'Native chiefs whom the mission have seen were concerned at the political and moral influence [the Polish refugees] had over the natives: there has been drink peddling, and land grabbing is feared if they are allowed to settle locally'.[412] Here again, the African officials feared the loss of land to the Poles. This concern came as no surprise, as the above-mentioned controversy around the Meru Land Case was at its height at this time. The chiefs' concern about a bad 'political and moral influence' is another interesting point. In the *East African Standard*, one concerned Kikuyu man from Kenya raised a comparable complaint against Italians in the colony in 1946, arguing for their removal.[413] In the case of the chiefs, two points might explain their tough stance. On the one hand, among those Poles remaining in 1950 there was a bigger proportion of petty criminals, drunkards and illicit distillers than in 1945. On the other, this statement must be seen in the light of growing political tension between the older, conservative chiefs and the younger generation of educated activists. The increased regimentation of the war years had made the chiefs more autocratic, and nationalist organizations challenging their position were starting to form.[414]

The Polish presence was thus not simply welcomed, but aroused concerns as well. Seen from today's perspective it is clear to all the interviewees that the Poles did *not* stay on and take away their land. This clearly has an influence on the memories that have survived.

Conclusion

It is impossible to summarize 'the' African perspective on the position of the Polish refugees within the hosting colonial societies. The picture is not clear-cut, as different actors saw and remember events differently. What emerges as a general assessment of the social position of the Poles is that they belonged to the privileged whites, but within this group they were placed closer to the Africans. While the British seemed arrogant and detached from Africans, the Poles were more approachable.

The refugees' material position developed from destitution upon arrival ('they came with bare hands') to their later role as employers who were able to give presents to Africans. The colonial policy of sustaining the Poles with a standard of living that was well above that of the average African seems to have worked quite well. One anecdote may serve to illustrate how the Poles' position differed from that of refugees elsewhere. One older Ugandan, who had been a diplomat later in life, told Edward Wakiku how he had met the Polish refugees once during his childhood. He had lived near a place where the Poles waited for the train during transit to camp. One day he went there and saw the largest group of whites he had ever seen. These refugees, who were waiting at the train station, gave him some sweet bread, which he still remembers to this day.[415] The refugees were the ones donating the bread given to them by the British, to members of the hosting population. One could read compassion and friendliness into this story; but at the same time it could be a story about white privilege, with British colonial officials supporting the Poles to lift them above the colonized.

Furthermore, the Poles were described as isolated under the control of the colonial rulers. The informants put all the blame on the British. The isolation was interpreted not as an intended segregation from the Africans, as with the British, but as a forced separation. The Poles remained politically powerless like the colonized, but materially better off. Apparently, most Poles did not conform to one of the central ingredients of colonial rule – the sense of superiority of the colonial official.[416] Their humiliating experience of deportation and dependence upon others seems to have instilled in them a humbler outlook. In the descriptions of their religious activities, one could even compare them to missionaries: benevolent whites who bring superior spiritual knowledge from Europe to Africa. This depiction conforms with Polish self-perceptions as missionaries. It must, however, be remembered that statements of this kind were mainly made in Uganda, a country where a quarter of the white population had been involved in missionary activities during colonial times.

Lwanga-Lunyiigo concludes a text about the Poles in Uganda, based on colonial sources and interviews with Africans, with the following statement: 'To the Africans this relationship with white people to some extent demystified whiteness and gave many of them the courage to demand their lost freedom'.[417] I would not go that far in the assessment of the Polish impact on the Ugandan independence movement. There were other socio-economic and global political factors that seem to have mattered more. The demystification of whiteness is, however, widely acknowledged as a side effect of the war.[418] Especially the experience of African soldiers fighting alongside less educated whites was revealing.[419] As Ousmane Sembène, the eminent Senegalese film director, author and former soldier, remembered: 'When a white soldier asked me to write a letter for him, it was a revelation – I thought all Europeans knew how to write. The army demystified the colonizer; the veil fell'.[420] Considering that nearly half of the rural population of pre-war eastern Poland was illiterate, the refugees could have made a similar impression on people living around the settlements.[421] The manifold interactions between Africans and lower-class Poles might have made a small contribution to the already growing activism and discontent with colonial rule.

The three perspectives I have sketched in these three subchapters all point to the Polish refugees being positioned on the margins of the white community. While Polish elites underlined their Europeanness and portrayed themselves as allied nationals on a par with the British colonizers, the lower-class Poles in the camps were less convinced about their superior position. For the colonial administrators and settlers, the Poles constituted a problematic peasant group that shared traits with other white subalterns. In the religious arena, the Poles occupied a position that showed some similarities with European missionaries. In my Conclusion chapter I will try to bring these perspectives together and critically evaluate my own approach, as well as my possible contribution to related discussions.

Notes

1. MSS Afr. s. 705, 'Welcome to Polish refugees', newspaper clipping of Charles M.A. Gayer, date and title of publication missing [most likely *East African Standard* in 1942].
2. Hall, 'The Local and the Global', 21.
3. Numbers from IRO: AJ/43/790/55/2, 'Refugees Remaining in Africa', Curtis, IRO, Nairobi to IRO HQ, Geneva, 9.02.49, p.4.
4. Thompson, *Governing Uganda*, 50–54.
5. Iliffe, *Modern History of Tanganyika*, 373, 450.
6. Smith, 'The Immigrant Communities', 460. In 1948 the biggest groups of non-British Europeans were the Greeks and the Germans.
7. When Germany joined the League of Nations in 1926, Germans were allowed to return to Tanganyika. See Pedersen, *The Guardians*, 137.
8. Pennington, 'Refugees in Tanganyika', 52. A further 2,000 Greek refugees transitted through Tanganyika en route to the Belgian Congo.
9. Shurmer-Smith, *Remnants of Empire*, 12f.
10. To make this clear, there were no Polish refugees in Nyasaland. It was planned, but they never came forth. In 1949 the Nyasaland government reclaimed expenditures for preparing the receipt of Polish refugees from the Colonial Office (PRO: CO 822/359, Director of Audit, Zomba, Nyasaland to Director General of Colonial Audit, CO 28.01.49).
11. The 'Closer Union' debate in East Africa went mainly from 1927 to 1931. See Pedersen, *The Guardians*, 222–25; Callahan, 'The Failure of Closer Union'. European settlers in Uganda, however, were opposed to a closer union with Kenya as they feared the competition as well as the political friction that Kenyan settlers stood for (Thompson, *Governing Uganda*, 177–80; Smith, 'The Immigrant Communities', 443f). The East African governments worked closely together. The seat of the East African Governors' Conference and the most important regional newspapers were located in Nairobi. In Central Africa, a possible amalgamation with Southern Rhodesia was the main political issue in Northern Rhodesia in the 1940s (Rotberg, *Black Heart*, 246). The Central African Federation was eventually made real in 1953 (Shurmer-Smith, *Remnants of Empire*, 15; Phiri, *Political History of Zambia*, 31).
12. Mlambo, *History of Zimbabwe*, 106.
13. Kennedy, *Islands of White*, 1.
14. Ibid., 8.
15. Ibid., 191f. On the elite composition of Kenya's settlers, see also Duder, 'Men of the Officer Class'.
16. Ochieng' and Atieno-Odhiambo, 'On Decolonization', xv.
17. McEwan, 'European Population of Southern Rhodesia', 429.
18. Mlambo, *History of Zimbabwe*, 140.
19. Harper and Constantine, *Migration and Empire*, 142.
20. Settlers in Kenya and Northern Tanganyika especially admired the Smuts government, and used the South African example to argue against the policy of the Colonial Office (e.g. EAS 03.01.44, 'The Future Of East Africa' by 'Group Of British Settlers', Arusha; EAS 25.08.44, 'Whither Are We Going? – Some Kenya Problems' by S.V. Cooke, Member for the Coast of the Legislative Council). Smuts is described by critics as 'probably the most distinguished of the leaders of white men's countries' (Lake and Reynolds, *Drawing the Global Colour Line*, 356).

21. Until 1912, South Africans had constituted the majority of white settlers in Kenya (Duder, 'Men of the Officer Class', 78).
22. Terreblanche, *History of Inequality*, 266–68. See also Butler, 'Afrikaner Women', 59; Cooper and Stoler, 'Between Metropole and Colony', 9.
23. Terreblanche, *History of Inequality*, 267.
24. Kennedy, *Islands of White*, 168.
25. Ibid., 91.
26. Ibid., 168. According to Kennedy, the other major reason for anxiety was the 'black peril'.
27. Hodder-Williams, *White Farmers in Rhodesia*, 159. But as far as I know, no group of Poles stayed for 'some months' in Nairobi. Instead, they stayed in one of the transit camps (Makindu or Dar es Salaam). Apart from this, the usual route for Polish refugees to Marandellas went through Beira port.
28. PRO: CO 822/145/5, 'Polish Refugees at Tengeru', T.W.E. Roche to J.B. Howard, Undersecretary of State, Aliens Department, Home Office, 16.06.50.
29. Acting Governor William Marston Logan in 1941, cited in Shapiro, *Haven in Africa*, 19.
30. The most prominent example in this case might be Philip Mitchell, who was governor of Uganda until 1940, and after an interlude in Fiji became governor of Kenya in 1944 (Thompson, *Governing Uganda*, 82).
31. PRO: CO 822/145/5, 'Polish Refugees at Tengeru', Thomas William Edgar Roche, Chief Immigration Officer, Home Office to J.B. Howard, Undersecretary of State, Aliens Department, Home Office, 16.06.50.
32. At least in retrospect this is how the the former director of refugees in Tanganyika, A.L. Pennington, summed it up. See Pennington, 'Refugees in Tanganyika', 52.
33. EAS 03.07.42, 'Polish Refugees from Persia', p.14.
34. EAS 30.06.42, 'Refugees from Persia', editorial.
35. EAS 28.07.42 'Ready for Refugees' Reception – Tanganyika to Give Homes to 5,000 Poles'; EAS 30.06.42 'Refugees from Persia', editorial.
36. KNA: AH/20/145, p.7, Memorandum of the East African Governors' Conference cited in a note by Director of Manpower, Nairobi, 17.07.45.
37. Ibid.
38. Especially Southern Rhodesia's prime minister (1933–53) Huggins was said to be against non-British settlement (Kennedy, *Islands of White*, 82).
39. Mlambo, 'Some Are More White'.
40. See Schutz, 'European Population Patterns'.
41. Iliffe, *Modern History of Tanganyika*, 263.
42. EAS 6.04.44, 'Housing' by 'Ex-Sergeant Major', Nairobi. The letter of this long-time Kenyan resident was motivated by his difficulties in finding accommodation after he was discharged from the army.
43. Cooper, 'Reconstructing Empire', 196.
44. Ibid., 199.
45. Iliffe, *Modern History of Tanganyika*, 475. In Southern Rhodesia, however, where the Colonial Office had less influence, African self-government was not an aim at all. The government kept the power in the hands of settlers, and clung to power until 1980.
46. KNA: AH/20/145, p.5, 'Refugees', note by Hyde-Clarke, Director of Manpower, 16.07.45. In the note he did not specify which refugees he meant, but the context suggests he was referring to the Poles.
47. KNA: AH/20/145, p.5, 'Refugees', note by Hyde-Clarke, Director of Manpower, 16.07.45.

48. IRO: AJ/43/790/55/2, M. Lush to Executive General PCIRO, Geneva, 27.11.47.
49. Ibid.
50. In the decolonization process, however, US Cold War concerns soon overrode anti-colonial convictions (see Louis, 'American Anti-Colonialism').
51. Eckert, 'African Nationalists', 292f. For the varied impact of the Second World War on Africa, see Killingray and Rathbone, *Africa and the Second World War*; Byfield et al., *Africa and World War II*.
52. Cooper, *Colonialism in Question*, 54.
53. Summary of a 1947 report by Sir Alan Pim, in PRO: CO 822/145/5 p.53, 'The Possibilities of Foreign Settlement in the Colonial Empire', n.d.
54. Ibid.
55. PRO: CO 822/145/5, 'Report of the British Mission to East Africa on Polish Refugees', T.W.E. Roche, Chief Immigration Officer, London Airport to J.B. Howard, Home Office, p.5, 6.7.50.
56. Holborn, *International Refugee Organization*, 418; Królikowski, 'Operation Polejump', 157f.
57. Smith, 'Immigrant Communities', 459.
58. Iliffe, *Modern History of Tanganyika*, 450. See also Hogendorn and Scott, 'East African Groundnut Scheme'; Scott, *Seeing Like a State*, 225–29.
59. Worsley, *Academic Skating on Thin Ice*, 60.
60. TNA: 24 /80/37 Vol.III, p.758, Biggs, Camp Commandant Ifunda to Director of Refugees, 17.04.48. The OFC staff seem to have liked music, as they also bought the piano of Dr Zamenhof, the Polish chief medical officer in Ifunda (TNA: 24 /80/37 Vol. III, p.742, F.N. Moore, John Mowlem and Co, Ltd., Lindi to DC Iringa, 11.02.48).
61. TNA: 69/782, Quartermaster Polish Refugee Camp Tengeru to Director of Refugees, 5.12.51; TNA: 69/782, Principal, Natural Resources School Tengeru to Provincial Commissioner Northern Province, Arusha, 6.10.52. Plans by the Overseas Food Corporation to move its headquarters to Tengeru had been abandoned, as it was deemed to be too expensive to convert the buildings (TNA: 69/782/IV, p.853, Chief Secretary, DSM to Provincial Commissioner, Arusha, 8.10.48).
62. TNA: 69/782, Principal, Natural Resources School Tengeru to Provincial Commissioner Northern Province, Arusha, 6.10.52.
63. Today the buildings still hold the Nyabyeya Forestry College, a government institution for forestry training.
64. Rupiah, 'History of the Establishment of Internment Camps', 152.
65. IRO: AJ/43/790/57/1, Pennington, Director of Refugees, Tanganyika to East African High Commissioner, 28.10.49. It is not entirely clear if his intention was really the creation of the school or if he used it as a pretext for the removal of the Poles.
66. Kennedy, *Islands of White*, 52.
67. Ibid.
68. KNA: AH/1/51, p.144, 'Employment of four Polish Refugees from Tengeru', Caldwell, Ag. Director of Aliens, Internees and War Refugees, Nairobi to Chief Secretary, 14.01.48.
69. See Chapter 2.
70. Fedorowich and Moore, *British Empire*, 49.
71. IRO: AJ/43/652/45/2, Curtis, IRO Nairobi to Warren G. Fuller, Resettlement Division, IRO Geneva, 1.06.50.
72. See Chapter 3.
73. Tavuyanago, Muguti and Hlongwana, 'Victims', 963; Zins, *Poles in Zambezi*, 83.

74. Rupiah, 'History of the Establishment of Internment Camps', 155.
75. Mlambo, 'Some Are More White', 144.
76. Quoted in EAS 28.08.44, 'No Unemployment in S. Rhodesia after the War – Every Returning Ex-Serviceman Guaranteed a Good Job'.
77. *Rhodesian Herald* article from 21.09.46, quoted in GP 20.10.46, 'Imigracja do Poludniowej Rodezji'. Here as elsewhere, I left the Polish newspaper captions as they were printed in the original, that is, mostly without the Polish diacritics.
78. Boucher, 'Limits of Potential', 922.
79. Tavuyanago, Muguti and Hlongwana, 'Victims'. See also Kennedy, *Islands of White*, 82.
80. Cited in Shurmer-Smith, *Remnants of Empire*, 14. On Welensky's loyalty to Britain, see Lowry, 'The Crown', 114.
81. Gore-Browne is mostly known for his support of the Zambian independence movement. On his life, see Rotberg, *Black Heart*.
82. PRO: CO 795/125/15, p.45, Report of Colonel Gore-Browne, Director of War Evacuees and Camps, Lusaka 3.7.1942. See also Chapter 1.
83. Rotberg, *Black Heart*, 236–37.
84. Cited in ibid., 237.
85. Tembo, 'Strangers in Our Midst'.
86. IRO: AJ/43/652/45/2, Curtis, IRO Nairobi to IRO HQ, Geneva, 31.01.49.
87. IRO: AJ/43/788/45/2, Wilkinson, Foreign Office, London to Arthur Rucker, IRO Headquarters, 11.04.49.
88. IRO: AJ/43/788/45/2, 'Polish Refugees (Official Communiqué)', Uganda Herald, n.d., attached to Curtis, IRO Nairobi to IRO Geneva, 10.03.49.
89. IRO: AJ/43/652/45/2, 'Polish Refugees', by F.J. Gorton, *Uganda Herald*, 15.02.49.
90. PRO: ED 128/101, 'Uwagi z akcji obozowej w Uganda', 10.11.46.
91. IRO: AJ/43/652/45/2, 'Refugees and Red Tape' by 'Mtu yule tena', *Uganda Herald*, 17.02.49. The alias translates from Kiswahili as 'This person again', but the content suggests he was not African, but rather British.
92. Thompson, *Governing Uganda*, 3.
93. Summers, 'Ugandan Politics', 498.
94. Thompson, *Governing Uganda*, 288f.
95. Ibid., 284.
96. IRO: AJ/43/788/45/2, 'Polish Refugees (Official Communiqué)', *Uganda Herald*, n.d., attached to Curtis, IRO Nairobi to IRO Geneva, 10.03.49.
97. British officials generally listened to the settler lobby as well as the Indian trader community (Thompson, *Governing Uganda*, 50f).
98. IRO: AJ/43/652/45/2, 'Refugees and Red Tape' by 'Mtu yule tena', *Uganda Herald*, 17.02.49.
99. At least one IRO official had heard this from undisclosed sources in the colonial administration. IRO: AJ 787/32/1 A+B, Curtis to The Director General, HQ Geneva, 05.05.49.
100. IRO: AJ/43/787/31/11, Director of Internment Camps and Refugee Settlements, Gatooma to Senior IRO Representative, Nairobi, 28.01.49. Maybe they were the refugees who were transferred from Northern to Southern Rhodesia in an attempt to stop the criminal activities mentioned in Rotberg, *Black Heart*, 237.
101. One woman was – apart from prostitution – charged for both offences (PRO: CO 822/146/1, Personal Summary, Zofia D., attached to Beryl Hughes, Home Office, London to Dawson, Colonial Office, 9.11.50).

102. One refugee was fined for this offence in Northern Rhodesia (PRO: CO 822/146/1, Personal Summary, Jozef K., attached to Beryl Hughes, Home Office, London to Dawson, Colonial Office, 9.11.50).
103. PRO: CO 822/146/1, Pennington for Governor of Tanganyika to Secretary of State, Colonial Office, 28.10.50.
104. PRO: CO 822/145/5, 'Polish Refugees at Tengeru', T.W.E. Roche to J.B. Howard, Undersecretary of State, Aliens Department, Home Office, 16.06.50. The thirty 'criminal family individuals' was misleading, as only sixteen of them were categorized as criminals. The remaining fourteen were their dependent family members.
105. PISM: Kol 147/11, 'Kronika – Afryka Rodezja Północna – Polskie osiedla uchodźce', chapter 'Katambora', n.p., n.d.
106. EAS 10.03.44, 'The Future of Kenya' by 'Permanent Resident', Kisumu.
107. TNA: 69/782/4, Provincial Commissioner, Arusha to all District Commissioners, Northern Province, 4.11.42.
108. TNA: 69/782/4, Camp Commandant, Tengeru to Provincial Commissioner, Arusha, 13.6.45.
109. TNA: 77/24/34, 'Mbeya Polish Refugee Fund', Manager Barclays Bank, Mbeya to A.A. Oldaker, Provincial Commissioner Mbeya, 17.09.47.
110. Barnes, *Humping My Drum*, 164.
111. Ibid., 165.
112. Hansen, *Distant Companions*, 7.
113. Ibid.
114. Barnes, *Humping My Drum*, 165.
115. Worsley, *Academic Skating on Thin Ice*, 60.
116. Brodhurst-Hill, *So This Is Kenya!*, 240. About Brodhurst-Hill, see Lorcin, *Historicizing Colonial Nostalgia*, 126–27.
117. Brodhurst-Hill, *So This Is Kenya!*, 126.
118. Ibid., 127.
119. Ibid., 126.
120. TNA: W3 /31798, p.1A, 'Ex-Service', Arusha to the Editor, East African Standard, Nairobi, forwarded to Chief Secretary, DSM on 1.12.43.
121. Jhaveri, *Dancing with Destiny*, n.p.
122. EAS: 31.08.42, '"Invasion" of East African Coast – Enemy Capture Zanzibar and Parts of Mombasa'. There were over seven hundred Germans in Kenya during the war (Nicholls, *Red Strangers*, 213).
123. EAS: 12.11.43, 'Tanganyika's Secret Hitler Shrine'. Another telling example is a longer article on German colonial plans for Africa in early 1942 (EAS: 28.08.42, 'Hitler's Plans for "German Africa". Greedy Eyes on Rich Prize of the Union').
124. In 1936 Tanganyika settlers even started organizing armed resistance units against a possible transfer of power to Germany (Ekoko, 'The British Attitude', 300). On the colonial revisionist movement and its changing relations to the Nazi state, see Linne, *Deutschland jenseits des Äquators?*
125. EAS: 10.07.42, 'Refugees' by John Williams, Kitale.
126. EAS: 21.07.42 'Refugees', by H. Weyl, Kisumu; and EAS 24.07.42, 'Refugees' by 'Give us the Chance', Ol Joro Orok.
127. EAS 5.06.46 ,'Reluctant Refugees', editorial.
128. An editorial in the Standard explained that the Italians were a cheap labour force during the war, but warned against the risk of creating a 'new poor white problem' by accepting them permanently (EAS 21.05.46, 'Italians in East Africa', editorial).

129. Huxley, *The Sorcerer's Apprentice*, 238.
130. Ibid., 237.
131. Cited from Chigume and Chakawa, 'The Media Weapon', 104. Unfortunately, the authors do not give clear references, but the published letter was most likely: The New Rhodesia, 13.12.46, 'Another view of Poles', by C. Olley, Salisbury, cited in Mlambo, 'Some Are More White', 19.
132. Hodder-Williams, *White Farmers in Rhodesia*, 159.
133. Ibid.
134. PRO: CO 822/145/5, 'Polish Refugees at Tengeru', T.W.E. Roche to J.B. Howard, Undersecretary of State, Aliens Department, HO, 16.06.50.
135. EAS 1.7.42, 'Finding Homes for Polish Refugees. "Orderly, Patriotic and Hardworking People"'.
136. Kennedy, *Islands of White*, 173.
137. PRO: AST 18/97, p.1, note by J.H.C. Ottley, National Assistance Board, London, 7.09.50.
138. Two sociologists made the observation of a growing cleavage between the clubbable and the non-clubbable members of the European community in East Africa in the late 1940s (i.e. Europeans who were allowed to join the European clubs and those who were barred from entry due to their lower socio-economic status). See Sofer and Ross, 'Some Characteristics of an East African European Population', 322.
139. Chakrabarty, *Provincializing Europe*, 11. He makes his point mainly in regard to post-colonial India, but draws links to subaltern colonial Indian historiography, where peasants are a central issue. I am not entering into the debate about the applicability of the term 'peasant' for the African context. The point here is the ascription of a class position and not an economic or anthropological analysis of peasant economies. For a glimpse into the debate, see Fallers, 'Are African Cultivators to Be Called "Peasants"?'; Cooper, 'Peasants, Capitalists, and Historians'.
140. Cresswell, *In Place/Out of Place*, 3.
141. Douglas, *Purity and Danger*.
142. NP 15.05.45, p.4, 'Rok 1943 – 25 Kwietnia', by Anna Suchnicka, Tengeru. Parts of this chapter are also contained in Lingelbach, 'Polish Refugees'.
143. Chappell and Milek, *Persian Blanket*, 146.
144. Brubaker and Cooper, 'Beyond "Identity"'. See the Introduction.
145. Brubaker and Cooper also mention Weber's German term 'Zusammengehörigkeitsgefühl' (ibid., 20).
146. It was the independent successor to the British-funded *Polak w Afryce* (Pole in Africa), which was liquidated after the de-recognition of the London-based Polish government-in-exile.
147. Stefania Buczak-Zarzycka and Janina Milek both lived on a small farm before being deported, and they published their life stories later. See Zarzycki and Buczak-Zarzycka, *Kwaheri Africa*; Chappell and Milek, *Persian Blanket*.
148. Piotrowski, *Polish Deportees*; and Tomaszewski, 'Shade'.
149. Gender is another important factor, which I have addressed in Chapter 4 already.
150. Chappell and Milek, *Persian Blanket*, 155.
151. Zins, *Poles in Zambezi*, 67.
152. Stewart Gore-Browne, Director of War Evacuees and Refugees, Northern Rhodesia (cited in Rotberg, *Black Heart*, 236).
153. Carlebach, *Jews of Nairobi*, 61. Matzo or matza is an unleavened bread that is part of Jewish cuisine and mainly eaten at the Passover festival.

154. MSS Afr s. 1652, p.12, 'A Polish Interlude in Africa – 1943–1944. A Personal Account of the Polish Refugee Settlements Established in Uganda during the War Years', by Rennie Bere, November 1978.
155. UN: S-1253-0000-0713, Report on Oudtshoorn, South Africa, by 'UNRRA representative', n.d.
156. PRO: CO 968/168/5, Bucharest to Foreign Office, secret diplomatic telegram, 8.10.44.
157. PRO: CO 968/168/5, C.W.F. Footman, CO to Paul Mason, FO, 9.09.44.
158. PRO: CO 968/168/5, Note by [Gerald] Creasy, CO, 7.09.44.
159. In a related way, Jewish Poles in the United States were not really considered to be part of the American Polish diaspora. See Jaroszyńska-Kirchmann, 'The Polish Post-World War II Diaspora', 48–49. On the close connection of Polish nationalism and Catholicism, see Porter-Szücs, *Faith and Fatherland*.
160. Interview with Simon Joseph, caretaker of the Polish cemetery in Tengeru, 19.04.2013; Jadwiga Morawiecka-Zabrowska in Piotrowski, *Polish Deportees*, 158.
161. IRO: AJ/43/790/55/2, Comprehensive report on Oudtshoorn by Emerson-Holcomb, UNRRA, December 1945, attached to 'The Problems in South Africa', M. Lush to IRO HQ, 17.01.49.
162. IRO: AJ/43/781, Curtis, PCIRO Nairobi to Ag. Chief PCIRO, 'Mr. Harazin's report on Polish Camps in Tanganyika', 29.08.47. Harazin's own background is unfortunately not clear. He was most likely Polish and close to the communist government. During his visit to Uganda he was met with suspicion and accused of being Russian by some of the refugees (IRO: AJ/43/781, 'Mr. Harazin's visit to Uganda', Curtis, PCIRO East Africa and Rhodesia to PCIRO Middle East HQ, Cairo, 15.09.47). A certain captain 'Harazim' [*sic*] is mentioned as IRO delegate touring the camps in October 1947 together with a representative of the communist Polish Foreign Ministry. See Królikowski, 'Operation Polejump', 163.
163. The Soviet authorities tried to restrict the evacuation of Polish citizens of Belarusian or Ukrainian nationality, therefore some of them changed their names in order to leave the USSR. See Mironowicz, 'Białorusini na Bliskim Wschodzie', 66; Grzybowski, 'Białorusini wśród uchodźców polskich', 329–30.
164. IRO: AJ/43/781, Curtis, PCIRO Nairobi to Ag. Chief PCIRO, 'Mr. Harazin's report on Polish Camps in Tanganyika', 29.08.47.
165. Cited in Grzybowski, 'Białorusini wśród uchodźców polskich', 340.
166. For example, one Tanganyika official admitted he had mixed up supporters of the London government-in-exile and the communist government in Warsaw among the refugees, stating 'it is most confusing!' (TNA: 176 /87, p.11, Skinner, Director of Refugees to O.A. Flynn, PC Southern Highland Province, Mbeya, 21.12.45).
167. Grzybowski, 'Białorusini wśród uchodźców polskich', 330, 341.
168. Gross, *Revolution from Abroad*, 4–5; Jolluck, *Exile and Identity*, 283.
169. According to Piotrowski, only half of the nearly 400,000 Polish citizens released during the amnesty were ethnic Poles (Piotrowski, *Polish Deportees*, 9).
170. For an in-depth analysis on the complicated issue of determining a DP's citizenship/nationality in the American-occupied zone of Germany, see Taylor, *In the Children's Best Interests*, chapter 10.
171. PRO: CO 822/146/1, Personal Summary, Anna Assen-Ajmer, attached to Beryl Hughes, Home Office, London to Dawson, Colonial Office, 9.11.50. By October 1950 she had left Tanganyika for an unspecified country, most likely French Morocco (PRO: CO 822/146/1, Pennington for Governor Tanganyika to Secretary of States for the Colonies, 28.10.50).

172. PRO: CO 822/146/1, Personal Summary, Karol Szustek, attached to Beryl Hughes, Home Office, London to Dawson, Colonial Office, 9.11.50.
173. Ibid.
174. PRO: CO 822/146/1, Pennington for Governor Tanganyika to Secretary of States for the Colonies, 28.10.50.
175. Immigration officer Roche about Karol Szustek. PRO: CO 822/145/5, 'Polish Refugees at Tengeru', TWE Roche, Chief Immigration Officer, Home Office to J.B. Howard, Undersecretary of State, Aliens Department, Home Office, 16.06.50.
176. Wójcik, 'Introduction to Chapter 6 Africa', 138. See also his travelogue about a trip from Lusaka to Dar es Salaam: Korabiewicz, *Kwaheri*.
177. The nickname was reportedly given to him by his friend and later Nobel Laureate Czesław Miłosz, because of his height and his passion for long walks (Panek, 'The Kilometre Who Sailed Thousands of Miles', 53).
178. Andrzej Szujecki in Piotrowski, *Polish Deportees*, 167.
179. PRO: CO 822/146/1, Pennington for Governor Tanganyika to Secretary of States for the Colonies, 28.10.50.
180. PRO: CO 822/146/1, Beryl Hughes, Home Office, London to Dawson, Colonial Office, 9.11.50.
181. PRO: CO 822/146/1, Pennington for Governor Tanganyika to Secretary of States for the Colonies, 28.10.50.
182. PRO: CO 822/146/1, Governor's Deputy, DSM to Secretary of State for the Colonies, 16.12.50.
183. PRO: CO 822/350, Ag. Governor Tanganyika to Secretary of State for the Colonies, 21.06.51.
184. TNA: 69/782, 'Polish Refugee Camp Tengeru Tanganyika. Nominal Roll in families as at 31st October, 1951'.
185. Panek, 'The Kilometre Who Sailed Thousands of Miles', 54.
186. Cited in ibid., 52.
187. Künzli, *L.L. Zamenhof*, 180, 333.
188. Wincewicz et al., 'Language and Medicine', 290.
189. Zamenhof graduated in medicine from Warsaw University in 1928 and received a diploma in Paris in 1932. PRO: FO 371/57902, Chief Secretary EAGC to Under Secretary of State for the Colonies, London, 28.08.46.
190. TNA: 69/782/IV, Pennington, for Director of Aliens and Internees to Camp Commandants Tengeru, Kondoa, Ifunda, 11.06.43.
191. TNA: 24 /80/37 Vol.III, p.779, E.K. Biggs, Camp Commandant Ifunda to T.M. Skinner, District Commissioner Iringa, 25.06.48.
192. Wincewicz et al., 'Language and Medicine', 289.
193. Commons Sitting of 21 February 1946, vol. 419, col. 1363, online. http://hansard.mill banksystems.com/commons/1946/feb/21/foreign-affairs#S5CV0419P0_19460221_ HOC_352. Last accessed 16 December 2019.
194. Taylor, *In the Children's Best Interests*, 304.
195. Ibid., 305.
196. Of the evacuated soldiers in the Polish army, 1,397 registered their nationality as Belarusian. Their number might likely be higher, because other Belarusians did register as Polish (Grzybowski, 'Białorusini wśród uchodźców polskich', 330).
197. See Jaroszyńska-Kirchmann, *Exile Mission*, 1; Davies, *Im Herzen Europas*, 152–55.
198. GP 20.10.46, 'Z Osiedli', p.10. See also Niedźwiecka, 'Armią Andersa', 38.

199. The lecture was held on the occasion of the visit by a delegate from the Polish government-in-exile to Ifunda (Piłsudski Archive, New York: Zesp.114, sygn. 249, no title, no date). My thanks to Katarzyna Nowak for providing me with these copies.
200. To give an idea of the content, here are some of the lectures in the YMCA club room in Tengeru: 'Stefan Żeromski', 'Stanisław Wyspianski'; 'Significance of the Seas'; 'Entry of the Second Corps into the Fighting in Italy'; 'Anniversary of Independence'; 'November Uprising'; 'Chopin's Life' (from GP 24.03.46, 'Z Osiedli', p.11).
201. Echo z Digglefold 44, No. 2, September 1944, p.2. Drawing on the same tradition but with a different political ideology, the Polish Women's Battalion fighting with the Red Army was called Emilia Plater as well (Cook, *Women and War*, 475).
202. Szostak, *American by Choice*, 90; Krolikowski, *Stolen Childhood*, 89. A photograph of the hedge is to be found in Wróbel, 'Polskie Dominium', 19.
203. See also Chapter 4.
204. Janowski, 'Food in Traumatic Times', 346.
205. Ibid., 339.
206. Gerald Mkindi, personal communication, Dar es Salaam, 28.03.13.
207. GP 01.12.46, p.3, 'Wracac czy dalej sie tulac?' by 'Jotes'.
208. For a general overview of the worldwide Polish diaspora, see Pacyga, 'Polish Diaspora'.
209. E.g. GP 26.05.46, p.1, 'Nasze Stanowisko' by Kazimierz Chodzikiewicz. Although it was not recognized any more, the government-in-exile stayed in London until December 1990.
210. Stanisław Kaczmarek was the Światpol representative for Southern Africa, and Kazimierz Chodzikiewicz was the representative for East Africa (MSS Afr. s. 1366/9, p.32, 'Swiatowy Zwiazek Polakow z Zagranicy ("Swiatpol") [*sic*] (World League of Poles Abroad)', 18.05.46). On Światpol and its relation to American Polonia organizations, see Blejwas, 'Old and New Polonias'.
211. Zins, *Poles in Zambezi*, 80. The surplus children's shoes were later sent with UNRRA to Poland (KNA: CS/2/7/40, p.222, Belcher, Commissioner EARA to Chief Secretary, Nairobi, 30.06.48).
212. NP Christmas 1947, 'Przewielebny Ksieze Dyrektorze!' by Władyslaw Słapa.
213. Jan Sliwowski and Antoni Wierzbiński were both sent from the US and served consecutively in Tengeru. Plawski, *Torn from the Homeland*, 151; IRO: AJ/43/781, Monthly report for November 1949 by Curtis to IRO HQ, p.4, 3.12.49; TNA: 69/782/IV, p.743, '"History" of Tengeru Camp', written by Miss Jowitt attached to Camp Commandant, Tengeru to EARA, Nairobi, 6.11.43.
214. NP 30.06.45, p.14, 'Z Osiedli. Korespondencja z Masindi'.
215. NP 30.06.45, 'Dzien 21 Maja 1945r. w Koji', by Zemoytel.
216. See Jaroszyńska-Kirchmann, *Exile Mission*, 56–57.
217. IRO: AJ/43/781, Monthly report for September 1948 by Curtis to IRO HQ, p.2, 21.10.48.
218. Zarzycki and Buczak-Zarzycka, *Kwaheri Africa*, 51.
219. IRO: AJ/43/790/55/2, 'Refugees Remaining in Africa', Curtis to IRO HQ, p.3, 9.02.49.
220. Malkki, *Purity and Exile*.
221. Ibid., 4.
222. See Carson, 'Quaker Internationalist Tradition', 74; Gatrell, *Making of the Modern Refugee*, 100.
223. Porajska, *From the Steppes*, 107; See also Krolikowski, *Stolen Childhood*, 84.
224. Hilton, 'Cultural Nationalism in Exile', 282.

225. PRO: CO 822/146/1, Acting Governor Uganda, 7.9.1950.
226. PRO: CO 822/146/1, p.278, Governor Tanganyika to Secretary of States for the Colonies, 4.12.50.
227. PRO: ED 128/107, M. Staszewski to Delegata Ministerstwo Wyznań Religijnych i Oświecenia Publicznego, Nairobi, 11.12.44. From the letter it remains open whether it was the consul in Kampala or Nairobi.
228. PRO: ED 128/107, C.L. Bruton, Commissioner EARA to Director of Refugees, 1.02.45.
229. The story of these children is covered in depth by Taylor, *Polish Orphans*. See also Kévonian, 'Histoires d'enfants, Histoire d'Europe'. For a first-hand account from the priest who accompanied the group to Canada, see Krolikowski, *Stolen Childhood*, 174–261.
230. IRO: AJ/43/616, Curtis, IRO Nairobi to IRO HQ, Geneva, 5.08.49.
231. Zins, *Poles in Zambezi*, 83. See also Chapter 1.
232. IRO: AJ/43/790/55/2, Lush, PCIRO Cairo to Executive General, PCIRO HQ, Geneva, 27.11.47.
233. Zins, *Poles in Zambezi*, 84–86.
234. For the construction of this difference, see Malkki, 'Refugees and Exile'.
235. Report by the official of a Canadian selection mission 'John A. Sharrar' (Sharrer in other IRO files), cited in Tomaszewski, 'From the Snows of Siberia'. It should be noted that local IRO officials explained the impression of the visiting Canadians with some unfortunate incidents: on the day of their arrival some boys went on a trip to the Ngorongoro crater; it was a Catholic holiday and furthermore the farewell party for Camp Commandant Minnery (IRO: AJ/43/788/45/2, Curtis, IRO Nairobi to Director of Refugees Tanganyika, p.3, 17.08.49).
236. In Masindi and Kidugala there were collections made for Poles and children from concentration camps in late 1945 (see GP 2.12.45, p.10, 'Z Osiedli').
237. EAS 05.06.46, 'Reluctant Refugees', editorial.
238. Chappell and Milek, *Persian Blanket*, 158.
239. Szostak, *American by Choice*, 100.
240. Julian Suski cited in Wróbel, *Uchodźcy polscy*, 162.
241. Over two-thirds of all houses in eastern Poland lacked sewer lines, water pipes, electricity and gas. Additionally, the Great Depression led to increased poverty and unemployment in the region. See Gross, *Revolution from Abroad*, 5.
242. NP 15.05.45, p.4, 'Rok 1943 – 25 Kwietnia' by Anna Suchnicka, Tengeru.
243. See Filomena Michałowska-Bykowska in Piotrowski, *Polish Deportees*, 162.
244. The Tanganyika director of refugees remarked that the system of three hours of 'free work' had already broken down in the first half of 1943 (PRO: FO 371/51150, 'Conference of the Directors of Refugees in East Africa' 6.–8.11.44) and one International Red Cross report on Rusape described the scheme as 'inoperative' there (PRO: FO 371/51150, 'Colonie de réfugiés polonais de Rusape. Visité le 4 septembre 1944 par M. G.C. Senn', 25.04.45).
245. KNA: AH/1/51, p.112/1(a), Reginald Caldwell, Director of Aliens and Internees and War Refugees, Nairobi to Camp Commandant Tengeru, 16.09.47.
246. Interview cited in Tomaszewski, 'Shade'.
247. Zarzycki and Buczak-Zarzycka, *Kwaheri Africa*, 72.
248. GP 02.06.46, p.14, 'Sladami "W Pustyni i w Puszczy"', by H. Czarnocka (Koresp. z Konga Belg.).
249. In May 1943, the *Rhodesian Herald* reported extensively on the Polish celebrations, and Zawisza's speech was broadcast on radio (Zins, *Poles in Zambezi*, 71f).

250. EAS 15.04.44, p.1, 'Polish Minister's Impressions of His E.A. Tour'.
251. See Chapter 3.
252. *Echo z Digglefold* 44, No. 2, September 1944, p.2.
253. In a report from Rongai school settlement, Polish officials underlined that the British commandant had agreed to put the Polish flag next to that of the British (PRO: ED 128/107, Seweryn Szczepanski, Chief Polish Educational Adviser and K. Chodzikiewicz, Ag. Chief Polish Adviser to Director of Aliens and Internees, Law Courts, Nairobi, 27.09.45).
254. MSS Afr. s. 705, 'Uganda's First Polish Village' by "Standard" correspondent, Kampala, newspaper clipping of Charles M.A. Gayer, date and title of publication missing [most likely *East African Standard* in 1942]. Unfortunately it is unclear who wrote the article.
255. TNA: 69/787, p.95–99, Tanganyika Government. Contract Agreement, 31.07.42.
256. TNA: 69/787, p.206, Divisional Engineer Public Works Department to Provincial Commissioner Northern Province, 29.12.43. The Greek contractors were reportedly unable to build the huts on time.
257. TNA: 69/787, p.142. Comments on the final report on Tengeru Refugee Camp submitted by Dr B.O. Wilkin, Senior Medical Officer by P.M. Huggins, District Commissioner Arusha, 15.04.43.
258. MSS Afr s 1378, Box 2, file 3, Report 'Tengeru Camp as seen on 22.12.42' by Bertram Wilkin, p.33.
259. MSS Afr. s. 1378, Box 2, file 8, Report 'Kidugalla [sic] Polish Refugee Camp as seen on 15.01.43' by Bertram Wilkin, Senior Medical Officer, p.14.
260. TNA: 69/787, p.178, Director of Refugees to Provincial Commissioner Northern Province, 24.06.43.
261. NP 15.04.46, 'Rusape' by Władyslaw Słapa.
262. NP 'Kwiaty, kwiaty...' by Podhalanin, n.d. [between 30.03.45 and 30.04.45].
263. TNA: 69/782/IV, p.743, '"History" of Tengeru Camp', by Miss Jowitt, attached to a letter from the Camp Commandant Tengeru to East African Refugee Authority, 6.11.43.
264. NP 15.04.46 'Rusape' by Władyslaw Słapa.
265. GP 31.03.46 'Z Osiedli. Fort Jameson' by 'Mieszkaniec Osiedla', p.12.
266. TNA: 69 /787, p.158, Notes on a Conference Held at Tengeru, 28.05.43.
267. Wisia Reginella, in Piotrowski, *Polish Deportees*, 156.
268. Observation on site (April 2013), where some houses still stand.
269. Maria Pawulska Rasiej cited in Wojciechowska, *Waiting to Be Heard*, 225.
270. TNA: 69 /787, p.144, Provincial Commissioner Northern Province to the Senior Medical Officer, Moshi, 12.05.43.
271. TNA: 69/782/IV, p.743, ""History" of Tengeru Camp", by Miss Jowitt, attached to a letter from the Camp Commandant Tengeru to East African Refugee Authority, 6.11.43.
272. NP 15.04.46 'Rusape', by Władysław Słapa.
273. Zarzycki and Buczak-Zarzycka, *Kwaheri Africa*, 30.
274. NP 15.05.47, 'Tengeru', p.7.
275. NP 15.10.46, 'Marandellas', by Władysław Słapa. The altar of the camp church featured a picture of the 'Black Madonna of Częstochowa' – a most revered and highly popular icon in Poland, with black skin colour.
276. NP 01.12.45, 'Wspaniały Kosciół zbudowano w Masindi', by Władysław Słapa.
277. While Masindi was part of Bunyoro, many of the workers came from other parts of Uganda and beyond.

278. Wanda Nowosiad-Ostrowska in Piotrowski, *Polish Deportees*, 173.
279. Zarzycki and Buczak-Zarzycka, *Kwaheri Africa*, p.40.
280. Sister Matilda (born in Poznań) was the Mother Superior of the Kilema mission and had arrived there back in 1904. See Krolikowski, *Stolen Childhood*, 154–60.
281. Zins, *Poles in Zambezi*, 52.
282. NP 15.01.47, 'Misja w Kasisi', by Halina Kenich.
283. Ibid.
284. NP 01.12.45, 'Swietlica Katolicka W.R.S. w Kondoa'; and Irena Bartkowiak-Drobek in Piotrowski, *Polish Deportees*, 161.
285. PISM: Kol 174/2, p.86, 'Duszpasterstwo w Ifundzie' by Jan Sajewicz, n.d.
286. For relationships between Italian men and Polish women, see Chapter 4.
287. NP 25.12.46, 'Czarni Swieci' by Jerzy Dołęga-Kowalewski. For a critical reassessment of the canonization of the Uganda martyrs, see Kassimir, 'Complex Martyrs'.
288. NP 25.12.46, 'Czarni Swieci' by Jerzy Dołęga-Kowalewski, p.8.
289. NP 08.12.46 'Takie duze czarne dzieci…' by Jerzy Dołęga-Kowalewski.
290. Ibid.
291. NP 30.06.45, p.15, 'Dzień 21 Maja 1945r. w Koji' by T. Zemoytel, citing from his speech at the 'Polish Countryside Celebration' on 21.5.45 in Koja.
292. An overview report describes YMCA activities for eleven of thirteen settlements: GP 18.11.45, p.10, 'Z Osiedli (z działalnośći YMCA)'.
293. GP 14.10.45, p.10, 'Z Osiedli'.
294. GP 18.11.45, p.10, 'Z Osiedli (z działalnośći YMCA)'.
295. Maria Gabiniewicz in Piotrowski, *Polish Deportees*, 171.
296. Romanko, 'From Russian Gulag', n.p.
297. Bohdan Ławiński in Piotrowski, *Polish Deportees*, 178.
298. See Zins, *Poles in Zambezi*. The Polish historian Henryk Zins worked at the University of Zimbabwe from 1985 to 1989. The original version of his book was published in Poland in 1988 as Zins, *Polacy w Zambezji*.
299. Interview with Luhende, Dar es Salaam, early 2009.
300. See Frankenberg, 'Introduction'; Steyn, *Whiteness Just Isn't What It Used To Be*.
301. Apart from the Poles, only about 0.05 per cent of the Ugandan population were white.
302. The only exception I found is the citation of one article about the Poles in a Ugandan newspaper, to which I will return later.
303. While it is called 'Masindi' in the Polish and British sources, the camp was in fact situated in the village of Nyabyeya, some 25 kilometres away from Masindi town. Ugandan informants usually called the camp 'Nyabyeya', therefore I will stick to this term in this subchapter.
304. My sincerest thanks go to Simon Joseph (Tengeru), Edward Wakiku (Koja) and Ochau Paito Caesar (Nyabyeya) for their time, hospitality, help and expertise.
305. The three interviews of 2009 were all conducted in Dar es Salaam in the homes of the informants, and the language was Kiswahili, for which no interpreter was needed. Of the Nyabyeya interviews, the one with Otwia Filimon was conducted in the Polish church, the others in the compounds of the informants' houses. Ochau Paito Caesar helped with the translation, as the Nyabyeyan Kiswahili was rather different from my coastal Tanzanian variant. In Koja the interview with Edward Sinabulya was in front of his house, the one with Mukeera Kasule next to a health station that had in part been financed by former Polish refugees and their descendants. Both interviews were translated from Luganda to English by Edward Wakiku, the caretaker of the Polish cemetery.

In Tengeru both interviews were conducted in Kiswahili in the memorial hall of the Polish cemetery.
306. See de Fina, 'Researcher and Informant Roles'.
307. Vansina, *Oral Tradition as History*, xii.
308. The Livestock Training Institute in Tengeru even received Polish development assistance later.
309. The artist Emma Wolukau-Wanambwa made this point to me in Berlin in April 2017. She has worked for some years on the Polish refugees in Uganda, and explained that most people who showed an interest in the story were Poles working for the church in Uganda.
310. Interviews conducted in Abercorn by Mary-Ann Sandifort are a valuable addition here, cited from her Master's thesis (Sandifort, 'World War Two'). Some side remarks in the historical and anthropological literature give further hints.
311. Interview with John Onega, Nyabyeya, 13.04.2013.
312. Ibid.
313. Interview with Teresa Tiko, Nyabyeya, 13.04.2013.
314. Cited and translated in Lwanga-Lunyiigo, 'Uganda's Long Connection', 9.
315. Ibid.
316. Irena Bartkowiak-Drobek in Piotrowski, *Polish Deportees*, 161.
317. Interview with Joshua Sinyangwe, Abercorn, cited in Sandifort, 'World War Two', 43.
318. Interview with Edward Sinabulya, Koja, 15.04.2013.
319. Ibid.
320. Rockenbach, 'Accounting for the Past'. On Uganda's refugee history, see also Gingyera-Pinycwa, 'Uganda's Entanglement'.
321. Pirouet, 'Refugees in and from Uganda', 239. Tanzania has a long history of refugee hosting as well. See Rosenthal, 'From Migrants to Refugees'. Chaulia, in his 'Politics of Refugee Hosting in Tanzania', did, however, omit the Poles in his historical sketch of this subject.
322. Interview with Simon Joseph, Tengeru, 19.04.2013. Unfortunately an attempted interview with the daughter could not be completed owing to time constraints. The grave of Anna Pietrutczyk Karaiskos (1915–2003) is to be found in the Polish cemetery of Tengeru.
323. Interview with Otwia Filimon, Nyabyeya, 13.04.2013.
324. Interview with Edward Sinabulya, Koja, 15.04.2013.
325. Interview with Mukeera Kasule, Koja, 16.04.2013.
326. Ibid.
327. White, 'Cars Out of Place', 28. On the interpretation of rumours as opposed to accepted 'facts', see also Stoler, 'In Cold Blood', 179, 182–83.
328. Interview with Patrick Kunambi, Dar es Salaam, early 2009.
329. Interview with Edward Sinabulya, Koja, 15.04.2013.
330. Interview with Mukeera Kasule, Koja, 16.04.2013.
331. Interview with Otwia Filimon, Nyabyeya, 13.04.2013.
332. Interview with John Onega, Nyabyeya, 13.04.2013.
333. Summers, 'Ugandan Politics', 487, fn.18.
334. Cited in Sandifort, 'World War Two', 45–46.
335. Jhaveri, *Dancing With Destiny*, n.p. Chapter 8.
336. Interview with Edward Sinabulya, Koja, 15.04.2013.
337. Interview with Otwia Filimon, Nyabyeya, 13.04.2013.
338. Interview with Edward Sinabulya, Koja, 15.04.2013.

339. Iliffe, *Modern History of Tanganyika*, 499.
340. Ibid., 500–501. See also Temu, 'Rise and Triumph of Nationalism', 205; Spear, *Mountain Farmers*, 209–35.
341. Iliffe, *A Modern History of Tanganyika*, 501.
342. See Chapter 3 on this issue.
343. Interview with Edward Sinabulya, Koja, 15.04.2013.
344. Interview with Ochau Paito Caesar, Nyabyeya, 12.04.2013.
345. Kassimir, 'Complex Martyrs', 360.
346. Professor Samwiri Lwanga-Lunyiigo, Entebbe, personal communication, 18.04.2013.
347. Interview with Simon Joseph, Tengeru, 19.04.2013.
348. Interviews with Otwia Filimon and John Onega, Nyabyeya, 13.04.2013.
349. In 1938, 570 of the 2,200 European residents in Uganda were attached to the missions. See Smith, 'Immigrant Communities', 442–43.
350. Own observation, April 2013, Tengeru. Unfortunately it was not possible to conduct a recorded interview.
351. Interview with John Onega, Nyabyeya, 13.04.2013.
352. Interview cited in Sandifort, 'World War Two', 45.
353. Interview with Otwia Filimon, Nyabyeya, 13.04.2013.
354. Ibid.
355. Interview with Edward Sinabulya, Koja, 15.04.2013.
356. The whole account is based on the narration of Edward Sinabulya.
357. Summers, 'Ugandan Politics', 480.
358. Thompson, 'Colonialism in Crisis', 642.
359. Ibid., 621.
360. GP 3.03.46, p.11, 'Osiedla jako rynki zbytu własnej produkcji' by M. Wagner (Korespondent w Kidugali).
361. TNA 69/782/IV, p.743, '"History" of Tengeru Camp' written by Miss Jowitt attached to Camp Commandant, Tengeru to EARA, Nairobi, 6.11.43.
362. TNA 69/787, p.8, R.S. Hickson-Mahony, Labour Commissioner, DSM to the Chief Secretary, DSM, 16.07.42.
363. PRO: FO 371/51150, p.14, Governor's Deputy, DSM to Secretary of State for the Colonies, London, 24.01.45.
364. Numbers for the Ugandan camps from Lwanga-Lunyiigo, 'Uganda's Long Connection', 7.
365. MSS Afr s. 1652, p.15, 'A Polish Interlude in Africa – 1943–1944. A Personal Account of the Polish Refugee Settlements established in Uganda during the War Years' by Rennie Bere, November 1978.
366. Interview with Mukeera Kasule, Koja, 16.04.2013.
367. Interview with Simon Joseph, Tengeru, 19.04.2013.
368. Interview with John Onega, Nyabyeya, 13.04.2013.
369. Interview with Ochau Paito Caesar, Nyabyeya, 12.04.2013.
370. Thompson, 'Colonialism in Crisis', 623.
371. TNA: W3 /31798, p.3, F.A. Montague, Ag. Chief Secretary to the Government, DSM to the Editor, East African Standard, Nairobi, 31.12.43.
372. Porajska, *From the Steppes*, 121.
373. Ibid. It was widespread for white settlers to call African men 'boy' regardless of age. On the racist implications of this practice see Mamdani, *Citizen and Subject*, 4; Morrell, 'Of Boys and Men', 616.
374. Porajska, *From the Steppes*, 121.

375. Ibid, 122.
376. Interview with Mukeera Kasule, Koja, 16.04.2013.
377. From interviews with former Polish refugees this seems likely, as they claimed they never ate African cooked food (Janowski, 'Food in Traumatic Times', 339).
378. Porajska, *From the Steppes*, 123.
379. Interview with Edward Sinabulya, Koja, 15.04.2013.
380. Iliffe, *Modern History of Tanganyika*, 370.
381. Byfield, 'Producing for the War', 37. For Northern Rhodesia, see Tembo, 'Coerced African Labour'.
382. Iliffe, *Modern History of Tanganyika*, 371.
383. Westcott, 'Impact of the Second World War', 151.
384. TNA: 9 /787, p.3, Partridge, Provincial Commissioner, Northern Province to Pennington, Compolice, DSM, 24.07.42. and p.6, Manpower, DSM to Provincer Arusha, 28.07.42.
385. TNA: 9 /787, 'Labour position – Tengeru Camp', n.d. [1942 or 1943].
386. TNA: 9 /787, p.172, District Commissioner Moshi to Camp Commandant Tengeru, 19.06.43.
387. According to Pennington, this overlap was due to problems with the Greek contractors. The last hut was not finished until December 1943. TNA: 9 /787, p.208, Pennington, Director of Refugees to Burloyanis and Mavrides, 22.02.44.
388. Westcott, 'Impact of the Second World War', 147.
389. Interview with Mukeera Kasule, Koja, 16.04.2013.
390. Interview with Simon Joseph, Tengeru, 19.04.2013.
391. There were repeated complaints that prices were rising and certain products completely selling out, especially around Tengeru settlement (see e.g. TNA: 5/28/1, Representative Economic Control Board to The Secretary, Economic Control Board, DSM, 5.04.44).
392. TNA: 5/28/1, 'Monthly requirements of Polish refugees camp Tengeru for about 3,734 inmates', no date [ca. 1944 or 1945].
393. TNA: 69/782/IV, p.804, Provincial Commissioner Northern Province to Proprietor, Baboo's Milk House, Moshi, 15.07.44.
394. TNA: 69/782/IV, p.743, '"History" of Tengeru Camp' written by Miss Jowitt attached to Camp Commandant, Tengeru to EARA, Nairobi, 6.11.43.
395. E.g. the incident in Ifunda, where Poles were accused of refusing to reveal their Indian suppliers, mentioned in Chapter 3.
396. TNA: 69 /787, p.142, Comments on the final report on Tengeru Refugee Camp submitted by Dr B.O. Wilkin, Senior Medical Officer by P.M. Huggins, District Commissioner, Arusha, 15.04.43.
397. Interview with Mukeera Kasule, Koja, 16.04.2013.
398. Interview with Edward Sinabulya, Koja, 15.04.2013.
399. Interview with Otwia Filimon, Nyabyeya, 13.04.2013.
400. TNA: 5/28/1, 'Monthly requirements of Polish refugees camp Tengeru for about 3,734 inmates', no date [ca. 1944 or 1945].
401. TNA: K6/31882, p.2, Ag. Chief Secretary to the Government to J.B. Wiercinski, Consul for Poland, DSM, 24.02.44.
402. Interview with Eliphase Mghoja, 19.04.2013.
403. Interview with the son of the late Philipo Jeto, Nyabyeya, 13.04.2013.
404. Interview with Edward Sinabulya, Koja, 15.04.2013.
405. Interview with Edward Wakiku, Koja, 15.04.2013.

406. Although not clearly related to the 'Joseph' from the interview, in the IRO files there is one 'Jozef P.' in Koja mentioned as an 'undesirable type of person'. According to one IRO official it was not clear 'whether he is really a social write-off, as many of the Poles in Koja seem to think, or if he is just a stupid fellow, too quick with his fists' (IRO: AJ/43/787/31/11, H.A. Curtis, IRO Nairobi to IRO Representative, Kampala, 06.04.50).
407. Interview with Simon Joseph, Tengeru, 19.04.2013.
408. Beattie, 'Spirit Mediumship', 161.
409. Ibid., 162.
410. MSS Afr. s. 1652, p.15, 'A Polish Interlude in Africa – 1943–1944. A Personal Account of the Polish Refugee Settlements established in Uganda during the War Years' by Rennie Bere, November 1978. Visiting painter Feliks Topolski made some fine drawings of the Mukama, reproduced in Topolski and Collis, *Three Continents*, 48–49.
411. On the lost counties campaign, and Mukama Winyi's prominent role therein, see Doyle, *Crisis and Decline*, 177–79.
412. PRO: CO 822/145/5, 'Resettlement of Refugees', Draft Notice on the Roche mission report, Appendix in Harris, Dawson, Scott, Rogers, Colonial Office to Cabinet, 26.7.50. Unfortunately it is not noted who these two chiefs were.
413. EAS 02.07.46, 'Italians in East Africa' by 'Astonished', Kisumu. The anonymous African writer wrote in his letter to the editor: 'These undesirable ex-enemy subjects have deteriorated Africans [sic] morally and socially. They have aggravated our racial problems'.
414. Iliffe, *Modern History of Tanganyika*, 357, 485.
415. Interview with Edward Wakiku, Koja, 15.04.2013.
416. Kirk-Greene, 'Thin White Line', 143f.
417. Lwanga-Lunyiigo, 'Uganda's Long Connection', 19.
418. See e.g. Mlambo, *History of Zimbabwe*, 139.
419. The spectacular victories of the Japanese army in 1941–42 are another factor that seriously damaged 'the prestige of white men', at least in Asia (Lake and Reynolds, *Drawing the Global Colour Line*, 341).
420. Cited in Killingray and Plaut, *Fighting for Britain*, 211.
421. Jolluck, *Exile and Identity*, 28. For more regional differentiation, see Gross, *Revolution from Abroad*, 5. Both draw on numbers from the 1931 census.

Conclusion

On the Edges of Whiteness

The history of the Polish refugees' sojourn in colonial Africa defies a Manichean understanding of colonial societies. Located on the edges of whiteness, they were neither colonizer nor colonized. The previous chapters have shown that their position within the hosting colonial societies was ambivalent and contested. The precarious position of Britain during the Second World War led to decisions that would never have been made under 'normal' conditions. Only the need for support from the Polish soldiers in the fight against Nazi Germany's aggression led to the subsequent need to take care of their 'dependants'. In an increasingly threatened British Empire, the East and Central African colonies were just the most feasible place to host them.

The arrival of this large group of white refugees brought the colonial administration into an uncomfortable situation. It went against earlier colonialist convictions that regarded the construction of an image of white superiority as paramount for the legitimization of colonial rule. The immigration of a group that consisted mostly of women and children furthermore contradicted the male-dominated world of colonial societies. It also went against nationalist calls from British settlers to keep their communities dominated by people of British descent. On top of that, the large influx of unskilled whites conflicted with postwar policies of 'developmental colonialism', which put an emphasis on the immigration of skilled Europeans and the gradual transfer of expertise and responsibility to Africans. Only a few of the Polish refugees found a place in this setting and were permitted to settle permanently.

The response of the colonial administration to these multiple complications resembled earlier responses to the problem of white subalterns (such as the poor, criminals and lunatics). First of all, the Poles were accommodated in rather isolated settlements, and their interaction with the rest of society was controlled and minimized. Secondly, they were lifted materially to a standard that distinguished them from the colonized. They arrived sick, emaciated and ragged, but their conditions soon improved. Their standards of food, clothing, housing, education and health care were higher than those of most of their African neighbours. Thirdly, colonial administrators were most eager to get rid of them after the war. Some were reluctantly accepted for permanent settlement, but most had to leave, despite efforts by Polish exile politicians, the International Refugee Organization and a few sympathetic officials and settlers.

While there is some literature on the Polish refugees' stay in Africa, *On the Edges of Whiteness* is the first study that traces their history comprehensively and from multiple sources. It covers all Polish camps in East and Central Africa, and pays attention to the specific historical circumstances. These Poles were not just one of many Polish diaspora groups, this time in a rather exotic setting. It was not only a story of suffering and national resilience set under the baobab tree, with lions roaring in the distance. It was an entangled history of people with diverse trajectories, convictions, affiliations and self perceptions, who were placed in diverging social categories. The peculiar position of the Polish refugee group as a whole was regarded differently by the different people involved. The unique contribution of this book lies in considering these multiple perspectives in light of a careful contextualization based on a broad range of literature on Polish, British and East and Central African history, refugee studies and the historiography of colonialism. As far as possible, I have tried to open up all the 'black boxes' of the groups involved. In contrast to their portrayal in a Polish national framework, the refugee group was not a homogeneous entity with common interests. Gender, class and religious affiliation formed the most important internal fault lines. The colonial administrators, the British settlers and their African neighbours were not homogeneous entities either.

While it facilitates a more nuanced understanding of the Poles' position within colonial societies, this marginal episode is also connected to general discussions related to their refugee status, their national background and their gender. For these three fields of research, the Poles have served as a kind of test case. First, I have argued that the International Refugee Organization (an important forerunner of the UNHCR) functioned in a largely imperial world and was confined to assisting white refugees only. Second, in regard to (post)colonial readings of Polish history, the Polish refugee elite's self-identification and attempts at being European would-be colonizers makes it impossible to regard Poland itself simply as a colony. And third, the role of the Polish women in colonial societies was ambiguous, as men disagreed about which community they should rightfully belong to. While some Polish women joined Polish or British men to re-create their community, others just went their own ways, trying to make the most of their situation. Especially when relationships crossed the colour-line, they were regarded as a threat to the colonial dichotomy, while at the same time exposing its fuzziness.

The multi-perspective approach to history writing offers the chance to sidestep the problematic of 'hierarchies of credibility'.[1] The main question we pose to contradictory sources should not be which version is true and which is false. Different actors experienced and interpreted the historical situation differently. While British colonial officials saw the Poles as subaltern whites, the Polish refugee elites understood themselves as European allies on a par with the British. Africans who worked in the camps regarded the Poles mostly as less arrogant and less detached employers than the other settlers. The officials of the IRO regarded refugees as numbers that needed to be reduced. Their task was to empty the camps before their own organization was disbanded. Bringing these perspectives together is a general challenge to writing global history in a manner that does not simply substitute Eurocentricity by privileging the 'Southern' perspective only.

It is furthermore important not to take all these groups as monolithic entities. They were assemblages of individuals with personal abilities, convictions and plans. Some divisions within the groups may explain the contrasting perceptions. The concern of some African leaders over the behaviour of especially the last few Poles stands in contrast to the recollections of former camp workers who seem to have enjoyed the time with their guests, who brought job opportunities and resources into the periphery. And while the African neighbours interacted mainly with the ordinary, 'peasant-class' refugees, the Polish newspapers were dominated mainly by the Polish elite in Nairobi. The latter's self-perception as European allies like the British, and the, in contrast, seemingly humbler self-perception of the ordinary refugees, point to the close connection between race and class. Polish peasants and workers had maybe more in common with African peasants and workers, whereas the Polish elites were closer to the colonial elites. The Poles' whiteness gave all of them, however, at least some tangible privileges.

History, like the present, is always seen differently from different angles. I am not, however, arguing for the acceptance of arbitrary 'alternative facts'. My analysis contains pieces of information that are reliably documented, most of which form the basis of my argument and were outlined in Chapter 2. However, the question of the social positioning of the Poles remains highly subjective and relational. I am aware that this may result in a *Rashomon story* – the term goes back to the film of the same name by Akiro Kurosawa

(1950), in which four different but plausible versions of the circumstances leading to the death of one person stand in contradiction when placed alongside one another.² In Stoler's words, a *Rashomon* story is 'a multistranded set of equally plausible claims'.³ In my case the contrasting evaluations from different angles complement each other, getting closer to what could be called the historical situation. This approach somehow resembles the good old triangulation, but insists on what Heider noted in regard to disputes among ethnographers: 'There is a shared reality, true, but differing truths may indeed be said about it'.⁴ These differences in told truths are closely related to differences in experience, which are connected to differing social positions. If this is true everywhere, it is especially true for colonial societies. As Burbank and Cooper note: 'The concept of empire presumes that different peoples within the polity will be governed differently'.⁵ These differing treatments led to differences in the experience of empire. Contrasting these differing perspectives, as I have done in the last chapter, may serve as a model for how to write entangled histories of colonialism.

There are certainly some issues I touched upon that deserve further research. One issue that I have raised only en passant is the current political and economic aspect of remembrance of the Polish refugees' odyssey.⁶ The silencing of this episode in the historiographies of all the nations involved and its post-communist recovery in Poland are worth further study. Already in the midst of the political transition in Poland, on 1 September 1989 the Polish ambassador in Tanzania laid a wreath at the Polish cemetery in Tengeru to commemorate the refugees and the fiftieth anniversary of the outbreak of the Second World War.⁷ The development of the small memorial complex around the still existing Polish cemeteries is a topic that could, furthermore, be revealing for the study of memorial tourism in peripheral regions.

Another aspect that I have not been able to address here is the perspective of African women on the whole story. They did not appear in any of the sources I read. My one interview with an elderly African woman in Nyabyeya did not produce much tangible information. My own position as a white male academic did not help to bridge the distance between me and this elderly Ugandan peasant woman. This dearth of sources on African women's perspectives had mundane reasons, but it also points to a general problematic already noted in Spivak's influential essay: 'If, in the context of colonial production, the subaltern has no history and cannot speak, the subaltern as female is even more deeply in shadow'.⁸

I hope *On the Edges of Whiteness* provides the reader with more than just information about an isolated historical episode. I think this story has relevance for at least two broader scholarly fields: the colonial history of Africa during and after the Second World War, and the history of refugee hosting outside Europe in the same period.

First of all, the role of the British Empire and Africa in the Second World War has recently moved into the focus of historians again.[9] The various economic, social and political effects of the war on imperial rule eventually contributed to its demise. The war exposed 'the hypocrisy of colonizing ideologies and the weakness underlying the apparent power of colonizing regimes'.[10] After the war, Britain was financially indebted to its dominions and colonies, and morally indebted to its colonial subjects, who demanded reforms and finally independence.[11] While evermore issues beyond direct military entanglements are being studied, the sheltering of European refugees is still an overlooked contribution of the empire to the allied war effort.[12] Hosting a large group of white refugees was shouldered not only by the British and Polish administrations but also by African workers and producers. Although the administrators made efforts to isolate the Poles, multiple interactions of ordinary refugees with Africans happened nonetheless. These encounters of peasants from the Polish periphery with peasants from the African periphery might have caused some further cracks in the carefully constructed image of white superiority.

The study may further serve as an inspiration for more empirically grounded historical research on the role of subaltern whites in the period of late colonial rule. While there is some literature on poor whites at the time of high colonialism, especially in the Indian context, less is known about this later period. The Second World War brought not only the Poles to East and Central Africa, but also Greek refugees and Italian internees and prisoners of war. The social impact of thousands of British soldiers and interned Germans has received only scant attention. A whole range of marginalized whites lived in the colonies during the war. Their interaction with the population remains largely unexplored. How were they perceived, controlled and treated? How did the former German settlers experience their situation in the internment camps? What was the social position of these differing groups? How did they interact with each other and with their hosts? The disputes about the suitability of Greek or Italian men for intimate relationships with Polish women have shed light on the ambiguous social (and thereby racial) position of these men at the edges of whiteness.

But there is a need for regional differentiation among the British colonies in Africa as well. The powerful Southern Rhodesian and Kenyan settler communities refused to accept large numbers of lower class, non-British whites. Both wanted more settlers, but not ones who threatened to lower the European standard of living and British predominance. In Uganda, by contrast, there was no sizeable settler community. Here the colonial government was more concerned with the reaction of the Ugandan elites to the introduction of white settlers. After the war, public discontent in Uganda was rife and colonial rule in serious doubt. In the end, the two colonies with a medium-sized white community were, in relative terms, the most willing to welcome the permanent settlement of Poles. The reasons are not entirely clear, but Tanganyika's history and status as a United Nations Trust territory had already led to a more diverse white community. British predominance was maybe less of an issue here. In Northern Rhodesia the postwar copper boom led to growing employment opportunities. In the South African Union, the 1948 change in government from the pro-white immigration policy of the Smuts administration to the nationalist Malan government led to a restrictive policy to safeguard Afrikaner domination. These nuances can only be understood with attention to the specific historical contexts.

The Poles stayed in Africa at a time when colonial rule was undergoing serious problems and reform. In all territories, white settlement and domination had, by the late 1940s, come under increasing pressure from its African subjects. Colonial governments had to react to this pressure, and the settlement of a substantial white community would have made the situation even more volatile. Colonial administrators (especially in the Colonial Office in London) adopted a rhetoric of 'racial partnership', and avoided bluntly racist depictions of Africans. The road to responsible African self-government had been set; it was not clear, however, when its end would be reached. The pace on the road varied between the different colonies, and some white settlers and officials hoped they would never arrive at its destination. In Southern Rhodesia, where the white minority ruled for nearly four more decades after the war had ended, officials were most clearly articulating the need to uphold the image of white superiority. In Uganda and Tanganyika, the rhetoric and policy were different. Nevertheless, a sense of possessing superior knowledge formed the basis of much of the administrative correspondence. For the time being, the colonial administration aimed at leading the Africans on this road. An image of white superiority was upheld until the very last days of colonial rule (and beyond). Other Europeans, even the most marginal, were generally in a privileged position.

The second of the two broader scholarly fields that I hope this book contributes to is the history of refugees and the international refugee regime. Over twenty years ago, Michael Marrus noted: 'Europe, not Africa or Asia, was once the continent of most of the world's homeless'.[13] In 2007, Philip Marfleet lamented the absence of history in refugee studies;[14] and in five years later, Holian and Cohen still noted in the introduction to a special issue on postwar refugee history: 'The Eurocentrism of the postwar refugee regime is well known. Nonetheless, the history of the critical early postwar period still remains to be written from a different optic'.[15] In recent years, refugees have received increasing public and academic attention, as many more of them have been reaching Europe from Africa and Asia. Showing once again that this has not always been the common direction of flight should help to place current-day anti-refugee politicians and activists in perspective. It furthermore highlights the importance of racism in refugee hosting. The postwar refugee regime privileged white refugees from Europe; the later reversal of flight directions led, in turn, to increasing restrictions that have profoundly undermined the right to asylum. This process is discursively underpinned by the historiographic differentiation between European postwar and later Third World refugees – the 'myth of difference'.[16] Writing the history of European refugees in Africa as both 'postwar refugee history' and 'African colonial history' may serve to bridge this divide.

But discrimination and government self-interest was also important in the treatment of different European refugee groups. The most obvious case in point is the reluctance by most countries, including Britain and its empire, to accept Jewish refugees from Nazi-occupied Europe. Emblematic is the shameful failure of the 1938 Evian conference, at which all represented countries – with the exception of the Dominican Republic – refused to open their doors to Jewish refugees. While the Colonial Office and private agencies made several investigations and attempts to find a place of refuge from Nazi persecution, all eventually failed. White settlers were reluctant to accept Jewish refugees, especially when they were of a lower class – the threat of a poor white class and of a non-British settler population concerned them. And while over fifty thousand applications were received to enter Kenya, only a tiny fraction (those with sufficient capital or secure employment) were approved.[17] As Marrus notes: 'In striking contrast to what was claimed about the Jews, namely, that there was no room anywhere for them, space was somehow found for the Polish civilian exiles, [who were] seen as cobelligerents against Hitler'.[18] Antisemitism was one reason for this reluctance, but so too was the strategic interest of the British government in the Polish army. Apart from humanitarian considerations, there are, in many cases, political or economic interests involved when refugees are hosted.

On a conceptual level, refugees are considered to be 'living on the edge', that is, in a status that makes them invisible and bereft of the rights that come with citizenship in a nation-state.[19] Living in liminal insecurity – no longer part of the society of origin but not yet part of the host society – is one of the defining features of the refugee experience.[20] Building on Mary Douglas's general observation that 'any structure of ideas is vulnerable at its margins', this marginal position makes refugees potentially dangerous to the existing order of society.[21] Following this interpretation, the Polish refugees in Africa were 'out of place' not only as white peasants but also as liminal refugees. They were placed on the edges as refugees *and* as marginal whites. This case once again urges refugee studies scholars to pay closer attention to the specific historical context. Not all refugees were or are the same, but their historically specific categorizations, self-understandings and connectedness play important roles in defining their room for manoeuvre. The importance of categorizations becomes apparent in current debates about refugees in Europe, which are more often than not about race, class, gender and religion. The ability of refugees to overcome seemingly closed borders and to organize against repressive policies often depends on their connectedness with other refugees and established diaspora members.

The materiality of the refugee camps, their construction and management in a colonial setting, shows the influence of local conditions and knowledges upon the seemingly universal technique of refugee hosting. Today most of the world's refugees live in Africa and Asia, and refugee camps are one of the main forms in which refugees are administered, sheltered and assisted.[22] The history of refugee camps is usually told as a story of the diffusion of a technique of population management and control from Europe into the rest of the world. But at the time, when DP camps were being set up by UNRRA in Europe, camps already existed in Africa hosting thousands of refugees.

When shifting the focus of refugee camp history from Europe to the African continent we can trace its development further back to an earlier British imperial setting, namely the South African War.[23] In such a recalibrated historiography of refugee camps, the Poles serve as an important case linking European postwar refugee history with colonial camp experiences in Africa.[24] As I have shown, the knowledge and skills of colonial administrators, Polish refugees and the African workers and neighbours all contributed to the building and maintenance of the refugee camps. The legislation that was passed to control the Poles in Tanganyika formed the basis for the legislation of postcolonial refugees in Tanzania.[25] And while the Polish refugees were allowed to freely enter and leave their camps, Africans were only allowed to enter with special permission. By contrast, in the late 1990s, Tanzanians were free to enter refugee camps while its Burundian inhabitants were not allowed to leave a four-kilometre zone around the camp.[26] These examples illustrate the need to further uncover the African history of today's most important means of refugee hosting, and not simply look towards Europe's postwar experience as the blueprint for today's refugee camps. The 'Polish' camps in Africa show that European and African refugee camp history have been entangled for a long time.

Notwithstanding my critical assessment throughout this book, it should not be forgotten that this was also a history of warmth and hospitality: ordinary people providing a safe place for other ordinary people – but people who had gone through hardships and suffering. There were instances of an unbiased encounter on an equal footing, despite the context of a racially segregated and hierarchized society. As the former refugee Irene Tomaszewski notes: 'About this last group, the "ordinary people" whose languages, cultures and appearance were so different, neither contemporary records nor the much later recollections reveal that they were anything other than kind and friendly, these qualities mixed with a natural and mutual curiosity marked by openness rather than suspicion'.[27] The memories of Polish refugees who regarded their stay as a time of relief and recreation are important in the light of current refugee movements from war zones and deprivation. Uganda, whose refugee legislation is considered to be 'among the most progressive in the world', may serve as an inspiration to other countries.[28] Geoffrey Aluma, a resident in northern Uganda, recently explained the reasons for his hospitality towards South Sudanese refugees: 'People here are very hospitable because at one time we were refugees in South Sudan. They hosted us until there was peace in Uganda'.[29] Aluma's statement, and the story of the Polish refugees in Africa, should thus serve as reminders of the importance of giving shelter to people who have been forced to flee their homes.

Notes

1. Stoler, 'In Cold Blood'.
2. For the film's influence on the social sciences, see a recent collection: Davis, Anderson and Walls, *Rashomon Effects*.
3. Stoler, 'In Cold Blood', 183. Stoler, however, distanced herself from this reading of the case she presented in her paper.
4. Heider, 'The Rashomon Effect', 74.
5. Burbank and Cooper, *Empires in World History*, 8.
6. I touch upon this issue in Lingelbach, 'Refugee Camps as Forgotten Portals'.
7. CCM Party Archives, Dodoma: CMM-OND-183-46, Vol. I – Poland, p.50, Embassy of the Polish People's Republic, DSM to Ministry of Foreign Affairs of the United Republic of Tanzania, 23.08.89. My sincerest thanks to Eric Burton for providing me with this chance discovery.
8. Spivak, 'Can the Subaltern Speak?', 287.
9. The most important pioneering volume is: Killingray and Rathbone, *Africa and the Second World War*. The renewed interest is manifest in two recent edited volumes focusing on Africa and the British Empire respectively: Byfield et al., *Africa and World War II*; Jackson, Khan and Singh, *An Imperial World at War*.
10. Cooper, *Africa since 1940*, 20.
11. India was its largest colonial creditor. See Thomas, *Fight or Flight*, 76.
12. For the increasing interest in the British imperial 'home front', see Crowley and Dawson, *Home Fronts*.
13. Marrus, *The Unwanted*, 4.
14. Marfleet, 'Refugees and History'.
15. Holian and Cohen, 'Introduction', 313. For a recent overview, see also: Kleist, 'History of Refugee Protection'.
16. Chimni, 'Geopolitics of Refugee Studies'. See also Mayblin, *Asylum after Empire*.
17. See Chapter 3. In regard to East Africa, this issue has hitherto not been well researched. For a comparable constellation in Northern Rhodesia, see Shapiro, *Haven in Africa*.
18. Marrus, *The Unwanted*, 246.

19. See the edited volume on refugees in 'Protracted Refugee Situations', Hyndman and Giles, *Refugees in Extended Exile*.
20. See e.g. Agier, 'Between War and City', 337; den Boer, 'Liminal Space'.
21. Douglas, *Purity and Danger*, 121. Building on Douglas's work, Liisa Malkki described refugees as 'out of place' in the national order. See Malkki, *Purity and Exile*, 7–8.
22. According to UNHCR statistics, in 2017 about one-third of all refugees were living in some form of camp (UNHCR, 'Global Trends', 60).
23. Aidan Forth convincingly shows how British colonial camp expertise was transferred from India to South Africa around the turn of the century. Forth, *Barbed-Wire Imperialism*.
24. Brett Shadle recently sketched such a narrative from the South African War to the Italo-Ethiopian War, in Shadle, 'Refugees in African History', 253–56.
25. The 1966 Tanzanian Refugee (Control) Act was derived from the Defence Regulations Act of 1946 and the 1949 Refugee (Control and Expulsion) Ordinance. See Daley, 'Refugees and Underdevelopment', 111.
26. Turner, 'Barriers of Innocence', 77.
27. Tomaszewski, 'From the Snows of Siberia', n.p.
28. UNHCR and World Bank, 'Assessment of Uganda's Progressive Approach', 2.
29. Byaruhanga, 'Why a Ugandan Farmer Gave Land to a Refugee'.

Bibliography

Primary Sources

Archives

Archives Nationales: Records of the International Refugee Organization, Paris (IRO)
Bodleian Libraries: Commonwealth and African Collections, Oxford (MSS Afr)
International Tracing Service, Bad Arolsen (ITS)
Kenya National Archives, Nairobi (KNA)
National Archives of the UK: Public Record Office, London (PRO)
Polish Institute and Sikorski Museum, London (PISM)
Tanzania National Archives, Dar es Salaam (TNA)
United Nations Archive, New York (UNA)

Newspapers

East African Standard, Nairobi (selected issues, 1942–1946) (EAS)
Głos Polski, Nairobi (October 1945 – March 1947) (GP)
Nasz Przyjaciel, Nairobi (January 1945 – December 1947) (NP)

Interviews

Patrick Kunambi, Dar es Salaam, early 2009
Luhende, Dar es Salaam, early 2009
Asman, Dar es Salaam, early 2009

Edward Wakiku, Koja, 15.04.2013
Edward Sinabulya, Koja, 15.04.2013
Mukeera Kasule, Koja, 16.04.2013

Ochau Paito Caesar, Nyabyeya, 12.04.2013
John Onega, Nyabyeya, 13.04.2013
Teresa Tiko, Nyabyeya, 13.04.2013
Otwia Filimon, Nyabyeya, 13.04.2013
Son of late Philipo Jeto, Nyabyeya, 13.04.2013

Simon Joseph, Tengeru, 19.04.2013
Eliphase Mghoja, Tengeru, 19.04.2013
Edward Wojtowicz, Arusha, 20.04.2013

Secondary Sources

Achebe, Chinua. 'An Image of Africa'. *The Massachusetts Review* 18(4) (1977), 782–94.
Adamczyk, Wesley. *When God Looked the Other Way: An Odyssey of War, Exile, and Redemption.* Chicago: University of Chicago Press, 2004.
Agier, Michel. 'Between War and City towards an Urban Anthropology of Refugee Camps'. *Ethnography* 3(3) (2002), 317–41.
Ahonen, Pertti, et al. *People on the Move: Forced Population Movements in Europe in the Second World War and Its Aftermath.* Oxford: Berg, 2008.
Allbrook, Maryon, and Helen Cattalini. *The General Langfitt Story*, 1995. Retrieved 17 December 2019 from https://web.archive.org/web/20130103115901/http://www.immi.gov.au/media/publications/refugee/langfitt.
Amar, Tarik Cyril. 'Sovietization as a Civilizing Mission in the West', in Balász Apor, Péter Apor and E.A. Rees (eds), *The Sovietization of Eastern Europe: New Perspectives on the Postwar Period* (Washington, DC: New Academia Publishing, 2008), 29–45.
Anders, Władysław. *An Army in Exile: The Story of the Second Polish Corps.* London: Macmillan, 1949.
Anderson, Benedict R. *Imagined Communities: Reflections on the Origin and Spread of Nationalism.* Revised edition. London: Verso, 2006.
Anderson, David. *Histories of the Hanged: The Dirty War in Kenya and the End of Empire.* London: Weidenfeld & Nicolson, 2005.
Applebaum, Anne. *Gulag: A History.* New York: Doubleday, 2003.
Arens, William. *The Man-Eating Myth: Anthropology and Anthropophagy.* New York: Oxford University Press, 1979.
Bakić-Hayden, Milica. 'Nesting Orientalisms: The Case of Former Yugoslavia'. *Slavic Review* 54(4) (1995): 917–31.
Bakuła, Bogusław. 'Colonial and Postcolonial Aspects of Polish Discourse on the Eastern "Borderlands"', 2007. Retrieved 17 December 2019 from http://www.postcolonial-europe.eu/index.php/en/studies/68--colonial-and-postcolonial-aspects-of-polish-discourse-on-the-eastern-borderlandsq.
Ballantyne, Tony. *Webs of Empire: Locating New Zealand's Colonial Past.* Wellington: Bridget Williams Books, 2012.
Barnes, J.A. *Humping My Drum.* Raleigh: Lulu.com, 2008.
Barnett, Laura. 'Global Governance and the Evolution of the International Refugee Regime'. *International Journal of Refugee Law* 14 (2002), 238.
Barrett, James R., and David Roediger. 'Inbetween Peoples: Race, Nationality and the "New Immigrant" Working Class'. *Journal of American Ethnic History* 16(3) (1997), 3–44.
Beattie, John. 'Spirit Mediumship in Bunyoro', in John Beattie and John Middleton (eds), *Spirit Mediumship and Society in Africa* (London: Routledge, 1969), 159–70.
Bhattacharjee, Anuradha. 'Polish Refugees in India: During and after the Second World War'. *Sarmatian Review* 34(2) (2013), 1743–57.
———. *The Second Homeland: Polish Refugees in India.* New Delhi: SAGE, 2012.
Bland, Lucy. 'White Women and Men of Colour: Miscegenation Fears in Britain after the Great War'. *Gender & History* 17(1) (2005), 29–61.
Blejwas, Stanislaus A. 'Old and New Polonias: Tensions within an Ethnic Community'. *Polish American Studies* 38(2) (1981), 55–83.
Blobaum, Robert. 'The "Woman Question" in Russian Poland, 1900–1914'. *Journal of Social History* 35(4) (2002), 799–824.

Borges, Jorge Luis. 'On Exactitude in Science', in *Jorge Luis Borges. Collected Fictions*, translated by Andrew Hurley (London: Penguin Books, 1999), 325.

Boucher, Ellen. 'The Limits of Potential: Race, Welfare, and the Interwar Extension of Child Emigration to Southern Rhodesia'. *Journal of British Studies* 48(4) (2009), 914–34.

Boucher, Leigh, Jane Carey and Katherine Ellinghaus. *Re-Orienting Whiteness: Transnational Perspectives on the History of an Identity*. New York: Palgrave Macmillan, 2009.

Bright, Charles, and Michael Geyer. 'Regimes of World Order: Global Integration and the Production of Difference in Twentieth-Century World History', in Jerry H. Bentley, Renate Bridenthal and Anand A. Yang (eds), *Interactions: Transregional Perspectives on World History* (Honululu: University of Hawaii Press, 2005), 202–38.

Brodhurst-Hill, Evelyn. *So This Is Kenya!* London: Blackie and Son, 1936.

Brodkin, Karen. *How Jews Became White Folks and What That Says about Race in America*. New Brunswick, NJ: Rutgers University Press, 1998.

Brubaker, Rogers. 'The Manichean Myth: Rethinking the Distinction between "Civic" and "Ethnic" Nationalism', in Hanspeter Kriesi et al. (eds), *Nation and National Identity: The European Experience in Perspective* (Zürich: Rüegger, 1999), 55–72.

Brubaker, Rogers, and Frederick Cooper. 'Beyond "Identity"'. *Theory and Society* 29(1) (2000), 1–47.

Burbank, Jane, and Frederick Cooper. *Empires in World History: Power and the Politics of Difference*. Princeton, NJ: Princeton University Press, 2011.

Burrell, Kathy. 'Male and Female Polishness in Post-War Leicester: Gender and Its Intersections in a Refugee Community', in Louise Ryan and Wendy Webster (eds), *Gendering Migration: Masculinity, Femininity and Ethnicity in Post-War Britain* (Aldershot: Ashgate, 2008), 71–87.

———. *Moving Lives: Narratives of Nation and Migration among Europeans in Post-War Britain*. Aldershot: Ashgate, 2006.

Butler, Jeffrey. 'Afrikaner Women and the Creation of Ethnicity in a Small South African Town, 1902–1950', in Leroy Vail (ed.), *The Creation of Tribalism in Southern Africa* (Berkeley: University of California Press, 1991), 55–77.

Byaruhanga, Catherine. 'Why a Ugandan Farmer Gave Land to a Refugee'. *BBC News*, 23 June 2017. Retrieved 18 December 2019 from http://www.bbc.com/news/world-africa-40365249.

Byerley, Andrew. 'Becoming Jinja: The Production of Space and Making of Place in an African Industrial Town'. Stockholm: Acta Universitatis Stockholmiensis, 2005.

Byfield, Judith A. 'Producing for the War', in Judith A. Byfield et al. (eds), *Africa and World War II* (Cambridge: Cambridge University Press, 2015), 24–42.

Byfield, Judith A., et al. *Africa and World War II*. Cambridge: Cambridge University Press, 2015.

Callahan, Michael D. 'The Failure of "Closer Union" in British East Africa, 1929–31'. *The Journal of Imperial and Commonwealth History* 25(2) (1997), 267–93.

Callan, Hilary, and Shirley Ardener. *The Incorporated Wife*. London: Croom Helm, 1984.

Callaway, Helen. *Gender, Culture and Empire: European Women in Colonial Nigeria*. London: Macmillan, 1987.

Carlebach, Julius. *The Jews of Nairobi, 1903–1962*. Nairobi: Nairobi Hebrew Congregation, 1962. Retrieved 17 December 2019 from http://ufdc.ufl.edu/AA00004166/00001.

Carson, Jenny. 'The Quaker Internationalist Tradition in Displaced Persons Camps, 1945–48', in Nick Baron and Peter Gatrell (eds), *Warlands: Population Resettlement and State Reconstruction in the Soviet–East European Borderlands, 1945–50* (Basingstoke: Palgrave Macmillan, 2009), 67–86.

Castro Varela, María do Mar and Nikita Dhawan. *Postkoloniale Theorie: eine kritische Einführung*. Bielefeld: transcript Verlag, 2005.
Cavanagh, Clare. 'Postcolonial Poland'. *Common Knowledge* 10(1) (2004), 82–92.
Chakrabarty, Dipesh. *Provincializing Europe: Postcolonial Thought and Historical Difference*. Princeton, NJ: Princeton University Press, 2000.
Chanock, Martin. *Unconsummated Union: Britain, Rhodesia and South Africa, 1900–45*. Manchester: Manchester University Press, 1977.
Chappell, Timothy Mark, and Janina Milek. *The Persian Blanket: The Life of Janina Milek*. Freemantle, WA: Fremantle Arts Centre Press, 2004.
Chatterjee, Partha. *The Nation and Its Fragments: Colonial and Postcolonial Histories*. Princeton, NJ: Princeton University Press, 1993.
Chaulia, Sreeram Sundar. 'The Politics of Refugee Hosting in Tanzania: From Open Door to Unsustainability, Insecurity and Receding Receptivity'. *Journal of Refugee Studies* 16(2) (2003), 147–66.
Chigume, Obert, and Joshua Chakawa. 'The Media Weapon: An Analysis of How the Rhodesian Government Used the Media to Handle the Polish Refugee Issue from 1940 to 1950'. *The Dyke: A Journal of the Midlands State University* 8(3) (2014), 93–107.
Chimni, Bhupinder S. 'The Geopolitics of Refugee Studies: A View from the South'. *Journal of Refugee Studies* 11(4) (1998), 350–74.
Christian, Mark. 'The Fletcher Report 1930: A Historical Case Study of Contested Black Mixed Heritage Britishness'. *Journal of Historical Sociology* 21(2/3) (2008), 213–41.
Chudzio, Hubert (ed.). *Z mrozów Syberii pod słońce Afryki: w 70. rocznicę przybycia polskich Sybiraków do Afryki Wschodniej i Południowej*. Kraków: Oficyna Wydawnicza Text, 2012.
Coe, David G., and E. Cyril Greenall. *Kaunda's Gaoler: Memoirs of a District Officer in Northern Rhodesia and Zambia*. London: Radcliffe Press, 2003.
Cohen, Gerard Daniel. *In War's Wake: Europe's Displaced Persons in the Postwar Order*. Oxford: Oxford University Press, 2012.
Conrad, Sebastian, and Andreas Eckert. 'Globalgeschichte, Globalisierung, multiple Modernen: Zur Geschichtsschreibung der modernen Welt', in Ulrike Freitag, Sebastian Conrad and Andreas Eckert (eds), *Globalgeschichte: Theorien, Ansätze, Themen* (Frankfurt: Campus, 2007), 7–49.
Conrad, Sebastian, and Shalini Randeria. 'Geteilte Geschichte – Europa in einer postkolonialen Welt', in *Jenseits des Eurozentrismus: Postkoloniale Perspektiven in den Geschichts- und Kulturwissenschaften* (Frankfurt: Campus, 2002), 9–49.
Cook, Bernard A. *Women and War: A Historical Encyclopedia from Antiquity to the Present*. Santa Barbara, CA: ABC-CLIO, 2006.
Cooper, Frederick. *Africa since 1940: The Past of the Present*. Cambridge: Cambridge University Press, 2002.
———. *Colonialism in Question: Theory, Knowledge, History*. Berkeley: University of California Press, 2005.
———. 'Peasants, Capitalists, and Historians: A Review Article'. *Journal of Southern African Studies* 7(2) (1981), 284–314.
———. 'Reconstructing Empire in British and French Africa'. *Past & Present* 210(6) (2011), 196–210.
Cooper, Frederick, and Ann Laura Stoler. 'Between Metropole and Colony: Rethinking a Research Agenda', in idem (eds), *Tensions of Empire: Colonial Cultures in a Bourgeois World* (Berkeley: University of California Press, 1997), 1–56.
Copeland, E.A. 'Louise W. Holborn Archives, Schlesinger Library, Radcliffe College'. *Journal of Refugee Studies* 10(4) (1997), 503–6.

Cresswell, Tim. *In Place/Out of Place: Geography, Ideology, and Transgression*. Minneapolis: University of Minnesota Press, 1996.
Crowley, Mark J., and Sandra Trudgen Dawson (eds). *Home Fronts: Britain and the Empire at War, 1939–45*. Suffolk, UK: Boydell & Brewer, 2017.
Curtis, Arnold (ed.). *Memories of Kenya: Stories from the Pioneers*, Introduction by Elspeth Huxley. London: Evans Africa, 1986.
Daley, Patricia. 'Refugees and Underdevelopment in Africa: The Case of Barundi Refugees in Tanzania'. PhD dissertation, University of Oxford, 1989.
Dall, Lesław. 'Generał Ferdynand Zarzycki (1888–1958). Doktor filozofii, nauczyciel, skaut, minister i senator', 2007. Retrieved 17 December 2019 from http://jpilsudski.org/arty kuly-personalia-biogramy/generalicja-oficerowie-zolnierze/item/1804-general-ferdynand-zarzycki-1888-1958-doktor-fiozofii-nauczyciel-skaut-minister-i-senator.
D'Arc, Mary. 'Colonia Santa Rosa in Mexico'. *Polish American Studies* 19(1) (1962), 45–56.
Davies, Norman. *Im Herzen Europas: Geschichte Polens*, translated by Friedrich Griese. Munich: C.H.Beck, 2000.
Davin, Anna. 'Imperialism and Motherhood'. *History Workshop* 5 (1978), 9–65.
Davis, Blair, Robert Anderson and Jan Walls (eds). *Rashomon Effects: Kurosawa, Rashomon and their Legacies*. London: Routledge, 2015.
de Fina, Anna. 'Researcher and Informant Roles in Narrative Interactions: Constructions of Belonging and Foreignness'. *Language in Society* 40 (2011), 27–38.
den Boer, Roselinde. 'Liminal Space in Protracted Exile: The Meaning of Place in Congolese Refugees' Narratives of Home and Belonging in Kampala'. *Journal of Refugee Studies* 28(4) (2015), 486–504.
Devlin, Julia. *Deportation und Exil: Eine polnische Odyssee im Zweiten Weltkrieg*. Berlin: Vergangenheitsverlag, 2014.
Dimitrakis, Panagiotis. *Military Intelligence in Cyprus: From the Great War to Middle East Crises*. London: I.B.Tauris, 2010.
Dodoo, Vincent, and Wilhelmina Donkoh. 'Nationality and the Pan-African State', in Toyin Falola and Kwame Essien (eds), *Pan-Africanism, and the Politics of African Citizenship and Identity* (London: Routledge, 2013), 151–71.
Donato, Katharine M., et al. 'A Glass Half Full? Gender in Migration Studies'. *The International Migration Review* 40(1) (2006), 3–26.
Douglas, Mary. *Purity and Danger: An Analysis of Concepts of Pollution and Taboo*. London: Routledge & Kegan Paul, 1966.
Doyle, Shane. *Crisis and Decline in Bunyoro: Population and Environment in Western Uganda 1860–1955*. Oxford: James Currey, 2006.
Duara, Prasenjit. 'Transnationalism and the Challenge to National Histories', in Thomas Bender (ed.), *Rethinking American History in a Global Age* (Berkeley: University of California Press, 2002), 25–46.
Du Bois, William Edward Burghardt. *The Social Theory of W.E.B. Du Bois*. Thousand Oaks, CA: Pine Forge Press, 2004.
Duder, C.J. '"Men of the Officer Class": The Participants in the 1919 Soldier Settlement Scheme in Kenya'. *African Affairs* 92(366) (1993), 69–87.
Dwyer, Claire, and Caroline Bressey. *New Geographies of Race and Racism*. Aldershot: Ashgate, 2008.
Easton-Calabria, Evan Elise. 'From Bottom-Up to Top-Down: The "Pre-History" of Refugee Livelihoods Assistance from 1919 to 1979'. *Journal of Refugee Studies* 28(3) (2015), 412–36.

Eckert, Andreas. 'African Nationalists and Human Rights, 1940s–1970s', in Stefan-Ludwig Hoffmann (ed.), *Human Rights in the Twentieth Century – A Critical History* (Cambridge: Cambridge University Press, 2010), 283–300.

Egan, Eileen. *For Whom There Is No Room: Scenes from the Refugee World.* New York: Paulist Press, 1995.

Ekoko, A. Edho. 'The British Attitude towards Germany's Colonial Irredentism in Africa in the Inter-War Years'. *Journal of Contemporary History* 14(2) (1979), 287–307.

Enloe, Cynthia. *Bananas, Beaches and Bases: Making Feminist Sense of International Politics.* Berkeley: University of California Press, 1990.

Evert, Helen. 'War Experiences: The Emotional Health and Wellbeing of Polish Elderly Immigrants'. PhD dissertation, University of Melbourne, 2007. Available at http://minerva-access.unimelb.edu.au/handle/11343/35766.

Fallers, L.A. 'Are African Cultivators To Be Called "Peasants"?' *Current Anthropology* 2(2) (1961), 108–10.

Fanon, Frantz. *Die Verdammten dieser Erde*, translated by Traugott König. Reinbek bei Hamburg: Rowohlt, 1969.

Fechter, Anne-Meike. 'Gender, Empire, Global Capitalism: Colonial and Corporate Expatriate Wives'. *Journal of Ethnic and Migration Studies* 36(8) (2010), 1279–97.

Fedorowich, Kent, and Bob Moore. *The British Empire and Its Italian Prisoners of War, 1940–1947.* Basingstoke: Palgrave Macmillan, 2002.

Feichtinger, Johannes, Ursula Prutsch and Moritz Csáky. *Habsburg Postcolonial: Machtstrukturen und kollektives Gedächtnis.* Innsbruck: StudienVerlag, 2003.

Fidelis, Malgorzata. 'Equality through Protection: The Politics of Women's Employment in Postwar Poland, 1945–1956'. *Slavic Review* 63(2) (2004), 301–24.

Fischer-Tiné, Harald. *Low and Licentious Europeans: Race, Class and 'White Subalternity' in Colonial India.* New Perspectives in South Asian History 30. New Delhi: Orient Blackswan, 2009.

Forth, Aidan. *Barbed-Wire Imperialism: Britain's Empire of Camps, 1876–1903.* Berkeley: University of California Press, 2017.

Frank, Matthew, and Jessica Reinisch (eds). *Refugees in Europe, 1919–1959: A Forty Years' Crisis?* London: Bloomsbury, 2017.

Frankenberg, Ruth. 'Introduction: Local Whitenesses, Localizing Whiteness', in Ruth Frankenberg (ed.), *Displacing Whiteness: Essays in Social and Cultural Criticism* (Durham, NC: Duke University Press, 1997), 1–33.

———. *White Women, Race Matters: The Social Construction of Whiteness.* Minneapolis: University of Minnesota Press, 1993.

Fraser, John Foster. *The Real Siberia: Together with an Account of a Dash through Manchuria.* London: Cassell, 1902. Retrieved 17 December 2019 from http://archive.org/details/cu31924023035912.

Furber, David. 'Near as Far in the Colonies: The Nazi Occupation of Poland'. *The International History Review* 26(3) (2004), 541–79.

Furedi, Frank. *Colonial Wars and the Politics of Third World Nationalism.* London: I.B.Tauris, 1994.

Fyfe, Christopher. 'Race, Empire and the Historians'. *Race & Class* 33(4) (1992), 15–30.

Gabaccia, Donna R. 'Is Everywhere Nowhere? Nomads, Nations, and the Immigrant Paradigm of United States History'. *Journal of American History* 86(3) (1999), 1115–34.

Gabiniewicz, Maria. 'Na tułaczym szlaku. Nazywano nas "dziećmi Andersa"'. *Kombatant* 5 (2006), 16–17.

Gann, Lewis Henry. *A History of Northern Rhodesia.* London: Chatto & Windus, 1964.

Gatrell, Peter. *Free World? The Campaign to Save the World's Refugees, 1956–1963*. Cambridge: Cambridge University Press, 2011.

———. 'From "Homeland" to "Warlands": Themes, Approaches, Voices', in Nick Baron and Peter Gatrell (eds), *Warlands: Population Resettlement and State Reconstruction in the Soviet–East European Borderlands, 1945–50* (Basingstoke: Palgrave Macmillan, 2009), 1–22.

———. *The Making of the Modern Refugee*. Oxford: Oxford University Press, 2013.

———. 'Putting Refugees in Their Place'. *New Global Studies* 7(1) (2013), 1–24.

Gatrell, Peter, and Nick Baron. 'Violent Peacetime: Reconceptualising Displacement and Resettlement in the Soviet–East European Borderlands after the Second World War', in Nick Baron and Peter Gatrell (eds), *Warlands: Population Resettlement and State Reconstruction in the Soviet–East European Borderlands, 1945–50* (Basingstoke: Palgrave Macmillan, 2009), 255–68.

Gingrich, Andre. 'The Nearby Frontier: Structural Analyses of Myths of Orientalism'. *Diogenes* 60(2) (2013), 60–66.

Gingyera-Pinycwa, A.G.G. 'Uganda's Entanglement with the Problem of Refugees in Its Global and African Contexts', in idem (ed.), *Uganda and the Problem of Refugees* (Kampala: Makerere University Press, 1998), 1–18.

Glasman, Joël. 'Seeing Like a Refugee Agency: A Short History of UNHCR Classifications in Central Africa (1961–2015)'. *Journal of Refugee Studies* 2(30) (2017), 337–62.

Goodwin-Gill, Guy S. 'The Politics of Refugee Protection'. *Refugee Survey Quarterly* 27(1) (2008), 8–23.

Gousseff, Catherine. 'Evacuation versus Repatriation: The Polish–Ukrainian Population Exchange, 1944–6', in Jessica Reinisch and Elizabeth White (eds), *The Disentanglement of Populations: Migration, Expulsion and Displacement in Post-War Europe, 1944–9* (Basingstoke: Palgrave Macmillan, 2011), 91–111.

Greenstein, Elijah. 'Making History: Historical Narratives of the Maji Maji'. *Penn History Review* 17(2) (2010), 60–77.

Gross, Jan Tomasz. *Revolution from Abroad: The Soviet Conquest of Poland's Western Ukraine and Western Belorussia*. Princeton, NJ: Princeton University Press, 1988.

Grzybowski, Jerzy. 'Białorusini wśród uchodźców polskich na Środkowym Wschodzie i w Afryce Wschodniej w latach II wojny światowej'. *Pamięć i Sprawiedliwość* 8(2) (2005), 329–45.

Haggis, Jane. 'Gendering Colonialism or Colonising Gender? Recent Women's Studies Approaches to White Women and the History of British Colonialism'. *Women's Studies International Forum* 13(1–2) (1990), 105–15.

Hall, Stuart. 'The Local and the Global: Globalization and Ethnicity', in Anthony D. King (ed.), *Culture, Globalization, and the World-System: Contemporary Conditions for the Representation of Identity* (Minneapolis: University of Minnesota Press, 1991), 19–40.

Hansen, Karen Tranberg. *Distant Companions: Servants and Employers in Zambia, 1900–1985*. Ithaca, NY: Cornell University Press, 1989.

Harper, Marjory, and Stephen Constantine. *Migration and Empire*. Oxford: Oxford University Press, 2010.

Harzig, Christiane. 'Domestics of the World (Unite?): Labor Migration Systems and Personal Trajectories of Household Workers in Historical and Global Perspective'. *Journal of American Ethnic History* 25(2/3) (2006), 48–73.

Heider, Karl G. 'The Rashomon Effect: When Ethnographers Disagree'. *American Anthropologist* 90(1) (1988), 73–81.

Hejczik, Anna. *Sybiracy pod Kilimandżaro. Tengeru. Polskie osiedle w Afryce Wschodniej we wspomnieniach jego mieszkańców*. Rzeszów-Kraków: Instytut Pamięci Narodowej, 2013.

Henkes, Barbara. 'Shifting Identifications in Dutch-South African Migration Policies (1910–1961)'. *South African Historical Journal* 68(4) (2016), 641–69.

Higonnet, Margaret R., and Patrice Higonnet. 'The Double Helix', in Margaret R. Higonnet et al. (eds), *Behind the Lines: Gender and the Two World Wars* (New Haven, CT: Yale University Press, 1987), 31–48.

Higonnet, Margaret R., et al. (eds). *Behind the Lines: Gender and the Two World Wars*. New Haven, CT: Yale University Press, 1987.

Hilton, Laura. 'Cultural Nationalism in Exile: The Case of Polish and Latvian Displaced Persons'. *Historian* 71(2) (2009), 280–317.

Hodder-Williams, Richard. *White Farmers in Rhodesia, 1890–1965: A History of the Marandellas District*. London: Macmillan, 1983.

Hoerder, Dirk. 'Migration Research in Global Perspective: Recent Developments'. *Sozial. Geschichte Online* 9 (2012). Retrieved 17 December 2019 from https://duepublico2.uni-due.de/receive/duepublico_mods_00029900.

Hogendorn, J.S., and K.M. Scott. 'The East African Groundnut Scheme: Lessons of a Large-Scale Agricultural Failure'. *African Economic History* 10 (1981), 81–115.

Holborn, Louise W. *The International Refugee Organization: A Specialized Agency of the United Nations, Its History and Work, 1946–1952*. London: Oxford University Press, 1956.

———. *Refugees: A Problem of Our Time. The Work of the United Nations High Commissioner for Refugees, 1951–1972*. Metuchen, NJ: Scarecrow Press, 1975.

Holian, Anna. 'Anticommunism in the Streets: Refugee Politics in Cold War Germany'. *Journal of Contemporary History* 45(1) (2010), 134–61.

Holian, Anna, and G. Daniel Cohen. 'Introduction'. *Journal of Refugee Studies* 25(3) (2012), 313–25.

hooks, bell. *Black Looks*. Berlin: Orlanda, 1994.

Hunczak, Taras. 'Polish Colonial Ambitions in the Inter-War Period'. *Slavic Review* 26(4) (1967), 648–56.

Huxley, Elspeth Joscelin Grant. *The Sorcerer's Apprentice: A Journey through East Africa*. London: Chatto & Windus, 1948.

Huxley, Elspeth Joscelin Grant, and Arnold Curtis (eds). *Pioneers' Scrapbook: Reminiscences of Kenya 1890 to 1968*. London: Evans Brothers, 1980.

Hyam, Ronald. 'Concubinage and the Colonial Service: The Crewe Circular (1909)'. *The Journal of Imperial and Commonwealth History* 14(3) (1986), 170–86.

———. 'The Political Consequences of Seretse Khama: Britain, the Bangwato and South Africa, 1948–1952'. *The Historical Journal* 29(4) (1986), 921–47.

Hyndman, Jennifer, and Wenona Giles. *Refugees in Extended Exile: Living on the Edge*. New York: Routledge, 2017.

Iliffe, John. *A Modern History of Tanganyika*. Cambridge: Cambridge University Press, 1979.

Jackson, Ashley, Yasmin Khan and Gajendra Singh. *An Imperial World at War: The British Empire, 1939–45*. London: Routledge, 2017.

Jackson, Will. 'Dangers to the Colony: Loose Women and the "Poor White" Problem in Kenya'. *Journal of Colonialism and Colonial History* 14(2) (2013).

Jacobson, Matthew Frye. *Whiteness of a Different Color: European Immigrants and the Alchemy of Race*. Cambridge, MA: Harvard University Press, 1999.

Janos, Andrew C. *East Central Europe in the Modern World: The Politics of the Borderlands from Pre- to Postcommunism*. Stanford, CA: Stanford University Press, 2000.

Janowski, Monica. 'Food in Traumatic Times: Women, Foodways and "Polishness" during a Wartime "Odyssey"'. *Food and Foodways* 20(3–4) (2012), 326–49.

Jaroszyńska-Kirchmann, Anna D. *The Exile Mission: The Polish Political Diaspora and Polish Americans, 1939–1956*. Athens: Ohio University Press, 2004.
———. 'The Polish Post-World War II Diaspora: An Agenda for a New Millenium'. *Polish American Studies* 57(2) (2000), 45–66.
Jhaveri, Urmila. *Dancing With Destiny: Memoir*. Gurgaon: Partridge Publishing, 2014.
Jolluck, Katherine R. *Exile and Identity: Polish Women in the Soviet Union during World War II*. Pittsburgh, PA: University of Pittsburgh Press, 2002.
Kassimir, Ronald. 'Complex Martyrs: Symbols of Catholic Church Formation and Political Differentiation in Uganda'. *African Affairs* 90(360) (1991), 357–82.
Kelly, Matthew. *Finding Poland: From Tavistock to Hruzdowa and Back Again*. London: Vintage, 2011.
Kennedy, Dane Keith. *Islands of White: Settler Society and Culture in Kenya and Southern Rhodesia, 1890–1939*. Durham, NC: Duke University Press, 1987.
Kesting, Robert W. 'American Support of Polish Refugees and their Santa Rosa Camp'. *Polish American Studies* 48(1) (1991), 79–90.
Kévonian, Dzovinar. 'Histoires d'enfants, Histoire d'Europe: L'Organisation Internationale des Réfugiés et la crise de 1949'. *Matériaux pour l'histoire de notre temps* 95 (2009), 30–45.
Killingray, David, and Martin Plaut. *Fighting for Britain: African Soldiers in the Second World War*. Woodbridge: James Currey, 2010.
Killingray, David, and Richard Rathbone. *Africa and the Second World War*. London: Macmillan, 1986.
Kirk-Greene, Anthony H.M. 'Colonial Administration and Race Relations: Some Research Reflections and Directions'. *Ethnic and Racial Studies* 9(3) (1986), 275–87.
———. 'The Thin White Line: The Size of the British Colonial Service in Africa'. *African Affairs* 79(314) (1980), 25–44.
Kiyaga-Mulindwa, D. 'Uganda: A Safe Haven for Polish Refugees: 1942–1951'. *Uganda Journal* 46(1) (2000), 67–72.
Kleist, J. Olaf. 'The History of Refugee Protection: Conceptual and Methodological Challenges'. *Journal of Refugee Studies* 30(2) (2017), 161–69.
Klobucka, Anna M. 'Desert and Wilderness Revisited: Sienkiewicz's Africa in the Polish National Imagination'. *The Slavic and East European Journal* 45(2) (2001), 243–59.
Kolchin, Peter. 'Whiteness Studies: The New History of Race in America'. *The Journal of American History* 89(1) (2002), 154–73.
Kołos, Anna. '"Wildness" as a Metaphor for Self-Definition of the Colonised Subject in the Positivist Period in Poland'. *The Journal of Education, Culture, and Society* 1 (2011), 81–95.
Kopp, Kristin. 'Arguing the Case for a Colonial Poland', in Volker Max Langbehn and Mohammad Salama (eds), *German Colonialism: Race, the Holocaust, and Postwar Germany* (New York: Columbia University Press, 2011), 146–63.
Korabiewicz, Wacław. *Kwaheri*. Warsaw: Iskry, 1958.
Kramer, Alan. 'Einleitung', in Bettina Greiner and Alan Kramer (eds), *Welt der Lager: Zur "Erfolgsgeschichte" einer Institution* (Hamburg: Hamburger Edition, 2013), 7–42.
Krolikowski, Lucjan. *Stolen Childhood: A Saga of Polish War Children*, translated by Kazimierz J. Rozniatowski. San Jose: Authors Choice Press, 2001.
Królikowski, Łucjan Zbigniew. *Skradzione dzieciństwo*. London: Veritas, 1960.
Królikowski, Roman. 'Operation Polejump'. *Zeszyty Historyczne (Paris)* 14 (1968), 150–88.
———. 'Polacy w Afryce Wschodniej'. *Kultura (Paris)* 9(26) (1949), 138–44.
———. 'Uhuru'. *Kultura (Paris)* 155(9) (1960), 84–92.
Kufakurinani, Ushehwedu. *Elasticity in Domesticity: White Women in Rhodesian Zimbabwe, 1890–1979*. Leiden: Brill, 2018.

Künzli, Andreas. *L.L. Zamenhof (1859–1917): Esperanto, Hillelismus (Homaranismus) und die 'jüdische Frage' in Ost- und Westeuropa*. Wiesbaden: Harrassowitz, 2010.
Kushner, Tony, and Katharine Knox. *Refugees in an Age of Genocide: Global, National and Local Perspectives during the Twentieth Century*. London: Frank Cass, 1999.
Lake, Marilyn, and Henry Reynolds. *Drawing the Global Colour Line: White Men's Countries and the Question of Racial Equality*. Cambridge: Cambridge University Press, 2008.
Lessing, Doris. *Landlocked* (Children of Violence series, 4). London: Granada, 1967.
Lester, Alan. 'Imperial Circuits and Networks: Geographies of the British Empire'. *History Compass* 4(1) (2006), 124–41.
Levine, Philippa. *The British Empire: Sunrise to Sunset*. London: Pearson Education, 2007.
———. 'Venereal Disease, Prostitution, and the Politics of Empire: The Case of British India'. *Journal of the History of Sexuality* 4(4) (1994), 579–602.
Limnios-Sekeris, Ioannis. 'Australia and the Intergovernmental Committee for European Migration: Racial Exclusion and Ethnic Discrimination in an Era of Universal Human Rights', in Lina Venturas (ed.), *International 'Migration Management' in the Early Cold War: The Intergovernmental Committee for European Migration* (Corinth: University of the Peloponnese, 2016), 191–216.
Lingelbach, Jochen. *Oyster Bay – Eine koloniale Heterotopie in Ostafrika und ihre postkoloniale Bedeutung*. Vol. 18. University of Leipzig Papers on Africa. Leipziger Arbeiten zur Geschichte und Kultur in Afrika. Leipzig, 2011.
———. 'Polish Refugees in Colonial Eastern Africa (1942–50): The Use of European Diaspora Sources for the Writing of African Colonial History', in Geert Castryck, Silke Strickrodt and Katja Werthmann (eds), *Sources and Methods for African History and Culture: Essays in Honour of Adam Jones* (Leipzig: Leipziger Universitätsverlag, 2016), 523–40.
———. 'Refugee Camps as Forgotten Portals of Globalization: Polish World War II Refugees in British Colonial East Africa'. *Comparativ. Zeitschrift für Globalgeschichte und vergleichende Gesellschaftsforschung* 3/4 (2017), 78–93.
———. '"Der Sturm trieb uns weit um die Welt..." Polnische Flüchtlinge in Ostafrika', in Elke Gryglewski and Cornelia Siebeck (eds), *Passagen, Brüche, Perspektiven: Flucht historisch denken lernen* (Berlin: Gedenk- und Bildungsstätte Haus der Wannsee-Konferenz, 2018), n.p.
Linne, Karsten. *Deutschland jenseits des Äquators? Die NS-Kolonialplanungen für Afrika*. Berlin: Ch. Links, 2008.
Loescher, Gil. 'The International Refugee Regime: Stretched to the Limit?'. *Journal of International Affairs* 47(2) (1994), 351–77.
Lorcin, Patricia. *Historicizing Colonial Nostalgia: European Women's Narratives of Algeria and Kenya, 1900–Present*. Basingstoke: Palgrave Macmillan, 2011.
Louis, William Roger. 'American Anti-Colonialism and the Dissolution of the British Empire'. *International Affairs* 61(3) (1985), 395–420.
Lowry, Donal. 'The Crown, Empire Loyalism and the Assimilation of Non-British White Subjects in the British World: An Argument against "Ethnic Determinism"'. *The Journal of Imperial and Commonwealth History* 31 (2003), 96–120.
Lukas, Richard C. 'Polish Refugees in Mexico: An Historical Footnote'. *The Polish Review* 22(2) (1977), 73–75.
Lush, Maurice Stanley. *A Life of Service: The Memoirs of Maurice Lush, 1896–1990*. London: Trinity, 1992.
Lwanga-Lunyiigo, Samwiri. 'Uganda's Long Connection with the Problem of Refugees: From the Polish Refugees of World War II to the Present'. Paper presented at the workshop 'Uganda and Refugee Problems', 20 December 1993, Makerere University,

Kampala. Retrieved 17 December 2019 from http://repository.forcedmigration.org/pdf/?pid=fmo:1145.

Macoun, Michael J. *Wrong Place, Right Time: Policing the End of Empire*. London: Radcliffe Press, 1996.

Madley, Benjamin. 'From Africa to Auschwitz: How German South West Africa Incubated Ideas and Methods Adopted and Developed by the Nazis in Eastern Europe'. *European History Quarterly* 35(3) (2005), 429–64.

Majd, Mohammad Gholi. *Iran under Allied Occupation in World War II: The Bridge to Victory and a Land of Famine*. Lanham, MD: University Press of America, 2016.

Malkki, Liisa. 'National Geographic: The Rooting of Peoples and the Territorialization of National Identity among Scholars and Refugees'. *Cultural Anthropology* 7(1) (1992), 24–44.

———. *Purity and Exile: Violence, Memory, and National Cosmology among Hutu Refugees in Tanzania*. Chicago: University of Chicago Press, 1995.

———. 'Refugees and Exile: From "Refugee Studies" to the National Order of Things'. *Annual Review of Anthropology* 24 (1995), 495–523.

Mamdani, Mahmood. *Citizen and Subject: Contemporary Africa and the Legacy of Late Colonialism*. Princeton, NJ: Princeton University Press, 1996.

Marfleet, Philip. 'Refugees and History: Why We Must Address the Past'. *Refugee Survey Quarterly* 26(3) (2007), 136–48.

Marrus, Michael Robert. *The Unwanted: European Refugees in the Twentieth Century*. Oxford: Oxford University Press, 1985.

Mayblin, Lucy. *Asylum after Empire: Colonial Legacies in the Politics of Asylum Seeking*. London: Rowman & Littlefield, 2017.

Mayblin, Lucy, Aneta Piekut and Gill Valentine. '"Other" Posts in "Other" Places: Poland through a Postcolonial Lens?' *Sociology* 50(1) (2014), 60–76.

McClintock, Anne. *Imperial Leather: Race, Gender and Sexuality in the Colonial Context*. London: Routledge, 1995.

McCulloch, Jock. *Black Peril, White Virtue: Sexual Crime in Southern Rhodesia, 1902–1935*. Bloomington: Indiana University Press, 2000.

McEwan, Peter J.M. 'The European Population of Southern Rhodesia'. *Civilisations* 13(4) (1963), 429–44.

McKeown, A. 'Global Migration, 1846–1940'. *Journal of World History* 15(2) (2004), 155–90.

Memmi, Albert. *The Colonizer and the Colonized*, translated by Howard Greenfeld. London: Earthscan, 2003.

Mironowicz, Antoni. 'Białorusini na Bliskim Wschodzie wobec spraw polskich w latach 1941–1945 w świetle pism ks. Michała Bożerianowa'. *Humanities and Social Sciences* 22(2) (2015), 63–86.

Mlambo, Alois S. *A History of Zimbabwe*. Cambridge: Cambridge University Press, 2014.

———. '"Some Are More White than Others": Racial Chauvinism as a Factor of Rhodesian Immigration Policy, 1890–1963'. *Zambezia* 27(2) (2000), 139–60.

Mohanty, Satya P. 'Drawing the Color Line: Kipling and the Culture of Colonial Rule', in Dominick LaCapra (ed.), *The Bounds of Race: Perspectives on Hegemony and Resistance* (Ithaca, NY: Cornell University Press, 1991), 311–43.

Moore, Bob. 'Unwanted Guests in Troubled Times: German Prisoners of War in the Union of South Africa, 1942–1943'. *The Journal of Military History* 70(1) (2006), 63–89.

Moore, David Chioni. 'Is the Post- in Postcolonial the Post- in Post-Soviet? Toward a Global Postcolonial Critique'. *Publications of the Modern Language Association of America* 116(1) (2001), 111–28.

Morawska, Ewa. 'Labor Migrations of Poles in the Atlantic World Economy, 1880–1914'. *Comparative Studies in Society and History* 31(2) (1989), 237–72.

Morrell, Robert. 'Of Boys and Men: Masculinity and Gender in Southern African Studies'. *Journal of Southern African Studies* 24(4) (1998), 605–30.

Nicholls, Christine Stephanie. *Red Strangers: The White Tribe of Kenya*. London: Timewell Press, 2005.

Niedźwiecka, Dorota. 'Z Armią Andersa – pod baobaby. Dzieci z Czarnego lądu'. *Zesłaniec* 49 (2011), 37–40.

Nowak, Katarzyna. '"We Would Rather Drown Ourselves in Lake Victoria": Refugee Women, Protest, and Polish Displacement in Colonial East Africa, 1948–49'. *Immigrants & Minorities* 37(1–2) (2019), 92–117.

Oberoi, Pia. 'South Asia and the Creation of the International Refugee Regime'. *Refuge: Canada's Journal on Refugees* 19(5) (2001), 36–45.

Ochieng', William Robert, and E.S. Atieno-Odhiambo. 'On Decolonization', in Bethwell A. Ogot and William Robert Ochieng' (eds), *Decolonization and Independence in Kenya, 1940–93* (London: James Currey, 1995), xi–xvii.

Osterhammel, Jürgen. *Die Verwandlung der Welt: eine Geschichte des 19. Jahrhunderts*. Munich: C.H.Beck, 2009.

———. *Kolonialismus: Geschichte, Formen, Folgen*. Munich: C.H.Beck, 1995.

Oyen, Meredith. 'The Right of Return: Chinese Displaced Persons and the International Refugee Organization, 1947–56'. *Modern Asian Studies* 49(2) (2015), 546–71.

Pacyga, Dominic A. 'Polish Diaspora', in Melvin Ember, Carol R. Ember and Ian A. Skoggard (eds), *Encyclopedia of Diasporas: Immigrant and Refugee Cultures around the World* (New York: Springer, 2005), 254–63.

Padmore, George. *Afrika unter dem Joch der Weissen*. Erlenbach-Zürich: Rotapfel Verlag, 1936.

———. *How Britain Rules Africa*. London: Wishart, 1936.

Padmore, George, and Dorothy Pizer. *How Russia Transformed Her Colonial Empire: A Challenge to the Imperialist Powers*. London: Dennis Dobson, 1946.

Panek, Bartosz. 'The Kilometre Who Sailed Thousands of Miles'. *International Maritime Health* 66(1) (2015), 52–54.

Parsons, Timothy. 'The Military Experiences of Ordinary Africans in World War II', in Judith A. Byfield et al., *Africa and World War II* (Cambridge: Cambridge University Press, 2015), 3–23.

———. *Race, Resistance, and the Boy Scout Movement in British Colonial Africa*. Athens: Ohio University Press, 2004.

Payseur, Monika Katarzyna. '"I Don't Want to Go Back": The Complicated Case of Polish Displaced Children to Canada in 1949'. *Theses and Dissertations*, Paper 489, 2009. Retrieved 17 December 2019 from http://digitalcommons.ryerson.ca/dissertations/489.

Peberdy, Sally. *Selecting Immigrants: National Identity and South Africa's Immigration Policies, 1910–2008*. Johannesburg: Wits University Press, 2009.

Pedersen, Susan. *The Guardians: The League of Nations and the Crisis of Empire*. Oxford: Oxford University Press, 2015.

Pennington, A.L. 'Refugees in Tanganyika during the Second World War'. *Tanganyika Notes and Records* 32 (1952), 52–56.

Peterson, Glen. 'The Uneven Development of the International Refugee Regime in Postwar Asia: Evidence from China, Hong Kong and Indonesia'. *Journal of Refugee Studies* 25(3) (2012), 326–43.

Phiri, Bizeck Jube. *A Political History of Zambia: From Colonial Rule to the Third Republic, 1890–2001*. Trenton, NJ: Africa World Press, 2006.

Piotrowski, Tadeusz (ed.). *The Polish Deportees of World War II: Recollections of Removal to the Soviet Union and Dispersal throughout the World*. Jefferson, NC: McFarland, 2004.

Pirouet, Louise. 'Refugees in and from Uganda in the Post-Independence Period', in Holger Bernt Hansen and Michael Twaddle (eds), *Uganda Now: Between Decay and Development* (London: James Currey, 1988), 239–53.

Piskorski, Jan M. *Die Verjagten: Flucht und Vertreibung im Europa des 20. Jahrhunderts*, translated by Peter Oliver Loew. Munich: Siedler Verlag, 2013.

Pittaway, Eileen, and Linda Bartolomei. 'Refugees, Race, and Gender: The Multiple Discrimination against Refugee Women'. *Refuge: Canada's Journal on Refugees* 19(6) (2001), 21–32.

Plawski, Czeslaw. *Torn from the Homeland: Unforgettable Experiences during WW II*. Bloomington, IN: AuthorHouse, 2011.

Polsgrove, Carol. *Ending British Rule in Africa: Writers in a Common Cause*. Manchester: Manchester University Press, 2009.

Porajska, Barbara. *From the Steppes to the Savannah*. London: Coronet Books, 1990.

Porter-Szücs, Brian. *Faith and Fatherland: Catholicism, Modernity, and Poland*. Oxford: Oxford University Press, 2011.

Prażmowska, Anita J. *Britain and Poland 1939–1943: The Betrayed Ally*. Cambridge: Cambridge University Press, 1995.

———. 'Polish Refugees as Military Potential: Policy Objectives of the Polish Government in Exile', in Anna Bramwell (ed.), *Refugees in the Age of Total War* (London: Unwin Hyman, 1988), 219–32.

Rabaka, Reiland. 'The Souls of White Folk: W.E.B. Du Bois's Critique of White Supremacy and Contributions to Critical White Studies'. *Journal of African American Studies* 11(1) (2007), 1–15.

Ray, Carina. *Crossing the Color Line: Race, Sex, and the Contested Politics of Colonialism in Ghana*. Athens: Ohio University Press, 2015.

———. 'Interracial Sex and the Making of Empire', in Ato Quayson and Girish Daswani (eds), *A Companion to Diaspora and Transnationalism* (Malden, MA: Wiley Blackwell, 2013), 190–211.

Reid, Eric. *Tanganyika without Prejudice: A Balanced, Critical Review of the Territory and Her Peoples*. London: East Africa, 1934.

Reid, Richard J. *Frontiers of Violence in North-East Africa: Genealogies of Conflict since 1800*. Oxford: Oxford University Press, 2011.

Reinisch, Jessica. '"Auntie UNRRA" at the Crossroads'. *Past & Present* 218, suppl. 8 (2013), 70–97.

———. '"We Shall Rebuild Anew a Powerful Nation": UNRRA, Internationalism and National Reconstruction in Poland'. *Journal of Contemporary History* 43(3) (2008), 451–76.

Rhode, Maria. 'Zivilisierungsmissionen und Wissenschaft. Polen kolonial?' *Geschichte und Gesellschaft* 39(1) (2013), 5–34.

Rockenbach, Ashley Brooke. 'Accounting for the Past: A History of Refugee Management in Uganda, 1959–64', in Kristin Bergtora Sandvik and Katja Lindskov Jacobsen (eds), *UNHCR and the Struggle for Accountability: Technology, Law and Results-Based Management* (New York: Routledge, 2016), 119–37.

Roediger, David R. *The Wages of Whiteness: Race and the Making of the American Working Class*. London: Verso, 1991.

Romanko, Maria Alina. 'From Russian Gulag to Alberta Prairies: The Story of Maria Alina and Aleksander Romanko'. Retrieved 17 December 2019 from http://www.romanko.net/book/book.htm.

Rosenthal, Jill. 'From "Migrants" to "Refugees": Identity, Aid, and Decolonization in Ngara District, Tanzania'. *The Journal of African History* 56(2) (2015), 261–79.

Rössel, Karl. '"Die Front ist die Hölle." Im Ersten Weltkrieg wurden Millionen Kolonialsoldaten eingesetzt (Teil 1)'. *iz3w* 340 (2014), 12–15.

Rotberg, Robert I. *Black Heart: Gore-Browne and the Politics of Multiracial Zambia*. Berkeley: University of California Press, 1977.

Rothberg, Michael. 'W.E.B. Du Bois in Warsaw: Holocaust Memory and the Color Line, 1949–1952'. *The Yale Journal of Criticism* 14(1) (2001), 169–89.

Rupiah, Martin R. 'The History of the Establishment of Internment Camps and Refugee Settlements in Southern Rhodesia, 1938–1952'. *Zambezia* 22(2) (1995), 137–52.

Ruthström-Ruin, Cecilia. *Beyond Europe: The Globalization of Refugee Aid*. Lund: Lund University Press, 1993.

Safran, William. 'The Jewish Diaspora in a Comparative and Theoretical Perspective'. *Israel Studies* 10(1) (2005), 36–60.

Sajewicz, Jan. 'Wspomnienia', 1986. Retrieved 17 December 2019 from http://www.polish winnipeg.com/przeboje/Ks.J.Sajewicz.htm.

Salvatici, Silvia. '"Help the People to Help Themselves": UNRRA Relief Workers and European Displaced Persons'. *Journal of Refugee Studies* 25(3) (2012), 428–51.

Sandifort, Mary-Ann. 'World War Two: The Deportation of Polish Refugees to Abercorn Camp in Northern Rhodesia'. Masters thesis, Leiden, 2015. Retrieved 17 December 2019 from https://openaccess.leidenuniv.nl/handle/1887/32948.

Schipper, Mineke. *Imagining Insiders: Africa and the Question of Belonging*. London: Cassell, 1999.

Schnell, Felix. 'Der Gulag als Systemstelle sowjetischer Herrschaft', in Bettina Greiner and Alan Kramer (eds), *Welt der Lager: Zur »Erfolgsgeschichte« einer Institution* (Hamburg: Hamburger Edition, 2013), 134–65.

Schulze, Rainer. 'Forced Migration of German Populations during and after the Second World War: History and Memory', in Jessica Reinisch and Elizabeth White (eds), *The Disentanglement of Populations: Migration, Expulsion and Displacement in Post-War Europe, 1944–9* (Basingstoke: Palgrave Macmillan, 2011), 51–70.

Schutz, Barry M. 'European Population Patterns, Cultural Persistence, and Political Change in Rhodesia'. *Canadian Journal of African Studies / Revue canadienne des études africaines* 7(1) (1973), 3–25.

Scott, James C. *Seeing Like a State: How Certain Schemes to Improve the Human Condition Have Failed*. New Haven, CT: Yale University Press, 1998.

Sequeira, James H. 'The Ethiopian Refugees in Kenya'. *Journal of the Royal African Society* 38(152) (1939), 329–33.

Shadle, Brett L. 'Refugees in African History', in William H. Worger, Charles Ambler and Nwando Achebe (eds), *A Companion to African History* (Hoboken: Wiley Blackwell, 2019), 247–64.

———. 'Reluctant Humanitarians: British Policy toward Refugees in Kenya during the Italo-Ethiopian War, 1935–1940'. *The Journal of Imperial and Commonwealth History* 47(1) (2019), 167–86.

———. *The Souls of White Folk: White Settlers in Kenya, 1900s–1920s*. Manchester: Manchester University Press, 2015.

Shapiro, Frank. *Haven in Africa*. Jerusalem: Gefen Publishing House, 2002.

Shurmer-Smith, Pamela. *Remnants of Empire: Memory and Northern Rhodesia's White Diaspora*. Lusaka: Gadsden Publishers, 2015.

Shutt, Allison Kim. *Manners Make a Nation: Racial Etiquette in Southern Rhodesia, 1910–1963*. Suffolk, UK: Boydell & Brewer, 2015.

Sikorska, Irena. 'Irena Sikorska's Biography'. Retrieved 17 December 2019 from http://irena.sikorska.free.fr/.

Sinke, Suzanne M. 'Gender and Migration: Historical Perspectives'. *The International Migration Review* 40(1) (2006), 82–103.

Skran, Claudena. *Refugees in Inter-War Europe*. Oxford: Oxford University Press, 1995.

Smith, Alison. 'The Immigrant Communities (1): The Europeans', in D.A. Low and Alison Smith (eds), *History of East Africa, Vol. III* (London: Oxford University Press, 1976).

Snochowska-Gonzalez, Claudia. 'Post-Colonial Poland: On an Unavoidable Misuse'. *East European Politics & Societies* 26(4) (2012), 708–23.

Sofer, Cyril, and Rhona Ross. 'Some Characteristics of an East African European Population'. *British Journal of Sociology* 2(4) (1951), 315–27.

Spear, Thomas T. *Mountain Farmers: Moral Economies of Land and Agricultural Development in Arusha and Meru*. Berkeley: University of California Press, 1997.

Spivak, Gayatri Chakravorty. 'Can the Subaltern Speak?', in Cary Nelson and Lawrence Grossberg (eds), *Marxism and the Interpretation of Culture* (Urbana: University of Illinois Press, 1988), 271–315.

Stadnik, Kateryna. 'Ukrainian–Polish Population Transfers, 1944–46: Moving in Opposite Directions', in Nick Baron and Peter Gatrell (eds), *Warlands: Population Resettlement and State Reconstruction in the Soviet–East European Borderlands, 1945–50* (Basingstoke: Palgrave Macmillan, 2009), 165–87.

Stańczyk, Ewa. 'Exilic Childhood in Very Foreign Lands: Memoirs of Polish Refugees in World War II'. *Journal of War & Culture Studies* (2017), 1–14.

Steyn, Melissa. *'Whiteness Just Isn't What It Used To Be': White Identity in a Changing South Africa*. Albany, NY: SUNY Press, 2001.

Stoler, Ann Laura. 'Carnal Knowledge and Imperial Power: Gender, Race, and Morality in Colonial Asia', in Micaela di Leonardo (ed.), *Gender at the Crossroads of Knowledge* (Berkeley: University of California Press, 1991), 51–101.

———. *Carnal Knowledge and Imperial Power: Race and the Intimate in Colonial Rule*. Berkeley: University of California Press, 2002.

———. '"In Cold Blood": Hierarchies of Credibility and the Politics of Colonial Narratives'. *Representations* 37 (1992), 151–89.

———. 'Making Empire Respectable: The Politics of Race and Sexual Morality in 20th-Century Colonial Cultures'. *American Ethnologist* 16(4) (1989), 634–60.

———. 'Rethinking Colonial Categories: European Communities and the Boundaries of Rule'. *Comparative Studies in Society and History* 31(1) (1989), 134–61.

———. 'Sexual Affronts and Racial Frontiers: European Identities and the Cultural Politics of Exclusion in Colonial Southeast Asia', in Frederick Cooper and Ann Laura Stoler (eds), *Tensions of Empire: Colonial Cultures in a Bourgeois World* (Berkeley: University of California Press, 1997), 198–237.

Stone, Tessa. 'Creating a (Gendered?) Military Identity: The Women's Auxiliary Air Force in Great Britain in the Second World War'. *Women's History Review* 8(4) (1999), 605–24.

Strobel, Margaret. *European Women and the Second British Empire*. Bloomington: Indiana University Press, 1991.

Sulkiewicz, Krystyna, Irena Bartkowiak-Drobek and Fundacja Archiwum Fotograficzne Tułaczy. *Tułacze dzieci. Exiled children*. Warsaw: Muza, 1995.

Summers, Carol. 'Ugandan Politics and World War II (1939–1949)', in Judith A. Byfield et al., *Africa and World War II* (New York: Cambridge University Press, 2015), 480–98.

Sunseri, Thaddeus. 'Exploiting the Urwald: German Post-Colonial Forestry in Poland and Central Africa, 1900–1960'. *Past & Present* 214(1) (2012), 305–42.

Sword, Keith R. *Deportation and Exile: Poles in the Soviet Union, 1939–48*. Basingstoke: Palgrave Macmillan, 1994.

———. '"Their Prospects Will Not Be Bright": British Responses to the Problem of the Polish "Recalcitrants" 1946–49'. *Journal of Contemporary History* 21(3) (1986), 367–90.

Szostak, Henryk. *American by Choice. A Life Story*. Bloomington: Xlibris, 2013.

Tambe, Ashwini. 'The Elusive Ingénue: A Transnational Feminist Analysis of European Prostitution in Colonial Bombay'. *Gender and Society* 19(2) (2005), 160–79.

Tavuyanago, Baxter, Tasara Muguti and James Hlongwana. 'Victims of the Rhodesian Immigration Policy: Polish Refugees from the Second World War'. *Journal of Southern African Studies* 38(4) (2012), 951–65.

Taylor, Lynne. *In the Children's Best Interests: Unaccompanied Children in American-Occupied Germany, 1945–1952*. Toronto: University of Toronto Press, 2017.

———. *Polish Orphans of Tengeru: The Dramatic Story of Their Long Journey to Canada 1941–49*. Toronto: Dundurn Press, 2009.

Tembo, Alfred. 'Coerced African Labour for Food Production in Northern Rhodesia (Zambia) during the Second World War, 1942–1945'. *South African Historical Journal* 68(1) (2016), 50–69.

———. 'Strangers in Our Midst: Polish Refugees in Northern Rhodesia (Zambia) during the Second World War', unpublished draft chapter.

Temu, A.J. 'The Rise and Triumph of Nationalism', in Isaria N. Kimambo and A.J. Temu (eds), *A History of Tanzania* (Nairobi: East African Publishing House, 1969), 189–213.

Terreblanche, Solomon Johannes. *A History of Inequality in South Africa, 1652–2002*. Scottsville: University of Natal Press, 2002.

Thomas, Martin. *Fight or Flight: Britain, France, and Their Roads from Empire*. Oxford: Oxford University Press, 2014.

Thompson, Ewa. *Imperial Knowledge: Russian Literature and Colonialism*. Westport, CT: Greenwood Press, 2000.

———. 'Whose Discourse? Telling the Story in Post-Communist Poland'. *The Other Shore: Slavic and East European Cultures Abroad, Past and Present* 1(1) (2010), 1–15.

Thompson, Gardner. 'Colonialism in Crisis: The Uganda Disturbances of 1945'. *African Affairs* 91(365) (1992), 605–24.

———. *Governing Uganda: British Colonial Rule and Its Legacy*. Kampala: Fountain, 2003.

Tomaszewski, Irene. 'From the Snows of Siberia to the Snows of Kilimanjaro'. *Cosmopolitan Review*, 11 February 2009. Retrieved 17 December 2019 from http://cosmopolitanreview.com/from-the-snows-of-siberia.

———. 'In the Shade of the Baobab Tree'. *Cosmopolitan Review* 6(3) (2014). Retrieved 17 December 2019 from http://cosmopolitanreview.com/baobab-tree/.

Topolski, Feliks, and Maurice Collis. *Three Continents 1944–45: England, Mediterranean Convoy, Egypt, East Africa, Palestine, Lebanon, Syria, Iraq, India, Burma front, China, Italian Campaign, Germany Defeated*. London: Methuen, 1946.

Turner, Frederick Jackson, and John Mack Faragher. *Rereading Frederick Jackson Turner: 'The Significance of the Frontier in American History', and Other Essays*. New Haven, CT: Yale University Press, 1994.

Turner, Simon. 'The Barriers of Innocence: Humanitarian Intervention and Political Imagination in a Refugee Camp for Burundians in Tanzania'. PhD dissertation, Roskilde University, 2001. Retrieved 17 December 2019 from https://forskning.ruc.dk/da/publications/the-barriers-of-innocence-humanitarian-intervention-and-political.

Uffelmann, Dirk. 'Buren und Polen. Metonymischer Manichäismus und metaphorische Autoafrikanisierung bei Henryk Sienkiewicz – Zur Rhetorik interkultureller Beziehungen', in Robert Born and Sarah Lemmen (eds), *Orientalismen in Ostmitteleuropa: Diskurse, Akteure und Disziplinen vom 19. Jahrhundert bis zum Zweiten Weltkrieg* (Bielefeld: transcript, 2014), 285–312.
UNHCR. 'Global Trends: Forced Displacement in 2017'. Geneva: UNHCR, 2018. Retrieved 15 March 2019 from https://www.refworld.org/docid/5b2d1a867.html.
UNHCR and World Bank. 'An Assessment of Uganda's Progressive Approach to Refugee Management', 2016. Retrieved 17 December 2019 from https://openknowledge.worldbank.org/handle/10986/24736.
Urbanek, Bogdan. 'Z nieludzkiej ziemi do afrykańskiego buszu'. *Temat Szczecinecki* (27 January 2011).
Vansina, Jan. *Oral Tradition as History*. Oxford: James Currey, 1985.
van Tol, Deanne. 'The Women of Kenya Speak: Imperial Activism and Settler Society, c.1930'. *Journal of British Studies* 54(2) (2015), 433–56.
Vargas, Nicholas. 'Off White: Colour-Blind Ideology at the Margins of Whiteness'. *Ethnic and Racial Studies* 37(13) (2014), 2281–2302.
Warach, Bernard. *Hope: A Memoir*. Bloomington, IN: iUniverse, 2011.
Webster, Wendy. 'Britain and the Refugees of Europe 1939–50', in Louise Ryan and Wendy Webster (eds), *Gendering Migration: Masculinity, Femininity and Ethnicity in Post-War Britain* (Aldershot: Ashgate, 2008), 35–51.
———. '"There'll Always Be an England": Representations of Colonial Wars and Immigration, 1948–1968'. *Journal of British Studies* 40(4) (2001), 557–84.
Weiss, Robert. 'Polish Children's Home, Oudtshoorn, South Africa 1942–47'. Paper presented at the FEEFHS Convention, Salt Lake City, 1997. Retrieved 19 December 2019 from https://feefhs.org/resource/poland-childrens-home.
Werner, Michael, and Bénédicte Zimmermann. 'Beyond Comparison: Histoire Croisée and the Challenge of Reflexivity'. *History and Theory* 45(1) (2006), 30–50.
Westcott, Nicholas. 'The Impact of the Second World War on Tanganyika, 1939–49', in David Killingray and Richard Rathbone (eds), *Africa and the Second World War* (Basingstoke: Palgrave Macmillan, 1986), 143–59.
White, Luise. 'Cars Out of Place: Vampires, Technology, and Labor in East and Central Africa'. *Representations* 43 (1993), 27–50.
———. *The Comforts of Home: Prostitution in Colonial Nairobi*. Chicago: University of Chicago Press, 2009.
Wilder, Gary. *Freedom Time: Negritude, Decolonization, and the Future of the World*. Durham, NC: Duke University Press, 2014.
Wilkin, David. 'Refugees and British Administrative Policy in Northern Kenya, 1936–1938'. *African Affairs* 79(317) (1980), 510–30.
Williams, Susan. *Colour Bar: The Triumph of Seretse Khama and His Nation*. London: Allen Lane, 2006.
Wilson, Dolly Smith. 'Gender, Race and the Ideal Labour Force', in Louise Ryan and Wendy Webster (eds), *Gendering Migration: Masculinity, Femininity and Ethnicity in Post-War Britain* (Aldershot: Ashgate, 2008), 89–103.
Wilson, Jeffrey K. 'Environmental Chauvinism in the Prussian East: Forestry as a Civilizing Mission on the Ethnic Frontier, 1871–1914'. *Central European History* 41(1) (2008), 27–70.
Wincewicz, Andrzej, et al. 'Language and Medicine in the Zamenhof Family'. *Acta Medico-Historica Adriatica* 8(2) (2010), 287–92.

Wojciechowska, Bogusia J. (ed.). *Waiting to Be Heard: The Polish Christian Experience under Nazi and Stalinist Oppression, 1939–1955*. Bloomington, IN: AuthorHouse, 2009.

Wójcik, Zdzisława. 'Introduction to Chapter 6 Africa', in Tadeusz Piotrowski (ed.), *The Polish Deportees of World War II: Recollections of Removal to the Soviet Union and Dispersal throughout the World* (Jefferson, NC: McFarland, 2004), 137–39.

Wolff, Larry. *Inventing Eastern Europe: The Map of Civilization on the Mind of the Enlightenment*. Stanford, CA: Stanford University Press, 1994.

Wolton, Suke. *Lord Hailey, the Colonial Office and the Politics of Race and Empire in the Second World War: The Loss of White Prestige*. Basingstoke: Palgrave Macmillan, 2000.

Woodbridge, George. *UNRRA. The History of the United Nations Relief and Rehabilitation Administration*, 3 vols. New York: Columbia University Press, 1950.

Worsley, Peter. *An Academic Skating on Thin Ice*. New York: Berghahn Books, 2008.

Wróbel, Janusz. 'Polskie Dominium w Afryce?' *Biuletyn IPN – Pamięć.pl* 7 (2012), 19–24.

———. *Uchodźcy Polscy ze Związku Sowieckiego 1942–1950*. Łódź: Instytut Pamięci Narodowej, 2003.

Wyman, David S. *Abandonment of the Jews*. New York: Pantheon, 1984.

Yuval-Davis, Nira. *Gender and Nation*. London: SAGE, 1997.

Zarycki, Tomasz. *Ideologies of Eastness in Central and Eastern Europe*. London: Routledge, 2014.

———. 'Orientalism and Images of Eastern Poland', in M. Stefański (ed.), *Endogenous Factors in Development of the Eastern Poland* (Lublin: Innovation Press, 2010), 73–88.

Zarzycki, Alicia A., and Stefania Buczak-Zarzycka. *Kwaheri Africa: A Polish Experience 1939–1950, from Deportation to Freedom*. Perth: n.p., 1986.

Zecker, Robert M. '"Negrov Lynčovanie" and the Unbearable Whiteness of Slovaks: The Immigrant Press Covers Race'. *American Studies* 43(2) (2002), 43–72.

Zetter, Roger. 'Labelling Refugees: Forming and Transforming a Bureaucratic Identity'. *Journal of Refugee Studies* 4(1) (1991), 39–62.

Zimmerer, Jürgen. 'The Birth of the Ostland out of the Spirit of Colonialism: A Postcolonial Perspective on the Nazi Policy of Conquest and Extermination'. *Patterns of Prejudice* 39(2) (2005), 197–219.

Zins, Henryk. *Polacy w Zambezji. Z Dziejów Polonii*. Lublin: Wydawnictwo Polonia, 1988.

———. *Poles in Zambezi*. Harare: Kloyes Enterprises Zimbabwe, 2007.

Zunes, Stephen, and Jacob Mundy. *Western Sahara: War, Nationalism, and Conflict Irresolution*. Syracuse, NY: Syracuse University Press, 2010.

Zyl-Hermann, Danelle van, and Jacob Boersema. 'Introduction: The Politics of Whiteness in Africa'. *Africa: The Journal of the International African Institute* 87(4) (2017), 651–61.

Index

Abyssinia. *See under* Ethiopia
Achebe, Chinua, 122, 128n133
African farmers, 30, 235–36. *See also* peasants: African
African neighbours, 11, 14, 104, 121, 218–19, 220–21, 224, 235, 258–59, 264
African workers
  building the Polish refugee camps, 20, 33–34, 36, 148, 212, 220, 232, 234, 264
  in the camps, 11, 14, 33, 38, 41, 115, 122, 147–48, 161, 210, 214, 218–20, 224, 226, 230–35, 259, 261, 264
  conscripted (*see under* conscript labour)
  See also domestic work: Africans employed in
Afrikaners, 28, 49, 64n302, 122, 173–74, 177–78, 181, 183, 185, 193, 228, 262
Algeria, 93, 103n237
'alien dilution', 191
Anders Army. *See under* Second Polish Corps
anti-colonial ideology, 106, 114, 116–17, 122, 179
anti-colonial movement, 112, 114, 116–17, 120, 123, 147, 153, 181, 185, 228–29, 239, 240, 224n81
antisemitism, 101n207, 105
  in Britain, 263
  among the Polish refugees, 73, 183, 198–99
  in settler societies, 26, 72, 90–91, 190–91
Americans. *See under* United States of America
Apartheid, 153

Arusha, 20, 32–33, 50, 56n136, 78, 154, 188, 190, 212, 219, 225, 234–35
Australia, 2–3, 5, 48, 78–79, 90, 101n205, 155, 183, 211

Bagshawe, Francis, 41–42, 61n242, 120, 128n128, 182
bakery, 33, 121–22
Barnes, John, 188–89
Bechuanaland, 153
Beira, 29, 39–41, 197, 242n27
Belarusians, 20, 31, 51n41, 113, 199–201, 203–4, 209, 247n163, 248n196
Belgian Congo, 58n171, 122, 216, 241n8
Bere, Rennie, 57n150, 147, 198–99
Bevin, Ernest, 203
'black peril', 144–45, 242n26. *See also* miscegenation
Brodhurst-Hill, Evelyn, 190, 245n116
Brubaker, Rogers, 10, 112, 195,
Buczak-Zarzycka, Stefania, 109, 118, 246n147
Buganda, 58n158, 185, 216, 224, 229, 231, 237
Bunyoro, 214, 237–38
Bwana Mkubwa, 39–40, 138, 150, 164n56, 217
Byelorusia. *See under* Belarusians

Caesar, Ochau Paito, 229, 252nn304–5
Caldwell, Reginald, 142, 150, 156–58
Canada, 2–5, 26, 31, 48, 79–80, 90, 97n90, 101n203, 136, 206, 208–9, 217, 250n235

categorization, 10, 20–22, 69–70, 89, 93, 119, 123, 132, 139, 142–43, 147, 153, 177, 191–92, 195–97, 199–201, 203–4, 209, 223, 228, 258, 263–64
Catholicism, 14, 26, 29–30, 33–35, 39, 45, 48, 60n210, 80, 83, 90, 110, 113, 115, 120, 137, 196, 198–200, 202, 206, 208–9, 212–19, 222, 225, 229–30, 247n159
  church buildings, 33–36, 38–39, 41, 137, 154, 199, 211–12, 213–15, 218, 220, 222, 225, 229–30, 251n275
cemetery, 33, 36, 64n304, 198, 221, 225, 229, 253n322, 260
Césaire, Aimé, 106, 125n57
Chakrabarty, Dipesh, 194, 246n139
children, 1–2, 4, 13, 19, 21, 23, 25–26, 28, 30–31, 33, 37–39, 41, 43, 49–50, 53n68, 78, 119–20, 130, 132–39, 141, 144–45, 147, 154, 156–57, 159–61, 173, 191–92, 196, 208, 210, 215–17, 224, 250n229, 257
Chipata. *See under* Fort Jameson
Chodzikiewicz, Kazimierz, 63n280, 74, 249n210
Christie, Janina, 138–39
Churchill, Winston, 23, 25, 120, 179
civilizing mission, 106, 109, 124n16, 124n31, 216
Cohen, Gerard Daniel, 90, 262
Cold War, 4, 46, 67, 70–1, 91, 93, 201, 204, 208
colonial division of labour, 13, 84–86, 88, 134, 147, 155, 157–58
Commonwealth war effort, 2, 26–27, 157, 176, 185, 193, 227, 231, 261
communists, 71, 92, 174, 204, 229
  in Poland, 2, 45–7, 67–8, 76, 108, 247n162 (*see also* Warsaw: communist government in)
  among the refugees, 116–17, 122, 194, 201–3, 228
Conrad, Joseph, 122
conscript labour, 14, 92, 234–35
Cooper, Frederick, 7, 10, 88, 107, 177, 195, 260
cosmopolitanism, 172, 196, 201–3

criminals
  European in colonial societies, 9, 186–87, 194, 258
  among the refugees, 40, 49, 78–79, 119, 150, 179–80, 186–87, 208, 239, 245n104
Curtis, Hubert Arnold, 45, 76–86, 88, 91, 99n158, 182, 200, 206
Curzon Line, 110, 203
Cyprus group, 24, 38, 40, 52n41, 183, 198
Czech, 151, 190

Dar es Salaam, 11, 19, 28–30, 38, 78, 119–20, 130, 134, 191, 202, 212, 219, 221, 226–27, 232
deportations (to the Soviet Union), 2–4, 9, 14, 20–22, 28, 42, 47, 50n11, 51n25, 69–70, 73, 75, 105, 108, 113–14, 119, 122, 130, 137, 199, 202, 208, 210, 215, 220, 240
developmental colonialism, 177–78, 180, 257
diaspora, 207, 264
  Polish, 3, 5–6, 13, 83, 136, 139, 194, 204–7, 209, 211, 214, 218, 249n210, 258
Digglefold, 42, 61nn235–36, 118, 135, 139, 159, 205, 211
Dillon, John, 83
displaced persons (DPs), 12, 48, 67–68, 70, 81, 90–91, 93, 99n139, 116, 120, 179, 200, 207, 209–10, 247n170
  camps, 6, 81, 142, 207, 209–10, 264
  'DP apathy', 81
Dołęga-Kowalewski, Jerzy, 216
domestic work, 136, 155–57, 189, 201
  Africans employed in, 39, 135, 157, 188–90, 232–34
  'nanny-companions', 156–57
  nursemaids, 84, 156
Douglas, Mary, 194, 266n21
Douglass, M.R., 56n122, 141–42
Du Bois, W.E.B., 7–8, 105, 114, 122

East African Campaign, 27, 174
East African Governors' Conference (EAGC), 28, 44
East African Refugee Authority (EARA), 25, 44–45, 62n255, 83

East African Standard, 25–26, 28, 47, 70, 156, 175–77, 190–91, 210–11, 238
Eden, Anthony, 25–26
Egypt, 25, 77, 82, 94n30, 97n90,
Ethiopia, 27, 30, 38, 68, 71, 83, 92, 94n21, 142, 168n168, 181, 203. *See also* Italo-Ethiopian war; refugees: Ethiopian
exile, 3, 5, 14, 26, 29, 31, 69, 85, 120, 123, 133, 136–39, 155, 160, 194–95, 204–5, 207–9, 214, 219, 263. *See also* diaspora

Fanon, Frantz, 6
Filimon, Otwia, 225, 227–28, 231, 236, 252n303
finances, 8–9, 27, 44, 72, 76, 114, 135, 206, 214, 229, 261
  reimbursement of expenditures for the refugees, 28, 47, 72–73
Fischer-Tiné, Harald, 9, 146, 154
food, 4, 20, 22–23, 26, 29, 33, 38–39, 41–42, 44, 71, 75, 79, 87, 89, 115, 187, 205, 210, 220, 224, 231, 233, 235–36, 258
Fort Jameson, 24, 38, 188–89, 213
France, 48, 57n142, 68, 125n57, 127n110, 152, 179, 201
Frankenberg, Ruth, 8
Furber, David, 106
Fyfe, Christopher, 111

Gatooma, 42, 76, 81, 87, 100n185, 182, 209
Gatrell, Peter, 82
'Gehenna', 22, 51n25, 115, 122, 215
gender, 1, 13–14, 82, 123, 130–36, 139, 141, 143, 146–47, 151, 155, 158–61, 189, 194–95, 258, 264
  gendered composition of the Polish refugee group, 133–34
  'womenandchildren', 159
  See also miscegenation; sexuality; white women
General Langfitt (ship), 48
Geneva, 68, 76, 78–79, 84, 168n168, 208
Germany, 13, 21–22, 25–26, 28–29, 31, 33, 42, 67–68, 70–71, 79, 81, 102n225, 104–7, 110–13, 116, 120, 124n8, 126n68, 133, 135, 142, 149, 152, 160, 172, 177, 179, 183, 190–91, 201, 207, 209–10, 228, 232–33, 245nn122–24, 257, 261
  German rule in Poland, 21, 104–7, 122
  See also internees: German; missionaries: German
Gingrich, Andre, 106
global history, 5, 13, 106, 259
Głos Polski, 11, 74–75, 135, 196, 205, 211
Gore-Brown, Stewart, 155, 183–84, 198, 244n81
Gorton, F.J., 184
government-in-exile (Polish), 2, 11, 22–23, 44–46, 67, 73–74, 120, 202–3, 206, 208, 217, 249n209
  derecognition of, 44–45
Greeks, 70, 119, 141–42, 148, 156, 165n80, 199, 212, 261. *See also* refugees: Greek
Grills, Shannon, 39, 164n56
groundnut scheme, 32, 55n114, 56n123, 180, 189
groupness, 10, 195, 209
guards, 45, 58n158, 220, 228, 232
Gulag, 21, 51n23. *See also* special settlements

Harazin, Franciszek, 199–200, 203, 247n162
Histoire Croisée, 6
Hitler, Adolf, 26, 106, 124n8, 191
Hitler–Stalin pact, 20
Hodder-Williams, Richard, 192
Hoima, 225
Holborn, Louise, 67, 82, 90, 101n201, 116
hospital, 31, 33–34, 36–37, 39, 43, 46, 147, 152, 180, 199, 202, 226, 234
humanitarianism, 23, 25, 71, 82, 90–93, 115, 122, 263
Huxley, Elspeth, 58n165, 99n158, 192

identification, 5, 8, 10, 123, 200, 215
identity, 10, 108–9, 130, 132, 136, 146, 161, 171, 195, 205
Ifunda, 31–33, 56n122, 81, 98n128, 115–16, 141, 151, 180, 189, 198, 203, 205, 215, 232, 249n199

India, 9, 146, 194, 202, 246n139, 261, 266n23
  independence, 9, 178–79
  partition refugees (*see under* refugees: Indian)
  Polish refugees in, 2, 26, 53n68, 56n125, 68, 75, 93, 94n30, 179, 201
Indians in Africa, 36, 38, 72, 85, 87, 89, 100n182, 116, 142, 149, 151–52, 167n135, 177, 179, 181, 185, 189, 193, 227, 231–33, 235. *See also* marriages: Polish-Asian
International Refugee Organization (IRO), 11–13, 37–38, 42, 45, 47–49, 65–66, 72, 75–93, 134, 138, 158, 178, 182, 184–85, 199–201, 206, 208–9, 250n235, 259
  eligibility for assistance, 66, 77–79, 97n97, 98n114
  establishment of, 68
internationalism, 79, 82, 90
internees, 4, 27, 53n71, 71, 154, 156, 180, 202
  German, 29, 31, 42, 71, 78–79, 177, 191, 232, 261
  Italian, 38, 42, 44, 71, 141–42, 261
interracial relationships. *See under* miscegenation
Iran, 22, 26
  Persian Corridor, 25
  Polish refugees in, 2, 19, 22–26, 28, 38, 43, 51n33, 52n56, 69, 72, 118, 183
Iringa, 81, 116, 141, 152
Italians, 30, 83, 120, 151, 180, 192, 218, 238
  prisoners of war, 26–27, 30, 37, 53n69, 142–43, 168n168, 172, 181, 190
  social position in colonial societies, 141–44, 152, 216, 245n128, 256n413
  See also internees: Italian; marriages: Polish-Italian; missionaries: Italian
Italo–Ethiopian war, 68, 71, 92, 143

Jackson, Will, 152
Jacobs, Sam, 73–74
Jewish, 20, 26, 28, 51n14, 53n62, 72–73, 85, 90–91, 105–7, 111, 113, 177–78, 182–83, 198, 201, 203, 209. *See also* antisemitism; refugees: Jewish

Jolluck, Katherine, 50n11, 132
Joseph, Simon, 225, 229, 232, 235, 237, 252n304

Kadoma. *See under* Gatooma
Kasule, Mukeera, 226–27, 230, 233, 235–37, 252n305
Katambora, 40, 60n212–16, 150, 153
Kazakhstan, 22, 127n102
Kennedy, Dane Keith, 173, 181, 194
Kenya, 8, 27–28, 36–37, 49–50, 65, 70–72, 80–81, 83–85, 87–88, 138, 148, 152, 155–58, 171–75, 177–82, 190–93, 234, 238, 261, 263
  reluctance to admit Polish settlers, 181–82
  See also Makindu; Mombasa; Nairobi; Rongai
Kidugala, 31–33, 46, 55n108, 63n280, 148, 203, 216, 232, 250n236
Kigoma, 38, 44, 234
Kirk-Green, Anthony, 16n49, 111, 168n161
Koja, 11, 20, 34–36, 47, 57n142, 76, 83, 120–22, 137, 140, 147, 149, 159, 175, 179, 184, 198–99, 205–6, 208, 213, 216, 220–22, 225–36, 256n406
Kolhapur, 179. *See also* India: Polish refugees in
Kondoa, 30–31, 33, 46, 54n97, 63n280, 200, 203, 215, 220, 224
Korabiewicz, Wacław, 202–3, 248nn176–77
'kresy'
  eastern borderlands, 20, 107, 109, 113, 125n44, 126n62, 206, 210, 250n241
  myth, 109
Krolikowski, Lucjan, 3–4, 15n6, 76, 115, 135, 137
Królikowski, Łucjan. *See under* Krolikowski, Lucjan
Królikowski, Roman, 49, 64n299
Kronika, 40, 187
Kunambi, Patrick, 226

L., Gracjan, 78
Lake Duluti, 154
Lake Victoria, 34, 159, 220
Lane, Marie D., 78
'Little Poland', 85, 137, 164n52

Livingstone (town), 24, 40, 52n48, 59n198, 197,
London, 10–11, 22, 49, 74, 78, 84–86, 92, 99n158, 106, 117, 139, 150, 153, 158, 173, 175–76, 179, 183, 190, 199, 201, 262
  Polish government in (*see under* government-in-exile (Polish))
Lorriman, F.J., 78–79
Luczyc, Helena, 116–17
Luhende, 219–20, 227, 230
Lusaka
  refugee camp, 39–40, 59n198, 76, 144, 175, 210, 215
  town, 24, 59n197, 144, 187, 202, 215
Lush, Maurice Stanley, 64n302, 65, 81–83, 86, 90–92, 100n159, 102n230, 178,
Lwanga-Lunyiigo, Samwiri, 4, 152, 229, 240

MacQuillan, Dr, 154
Makindu, 37, 58n171, 59n176, 147, 181, 207
Makowski, Michał, 57n142, 57n150, 198
Malkki, Liisa, 88, 207, 266n21
Marandellas, 41–42, 61n226, 144–45, 174, 192–93, 209, 213–14, 242n27, 251n275
Marczuk, Tekla, 139
Marondera. *See under* Marandellas
marriages, 78, 117, 135–36, 148–49, 153, 158, 160, 164nn59–60, 203
  Polish-African, 17n56, 50, 114, 148–49, 166n120, 225 (*see also* miscegenation)
  Polish-Asian, 114, 149–50, 159–50
  Polish-British, 138–40, 148, 155
  Polish-Italian, 141, 143, 148, 216, 261
Marrus, Michael, 26, 262–63
Masindi, 11, 20, 29, 34–35, 50, 135, 137, 154, 159, 175, 180, 192, 197, 198, 206–7, 211, 213–14, 218, 220–21, 238. *See also* Nyabyeya
Masiuk, Bernard, 117
Mbala. *See under* Abercorn
McClintock, Anne, 153, 168n155
Meru, 32, 116, 229
  Meru Land Case, 228–29, 238
Mexico, 26, 53n66
Michałowska-Bykowska, Filomena, 115

Mickiewicz, Adam, 205
Middle East Relief and Refugee Administration (MERRA), 19, 70, 194
Milek, Janina, 155, 246n147
Minnery, John, 33, 56n136, 80, 215, 250n235
miscegenation, 143–146, 152, 156
  legislation prohibiting, 152
missionaries, 30, 33, 220, 230
  German, 31, 55n108
  Italian, 30–31, 39, 215–16, 218
  missionary outlook, 215–18, 230, 240
  Polish, 215, 218–19, 222
  self-description of refugees as, 14, 240
Mlambo, Alois, 28, 182
Mombasa, 29, 36–37, 47–48, 75–76, 149, 151, 167n139, 181, 207, 211
Moore, David Chioni, 107, 123
Morogoro, 30, 33, 220–21, 226
motherhood, 23, 132–33, 135, 144, 149, 208
  'Matka Polka', 132–33, 136
  single mothers, 137, 149
Mozambique, 29, 40, 142

Nairobi, 6, 11, 13, 19, 25, 29, 32, 36–37, 44–47, 49, 73, 75–76, 82, 85, 87–89, 91, 118–20, 134–37, 142–43, 148, 150, 155, 157–58, 171, 173–75, 177, 179, 190, 192, 196, 198, 200, 206, 208, 211, 259
Najman, Genowefa, 149
Nasz Przyjaciel, 11, 63n269, 196, 206, 212
Ndola, 39, 217
Njombe, 31
Northern Rhodesia, 4, 24, 26–27, 38–40, 49, 144–45, 150, 154–57, 172–74, 183–84, 186–89, 193, 197–98, 262
  Copperbelt, 38–39, 172
  See also Abercorn; Bwana Mkubwa; Fort Jameson; Katambora; Lusaka
Nyabyeya, 34–35, 180, 221–22, 224–25, 227–33, 236–37, 252n303. *See also* Masindi
Nyasaland, 38, 173, 183, 241n10

Onega, John, 224, 227, 230, 232
'Operation Polejump', 48, 149
oral history, 11, 221–23

orientalism, 1, 90, 106–7, 110, 143
orphans, 3–4, 30, 33, 37, 48, 134–35, 137, 188, 198, 208, 215
Orthodox, 33, 110, 209
  among the Polish refugees, 198–200
osadnicy, 21
Othering, 106–9, 171, 216
Oudtshoorn, 43, 49–50, 73, 199, 217

Padmore, George, 106–7, 124n8, 124n23
Paris, 11, 203, 205–6
peasants
  African, 228, 236, 259, 261
  concept, 194, 246n139
  Polish, 8, 14, 20, 69, 120, 145, 154, 158, 171, 179–80, 183, 188, 190, 192–94, 196, 198–99, 209–10, 213, 220, 240, 259, 261, 263
Pennington, A.L., 43, 74, 80, 186, 202, 242n32
Persia. *See under* Iran
Peterson, Glen, 93
Pierce, C.M., 74
Piotrowksi, Tadeusz, 3, 15n3, 50n11, 247n169
Pławski, Teresa, 114
police, 19, 32, 37, 40, 46, 59n176, 60n212, 74–75, 111, 115–17, 120, 135, 141–43, 147–48, 150, 233
Polish Civic Committee (Polski Komitet Obywatelski), 44, 62n264
Polish colonial attempts, 111, 120–21
Polish milieu, 137, 139, 195, 205, 161. *See also* 'Little Poland'
Polish partition period, 104, 106, 119, 122–23, 138, 228
'Polish quota', 49, 64n299, 84, 86, 184, 193
Polish–Soviet War, 20–21, 96n80, 109
Polonia. *See under* diaspora: Polish
poor white, 8–9, 143, 174–175, 177, 190, 245n128, 261, 263
  in South Africa, 174
  Polish refugees as, 2, 7, 86–87, 158, 174, 189, 193–94, 229
  See also subaltern whites
Porajska, Barbara, 135, 207, 233
postcolonial, 5, 13, 104–9, 113, 222, 246n139, 264

prisoner of war (POW). *See under* Italians: prisoners of war
prostitution, 21, 150
  of African women, 155
  of Polish women, 37, 40, 141, 150–52, 154, 156, 161, 167n150, 194
  of white women in colonies, 9, 166n109, 132, 151–52, 168n155

Red Cross, 12, 36, 41, 45–47, 62n267, 141, 144, 183
refugee camps, 1, 19–20, 29, 93, 104, 139, 153, 161, 189, 237, 264
  in Africa (not Polish), 225, 263–64
  conditions in the Polish camps in Africa, 2, 6, 198, 210, 212–13, 220
  description of the different Polish camps in Africa, 28–43
  in Europe (*see under* displaced persons (DPs): camps)
  internal organization, 43, 45–46
  Polish terminology for, 207
refugees
  Baltic, 90–91, 101n209
  Chinese, 92–93, 94n20, 102n232
  Ethiopian, 71–72, 92
  Greek, 30, 58n171, 70, 94n10, 156, 172, 241n8, 261
  Indian, 92
  Jewish, 21, 26, 72, 86, 90, 92, 95n55, 101n207, 174, 181, 190–91, 199, 263
  legislation, 70–71, 264–65
  liminality, 263
  registration, 73, 200, 248n196
  repatriation, 36, 45, 47, 67–68, 70, 73–77, 92, 136, 199–200
  Russian, 92, 117
Roche, Thomas William Edgar, 175, 186
Roediger, David, 7
Rogiński, Piotr, 75, 96n80
Romanko, Maria Alina, 135, 217
Rongai, 30, 37, 138, 143, 163n45, 181, 208, 251n253
Rucker, Arthur, 84, 86
Rule, Mollie, 42, 61n247, 82
Rusape, 41, 139, 213–14, 250n244

Salisbury, 40–42, 86, 192
Sander, Karol, 143

Sapieha, Prince Eustachy, 36, 47, 58n161, 62n267
school, 29, 31, 33–34, 36–37, 39–44, 46, 118–20, 134–35, 137, 139, 143, 180–81, 191–92, 194, 208, 217, 220, 230
scouts, 42–43, 61nn239–40, 137, 163n49, 184, 205, 211
Second Polish Corps, 2, 22–23, 25, 47, 51n32, 69, 73, 120, 135–36, 139, 160, 204, 257
  correspondence of refugees with soldiers in, 135–136
Second Polish Republic, 20, 36, 51n14, 113, 123
self-identification, 10, 13–14, 71, 108–9, 111, 119, 122, 132, 161, 195–96, 203, 207, 209, 211, 218–19, 240, 258–59, 263
semi-skilled, 65, 83, 87, 149, 185. *See also* colonial division of labour
sexuality, 114, 131, 140–42, 144–46, 151, 155–57, 161, 188
  interracial, 111, 131, 142, 146, 152–53, 161, 225–26 (*see also* miscegenation)
  promiscuity, 145
  See also marriages; prostitution
Seychellois, 85, 149–50, 152, 167n139
Shadle, Brett, 8, 266n24
Siberia, 115, 122, 155, 215. *See also* deportations (to the Soviet Union)
'Sybiracy', 51n25. *See also* Siberia
Sienkiewicz, Henryk, 118, 122, 127n106, 128n135, 129n136
Sikorski-Maisky Agreement, 2, 22, 200
Sinabulya, Edward, 224–26, 228–29, 231, 234–36, 252n305
Skran, Claudena, 66, 70
Słapa, Władysław, 45, 63n269, 196
Smuts, Jan, 49, 64n302, 241n20, 262
Snochowska-Gonzales, Claudia, 109
soldiers, 19–20, 111, 144, 155, 158, 168n168, 182, 240
  British, 25, 29, 155, 261
  colonial, 30, 144, 127n110, 118–19, 185, 231, 240
  Polish (*see under* Second Polish Corps)
  Polish women in British auxiliary units, 155–56

South African War, 122, 128n128, 264, 266n24
Southern Rhodesia, 4, 27–28, 40–42, 49, 71, 86–87, 120, 135, 138, 144, 152–53, 155, 158, 173–74, 177, 181–83, 193, 211, 234, 261–62. *See also* Digglefold; Gatooma; Marandellas; Rusape; Salisbury
Soviet Union, 7, 13, 19–23, 25, 28, 47, 67–70, 73–74, 76, 79, 104–12, 115–17, 122, 124n23, 126n62, 132, 154–55, 161, 176, 178–79, 199–201, 203, 205–6, 210, 214, 220, 228–29, 235. *See also* deportations (to the Soviet Union)
South Africa. *See under* Union of South Africa
special settlements, 2, 21–22, 47, 51n23, 130, 220
Stephan, C., 79–80, 98n128
Stoler, Ann Laura, 6, 8–9, 131, 140, 143, 260, 265n3
Story, Herbert, 73, 95n45, 96n68
subaltern whites, 9, 13, 194, 240, 258–59, 261
Suchnicka, Anna, 195, 210
Szustek, Karol, 201

Tabora, 44, 71, 141
Tanga, 29, 32–33, 134, 195
Tanganyika, 4, 26–28, 30–33, 43, 49, 70, 78–81, 113, 116, 142, 148–50, 172–73, 177, 184, 186–88, 191, 193, 202, 234–35, 262, 264. *See also* Dar es Salaam; Ifunda; Kondoa; Kidugala; Morogoro; Tengeru
Tanzania. *See under* Tanganyika
Tehran, 23, 118. *See also* Iran
Tengeru, 3, 11, 30, 32–33, 36, 47, 50, 56nn132–34, 71, 73, 75–76, 79–82, 85, 90, 98n114, 114, 116–17, 119, 133–34, 142, 146, 150–51, 154–55, 180–81, 186, 190, 198–201, 203–6, 208–10, 212–15, 218, 221–23, 225, 228–30, 232–38, 249n200, 260
Thompson, Ewa, 108
Tiko, Teresa, 224
Topolski, Feliks, 238, 265n410

trade, 21, 69, 149, 151, 154, 235–36
  illicit, 114, 116, 126n82, 235
transnational history. *See under* global history

Uganda, 4, 26–28, 33–36, 49, 85–87, 139, 172–73, 184–86, 192–93, 208, 224–25, 227–34, 239–40, 260–62, 265. *See also* Buganda; Bunyoro; Kampala; Koja; Masindi; Nyabyeya
'Uganda Disturbances', 120, 185, 227, 231–32
Uganda Herald, 184
Ukraine, 20, 109, 126n68
Ukrainians, 199–200, 203, 247n163
Union of South Africa, 26, 28, 43, 49–50, 85, 139, 153, 172–75, 181, 183, 198, 217, 262. *See also* Afrikaners; Oudtshoorn
United Nations, 12, 65, 68, 94n12, 110, 172, 228, 262
United Nations High Commissioner for Refugees (UNHCR), 93, 102n233, 103n237, 258, 266n22
United Nations Relief and Rehabilitation Administration (UNRRA), 12, 37, 45, 47, 67–68, 72–77, 82, 87, 89, 94n12, 199, 264
United States of America, 4, 8, 26, 45, 63n269, 68, 73, 76, 81, 83, 97n90, 101n203, 105–7, 141, 183, 205–6, 243n50
universalism, 12, 65–66, 89, 93

Wakiku, Edward, 236, 239, 252nn304–5
Walden, Stanley, 81, 141–42
War Relief Service (WRS), 45, 60n210
Warsaw, 17n72, 34, 114, 203
  communist government in, 46, 67, 73–6, 202, 208, 217
Washington, 74, 94n15

Webster, Wendy, 146
Welensky, Roy, 183, 244n80
white prestige, 8–9, 143–45, 160, 193
White Russia. *See* Belorusians
white women, 13, 123, 143, 147, 153, 156–57, 160–61, 189
  stabilizing colonial rule, 131, 138
  transgressive, 8, 114, 131–32, 146, 151–52
  welfare organizations, 41, 134, 140–41, 143–45
White, Luise, 167n150, 226
whiteness, 119, 130–31, 140, 219–20, 230, 257, 259
  in colonial societies, 8, 10, 16n43, 153, 157–58, 160, 209, 240
  and gender (*see under* white women)
  marginal, 15, 145, 152, 261 (*see also* poor white)
  studies, 7–8
Wielka Emigracja, 205
Wierzbiński, Antoni, 38, 59n194, 81, 249n213
Wilkin, Bertram, 212
Williams, J.P., 63n280, 80
Woodbridge, George, 89
Worsley, Peter, 55n114, 189
Wróbel, Janusz, 3, 137

Yalta, 113, 126n63
YMCA, 29, 31, 39–40, 43, 45, 206, 216–17, 252n292
Yugoslavia, 70, 110
Yuval-Davis, Nira, 132, 159

Zambia. *See under* Northern Rhodesia
Zamenhof, Julian, 31, 63n280, 203, 243n60, 248n189
Zarzycki, Ferdynand, 42, 61n238
Zimbabwe. *See under* Southern Rhodesia
Zins, Henryk, 198, 218, 252n298

www.ingramcontent.com/pod-product-compliance
Lightning Source LLC
Chambersburg PA
CBHW072046110526
44590CB00018B/3059